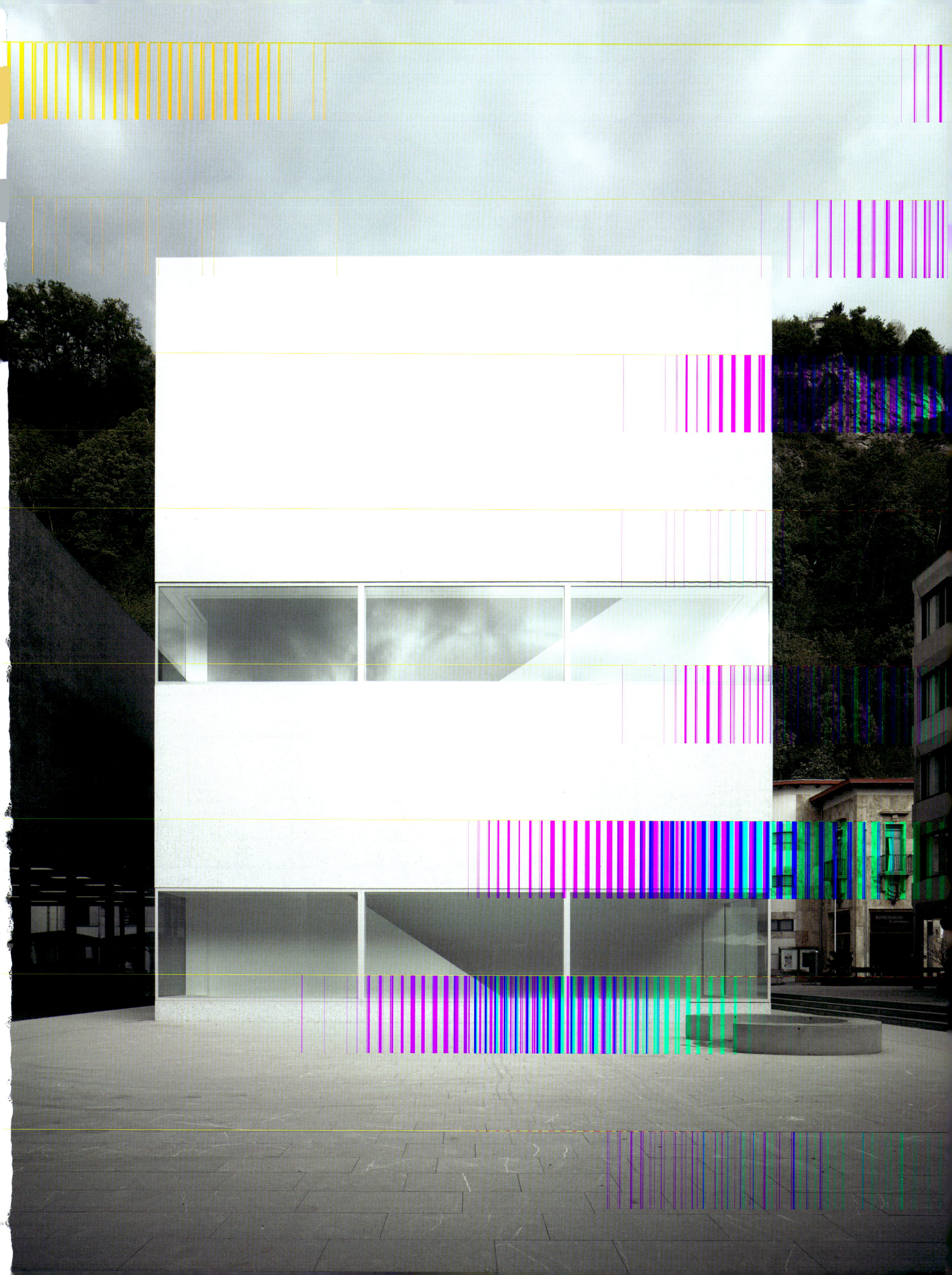

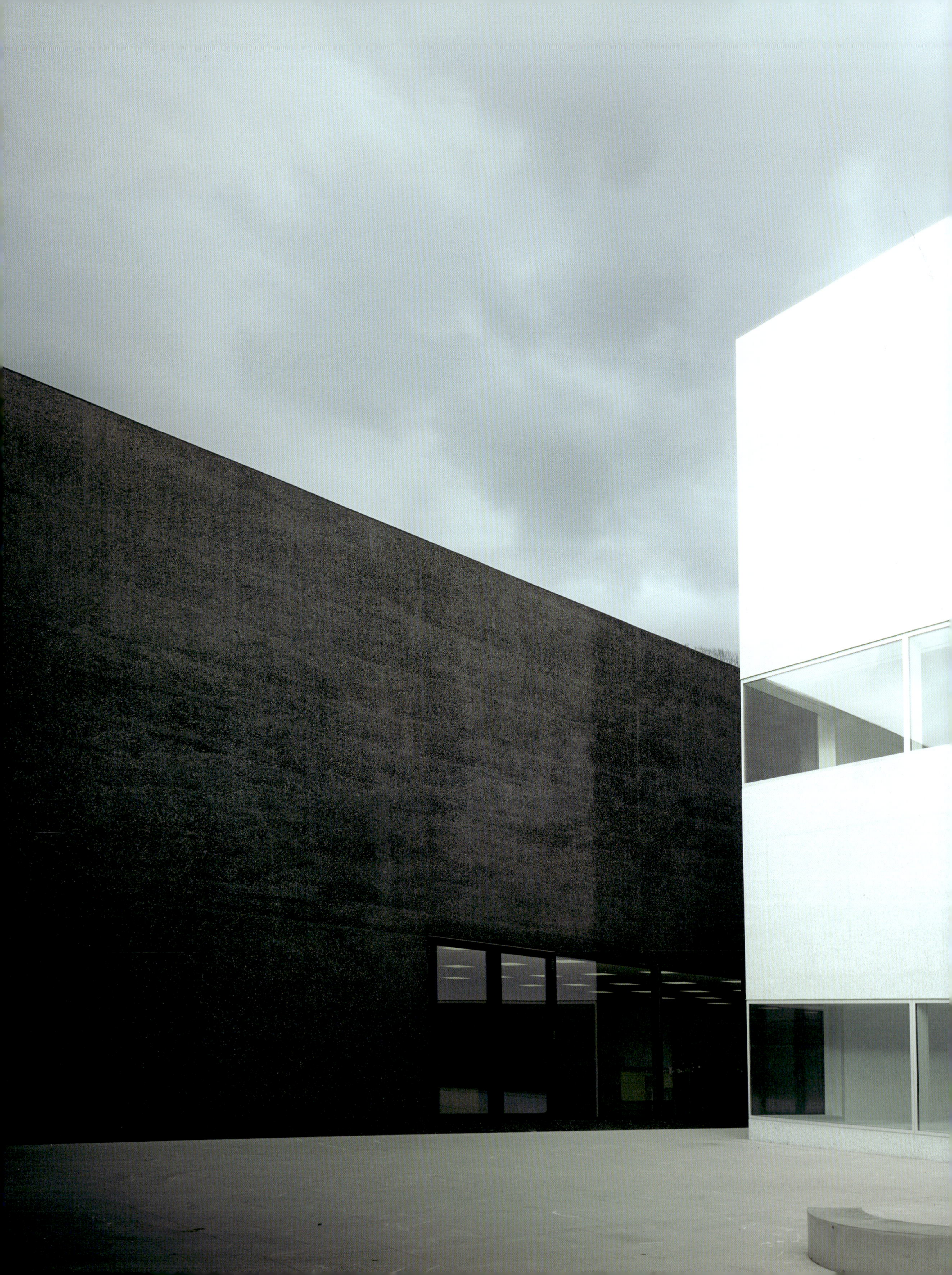

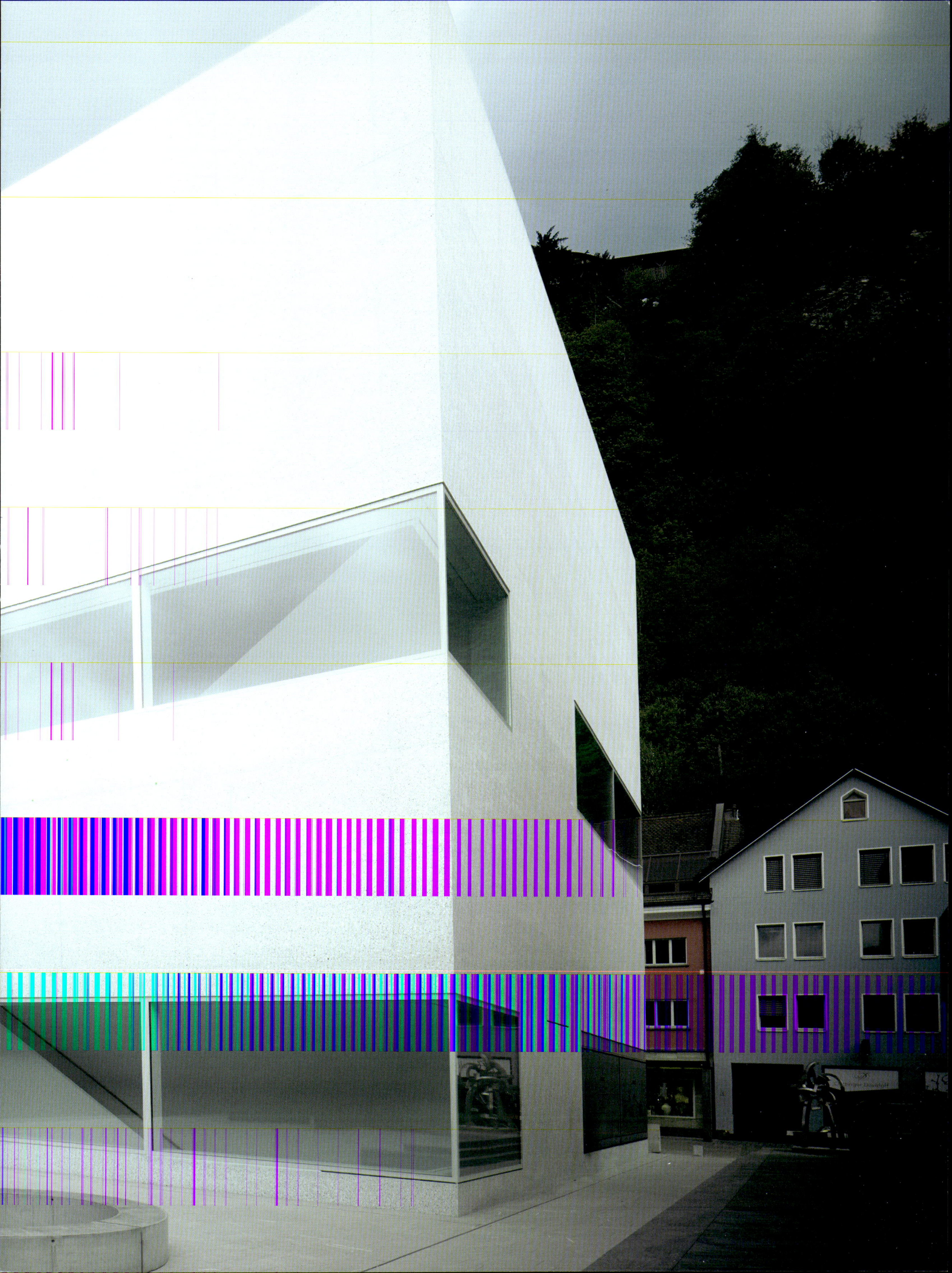

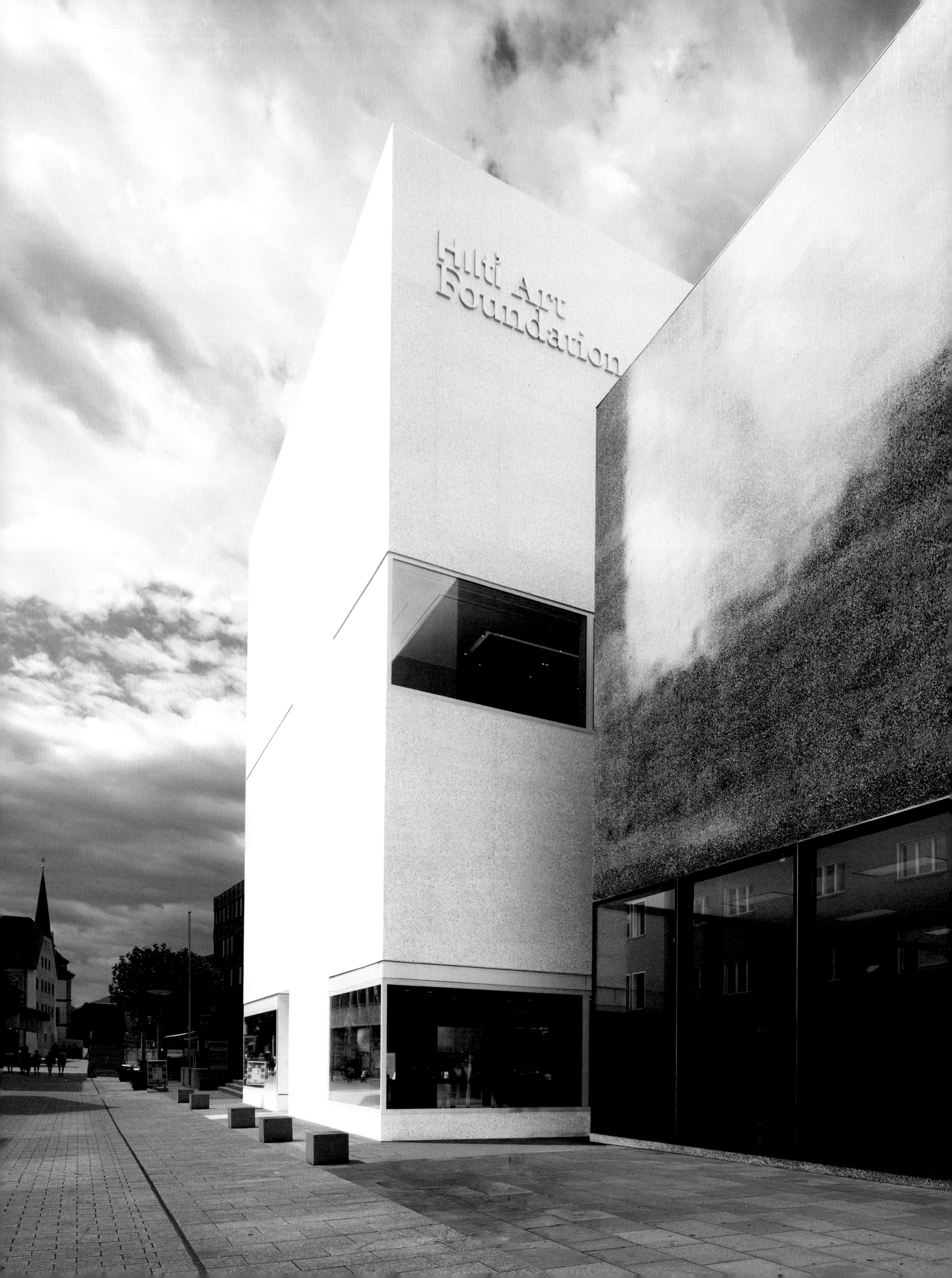
Hilti Art
Foundation

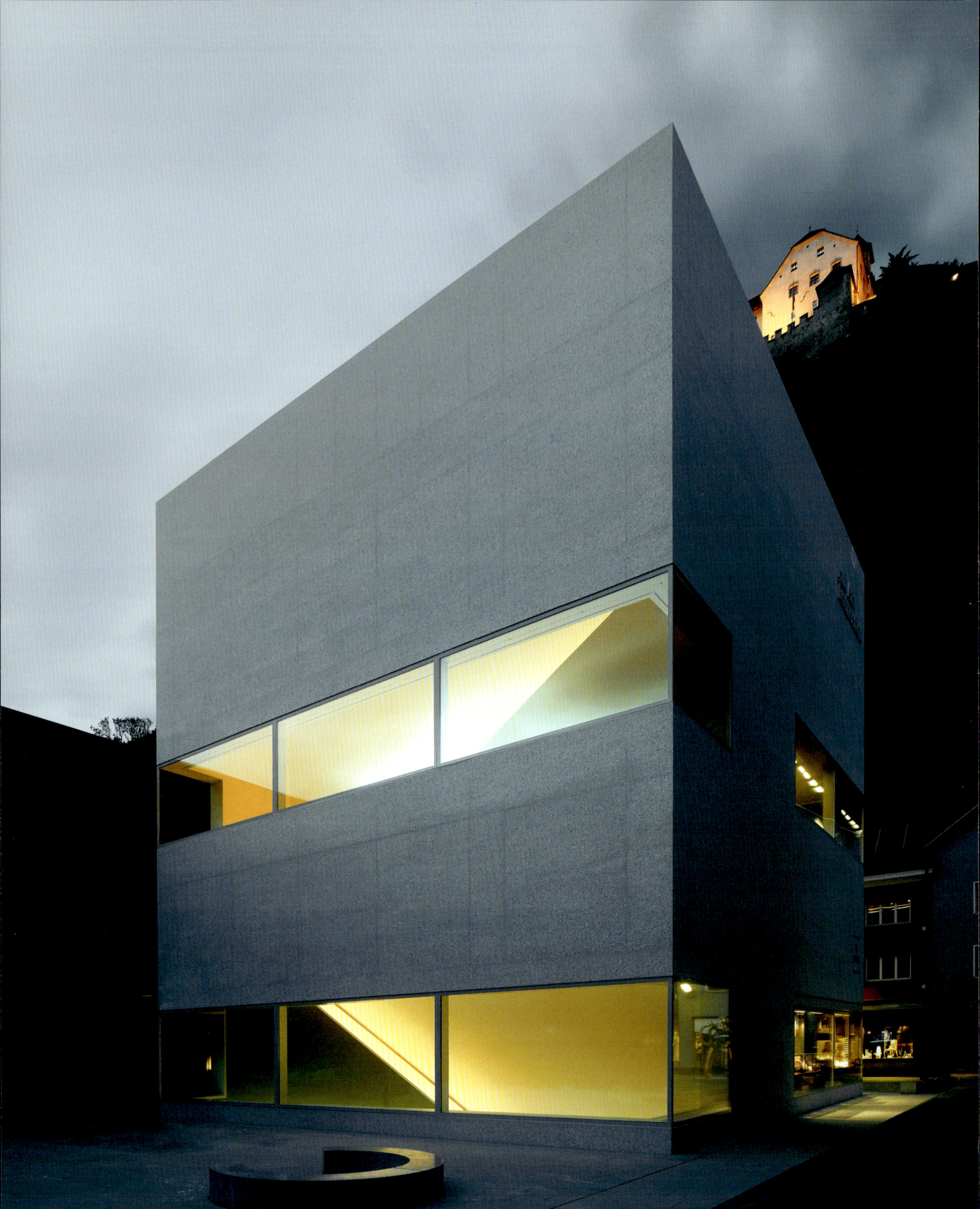

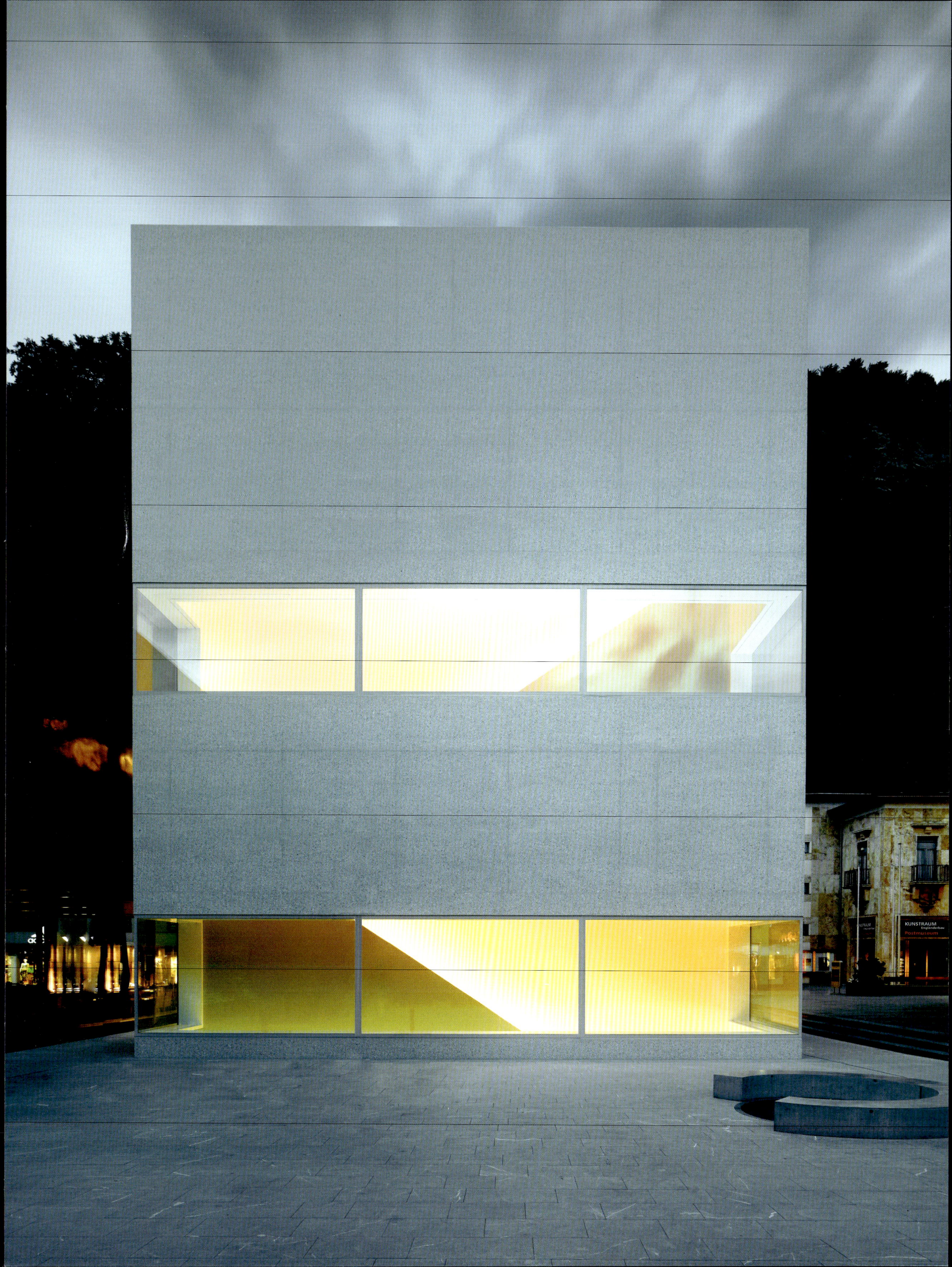
KUNSTRAUM
Engländerbau
Postmuseum

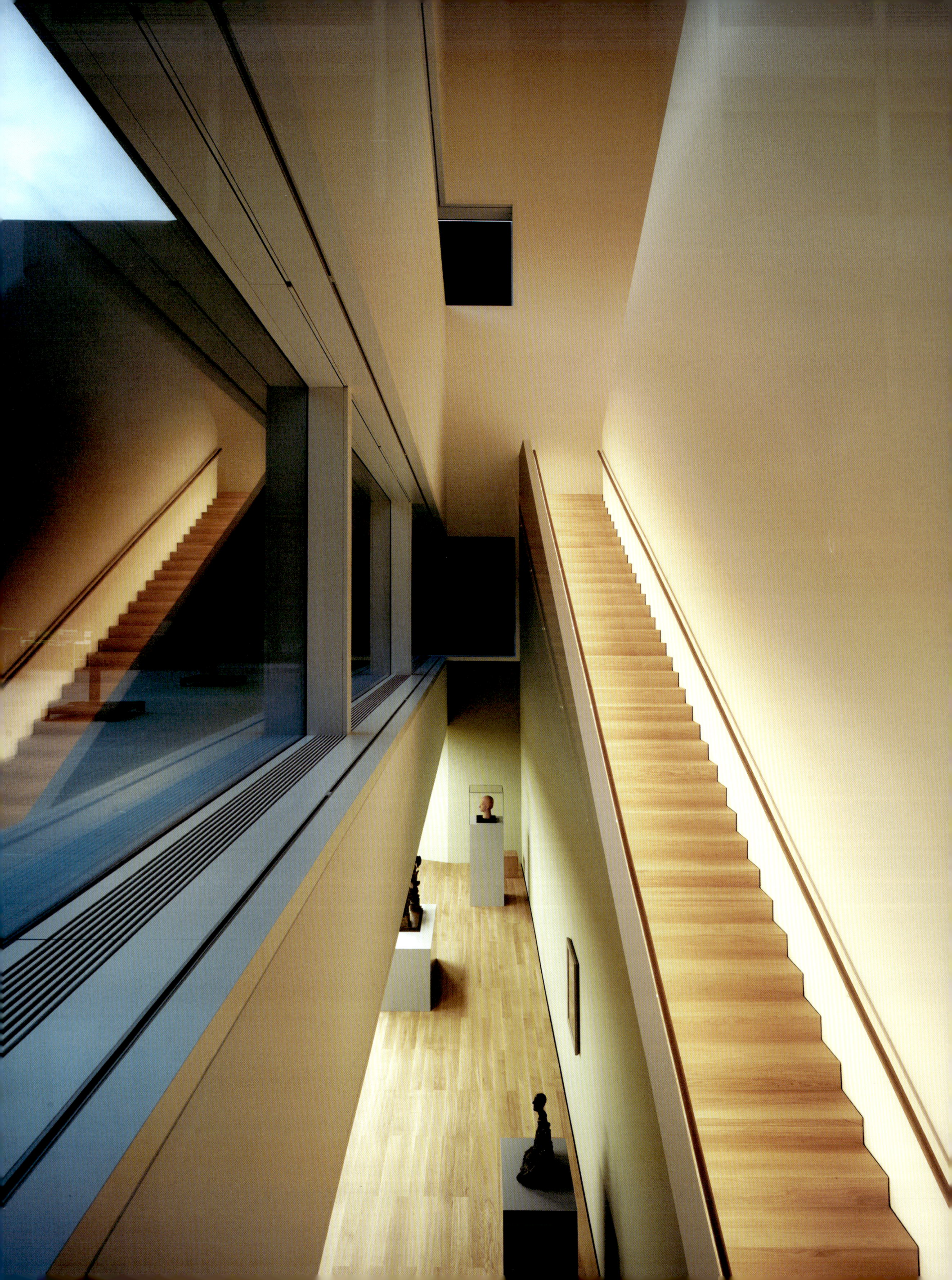

The question "Are we to compare or not to compare when considering works of art" is one we would like to answer as follows: the trained connoisseur should make comparisons, for he has a general idea, a preconceived notion of what could be and should be achieved; the amateur, still involved in the process of being educataed, can make the best progress if he does not compare but judges each achievement on its individual merit: this gradually forms an instinct and idea for the general situation. Comparison by the unknowing is really only a lazy and conceited way of avoiding judgement.

Johann Wolfgang von Goethe

Maximen und Reflexionen, 783

Hilti Art Foundation

The Collection Vol. I

Classical Modernism 1880–1950

HIRMER

Preface
Michael Hilti

For the first time in 2005, we ventured to present some 60 works from our family collections, newly named the Hilti Art Foundation, to a larger public at the Kunstmuseum Liechtenstein. The collections have been growing steadily ever since, and in 2015 we mounted a second exhibition of selected works, this time in the galleries of our own museum. These developments were inspired by the wish to make the collections permanently accessible to the public in the form of changing exhibitions. When I speak of family collections presented under the name of the Hilti Art Foundation, I am referring to the Martin Hilti Family Trust, into which the collection of my sister Ursula Zindel-Hilti was integrated when she passed away in 2016, as well as the collection belonging to myself and my wife Caroline. We have now taken the next step of publishing a comprehensive catalogue to allow in-depth study of our collections and provide greater insight into their development through the inclusion of acquisition dates.

It is perhaps of interest to trace the emergence of our collections. My parents always had works of art at home, not with the intention of building a collection but simply because they loved living with art. These were largely works by masters of earlier periods. It was only late in life that our father acquired two paintings by Emil Nolde, *Dunkles Meer* and *Mädchen im Blumengarten* as well as Paul Gauguin's *Entre les Lys*. Upon his death in 1997, our family decided to keep the collected work intact, rather than dividing it up, with the objective of using it as the wellspring of a family collection devoted to classical modernism. My wife Caroline's private collection stems from her delight in art and from encounters with our English friend and art dealer Richard Nathanson, whom we met through my work in London in 1974.

Private collectors have the privilege of being able to pursue goals that are different from those of public institutions. We need not be guided primarily by art historical considerations; we are free to decide. Our collections are an expression of this freedom; they testify to our preferences, to what we consider important and outstanding. A closer look at our work will reveal that we have always aimed to collect art that is informed with a certain sense of harmony and balance, art that not only stimulates perception and inspires new thoughts, but that is, above all, a joy to look at – in short, art that is a pleasure to live with. For us, collecting has never meant speculation; it has always been a matter of affinity and quality – art as part of everyday life, self-evident, loved and integrated. In this spirit, I hope that you, too, will share the emotion and passion that we feel for these works when you study our catalogue.

I would like to take this opportunity to thank our curator Uwe Wieczorek for his invaluable support over the past 16 years in building up and expanding the collections, the advisory board of the Hilti Art Foundation, Angela Schneider and Claudia Steinfels, as well as the galleries and auction houses for repeatedly drawing our attention to interesting works.

The Art Collection
of the Hilti Art Foundation

Uwe Wieczorek

Curator

Since it was established in 1998, the Hilti Art Foundation has functioned as the umbrella organization for two separate in-house collections, treated in public as a single entity: the Martin Hilti Family Trust, comprising art of classical modernism from approximately 1880 to 1950, and the collection of Michael and Caroline Hilti, which extends beyond modernism into the present day. In both cases, acquisitions are not merely governed by artistic reputation but equally by materials, aesthetics and subject matter as well as the manner in which they reflect the spirit of their times. Currently, the two steadily growing collections encompass over 200 paintings, sculptures, objects and photographs. Since May 2015 the museum of the Hilti Art Foundation, which conjoins the Kunstmuseum Liechtenstein in Vaduz, has been organizing exhibitions for the public of selected works from the collection.

To do justice to the quality and quantity of the art, the Hilti family and all of those responsible for the collection felt it appropriate to present the most important works from the late 19th century to the present day in book form. The two-volume publication includes meticulously rendered reproductions, texts and details, offering not only visitors to the museum but also art lovers further afield an in-depth source of information for their personal use. The present volume contains 80 works of classical modernism, starting in the 1880s and represented by such trailblazing artists as Georges Seurat, Paul Gauguin and Medardo Rosso, whose art still shows the influence of Impressionism, and moving forward into the mid-20th century with such artists as Alberto Giacometti, Jean Dubuffet and Wols and into the 1970s with Willem de Kooning. Despite the caesura of the Second World War, the two major currents of classical modernism, the figurative and the abstract, continue to resonate with great individuality in the oeuvres of these artists. Cubist, Futurist, Expressionist and Surrealist artists represent significant highlights within this temporal spectrum. In addition, the collection holds groups of work by such artists as Pablo Picasso, Paul Klee, Ernst Ludwig Kirchner, Max Beckmann and Alberto Giacometti.

As a whole, the works presented in this volume encapsulate the most important stylistic and iconographic aspects of art from the late 19th through the first half of the 20th century. The blurring of boundaries between the natural sciences and the humanities and the accelerated advance of worldwide economies, technologies and traffic have led to an unprecedented revolution in our understanding of the world and reality, unleashing radical reactions and experimentation with new forms of artistic expression. Thus, Cubism, as devised by Pablo Picasso (cat. 63) and Georges Braque, no longer depicts the empirical world but instead aims to render autonomous configurations based on stereometric forms, demonstrated as well by Juan Gris and Fernand Léger (cat. 32, 33). Exploiting multiple perspectives in the treatment of space and subject matter, the Cubists abandoned the laws of central perspective that had prevailed for centuries. Artists like Piet Mondrian, Friedrich Vordemberge-Gildewart and Rudolf Belling (cat. 34–36) drew their own consequences, devoting themselves to abstract or purely constructive, non-figurative compositions based on universal geometrical shapes. Futurism's enthusiastic embrace and glorification of modern life is exemplified by an artistic focus on movement, technology and machines. Umberto Boccioni's (cat. 30) *Forme uniche* was considered quintessentially Futurist for its embodiment of a figure entirely divested of individuality through speed.

In contrast, a sceptical view of civilization motivated artists like Paul Gauguin (cat. 2), Karl Schmidt-Rottluff, Ernst Ludwig Kirchner and Erich Heckel (cat. 14–19) to seek virgin sources of inspiration in so-called primitive cultures outside of Europe, whose content and style they assimilated into their own quest for new forms of expression. The Expressionist artists associated with the Brücke (cat. 19) and the Blaue Reiter (cat. 22, 23) discovered untouched nature as an alternative to urban life and as a place of creaturely existence that nurtures both physical and spiritual regeneration.

Poetry and magic, play and Eros, and above all the unfathomable depths of the unconscious were both source material and hunting grounds for Surrealists like Yves Tanguy, René Magritte, Max Ernst, Joan Miró (cat. 41–43, 48) and Julio González (cat. 51), while Paul Klee, Louis Soutter and Jean Dubuffet (cat. 47, 49, 78) drew on visible reality, on their own powers of the imagination and even on the creative worlds of the mentally ill and of children for inspiration in composing their emblematic works.

The art of Max Beckmann (cat. 67, 68) and Germaine Richier (cat. 72) exemplifies the dire experience of war and suffering that marked the 20th-century. Beckmann's self-portrait ranks among art's greatest testimonials to personal succour between despair and hope, manifesting the incontrovertible willingness to see and speak untarnished truths in the face of historical events. In the wake of the global catastrophes of the 1930s and 1940s, the very existence of humankind was shaken to the roots, both physically and morally. Within this context, Alberto Giacometti (cat. 73–76) attempted to render in his art the essence of what it means to be a human being. Wols (cat. 77), in turn, gazing both within and without, reacted to the turbulence of the times and the instability of his own life by renouncing figuration altogether. In his deliberately small-format paintings, the informal gesture of line and colour suffice to represent emotional impulses with an immediacy as sensitive as it is forceful. And finally – complementing the sculptures of Medardo Rosso, Alexander Archipenko, Wilhelm Lehmbruck, Pablo Picasso, Umberto Boccioni, Ernst Ludwig Kirchner, Raymond Duchamp-Villon, Max Beckmann, Henri Laurens, Germaine Richier and Alberto Giacometti – Willem de Kooning's figure (cat. 80) refers once again to the vulnerable, changeable and existentially precarious nature of humankind, rendered with such vibrancy and intensity in this section of the collection.

Despite gaps, the salient features of the collection, briefly outlined here, attempt to encompass the most important aspects of this period in art history. By enlarging and elaborating on our understanding of those years with all their upheavals, turbulence and achievements, by revealing all that is bound in time and timeless, irrevocably past enduring, this art ultimately fosters a better understanding of our own times. The works of art reproduced in this catalogue and on view at the museum of the Hilti Art Foundation are buoyed by the conviction that collecting art is not simply a matter of personal pleasure and even less so of inappropriate personal gratification. Above all, the collection reflects the desire to demonstrate the ability of art to reveal the best qualities in society and the abiding creative potential of humankind. A sense of responsibility and active citizenship has invested a *res privata* with the character of a *res publica*.

My heartfelt gratitude goes to the following people for their commitment, professionalism, reliability and support: Caroline, Michèle and Michael Hilti, all of the members of the Hilti family, the Martin Hilti Family Trust and also, in alphabetical order, to Marco Auderset, Siegfried Brugger and all the staff of the MuseumsPartner, Claudia Büchel, Kurt Dornig, Isabel Fehr, Shandor Hayde, Valentin Jeck, Günter König, Heinz Preute, Martin Rogy-Hinse, Catherine Schelbert, Angela Schneider, Louise Stein, Claudia Steinfels, Cornelia Wieczorek, Thomas Zuhr and the staff of Hirmer Verlag and all those, even unnamed, who have been indispensable to this project.

The Authors

Dr. Angela Schneider
studied art history, classical archaeology and history at the University of Munich. From 1973 to 2008 she worked at the National Gallery in Berlin, first as a curator and from 1999 additionally as Deputy Director. There she planned and mounted numerous exhibitions of 20th century international art, including one-person shows of such artists as Pablo Picasso, Alberto Giacometti, Francis Bacon, Walter de Maria and Jannis Kounellis.
AS

Dr. Uwe Wieczorek
studied art history, classical archaeology and history of bookmaking at the University of Mainz. He worked for the Berlin State Museums, and from 1992 to 2003 he was director of The Collections of the Prince of Liechtenstein. Since 2003 he has been the curator of the Hilti Art Foundation in Schaan, Liechtenstein. He planed and mounted exhibitions on art from the Renaissance to the 20th century, as well as solo presentations of such artists as Franz Erhard Walther, Sean Scully, Gottfried Honegger and Gotthard Graubner.
UW

Works of Classical Modernism

Georges Seurat
Le tas de pierres
c. 1882–1884

001

Georges Seurat
1859 Paris – 1891 Paris

Oil on canvas
33.2 × 41.3 cm

Inv. no. P44T / Acquired 2010

A man wearing dark trousers, a white shirt, and a straw hat is stoutly hacking away at stones in the earth. A second person is picking up the stones and putting them in a pile. Green vegetation provides the backdrop to this tightly framed scene. Seurat observes people hard at work in rural surroundings with the eye of an impressionist and, by the look of it, directly on-site. For he has rendered the relatively small format and therefore easily portable painting entirely in the style of Impressionism, that is, with rapidly executed brushstrokes, allowing the colours to blend before the paint dries and imbuing the whole with the sense of a moment arrested. The contours are blurred in the bright light and shimmering air; the shadows are coloured and the contrasts complementary. The two people are depicted without individualizing features.

Seurat was already familiar with Barbizon painters like Corot and Millet, as well as Courbet, whose works depicted natural environs and human labour. But when he saw the work of Manet and Pissarro at the Fourth Impressionist Exhibition of 1879 in Paris, he was so deeply impressed that he gave up studying at the Academy and, from then on, sought out the motifs of his art in the real world, in both city and country. In the early 1880s, he was drawn to the outskirts of Paris, in particular Le Raincy, where his father lived. There he observed people at work, capturing them in drawings and small oil studies that would later provide source material for the execution of larger paintings in the studio.

Early on, Seurat studied the phenomenon of colour. Insights gleaned from reading Charles Blanc's *Grammaire des arts du dessin* (1867) and Michel-Eugène Chevreul's *De la loi du contraste simultanée des couleurs* (1839) led in the mid-1880s to an increasingly systematic application of colour in his paintings. Seurat was particularly interested in the "optical blend" generated by the side-by-side of very small dabs of pure, unmixed pigments, which blend in the eyes of beholders so that they perceive the desired colours. Through this method, for which art criticism invented the terms Pointillism or Neo-Impressionism, Seurat underpinned Impressionism with theoretical and rational foundations – and simultaneously surmounted them. The method was to exert an exceptionally great influence on many contemporaries and successors of Seurat and was to rank him among the trailblazers of modern art next to Cézanne, Gauguin and van Gogh. Although Seurat did not yet apply his new method to *Le tas de pierres* (The Stone Heap), the painting does exhibit the qualities that would characterize his greatest and most enduring creations – a serene, detached and occasionally witty faculty for observation that subtly registers the constantly changing appearances in nature and modern civilization.

UW

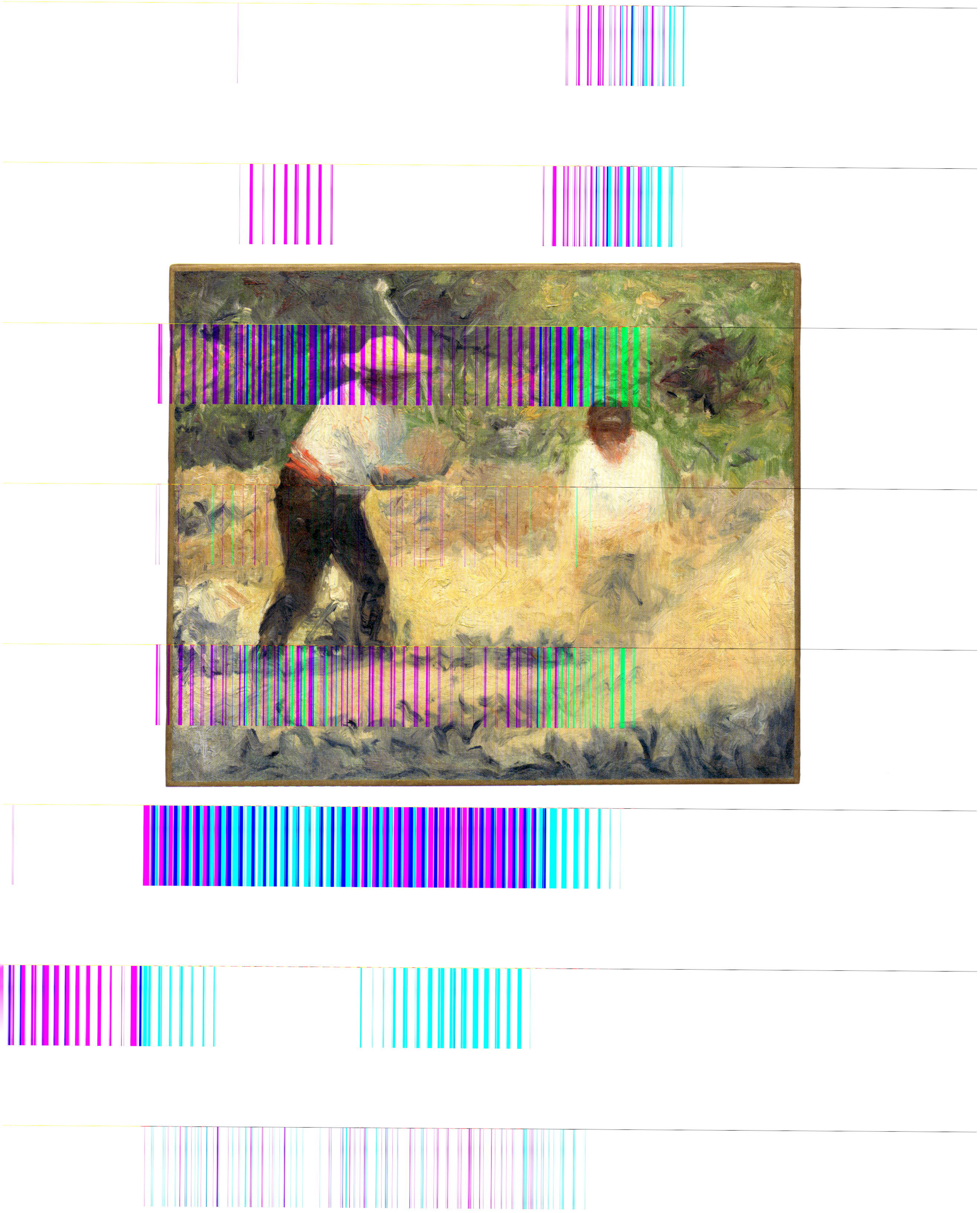

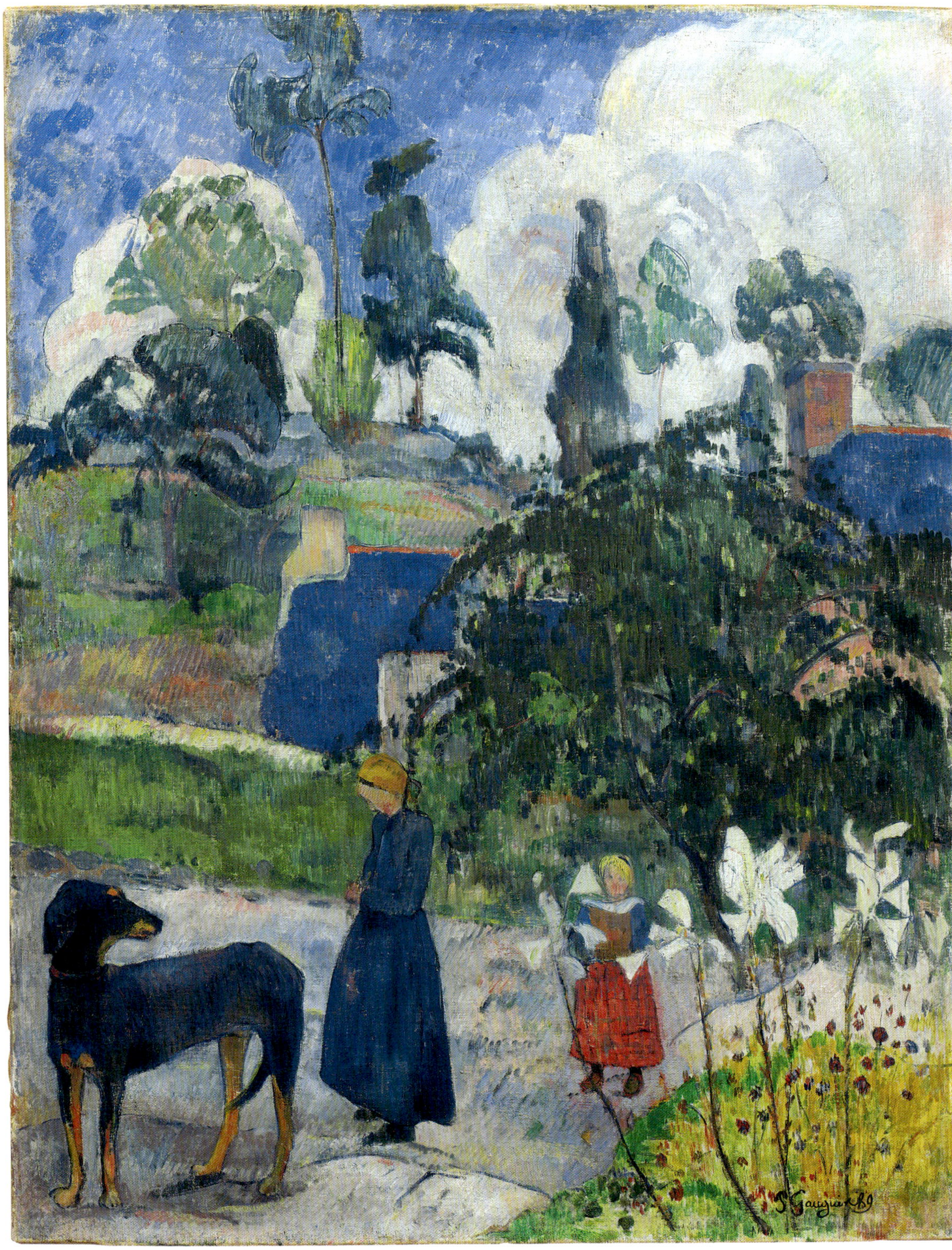

002

Paul Gauguin
1848 Paris – 1903 Hiva Oa / Marquesas Islands

Oil on canvas
Signed and dated lower right: P Gauguin 89
92 × 73.5 cm

Inv. no.: P19T / Acquired 1997

Paul Gauguin
Entre les lys
1889

When Gauguin moved to Brittany from Paris in 1886, he encountered the primal life ("la vie sauvage") that he had always longed to find and that ultimately took him to the South Seas. In the nineteenth century, Brittany was a remote region, untouched by urban civilization, where women wore traditional folk dress and still embodied the ancient myths. Life was inexpensive there and soon attracted an international colony of diverse artists with Gauguin at its core, first in Pont-Aven and later in Le Pouldu.

Gauguin painted *Entre les lys* (Among the Lilies) in the year 1889, when he had tired of the tourism in Pont-Aven and was commuting between the two villages. Although it cannot be unequivocally identified, the landscape he chose to paint in *Entre les lys* shows the low-lying hills and slate-roofed houses typical of the region. A curious procession – a dog looking back at two girls in Breton folk costume – is on its way out of the village, which the artist has framed and partially hidden behind a few trees. The dog is a nod to the great realist painter Gustave Courbet, who gave the animal pride of place in the foreground of his history painting *A Burial at Ornans* (1849). Whether the motif of a procession is also indebted to Courbet or rather motivated by Paul Gauguin's quest for a Symbolist visual idiom, which was gaining prominence in his work at the time, is a moot question.

The dog acquires special significance in comparison to a work painted shortly afterward, *The Loss of Virginity* (The Awakening of Spring), 1890–91, in which a fox plays the role of seducer. In *Entre les lys*, Gauguin presents the dog not only as protector but also suggests the animalistic drive that lures the still innocent girls out into world, passing by white lilies, the Christian symbol of purity, and away from the village flourishing in the warmth of summer.

AS

Medardo Rosso
Bambino ebreo
c. 1892–93

003

Medardo Rosso
1858 Turin – 1928 Milan

Wax on plaster
Signed: Rosso
Height: 22 cm

Inv. no. S183M / Acquired 2007

Representations of children feature prominently in the oeuvre of Medardo Rosso – from the nursing infant to girls and boys whose young lives still embody all the potential of growth and development. He pictures children who know the joy of maternal love and those whose only sustenance is the soup kitchen, children full of laughter and those suffering illness. All of them are children that he encountered in real life. In 1885 he became the father of a son.

Medardo Rosso was not only a keen observer of children and young people. As a rule he would direct his attention to the head of his subject, concentrating above all on the fleeting moment of his first impression and the visual surprise that comes directly prior to the intellectual impulse of seeking recognition. Rosso felt that the truth of that first, profoundly poetic and enigmatic impression was infinitely more meaningful than a truth based on our accumulated knowledge of dry facts. That first impression, conveyed in his sculptures, includes the spatial context around his sitters, the light in which they are standing, the tonality of the atmosphere around them, in other words, those factors that, according to the artist, enable us to forget and transcend matter.

Rosso, described by contemporary art critics as a genuine Impressionist of sculpture, experienced the fleeting moment of the first impression as a painter would, inasmuch as the salient perception of the subject captured in the work precludes looking at it from several angles. For Rosso, it makes no more sense to walk around a sculpture than it does around a painting. Nor should sculpture be touched; it should be appreciated from a distance and from the angle prescribed by the artist. This was a radical departure from an idea that has prevailed since the 16th century, namely that sculpture should be equally beautiful from all sides. *Bambino ebreo* (Jewish Child) is no exception to Rosso's rule, for it is not to be viewed from all sides. The left side and the back of the head are "unfinished". The artist's own photograph of the work shows only the right side of the face.

Rosso had some 50 copies made of this work; it meant a great deal to him and he often gave it away as a present, executed in wax on a stabilized plaster core or in bronze. The child's face features the same physiognomy, but each is different in the way it has been cast, in the use and effects of different materials, as well as the colouring, so that they are ultimately each unique. Whether the sculpture pictures Oscar Ruben Rothschild, born in 1888, whose family Rosso knew and mentioned in a letter, can only be surmised. The child clearly shows individual, almost melancholy characteristics, sensitively rendered in the soft wax with a profound appreciation of the subject's tender age.

Rosso created this particular head in Paris where he had been living since 1889. In 1893, shortly after making *Bambino ebreo*, he presented it (most probably in a different cast) at Galerie La Bodinière alongside ten other works of his. The sculptor Auguste Rodin was among those who attended this exhibition, and the two artists struck up a friendship although it was not always without undertones of jealous rivalry.

UW

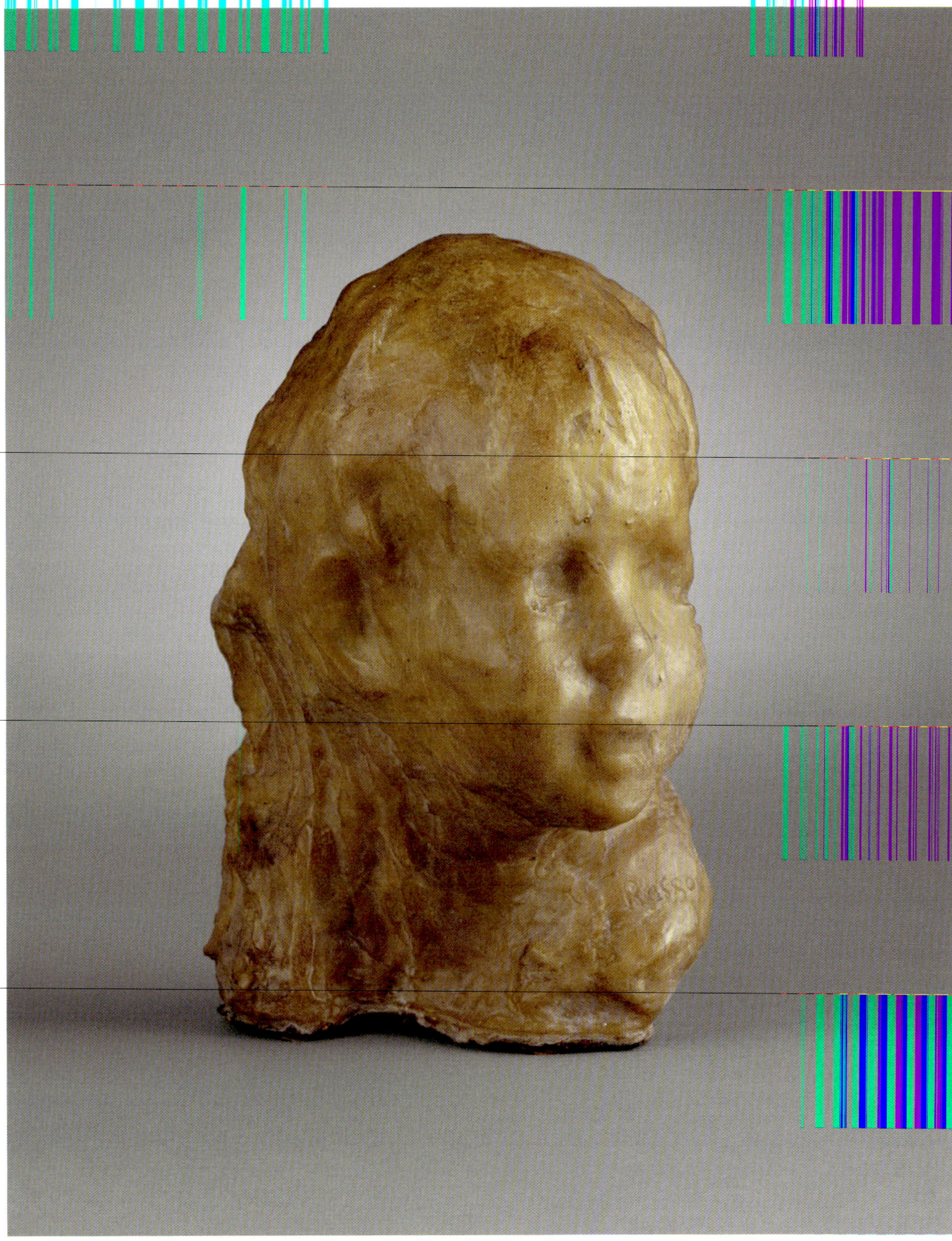

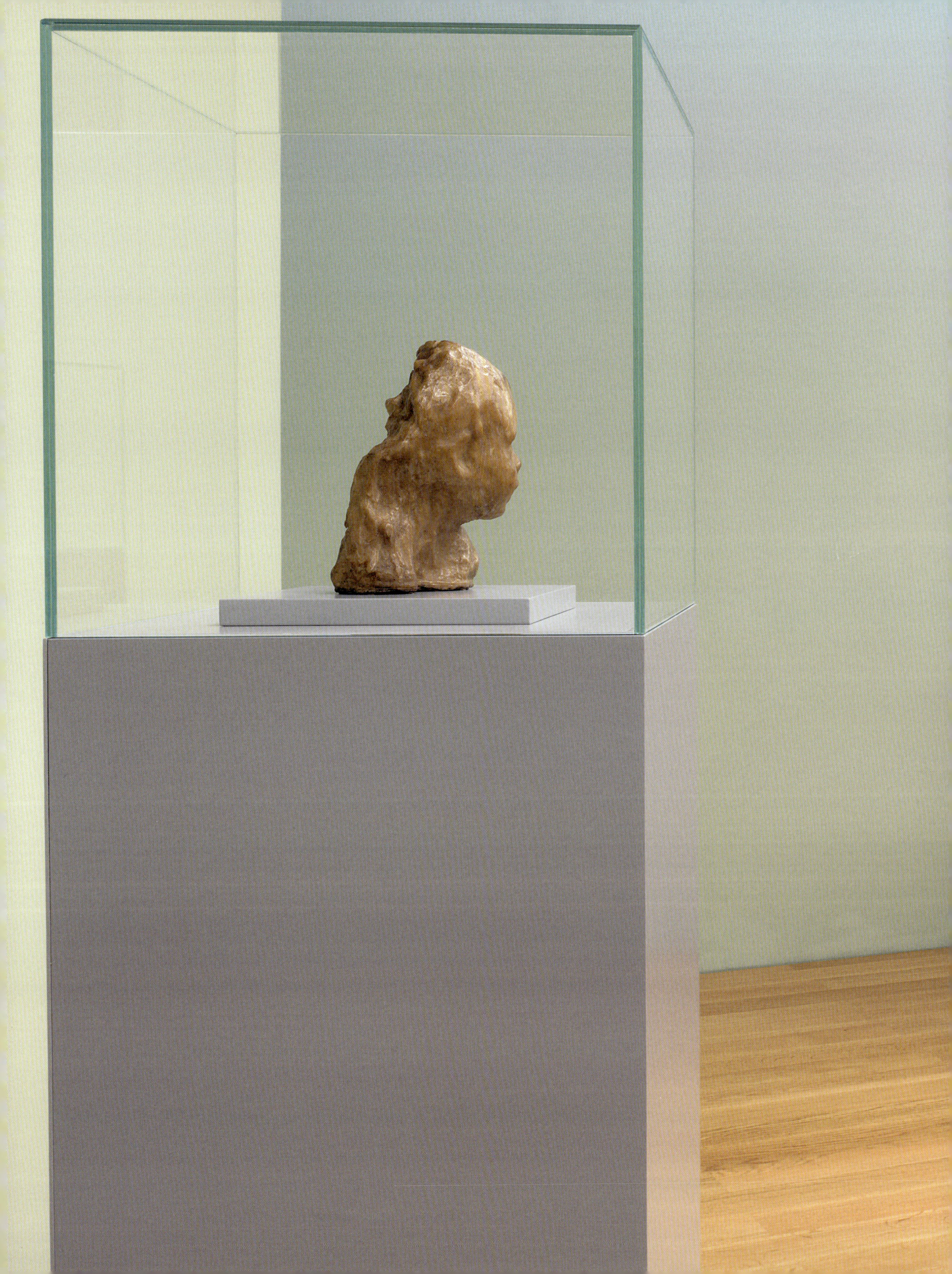

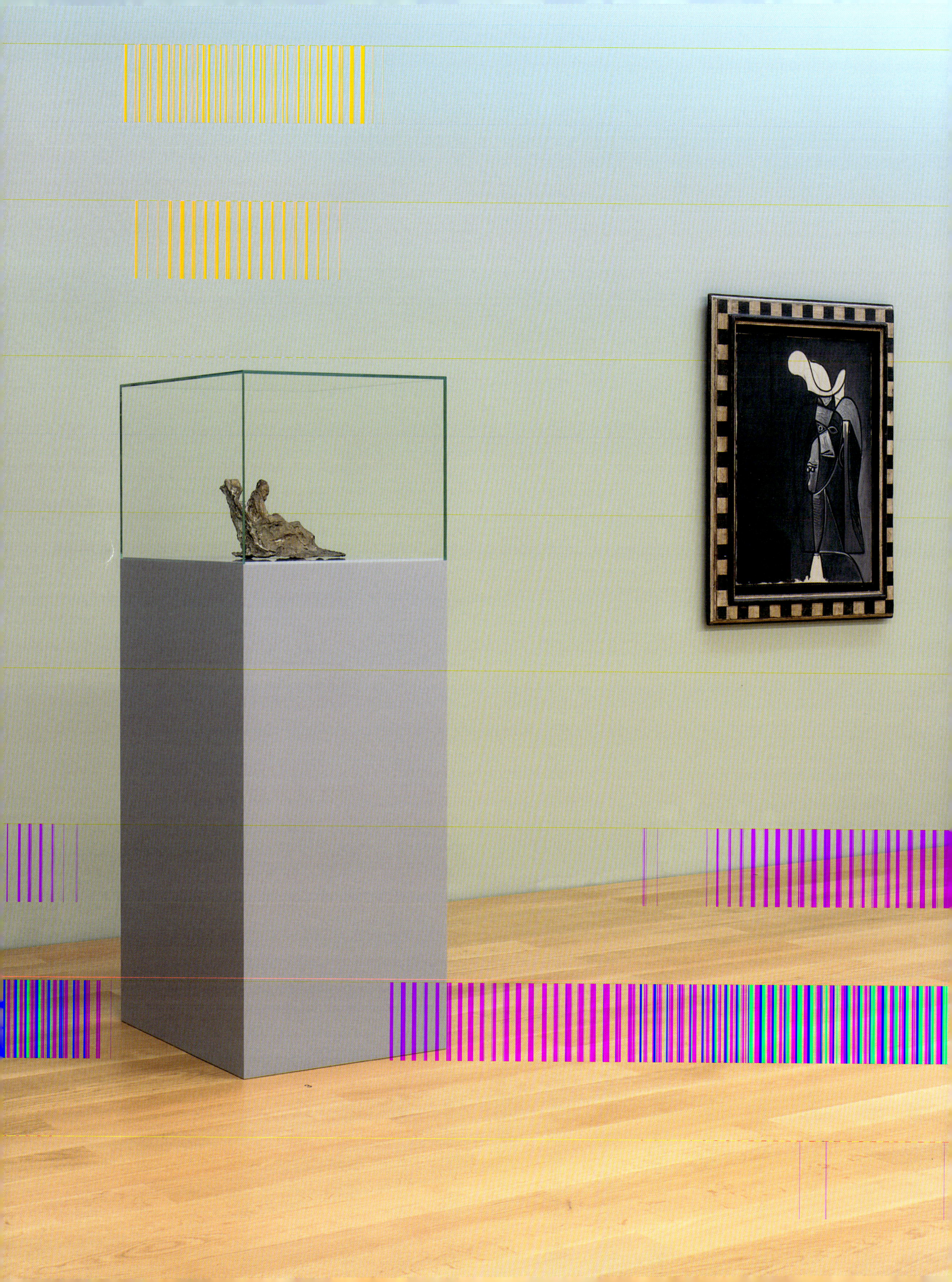

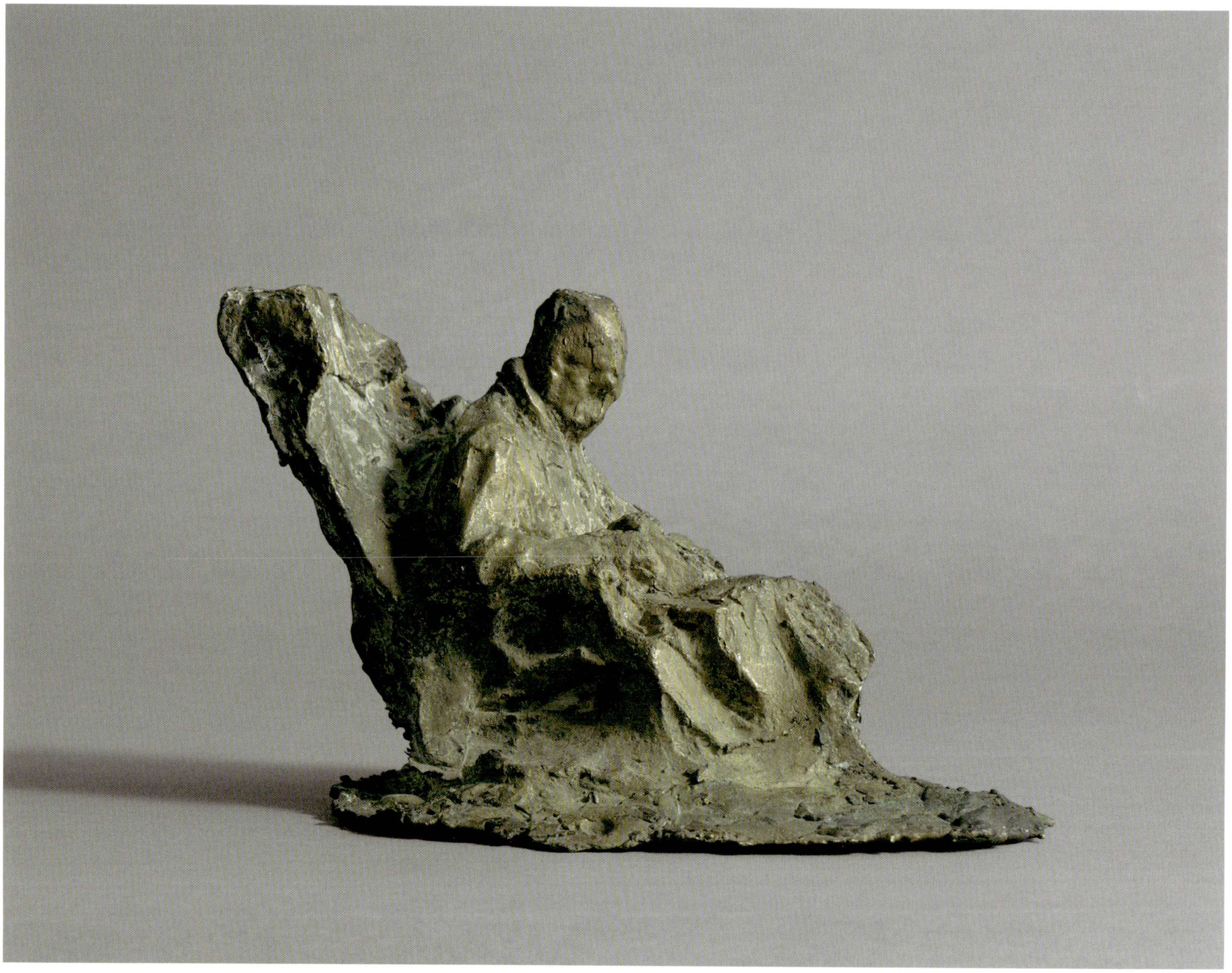

004

Medardo Rosso
1858 Turin – 1928 Milan

Bronze with plaster remnants (cast c. 1906)
Signed: Rosso (on the cast)
Height: 19.7 cm

Inv. no. S68T / Acquired 2017

Medardo Rosso
Malato all'ospedale
1889

Medardo Rosso's bronze sculpture *Malato all'ospedale* (Après la visite) superbly complements the artist's wax figure *Bambino ebreo* in the collection of the Hilti Art Foundation (cat. 3). Created in 1889 at the age of 31, it was the artist's response to his observation of an old, ailing man while he himself was a patient at the Parisian Hôpital Lariboisière. It is the first work Rosso made after moving to the French capital and may have been inspired by Vincenzo Vela's sculpture *Les derniers jours de Napoléon* (1866).

As so often in Rosso's oeuvre, *Malato all'ospedale* captures a scene from everyday life. The man is sitting in an armchair – hunched over, too weak to straighten up, as if reduced entirely to waiting for the end of his life. As in *Bambino ebreo*, Rosso is motivated by the quest for the truth of the first impression. Once again and undoubtedly in the spirit of Impressionism, he seeks to render the light and tonality of the entire atmosphere around the figure. And indeed, the ailing man merges inseparably with the material and immaterial elements of his existence, with his clothing, the armchair, the floor and with the entire light- and air-filled space of the artist's first impression.

The old man's face shows hardly any individual traits. What's more, the possibility of concrete interpretation is overlaid by the formlessness that emerges when viewers change their vantage point. Typically, *Malato all'ospedale* is not a full sculpture in the round, testifying to Rosso's conviction that one cannot do justice to the truth of the first impression if a sculpture is complete on all sides. The back remains unfinished. Logically therefore, Rosso's own photographs of *Malato all'ospedale*, although shot from different heights and angles, show only the front of the sculpture.

In 1906 and until his death, Rosso stopped producing new compositions, devoting himself instead to variations of sculptures he had already made and having them cast in foundries or casting them himself. In 1896 he had already acquired a small foundry of his own in Paris. As in the present work, he rarely smoothed or eliminated the traces of the casting process, preserving them as detailed evidence of the creative composition and the process of casting. He produced *Malato all'ospedale* in bronze, plaster and wax with variations in the painted coat or patina.

UW

Pierre Auguste Renoir
Portrait de Nini Lopez
1876

005

Pierre Auguste Renoir
1841 Limoges – 1919 Cagnes-sur-Mer

Oil on canvas
Signed upper right: Renoir
27 × 22 cm

Inv. no. P73T / Acquired 2005

Nini Lopez, her head inclined, is as bashful as she is charming, freshly captured with vibrant strokes of the brush, entirely in the style of French Impressionism, by one of the movement's most renowned representatives, Pierre Auguste Renior. The young woman lived in Montmartre in Paris, where Renoir had met her in the early 1870s and subsequently asked her to pose for him.

She made her first appearance as Renoir's model in *La Loge*, painted in 1874 on the occasion of the first Impressionist exhibition that same year and presented in photographer Félix Nadar's studio on Boulevard des Capucines 35 in Paris. There she is seen, elegant and stylish, in an opulent setting, while this portrait, small in format, tightly framed and with portions of it "unfinished", has the character of an intimate, spontaneous likeness. Bright daylight illuminates the gentle blush of her cheeks, emphasizing the youthful traits of the young woman's countenance. These appealed to Renoir so much that he repeatedly painted Nini Lopez in ever new settings and changing roles.

As observed by Georges Rivière, a French art critic and friend of the artist, Renoir's model was not only grave and discreet; she also had a superb head with a classical profile, beautifully glossy hair and long eyelashes under shapely eyebrows. For Renoir, Nina Lopez was the ideal embodiment of feminine beauty. She left him in 1887 to marry an actor from Montmartre.

UW

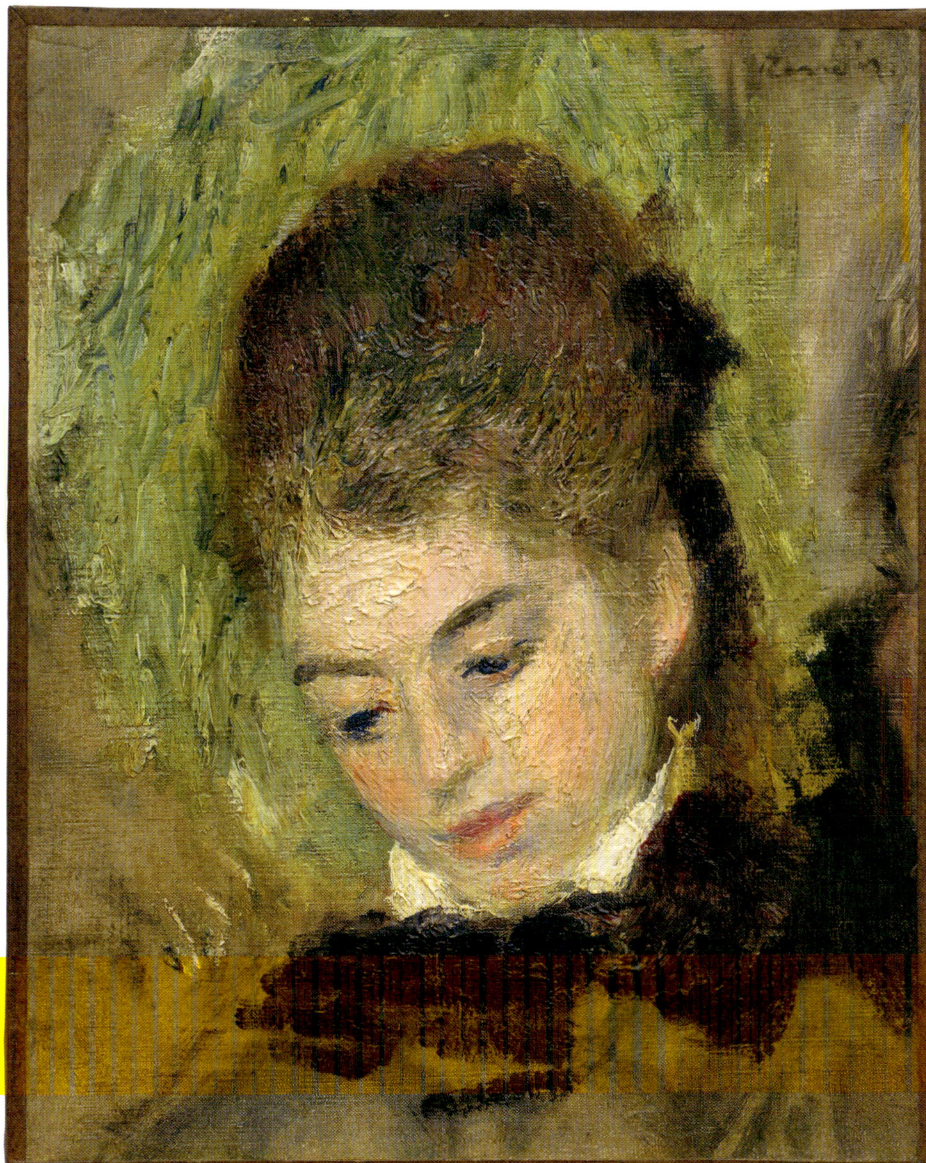

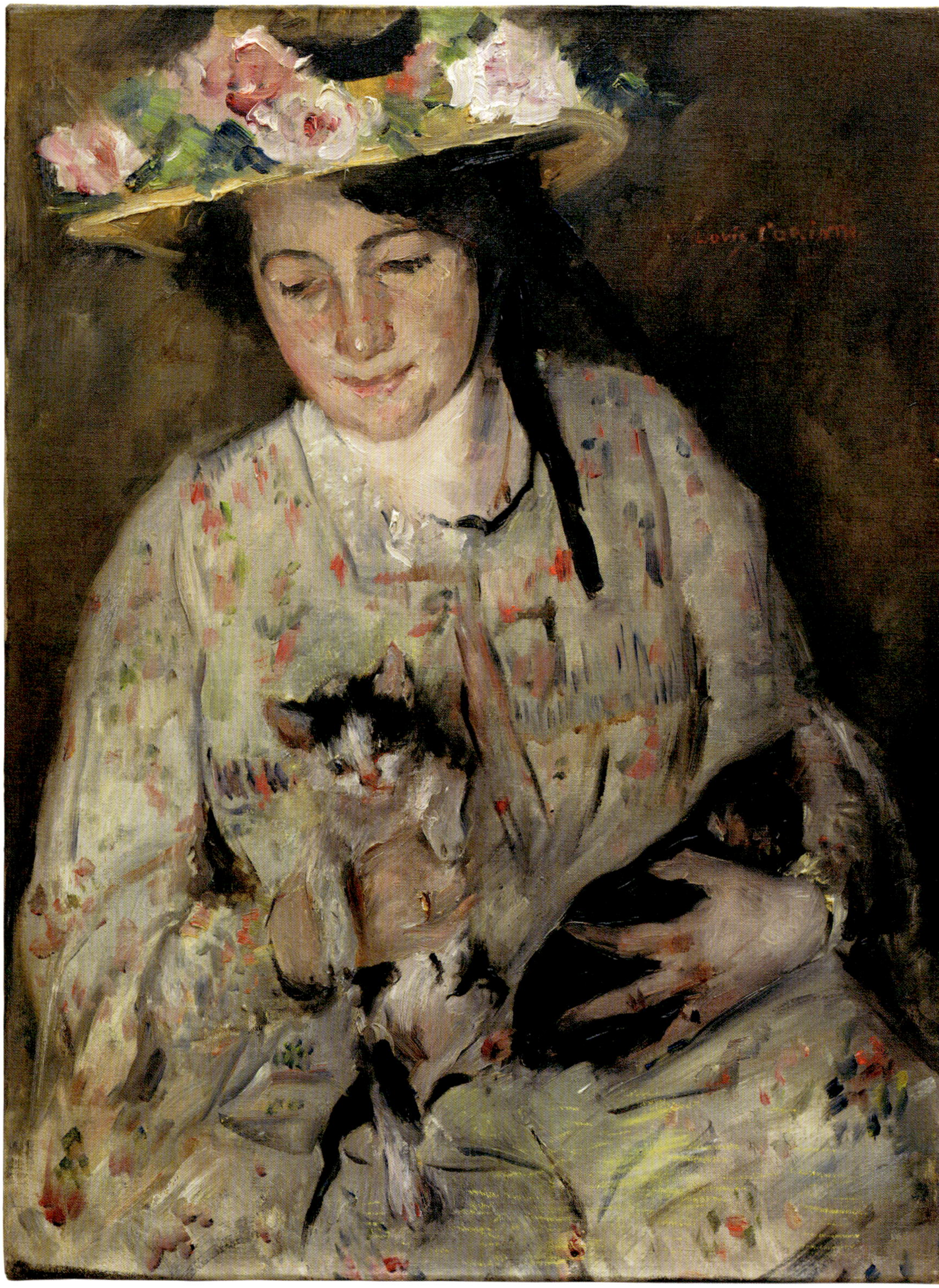

Lovis Corinth
1858 Tapiau – 1925 Zandvoort

Oil on canvas
Signed upper right: Lovis Corinth
78.5 × 60 cm

Inv. no. P75T / Acquired 2012

Lovis Corinth
Junge Frau mit Katzen (Charlotte Berend-Corinth)
1904

When Lovis Corinth painted this intimate and sensuous portrait of 24-year-old Charlotte Berend in 1904, the two had just been married. The young woman's wedding ring is clearly visible on her right hand. Artistically talented, she began taking art lessons in 1901 from the painter, more than two decades her senior, who had become a member of the Secession in Berlin that same year, after previous sojourns in Paris and Munich. Charlotte Berend, already pregnant when the two were wed, did not relinquish her family name, but instead appended that of her husband. Their son Thomas was born on 13 October 1904. Hence, the young woman in the present painting was not only a newlywed but also happily expecting.

Her charming appearance is equally indebted to the loving but also "painterly" eye of the artist. Corinth has captured Charlotte in close up, picturing her slightly from above against a dark ground. Wearing a light, filmy summer dress and a lavishly decorated floral hat, she is cuddling two kittens with tender care. Pensive and introverted, she is gazing neither at the viewer nor at the kittens. An atmosphere of peaceful happiness embraces her, beautifully expressed in the understated, Impressionist execution of the painting. The painter pays homage to his young wife as a woman and also, through her sensuous presence, to the future life budding within her. In 1909 she gave birth to their second child, a daughter Wilhelmine.

Corinth painted numerous portraits of Charlotte Berend, born in 1880, the second daughter of a well-to-do family in Berlin. She served as his model in other contexts as well. Although she devoted herself selflessly to her family and her husband's life as an artist, and even more so after he suffered a stroke in 1911, she continued to engage in her own work as painter, illustrator of books and writer. In 1906, she also joined the Secession in Berlin and exhibited her paintings there. After her husband died, she managed his estate, published a biography in 1926, and in 1958 a catalogue raisonné of his paintings, commemorating his 100th birthday. Being Jewish, she fled via Switzerland to the United States in 1939. She died in New York in 1967.

UW

Lovis Corinth
Apfelblüten und Flieder
1920

007

Lovis Corinth
1858 Tapiau – 1925 Zandvoort

Oil on canvas
Signed upper left: Lovis Corinth. 1920.
99.5 × 82.5 cm

Inv. no. P74T / Acquired 2007

The genre of the still life is associated with the thought that all things earthly are transient, and Corinth's painting *Apfelblüten und Flieder* (Apple Blossoms and Lilac) of 1920 is no exception. No matter how exuberant the rendering of the apple and lilac branches, their beauty is inevitably of brief duration. The first petals already lie scattered next to the vase on the table. The elongated branches have been placed in a crystal vase, according to Charlotte Berend-Corinth's brief description in the catalogue raisonné of her husband's paintings, which she wrote and published in 1958. She also mentions the white tissue paper underneath the vase as well as a box of watercolours with paintbrush and a glass of water. In addition, we learn that Corinth painted this still life at Klopstockstrasse in Berlin, where he had been living and working since 1901.

From the letters Corinth wrote or received, published in a documentation by his son Thomas Corinth in 1979, we learn about the specific circumstances of pictures painted around 1920. Thus, for example, an import-export businessman from Hamburg commissioned still lifes of flowers in exchange for the delivery of foodstuffs, such as cocoa, sugar and coffee, which were in short supply in Germany after the First World War. *Apfelblüten und Flieder* may have been one such painting although the title is not explicitly mentioned since, as a rule, the client gave the artist carte blanche in his choice of subject matter.

Still lifes, depicting flower arrangements in particular, are the most prolific genre in Corinth's late oeuvre, amounting to more than seventy paintings. Like his series of Walchensee landscapes, they demonstrate the artist's extraordinary mastery and freedom in the treatment of colour. From the very beginning, colour played a crucial role in Corinth's compositions, as also revealed in his history and genre paintings. As in *Junge Frau mit Katzen* of 1904 (cat. 6), *Apfelblüten und Flieder* combines darker hues with a light, Impressionist palette. At the same time, the pigments, applied with great sensitivity and a nervous hand, invest the painting with an air that would seem to show more affinity with Expressionism than with Impressionism. Basically, Corinth addressed the great themes of painting with a temperament as sensuous as it is robust. A stroke in 1911 which paralyzed his left side, critically undermined his vitality. After physically recovering and returning to his art, Corinth suffered gradual, insidious change described by his wife, in 1920 – the year he painted this picture: "His state of mind was very unsteady. Time and again he was in despair, sensing that he had not achieved what he had set out to do." The slanting, unsteady stroke of the brush and the dissolution of all con-tours lend the subject matter of Corinth's late work a transience that seems to consume all substance and, upon looking at his last self-portraits, even the artist himself.

UW

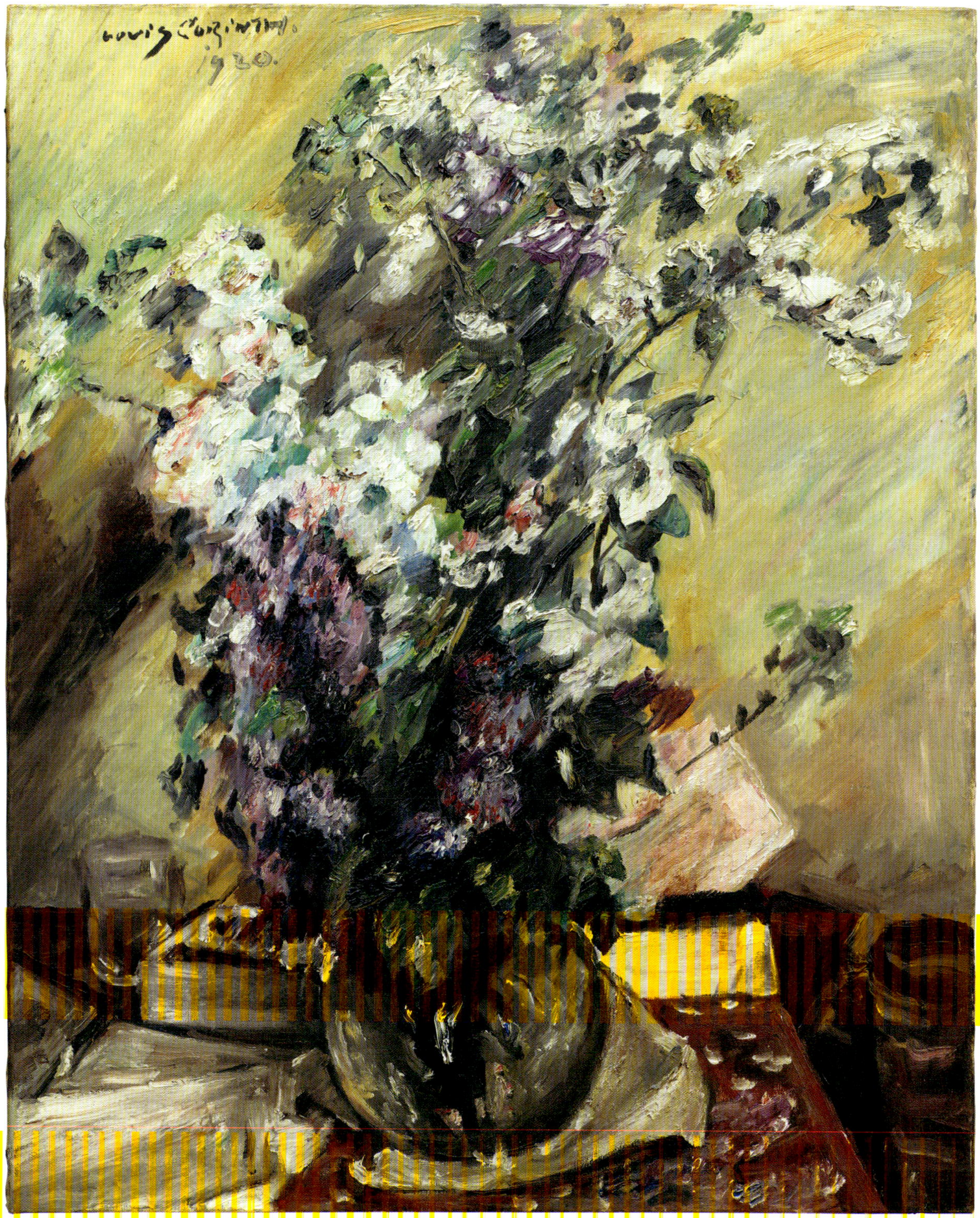

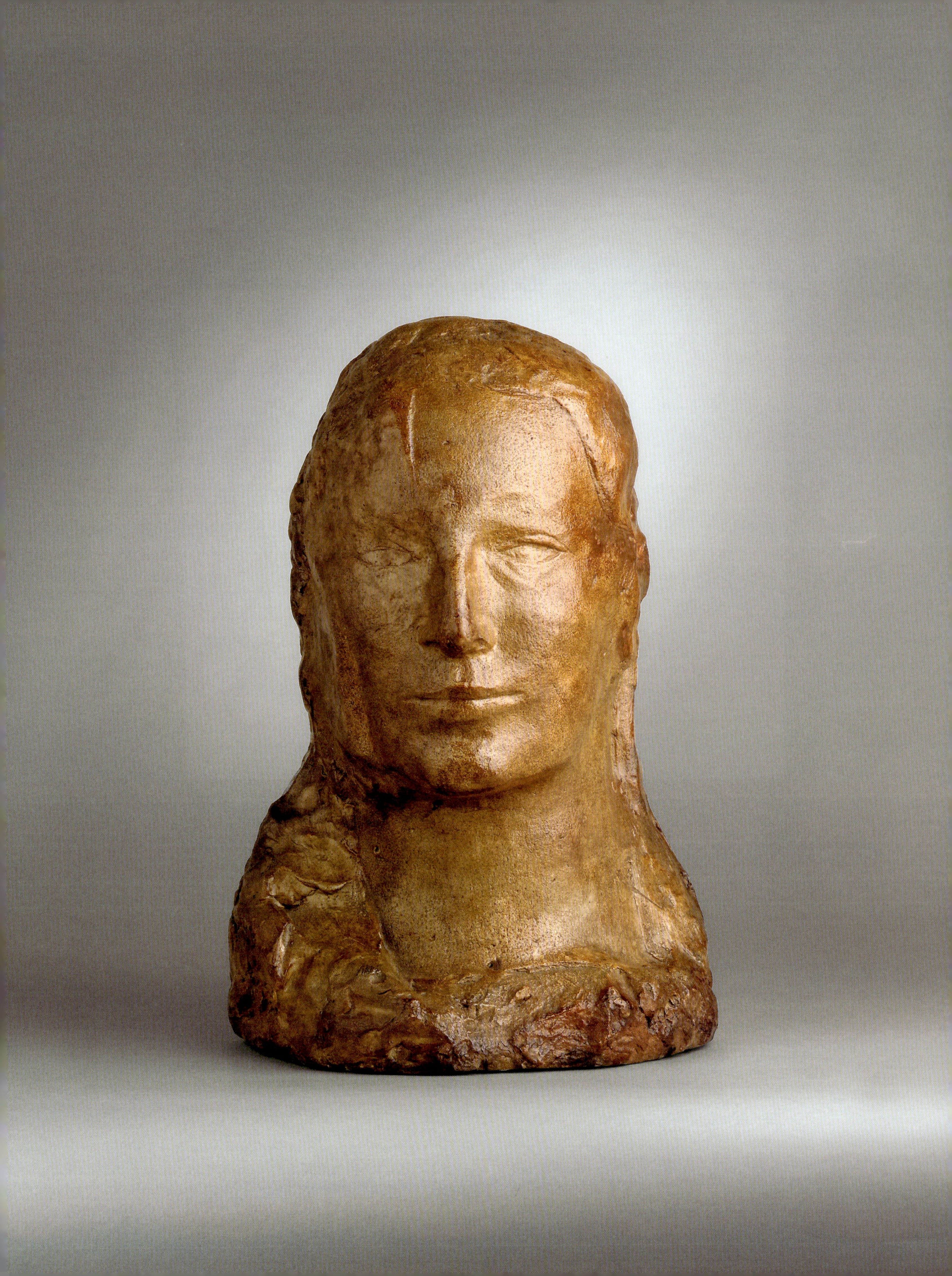

Pablo Picasso
1881 Málaga – 1973 Mougins / Cannes

Plaster, shellac
Signed on verso: Picasso
Height: 36.3 cm

Inv. no. S1T / Acquired 2001

Pablo Picasso
Tête de femme (Fernande)
1906

Picasso's sculptural oeuvre encompasses 664 works. Although much less familiar, apart from a few exceptions, than his body of paintings, it is similarly characterized by ceaseless change in form, content and expression. The artist created *Tête de femme (Fernande)* in the first half of 1906 during a time of artistic upheaval. He had just abandoned his blue and pink periods to devote himself to "primitivism", Gauguin and early Iberian sculpture.

Tête de femme is the first full sculpture made by Picasso of the head of his then lover Fernande Olivier, who shared with him the years he spent at Montmartre in the Bateau Lavoir. In 1904–05, the sensual young woman with almond-shaped eyes began making frequent appearances in drawings and paintings. Fernande, said to have had a weakness for perfume and furs, gazes at us head on with elegant noblesse. Her hair frames her face and falls loosely to her shoulders. This face, accentuated by a narrow, slightly curved nose and a distinctive mouth, is composed of two different halves. The right side is rougher, less finished, and the tactile surface appeal of the material emphasized. Picasso presumably achieved this effect by pressing gauze into the damp plaster. The right eye engraved in the surface appears to be blind, at least in the bronze version, in contrast to the sculpted and clearly seeing left eye. The asymmetry of the two halves is more than a formal distinction. It demonstrates the fact that the two sides of our faces are dissimilar by nature and refers, of course, to that same phenomenon in the sitter's face, where they might be described as clear and diffuse. The principle of uneven facial features was to play a prominent role in Picasso's oeuvre and recurred with great virtuosity in the decades that followed.

The painterly version of *Tête de femme* echoes the tradition of Auguste Rodin and Medardo Rosso, whose sculptures Picasso had seen in 1904 and 1905. The windblown hair around Fernande's face establishes her as a "creature of nature", redolent of the melancholy mood that marked the turn of the century.
AS

Wilhelm Lehmbruck
Torso der Grossen Stehenden
1910

009

Wilhelm Lehmbruck
1881 Meiderich / Duisburg – 1919 Berlin

Stone cast
Signed on right thigh: LEHMBRUCK
Height: 118 cm

Inv. no. S55T / Acquired 2013

Wilhelm Lehmbruck went to Paris in 1910 after completing a conventional academic education in Düsseldorf. Having become a member of the *Societé Nationale des Beaux-Arts* in 1907, he was familiar with the French capital through his participation in the annual exhibitions. In 1910, he began contributing to the *Salon d'Automne*, where he made the acquaintance of important artists such as Archipenko, Brancusi, Derain, Léger and Modigliani. In 1904, Lehmbruck had already seen a large retrospective of Rodin's work at the International Art Exhibition in Düsseldorf.

At the *Salon d'Automne* of 1910, he exhibited his larger-than-life *Grosse Stehende* (Large Standing Nude), cast in tinted plaster. It was the twenty-nine-year-old artist's first major work. The elongated limbs of this full-length figure were to become characteristic of sculptures made between 1911 and 1918. That same year Lehmbruck made his *Torso der Grossen Stehenden* (Torso of the Large Standing Nude). As Dietrich Schubert explains, the decision to depict only the torso enabled the artist to capture the quintessence of the figure by reducing it to essentials. The exquisitely balanced result clearly embodies Lehmbruck's artistic principle: "All art is scale, scale against scale, that is all." As in the work of Hans von Marées, to whom he was deeply indebted by his own account, Lehmbruck constructed the body as a piece of architecture seen from the front, with an axial skeleton around which the classically moulded thighs, hips, breasts, and shoulders are grouped. The contours of the figure reinforce the harmony of its self-contained presence. The inclined head and lowered eyes are not so much an expression of melancholy, as often observed, but rather a sign of inner peace and concentration. In comparison to Maillol's nudes – Lehmbruck studied them in Paris – the nude torso is neither erotically seductive nor overly modest. The artist has made a visual statement of existential and serene beauty.

This *Torso der Grossen Stehenden* is one of the two casts produced in Lehmbruck's lifetime. Parts of the grey "stone mass", as he called it, show a flesh-tinted pink, quickening the torso with a touch of animate life.

AS

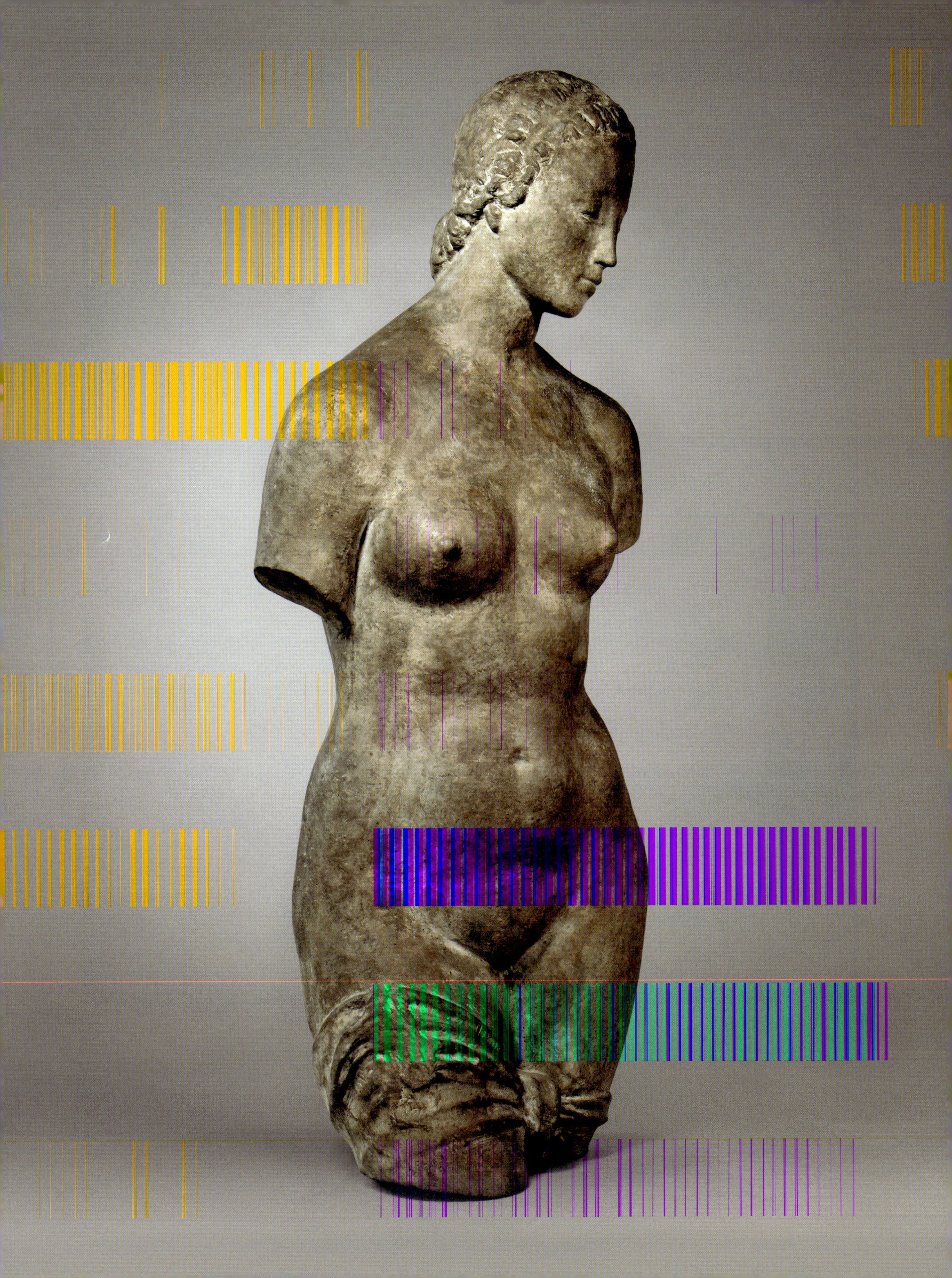

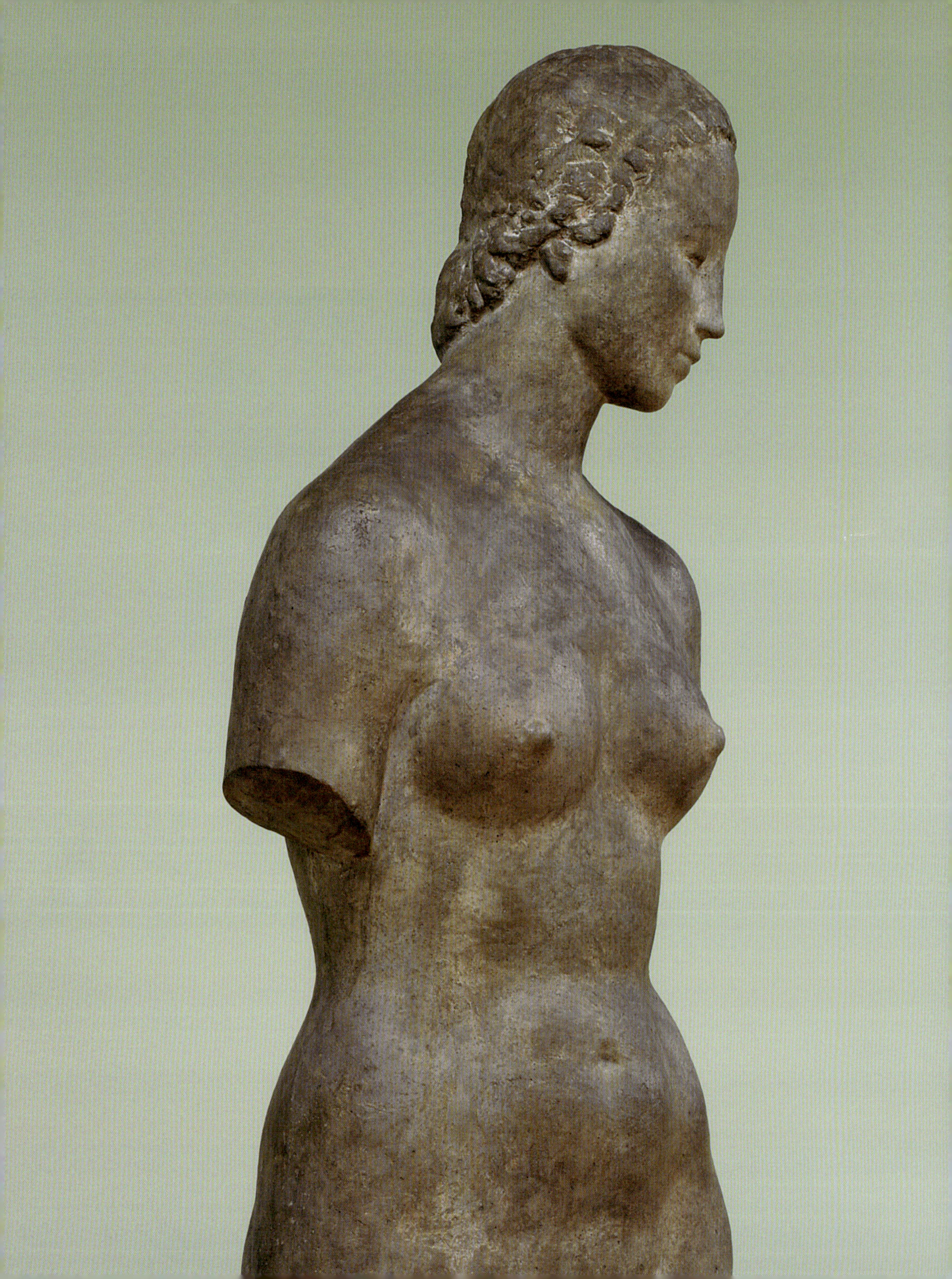

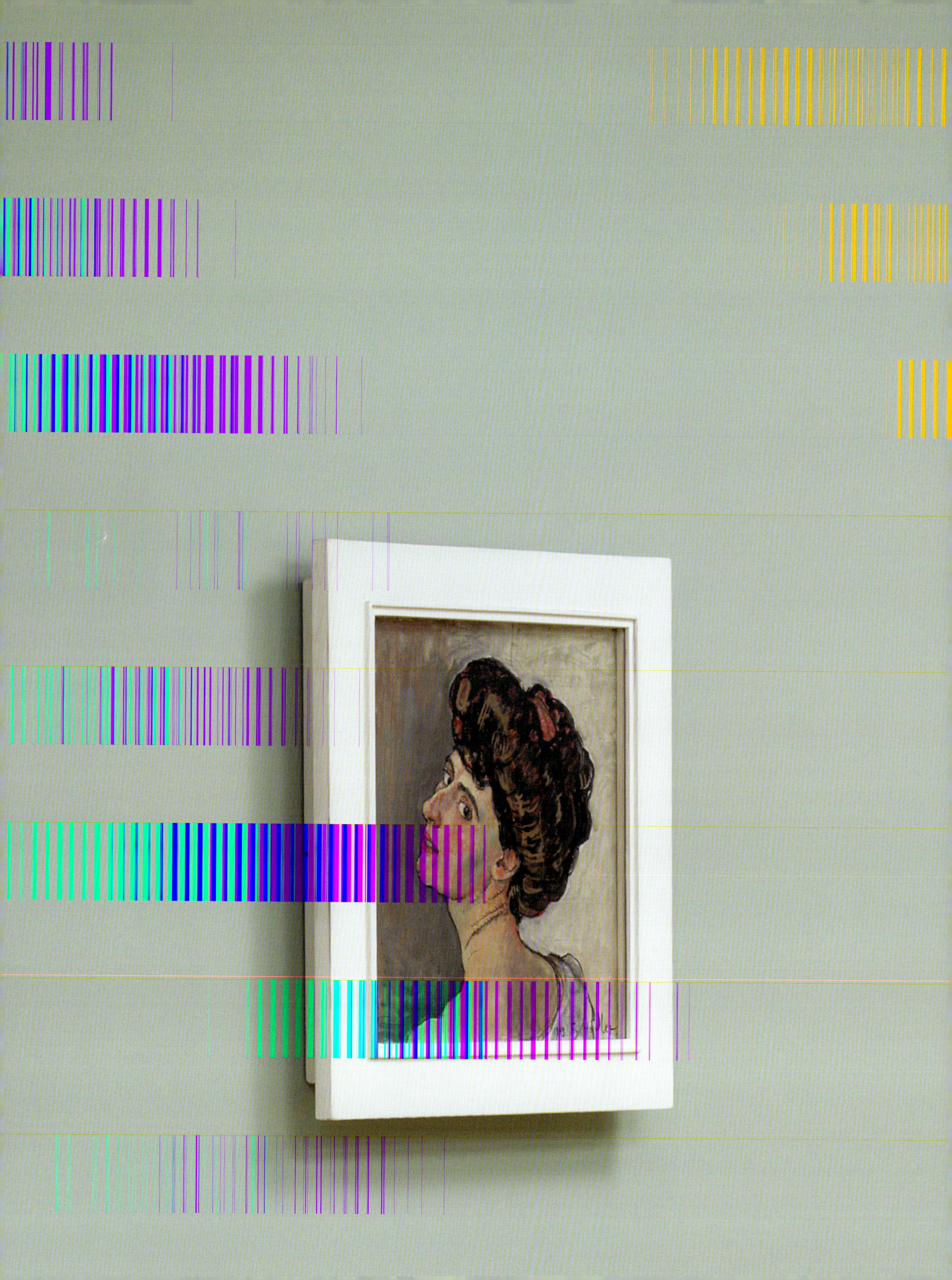

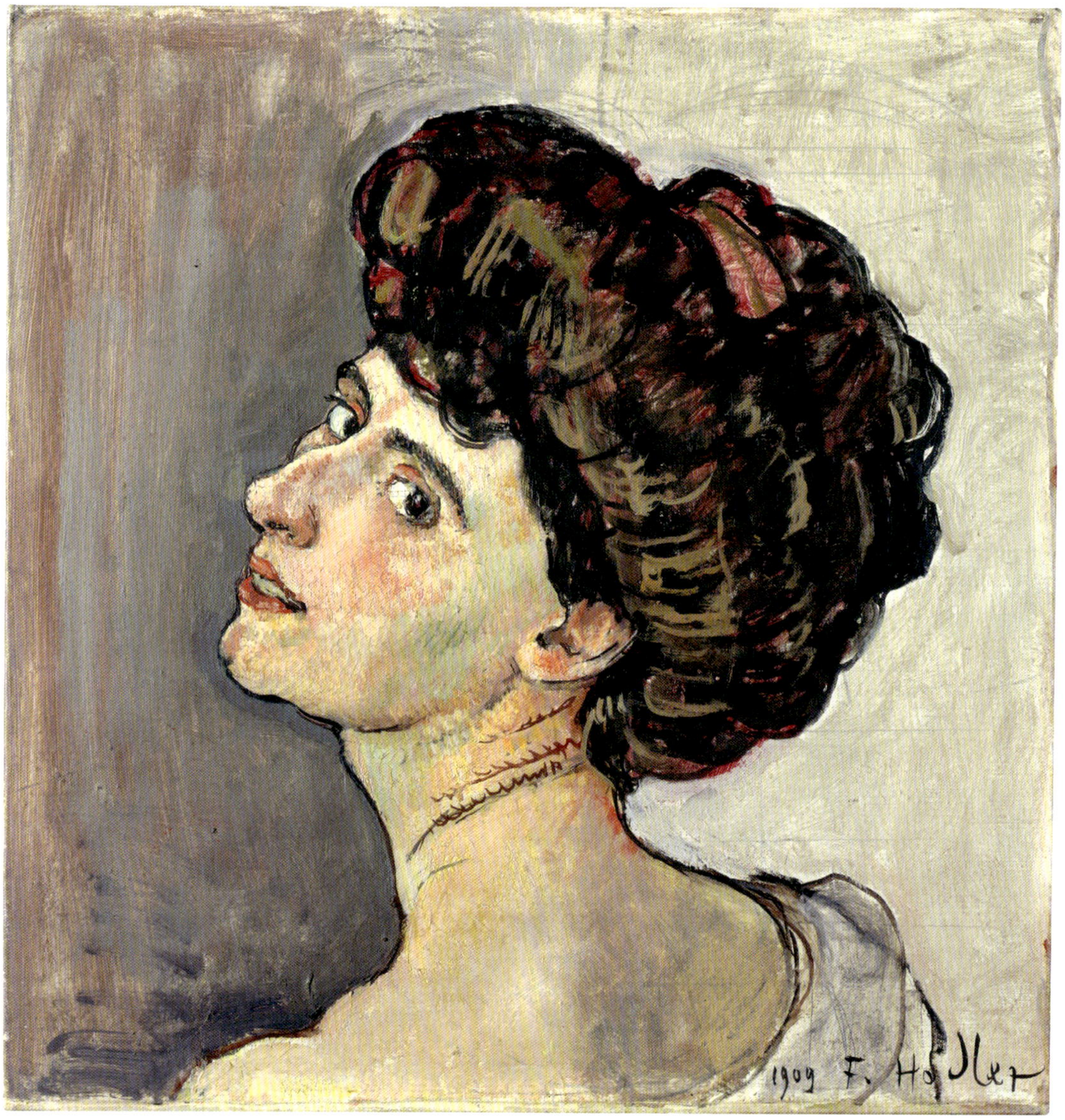

010

Ferdinand Hodler
Bildnis Valentine Godé-Darel (La Parisienne I)
1909

Ferdinand Hodler
1853 Bern – 1918 Geneva

Oil on canvas
Signed and dated lower right:
1909 F. Hodler
41.8 × 40.5 cm

Inv. no. P52T / Acquired 2012

Hodler presumably first met the actress and porcelain painter Valentine Godé-Darel in Geneva in 1908. Born in Paris in 1873, Godé-Darel was much younger than her lover for whom she was muse, model, and finally the mother of their daughter Paulette. Hodler's love affair was no doubt painful for his wife Berthe, but after Valentine's premature death, she raised Paulette with the help of a governess. Godé-Darel is known to the world primarily through the numerous paintings Hodler made of her agonizing death. His analytic gaze captures all the phases of an illness that broke out just a few weeks after the birth of their daughter and led to Valentine's death two years later in January 1915.

For Hodler, Valentine was the love of his life. In *La Parisienne*, as she was called, he pictures her as a beautiful woman in the prime of life, with sensitive features and yet subtly flirtatious, as she glances at the viewer over her bare left shoulder, her red lips slightly open and her luxurious hair exquisitely coiffed. The intimate portrait bust is preceded by nude studies made in connection with the painting *Linienherrlichkeit* (Linear Glory, 1908) and showing Valentine's body in eurythmic movement with her head similarly positioned. The almost square painting features the face and shoulders of the sitter, clearly outlined but executed with painterly and in part rather sketchy brushstrokes against a reddish grey ground. The richly nuanced colouring of her complexion seems to mirror a gently excited state of mind. Hodler painted a variation on this picture of the same size against a greenish grey ground followed by a third, smaller version that clearly emphasizes the sitter's refinement, for she is pictured wearing a fashionable high-collared garment and a lavish hat.

This first version of *La Parisienne*, combining aspects of neo-Impressionism, Art Nouveau, and Expressionism, probably gives the closest impression of the intimate relationship between painter and sitter. Knowing the tragic fate that awaited Valentine Godé-Darel, one cannot banish the sorrowful thought that a premonition of the imminent end of their love lies in the ephemerality of her gaze.

UW

Emil Nolde
Blumengarten (Kleines Mädchen)
1908

Emil Nolde
1867 Nolde – 1956 Seebüll

Oil on canvas
Signed and inscribed on verso: Emil Nolde "Blumengarten" (Kleines Mädchen)
60.5 × 70 cm

Inv. no. P21T / Acquired 1995

Nolde, the erratic, excitable and reclusive Expressionist from the Frisian north of Germany, travelled to Paris in 1899. The nine months he spent there seminally altered his artistic orientation. After sombre, clayey beginnings echoing the nature lyricism of artistic circles from Munich and Dachau, his art burst into a sumptuous array of bright, unbroken colours through his encounter with French painting – initially Manet and the Impressionists, later the "ice-breakers" Cézanne, van Gogh, Gauguin and Signac.

But it was not until 1903, when he was already in his late forties, that his palette became visibly brighter and his skills and experiences took distinctive, singular shape in his paintings. Nolde had rented a house on the Danish Baltic island of Als with his wife, the actress Ada Vilstrup. There he painted the first pictures of gardens and flowers in refreshing, colourful hues. "It was in Als in the middle of summer. The colours exerted an irresistible attraction and suddenly I was there painting... The blossoming colours of the flowers and the purity of these colours, I loved them." *Blumengarten* (Flower Garden), with the little girl in the blue dress, is one of 25 paintings of gardens and flowers created in the year 1908. Impetuously, Nolde applied his paint to the canvas – pastose and yet flat, carpet-like in effect. The child can barely be distinguished in the sea of flowers that fills the entire canvas. It is as if she were part of it, part of exuberant, fruitful nature. Despite the affinity to late Impressionism, which Nolde clearly gave an Expressionist slant, the sumptuously colourful, undeniably bright and fresh array of flowers and blossoms seems to have been born not of the immateriality of light but rather of the weighty substantiality of the earth.

UW

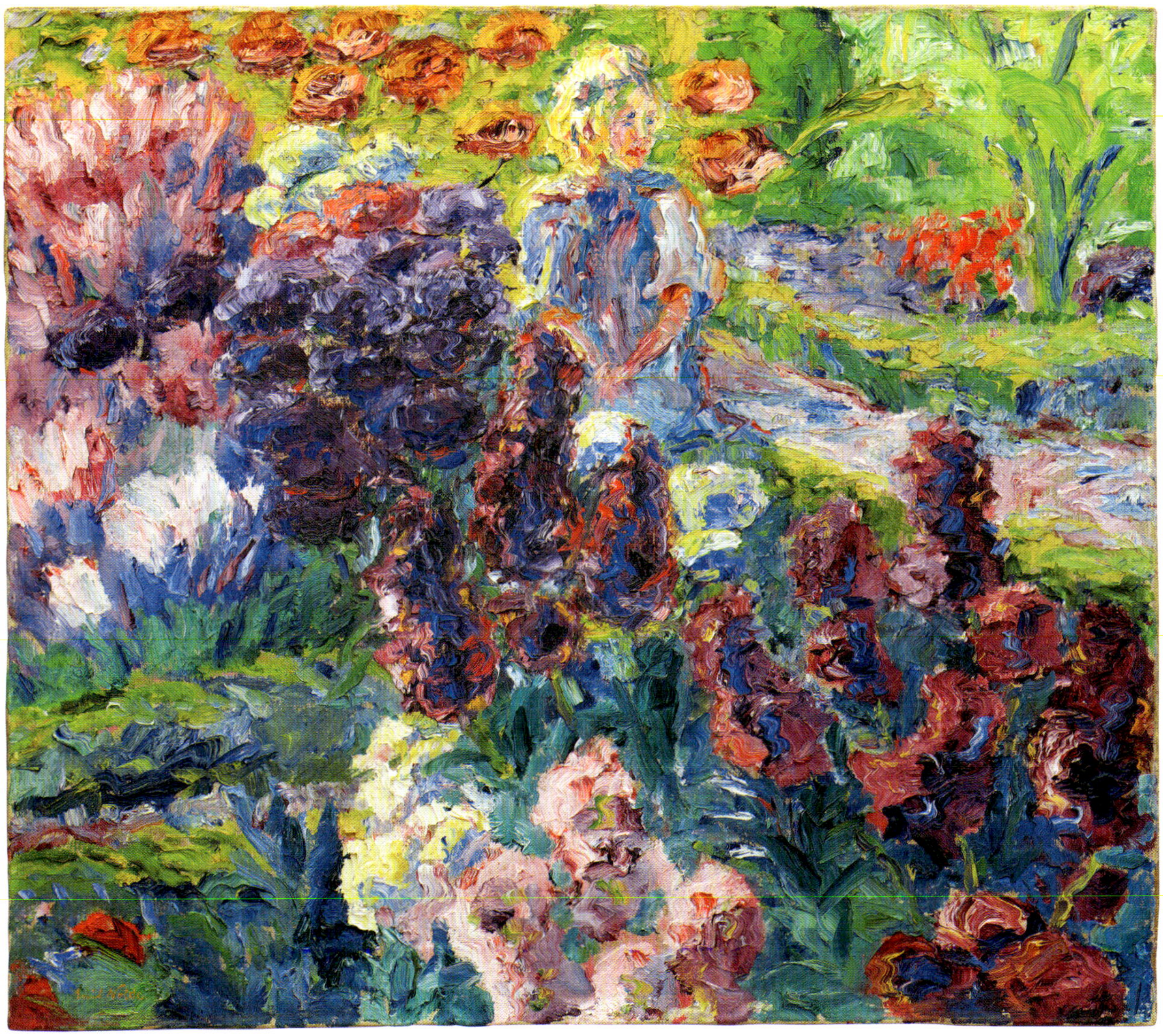

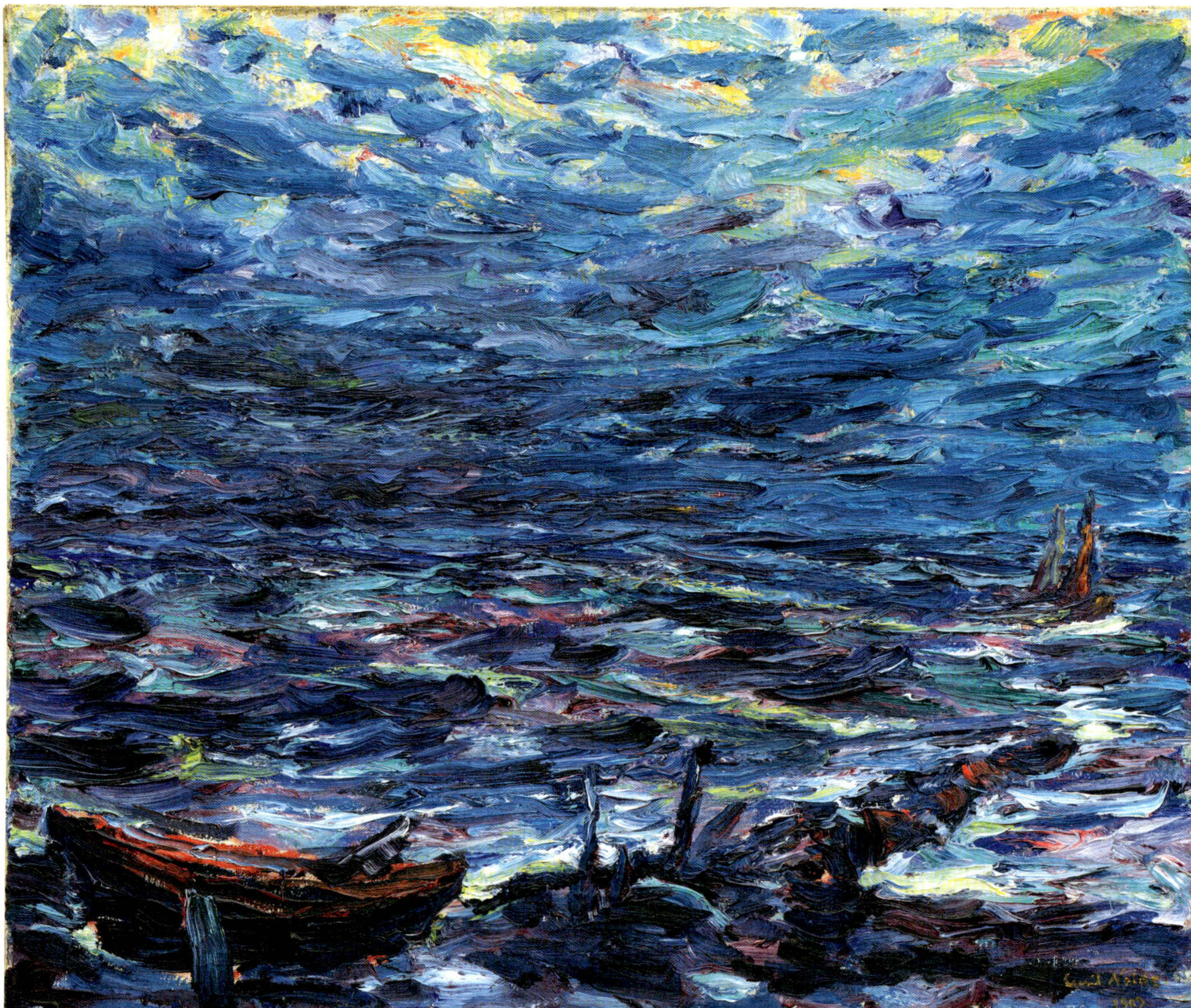

Emil Nolde
Dunkles Meer
1909

Emil Nolde
1867 Nolde – 1956 Seebüll

Oil on canvas
Signed and dated lower right:
Emil Nolde 1909
Signed and inscribed on verso:
Emil Nolde: Dunkles Meer
71 × 87 cm

Inv. no. P18T / Acquired 1995

We do not know for certain where Nolde painted this seascape in 1909. He spent part of that year on Als, an island in the Baltic Sea, where he had rented a fisherman's house near the beach, and he spent the summer in Ruttebüll, a small village in West Schleswig not far from the coast of the North Sea. The painting has no topographic features by which its location might be identified. The composition consists largely of sky and water, separated by a barely perceptible horizon line. A boat is pulled up on the shore next to a breakwater reaching into the waves like an index finger. Two boats with sails set are drifting on the water – the only sign of human life. The elements are agitated as if presaging a storm or, to the contrary, as if the storm had just passed, permitting the dark, turbulent clouds to part at the zenith of the warm sunlight. A saturated blue dominates the seascape, intensified into purple here and there or with white highlights where the spray leaves a trail in the water, on which occasional yellow, red and green reflexes are seen, conversing with the colours of the sky.

The painting might be said to prefigure the series of autumn seascapes of 1910 and 1911. Nolde had adapted the brushstroke entirely to the turbulence of his subject matter. As in *Blumengarten* (Flower Garden, No. 11), the animation and vibrancy of late Impressionism still reverberates. However, although the stylistic devices of Impressionism had pointed the way, he felt they had not led to a satisfactory goal. In his own words,"Nature rendered faithfully and precisely does not yield a work of art. ... Nature reinvented through the addition of one's own soul and spirit turns it into a work of art." *Dunkles Meer* (Dark Sea) thus stands on the threshold of painting increasingly governed by the subjective expression of inner experience: it stands on the threshold of Expressionism, whose groundwork had been laid by such artists as Gauguin and van Gogh. 1909 also saw a new direction in the subject matter of Nolde's art, for it was in Ruttebüll that he first began painting religious works. Throughout his life, he still remained faithful to the landscape, in particular the sea, for his soul never ceased to be captivated by "everything primal" because, as he said, "the great, tempestuous seas are still in a primal state".

UW

Max Pechstein
Geteerte Kähne
1909

Max Pechstein
1881 Eckersbach / Zwickau – 1955 Berlin

Oil on canvas
Initialled upper right: HMP 09
Signed, dated and inscribed on verso:
Nidden 09 / Pechstein / Geteerte Kähne
65 × 50 cm

Inv. no. P72T / Acquired 2001

The discovery of Vincent van Gogh's paintings, on view in 1905 and 1908 at Galerie Arnold in Dresden, seminally impacted Pechstein's artistic development. Through them, he found a simplified approach to rendering objects entirely through the cogency of colour. This attracted the attention of Erich Heckel, who had founded the artists' group *Die Brücke* in 1905 together with Ernst Ludwig Kirchner, Karl Schmidt-Rottluff and Fritz Bleyl.

In 1906 Heckel persuaded Pechstein to join the group, which was active until 1913 and was essentially the very embodiment of German Expressionism. The *Brücke* artists worked primarily in the urban centres of Dresden and Berlin but regularly sought out the simple life in what they perceived to be the untouched natural surroundings of the countryside. Gauguin had already taken delight in escaping the sophisticated life of Paris by withdrawing to the small fishing village of Pont-Aven in Brittany, a place, "of archaic customs, of an atmosphere that is so distinct from our over-civilized environs".

Pechstein also found respite from city life, in his case at the Baltic Sea in the fishing village of Nidden on the Curonian Spit. After 1909, he regularly spent his summers there and in 1913 Schmidt-Rottluff came to visit him. It was during Pechstein's first visit that he painted *Geteerte Kähne* (Tarred Boats). To the left, five fishing boats are pulled up on the sand and to the right, cut off at the edge of the picture, a sixth boat with sails set is seen afloat on the calm waters. The village is marked by a few houses, crouching low in the shelter of the vegetation. An almost cloudless sky spreads out above the deserted scene and the sun has probably reached its zenith for the day. Although the view is directed inland and not toward the open sea, the subject matter recalls van Gogh's *Fishing Boats on the Beach at Les Saintes-Maries-de-la-Mer* painted in southern France in 1888.

The peace and tranquillity of the scene stands in conspicuous contrast to the vibrant colouring of the composition, which is indebted not only to van Gogh but also to the French Fauves. Strong colours, largely unmixed, have been applied to the canvas, its weave occasionally appearing between the pastose strokes of the paintbrush. Yellow is juxtaposed with blue and orange with green. Olive, brown and pink generate in-between hues, interspersed with occasional accents in white and black. The expressive intensity of the palette as a whole lends the subject matter a vehement, almost raw immediacy. Pechstein has invested this painting with the entire weight of his emotions and his "longing for exhilarating experiences".

UW

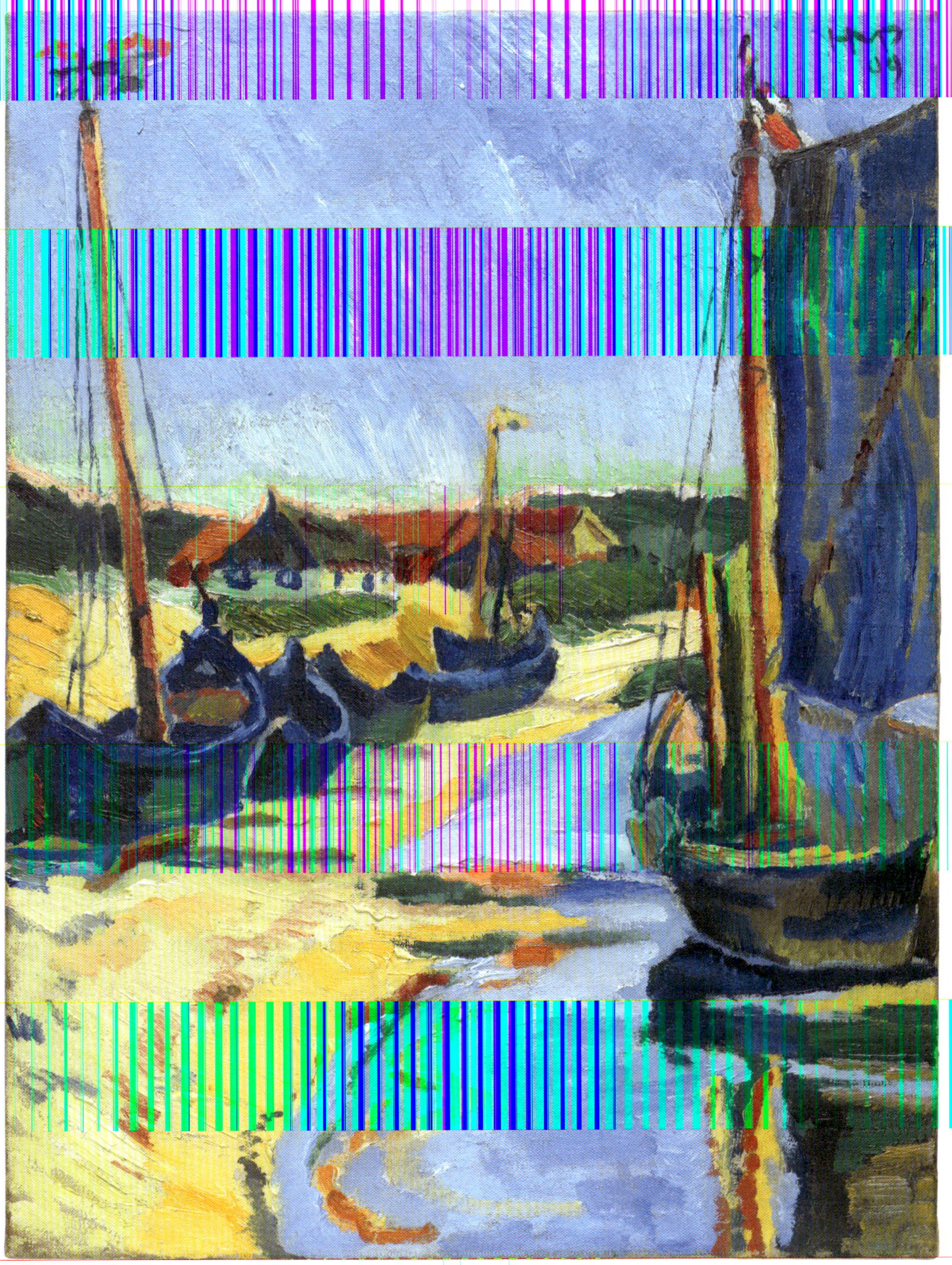

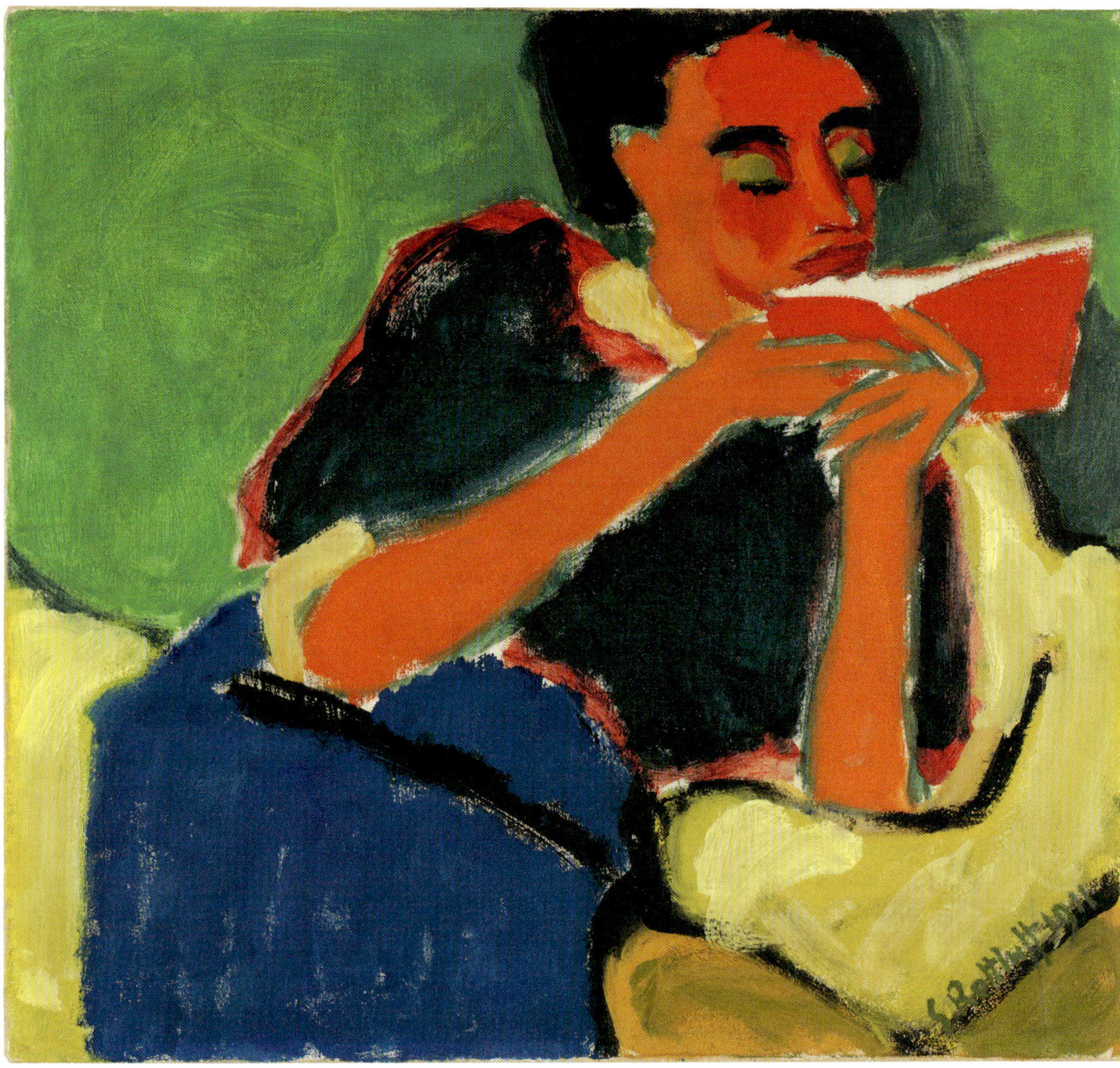

Karl Schmidt-Rottluff
1884 Rottluff / Chemnitz – 1976 Berlin

Oil on canvas
Signed and dated lower right:
S. Rottluff 1911
77 × 85 cm

Inv. no. P3T / Acquired 2001

Karl Schmidt-Rottluff
Die Lesende
1911

On 7 June 1905, Fritz Bleyl, Erich Heckel, Ernst Ludwig Kirchner, and Karl Schmidt-Rottluff founded the artists' group *Brücke* in Dresden. In their brief and emphatic manifesto, the artists, once students of architecture, declared, "Anyone who depicts, with immediacy and candour, that which compels him to create belongs to us." Although they each clearly represented a distinctive artistic temperament of their own, they shared developments during their first years in Dresden that by 1910–11 had led to the flatness that distinguishes *Brücke* paintings.

It was during this period that Schmidt-Rottluff painted *Die Lesende* (Woman Reading). He depicts his young sitter with expansive and monumental gesture. The extreme close-up, essentially a photographic device, is achieved by cropping the figure and squeezing it into the rectangular picture plane. The woman, probably seated on a sofa and engrossed in her book, does not establish eye contact with the viewer. She keeps her distance despite the proximity and informality of her attitude. Her eyes are lowered in full concentration on the book that she is holding in her slender, plant-like hands. The composition converges in this part of the canvas; the shapes are more complex and smaller as opposed to the large flat fields of colour that characterize the rest of the painting. Instead of being placed seamlessly side-by-side, the colours are outlined in the nature of a preliminary sketch. Schmidt-Rottluff borrowed the device from woodcutting, a medium of great interest to him. The colours, clear cut at first sight, radiate an inner luminosity that stems from subtle combinations of primer and superimposed layers of paint, such as green on yellow or petrol on red. The tension and excitement generated by the strong yellows and reds heightens the casual, relaxed pose of the reader.

Die Lesende is one of Schmidt-Rottluff's first large-format works. The sitter cannot be conclusively identified. It may be Nelly, one of the three black models along with Sam and Milly, who were frequent guests at Ernst Ludwig Kirchner's studio in Dresden, where they used to dance. The work shows similarities in physiognomy with a lithograph (*Drei Negerakte / Three Black Nudes*) and a portrait (*Nelly*), both made by Kirchner that same year in 1911, and with a photograph of *Nelly and Siddi Riha dancing in Erich Heckel's studio*, 1910–11. The mask-like countenance of the young woman with her pointed chin and full lips is reminiscent of West African tribal art, specifically the sculptures made by the Fang people. *Die Lesende* exemplifies the "primitivism" practiced by *Brücke* artists, whose interest in the art of Oceania and Africa was initially inspired by visits to the Dresden Museum of Ethnology. The treatment of plane and the atmosphere of Schmidt-Rottluff's painting evokes Paul Gauguin's paintings of the South Seas while the countenance of his sitter references the heritage of Africa.

AS

Erich Heckel
Stilleben mit blauer Vase
1912

015

Erich Heckel
1883 Döbeln – 1970 Radolfzell

Oil on canvas
Signed and dated left margin and on verso:
Erich Heckel 12
48.5 × 55.5 cm

Inv. no. P67T / Acquired 2016

The painting *Stilleben mit blauer Vase* (Still Life with Blue Vase) exemplifies the interest in extra-European cultures, in particular African art, that Erich Heckel shared with other members of the *Brücke* artists group. The wall hanging, designed by Heckel himself and depicted as a tablecloth in the painting, shows a frieze with gazelles. To the right behind the blue vase that dominates the centre of the composition, a round, three-legged Hehe or Makonde stool can be seen on the table, or rather, on the tablecloth. Heckel acquired such objects through his brother Manfred Heckel, who spent several years working as a railway engineer in German East Africa (now Tanzania). In the upper right-hand corner, behind the stool, we see Heckel's *Hockende* (Museum Folkwang, Essen), a squatting woman carved out of lime wood in the style of primitivism.
UW

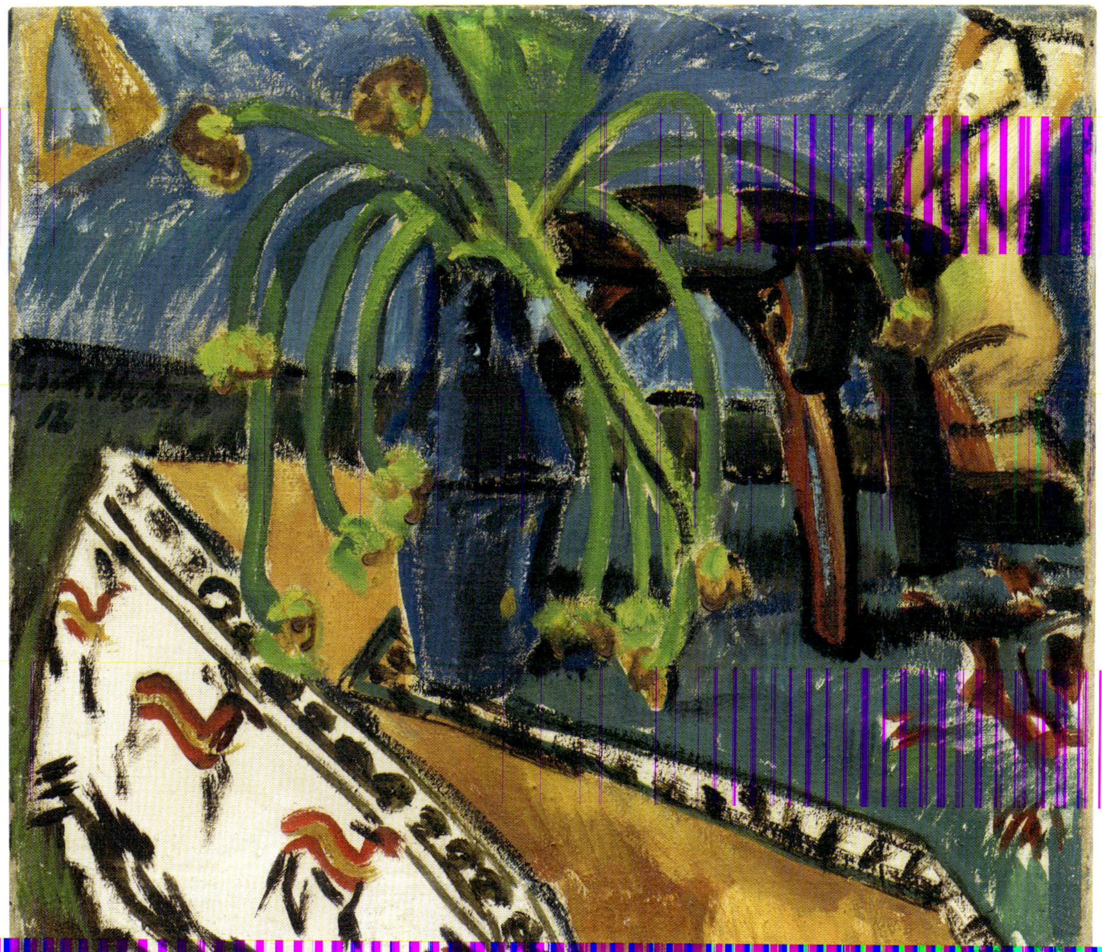

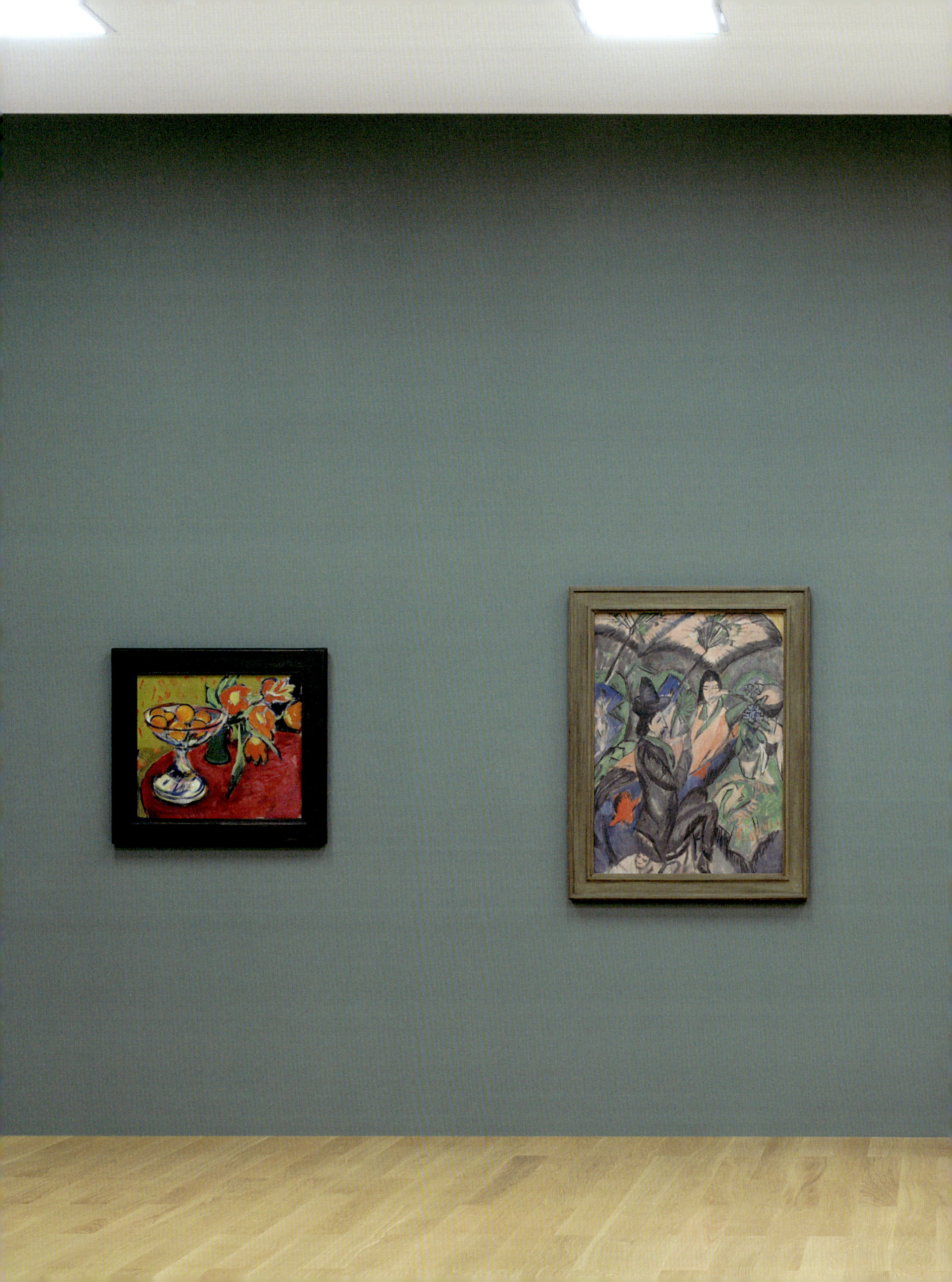

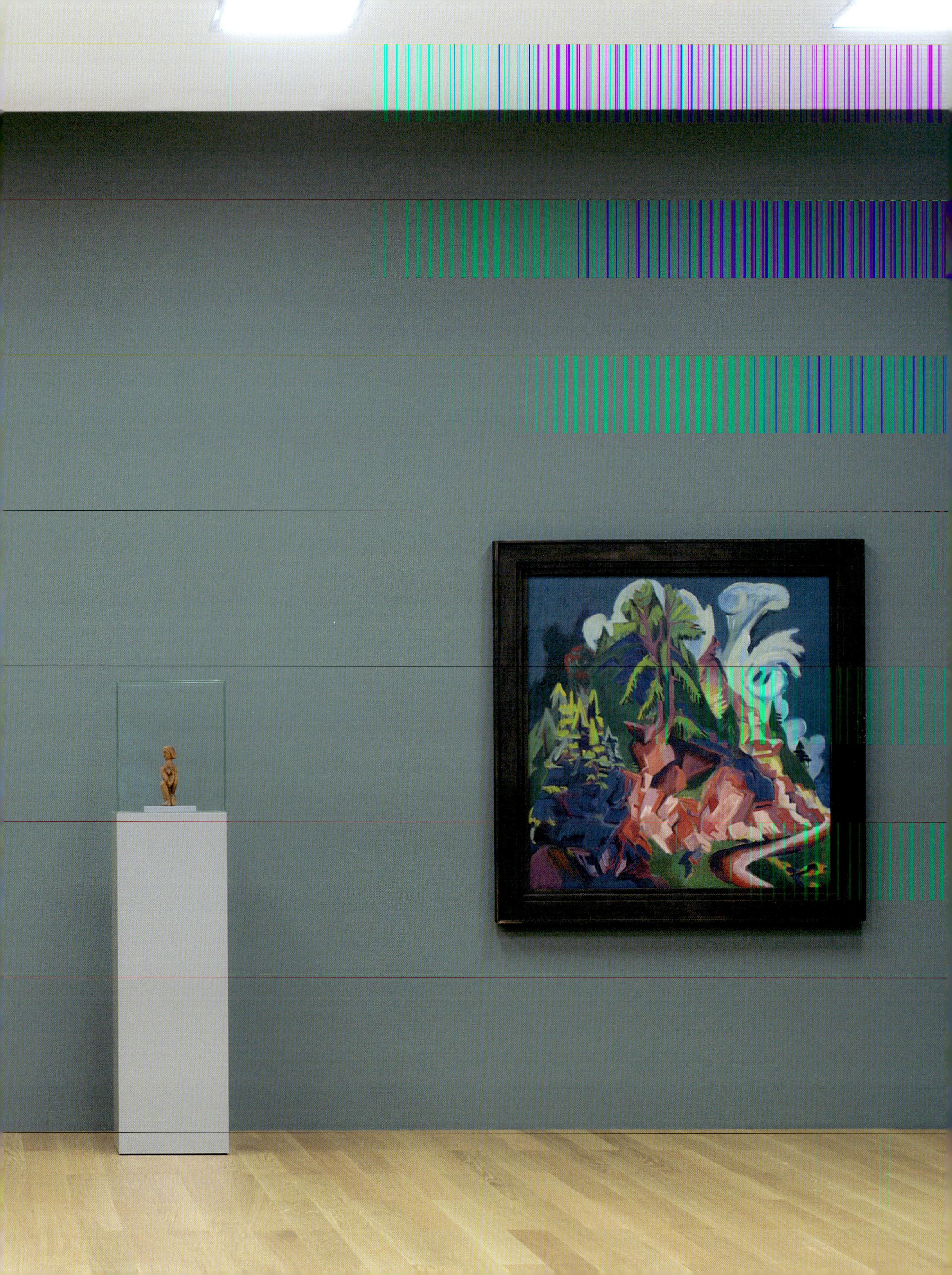

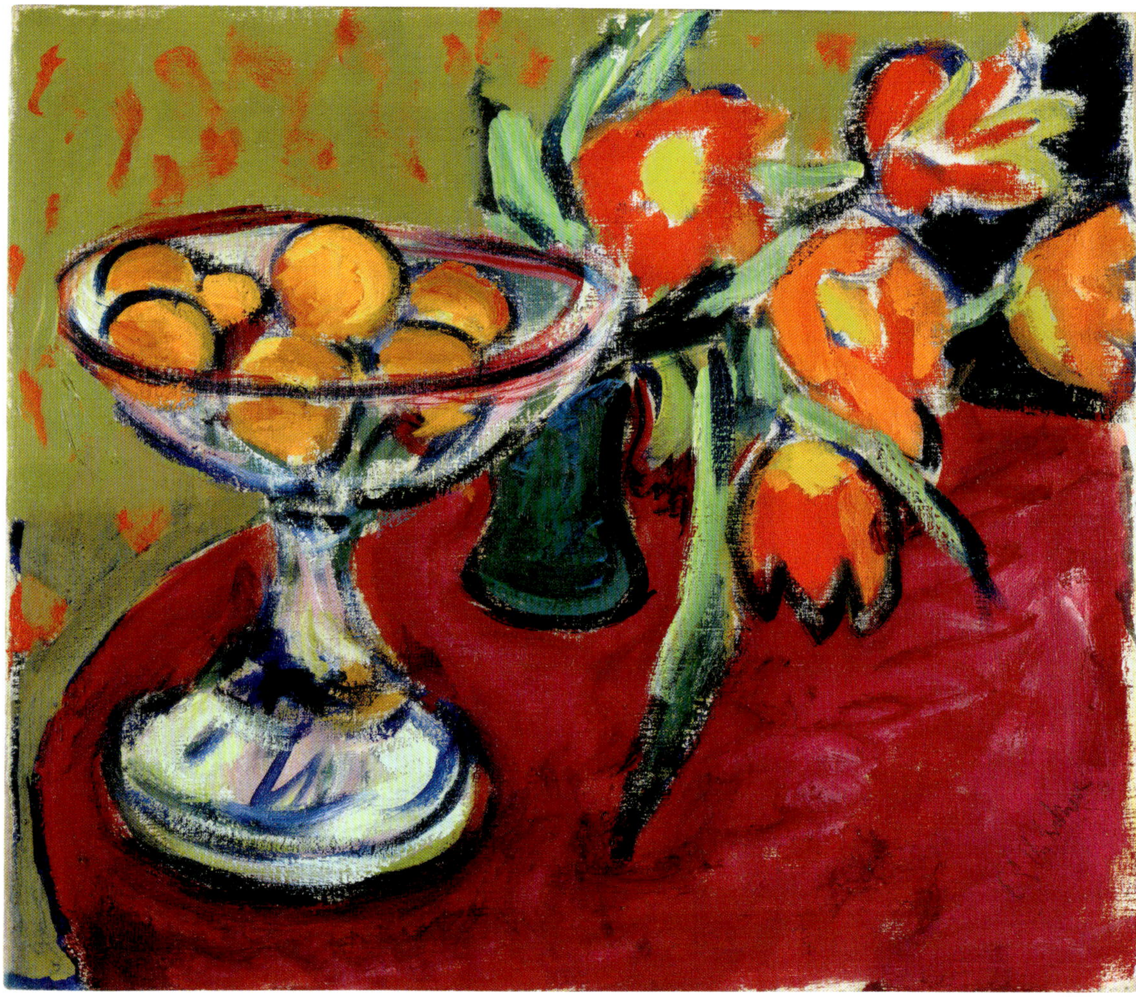

Ernst Ludwig Kirchner
1880 Aschaffenburg –
1938 Frauenkirch-Wildboden / Davos

Oil on canvas
Signed lower right and verso:
E. L. Kirchner
55 × 65 cm

Inv. no.: P29T / Acquired 2005

Ernst Ludwig Kirchner
Stilleben mit Orangen und Tulpen
1909

After studying architecture and receiving a degree in engineering at the Institute of Technology in Dresden in 1905, Ernst Ludwig Kirchner chose to take up painting, motivated by the "audacious idea …of renewing German art". While still at the Institute, he and his fellow students of architecture, Fritz Bleyl, Erich Heckel and Karl Schmidt-Rottluff, started drawing and painting, acquiring their first experiences in art. On 7 June 1905, the young painters founded the artists' group *Brücke*. Their manifesto, largely penned by Kirchner in 1906, called for a new era of freedom to be established for young people as bearers of the future, emphatically declaring that "Whoever renders directly and authentically that which impels them to create is one of us."

The natural and spontaneous nature of human existence was central to Kirchner's artistic agenda. In unfiltered immediacy, his paintings and drawings record the uninhibited atmosphere in the artists' studios, peopled with posing, sprawling, frequently nude models, girlfriends and many different dancers.

The colourful *Stilleben mit Orangen und Tulpen* (Still Life with Oranges and Tulips) is an exception among the works created in the early *Brücke* years. It is of significance in another respect as well since it reveals Kirchner's appreciation of contemporary French art, in particular Cézanne and especially Matisse. After he and his friend Max Pechstein went to see a Matisse exhibition at Paul Cassirer's Art Salon in Berlin in January 1909, he wrote a postcard to his friend Erich Heckel, 12 January 1909, commenting, "Matisse pretty daring at times."

Cézanne and Matisse often painted still lifes picturing bowls of fruit and flowers as embodiments of a joie de vivre. The subject matter of Kirchner's *Stilleben mit Orangen und Tulpen* is comparable above all to paintings by Henri Matisse. He shows a bolder, more carefree and perhaps even more boisterous touch in the buoyancy of his rapid, spontaneous brushstroke and his intensely glowing palette that contradicts the tradition of French *peinture* – an approach that did not escape the notice of contemporary art critics. Expansive, lucid patches of colour dominate the composition while the contrast of dark red, orange and green hues evoke Renaissance painting in Germany up to Holbein, which Kirchner admired so deeply. The tulips are already in full bloom and reach for the light like dancing figures.

The painting, alternately titled *Stilleben mit Schale und Blumen* (Still Life with Bowl and Flowers), was shown in 1917 at the Kunstverein Jena. The exhibition had been organized by the philosopher Eberhard Grisebach to finance Kirchner's move to Davos in 1918, where the artist would spend the remainder of his life until his suicide in 1938.

AS

Ernst Ludwig Kirchner
Kniende, nach links gewandter Kopf, rechte Hand auf der linken Brust
1912

017

Ernst Ludwig Kirchner
1880 Aschaffenburg –
1938 Frauenkirch-Wildboden / Davos

Wood (Swiss stone pine)
Initialled on stand: ELK
Height: 21.6 cm

Inv. no.: S56T / Acquired 2013

Some 80 of the 140 sculptures definitively attributed to Kirchner have survived. With few exceptions, they are made of wood and carved directly out of the tree trunk, so that marks left behind in the wood allow us to trace the development of the works. Forty of these sculptures, showing active and often unusual poses, were made while Kirchner was living in Berlin. In his own words, they make no reference to antiquity. This includes the small, kneeling woman of 1912, one of the few sculptures with a monogram. She is not only pictured in a photograph that Kirchner took in 1913; she also appears in a painting of 1912, *Stilleben mit Plastiken and Blumen* (Still Life with Sculptures and Flowers).

The small, unquestionably regal figure with the aloof gaze of a Sphinx is reminiscent of Egyptian statuettes and commands respect. The uneven, convoluted arrangement of her arms and legs yields completely different views of this squatting figure. She may, for instance, appear to be in movement or at rest, one of many impressions inspired by the artist's study of nature and, as he himself wrote in retrospect, by his "experience of the figures of contemporary life". Transposing that experience into art led to what Kirchner termed a hieroglyph.

In addition to the vibrancy and lifelike intimacy expressed by the *Kniende* (Woman Kneeling, Head Facing Left, Right Hand on Left Breast), one can identify diverse references to art history, as in many of Kirchner's works. While the tribal art of Africa reverberates in the choice of material and the kneeling pose – Kirchner's interest in the sculpture of Cameroon is well documented – the inspiration of French nineteenth-century painting is also unmistakable, for instance, Delacroix's *Women of Algiers*, Degas's paintings of *Women Bathing*, or Gauguin's *Squatting Women* in his paintings of the South Seas. The conspicuously asymmetric position of the legs does not typically feature in African tribal art but is occasionally seen in works by the above-mentioned painters, referring in turn to forms of life outside of Europe. However, the right hand of the *Kniende*, resting on her left breast, echoes the traditional gesture of a Venus pudica, a chaste Venus covering her breasts and private parts. Revealing and concealing, seducing and rebuffing: these are ancient modes of female existence.

AS

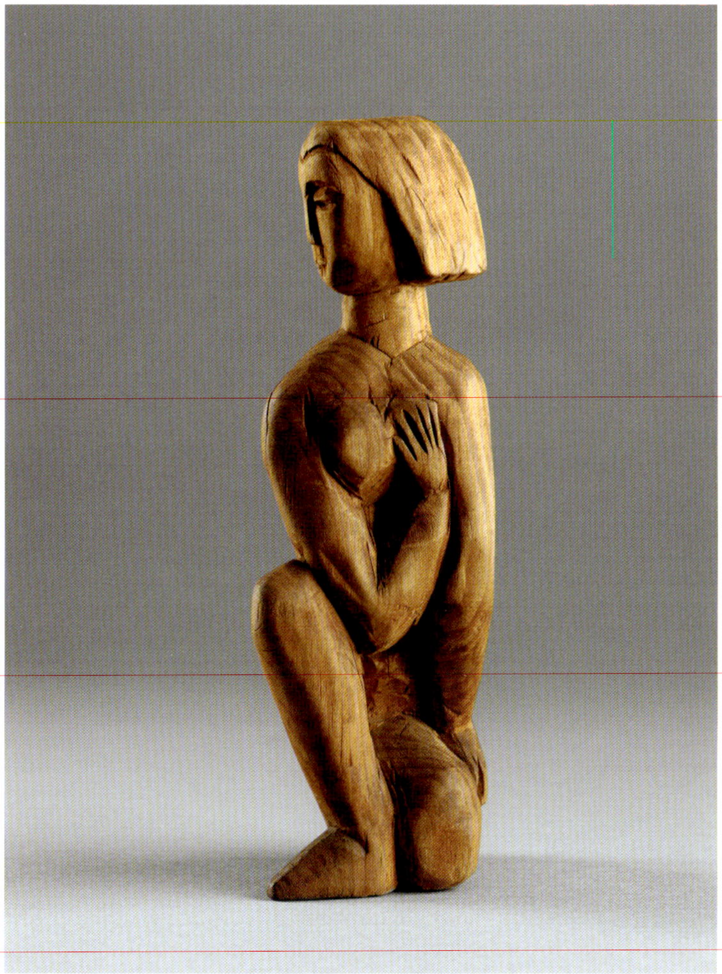

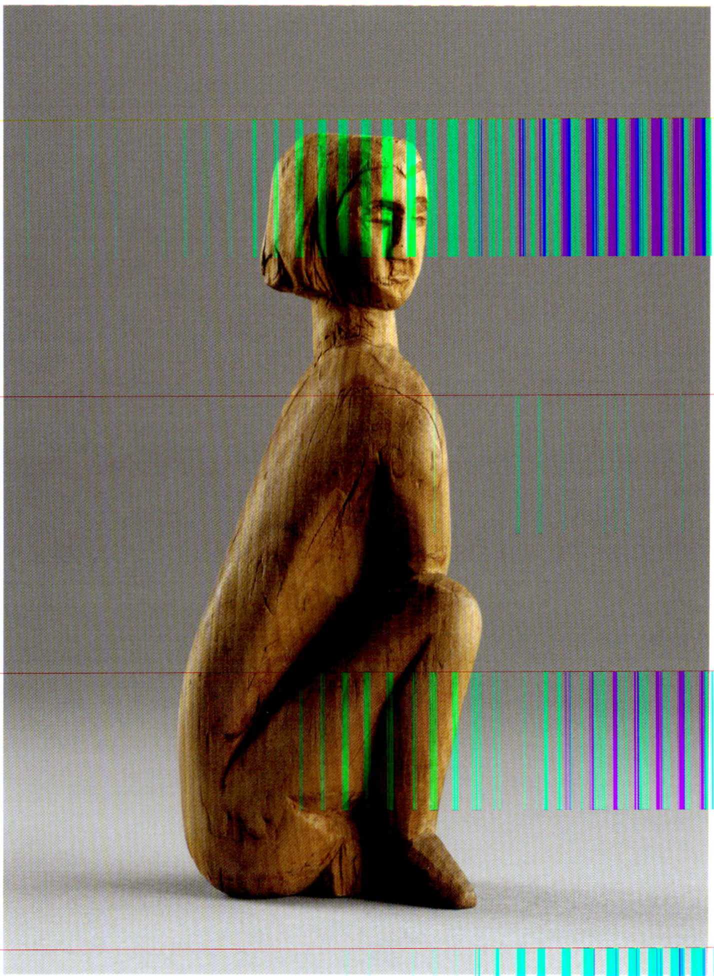

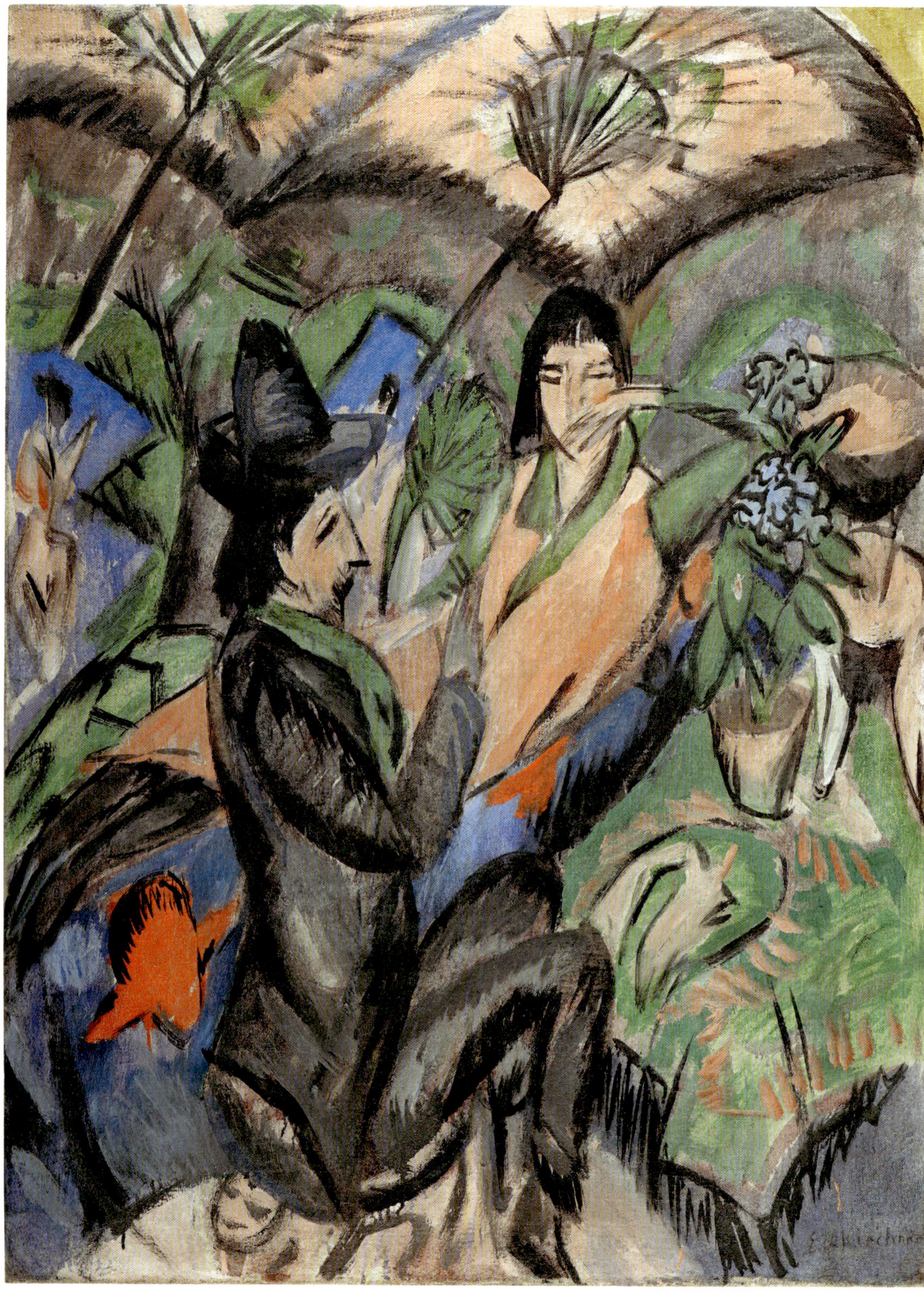

Ernst Ludwig Kirchner
1880 Aschaffenburg –
1938 Frauenkirch-Wildboden / Davos

Oil on canvas
Signed lower right: E. L. Kirchner
100 × 75.5 cm

Inv. no. P37T / Acquired 2007

Ernst Ludwig Kirchner
Paar unter Japanschirm
1913

Kirchner painted *Paar unter Japanschirm* (Couple under Japanese Umbrella) in 1913 during extremely productive years, beginning when he moved to Berlin from Dresden in 1911 and drawing to a close in the spring of 1915 when he was called up for military duty. The year 1913 was devoted in particular to the large works painted on the Baltic island of Fehmarn and to the artist's important street scenes, culminating in *Der Potsdamer Platz* (Potsdam Square, 1914). *Paar unter Japanschirm* belongs to a third complex of works that is central to Kirchner's oeuvre: paintings of friendship and conversations in his studio.

There is a hint of Arcadia in the relatively tight framing of the composition, picturing the painter Otto Mueller with his wife Maschka, also a painter. We cannot tell at first sight if this is an interior or a scene on the Baltic Sea, but a 1912 photograph of Kirchner's first studio in Berlin at Durlacher Strasse 14 provides the answer. The painted wall hanging as well as other items can be clearly identified. They testify to Kirchner's avid interest in other cultures. The umbrellas illustrate the great popularity of Japanese fashions that spread from Paris to the rest of Europe; the tablecloth is of Coptic origins, and the leopard stool, on which Mueller is sitting straight as a ramrod, reflects the artist's interest in "primitive" art. The stool, already among the furnishings of Kirchner's studio in Dresden, was probably brought back from Africa by Erich Heckel's brother Manfred.

The picture is painted in the graphic style cultivated by Kirchner in the years 1913–14. The nervous brushstroke applies not only to the contours of the figures and objects but to the entire painting, its vibrant rhythm an artistic equivalent to the hectic urban climate that prevailed prior to World War I. In contrasts, the subtle, understated palette of blues, greens, and a matt pink reference nature and are no doubt indicative of an intentional link between indoors and outdoors, underscored by the fact that the wall hanging resembles an arcade. In the blue segments under the arcades – they might be interpreted as sky or sea – we see nudes, as in Arcadia, which feature in many of Kirchner's paintings. The joyous mood in *Paar unter Japanschirm* evokes not only the happy times spent with the Muellers on Fehmarn, but also the summertime mood in the works of the Impressionists and Matisse. It is quite possible that Kirchner had seen Manet's painting *Im Wintergarten* (In the Winter Garden, 1879) at the National Gallery in Berlin.

AS

Ernst Ludwig Kirchner
Weg zur Staffel
1919

019

Ernst Ludwig Kirchner
1880 Aschaffenburg –
1938 Frauenkirch-Wildboden / Davos

Oil on canvas
Signed lower right: E. L. Kirchner
Signed and inscribed on verso:
E. L. Kirchner / Weg zur Staffel [sic!]
120 × 120 cm

Inv. no. P51T / Acquired 2012

The first time Kirchner spent the summer months on the Stafelalp in the Davos Alps was in 1917. Following the advice of friends and physicians, he had gone there in an attempt to overcome the anxiety attacks caused by the war. After a prolonged stay at Dr. L. Binswanger's sanatorium on Lake Constance, he returned to Davos in 1918, spending the summers in the Alps and the winters down below, in the "Haus in den Lärchen" in Frauenkirch.

"The experience in the mountains" was, as he wrote under the pseudonym of author Louis de Marsalle, the main subject matter of his art during those years. Commenting on his own work in 1925, he wrote, "The years 1917 to 1920 again contain a fanatic study of nature on a new basis, while at the same time, the inner wealth of forms thus achieved give the artist more and more freedom so that he can easily make the transition to compositions of free invention."

1919 saw the creation of such poetic and emotionally charged paintings as *Winterlandschaft* (Winter Landscape), *Stafelalp bei Mondschein* (Stafelalp in Moonlight) and *Weg zur Staffel* (Path to Staffel). The latter shows a more complex and faceted composition than is seen in the other paintings. The mountains in the foreground to the left of the Stafelberg and the Tinzenhorn in the distance to the right take the classic shape of pyramids. They are broken up and framed by a diversity of single shapes – stylized pine trees, cubes for the boulders and bulging circles for the billowing clouds. Kirchner takes the unfiltered appearance of nature and its infinitely varied forms as his point of departure and, in the process of painting, he gradually transforms them into a distinctive, independent art form. As he defines it, "They are hieroglyphs inasmuch as they render the forms of nature in the planarity of simpler forms that suggest their meaning for viewers."

Weg zur Staffel presages an artistic turn in the artist's oeuvre that has been described as his "carpet style". Kirchner's love of valuable oriental carpets is well known and to his pupil, Nele van de Velde, the daughter of Henry van de Velde, he said, "Nele, I put this Persian carpet down next to every picture that I think I have finished. If the picture can hold its own, I am content."

The expressive, indeed explosive character of the painting is indebted not only to its formal structure but also and especially to the flamboyant colouring with patches of cliffs so red that they seem to be ablaze. According to his friend and early patron, the archaeologist Botho Graef, the works "are never about pure subject matter, they always deal with the soul." Kirchner himself explained the philosophy behind his art in a letter that he wrote to the philosopher Eberhard Grisebach in 1918. Three things had determined his work: "Dream, life and knowledge or, if you wish, vision, sensuality and psyche."
AS

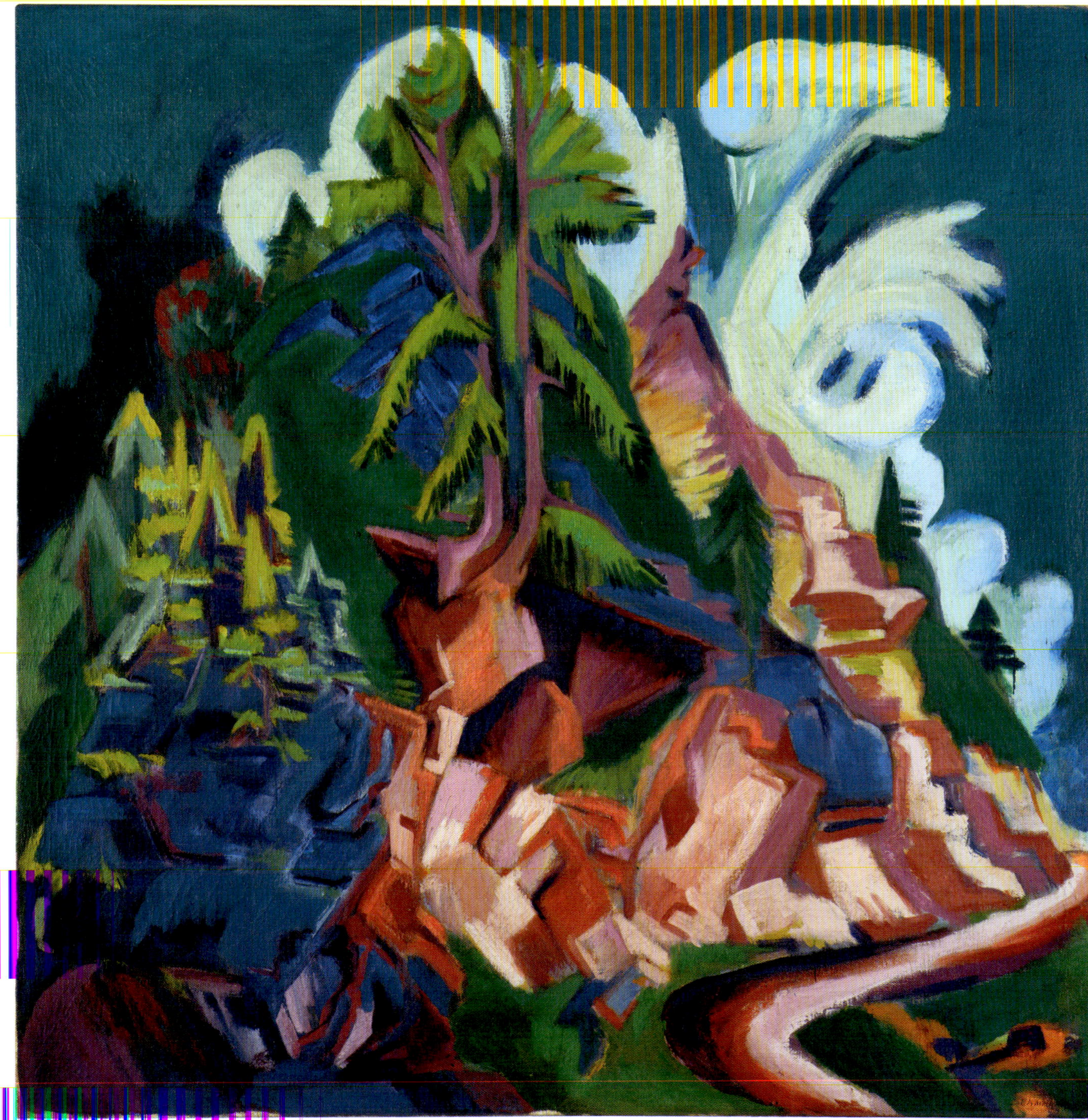

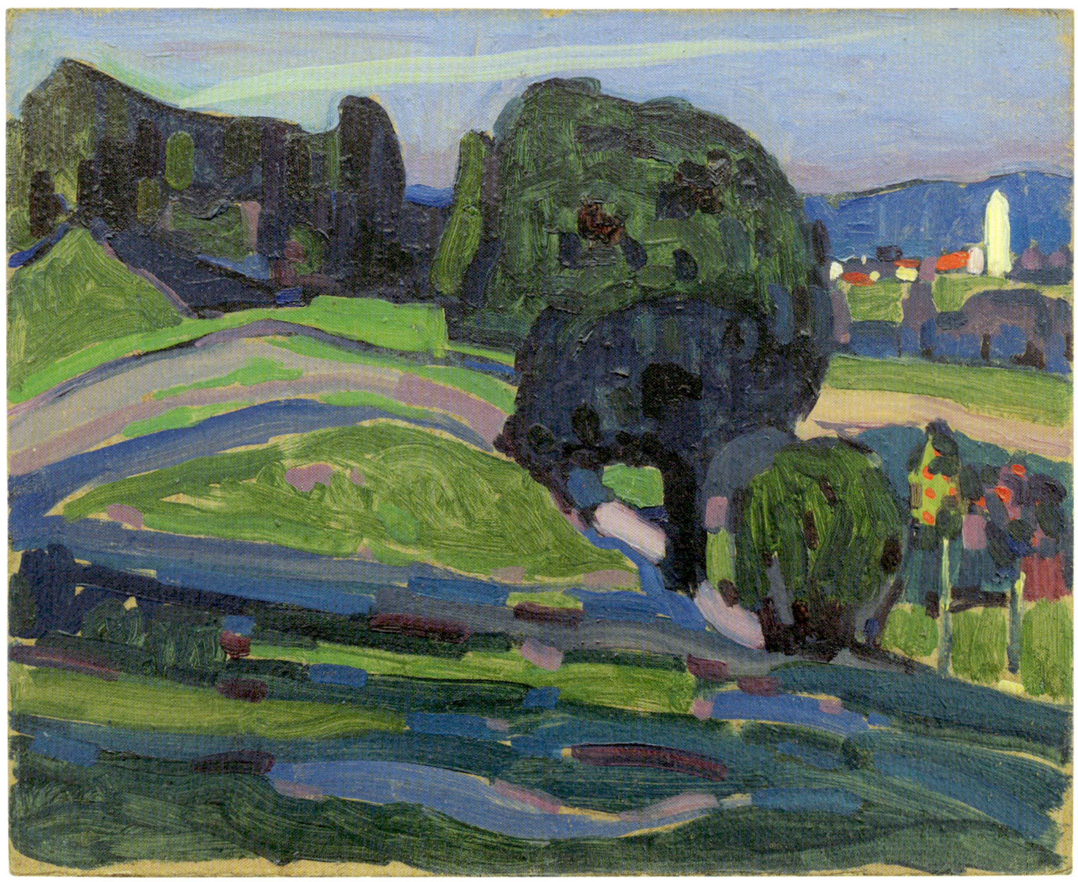

020

Wassily Kandinsky
Paysage à Murnau (Landschaft mit dunklem Baum)
1908

Wassily Kandinsky
1866 Moscow – 1944 Neuilly-sur-Seine

Oil on canvas
Inscribed and dated (by Kandinsky?) on verso:
Kandinsky 1908
32.8 × 41 cm

Inv. no. P4T / Acquired 1998

Wassily Kandinsky moved from Moscow to Munich in 1896 and shortly afterwards attended the Art Academy run by the painter Anton Ažbé from Laibach (Ljubljana). When Kandinsky in turn founded the *Phalanx School of Art* in 1902, Gabriele Münter was one of his first students. They soon entered into a relationship which would last until the First World War. In 1908, the two travelled to the Bavarian Prealps where they discovered the town of Murnau am Staffelsee. They purchased a house there the following year, where Alexej Jawlensky and Marianne von Werefkin were to become frequent guests (cat. 21). Their delight in exploring the surrounding countryside is recorded in numerous, mostly small-format paintings.

In *Paysage à Murnau* (Landscape near Murnau), the features of a neo-Impressionist style dominate: the artist's treatment of light and colour is reduced to relatively coarse lines and dots, the colours unmixed and placed side-by-side. On the other hand, the ornamental linear flow of Art Nouveau can be detected in the rhythmically undulating landscape dotted with trees. One cannot say for certain whether the town that appears in the background to the right is Murnau. Kandinsky's paintings also picture other, smaller villages in the environs of Murnau. Lush greens and cool blues interspersed with shades of purple dominate, accentuated by a few small but distinctive patches of white and red. A late summer afternoon has probably been captured here, where the shadows, though already dark, are still colourful, a phenomenon exquisitely exploited by the Impressionists. In this intimate, planar painting, Kandinsky has already largely liberated colour from subject matter. The landscape was largely an excuse for Kandinsky to hold the viewer's soul in thrall through colour alone, through the enchantment of its sound. What the artist wrote about Cézanne applies equally to his own work: "Not a man, not an apple, not a tree is represented but rather, all of that is ... required for the creation of an inner painterly something that is called 'picture'." Just a few years after painting *Paysage à Murnau*, Kandinsky passed the threshold to pure abstraction, to the complete, unadulterated liberation of colour from subject matter.

UW

Alexej Jawlensky
Landschaft bei Murnau
c. 1910

Alexej Jawlensky
1864 Torschok – 1941 Wiesbaden

Oil on canvas
Signed lower left: A. Jawlensky.
Inscribed on verso: Gelbe Abendwolken
33.2 × 41.2 cm

Inv. no. P8T / Acquired 1999

In 1896, Alexej Jawlensky and Marianne von Werefkin moved from St. Petersburg to Munich. There, Alexej Jawlensky attended Anton Ažbé's Art Academy where Wassily Kandinsky would also become a student a year later. However, it was not until 1909 that the relationship between the two developed into a close friendship. Having purchased a house in Murnau (cat. 20), Kandinsky and Gabriele Münter frequently welcomed Jawlensky and von Werefkin as guests. The ideas that flourished in this amicable and creative atmosphere would soon take concrete shape in the artwork of the *Blaue Reiter* (Blue Rider) artists group.

The simplification of form and the dominance of colour are the most conspicuous features in the paintings of these four artists. Unlike Kandinsky, Jawlensky had discovered the work of Van Gogh and Cézanne when he was still at the Academy in St. Petersburg and also through his acquaintance with the Russian painter Ilya Rjepin. In addition, the monk and artist Jan Verkade (Father Willibrord) from Beuron, whom he met in 1906, introduced him to the flat style cultivated by the French artists group, Les Nabis, who followed Paul Gauguin. The previous year, Jawlensky had already met Henri Matisse in Paris and Ferdinand Hodler in Geneva. Thus, he was not only the elder but also the more experienced artist among the group in Murnau, and his influence is clearly discernible in the work of his friends. Although, unlike Jawlensky, Kandinsky turned to pure abstraction in 1913, he never failed to profess his gratitude to the older artist for "teaching me" during their Murnau days.

Murnau is pictured against an Alpine massif with an open field in the foreground. The church of St. Nikolaus, still a dominant feature in Murnau today, rises to the right above the silhouette of the town. The deep purple of the mountains and the church is set off against the complementary lush yellow of the evening clouds. Strong accents in blue and orange as well as red and green accompany this dramatic tonality. The animated gesture of the paint applied to the cardboard is largely kept in check by the contouring, which Jawlensky had summarily painted dark blue first, generating the impression of *cloisonné*, a decorative technique of enamel compartments enclosed in precious wire or metal. Emile Bernard and Paul Gauguin had discovered this *cloisonné* technique for their painting and treated the dark contours as an expressive device. This impacted the style of many artists as did their "synthesism", that is, the practice of establishing a synthesis between simple shape and clear, non-descriptive colour. Jawlensky often spoke about synthesis in discussing art theory, and *Landschaft bei Murnau* excellently illustrates his understanding of the term. Gabriele Münter succinctly summed up the objectives pursued at that time: "Stop making Impressionist copies of nature and start feeling the content, abstracting it – expressing the extract." It is through this extract that the transformation of an outside impression into an inner experience acquired visible shape.

UW

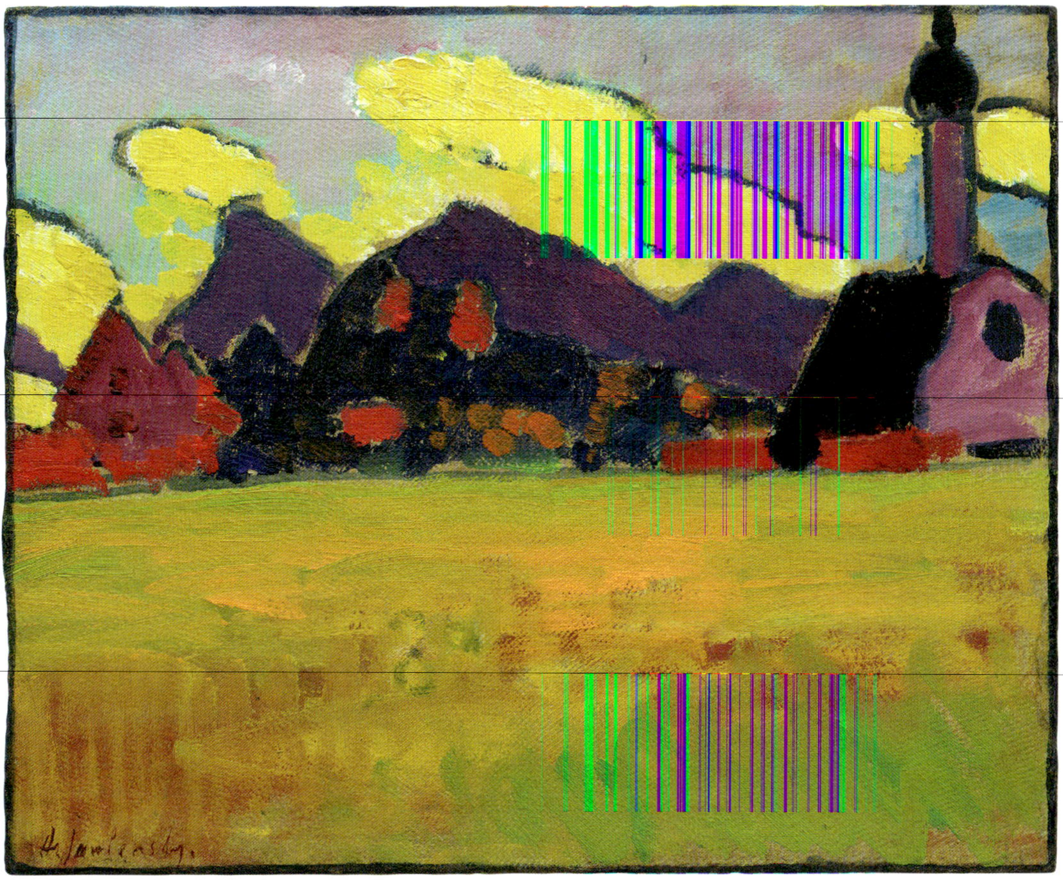

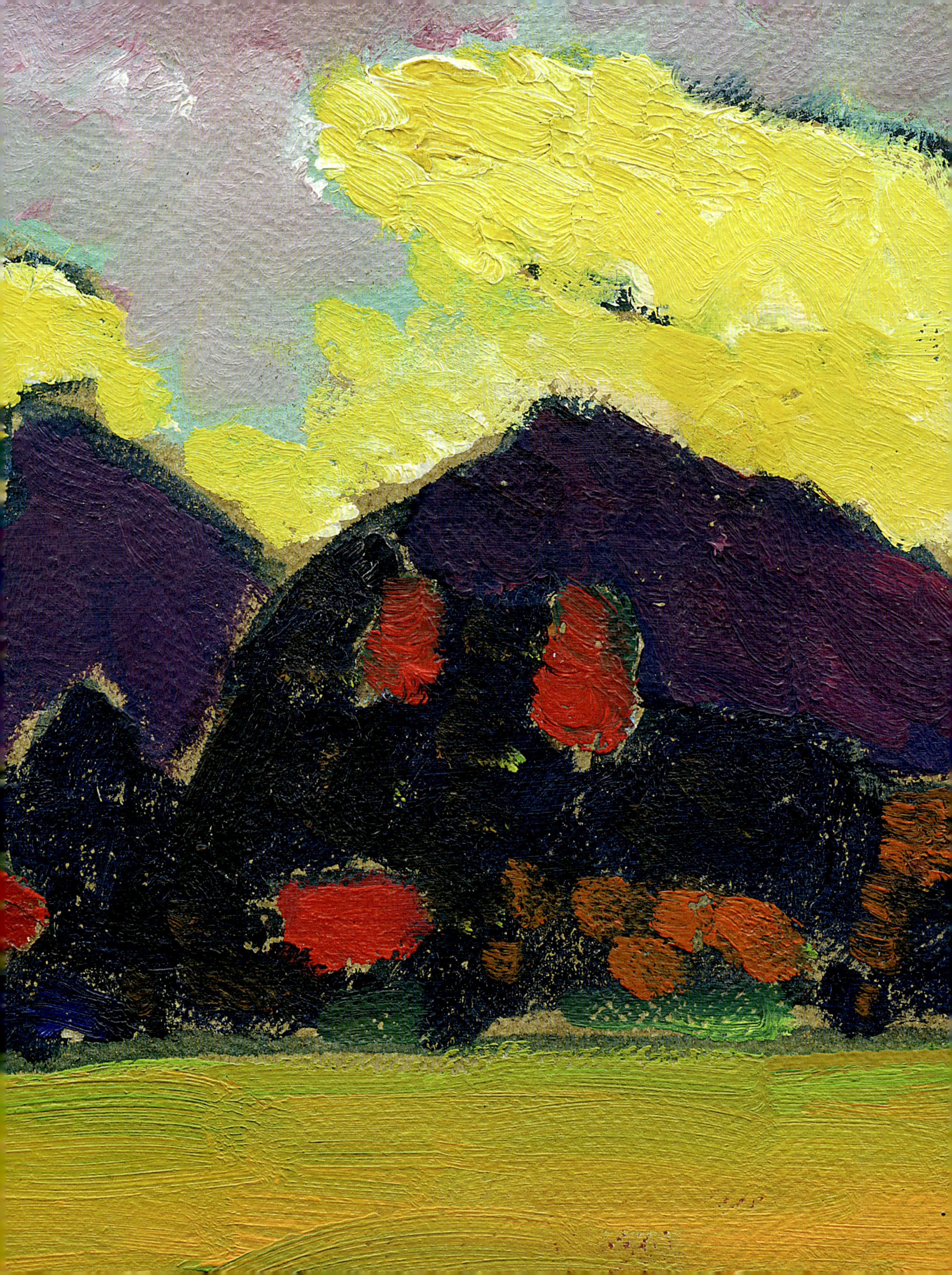

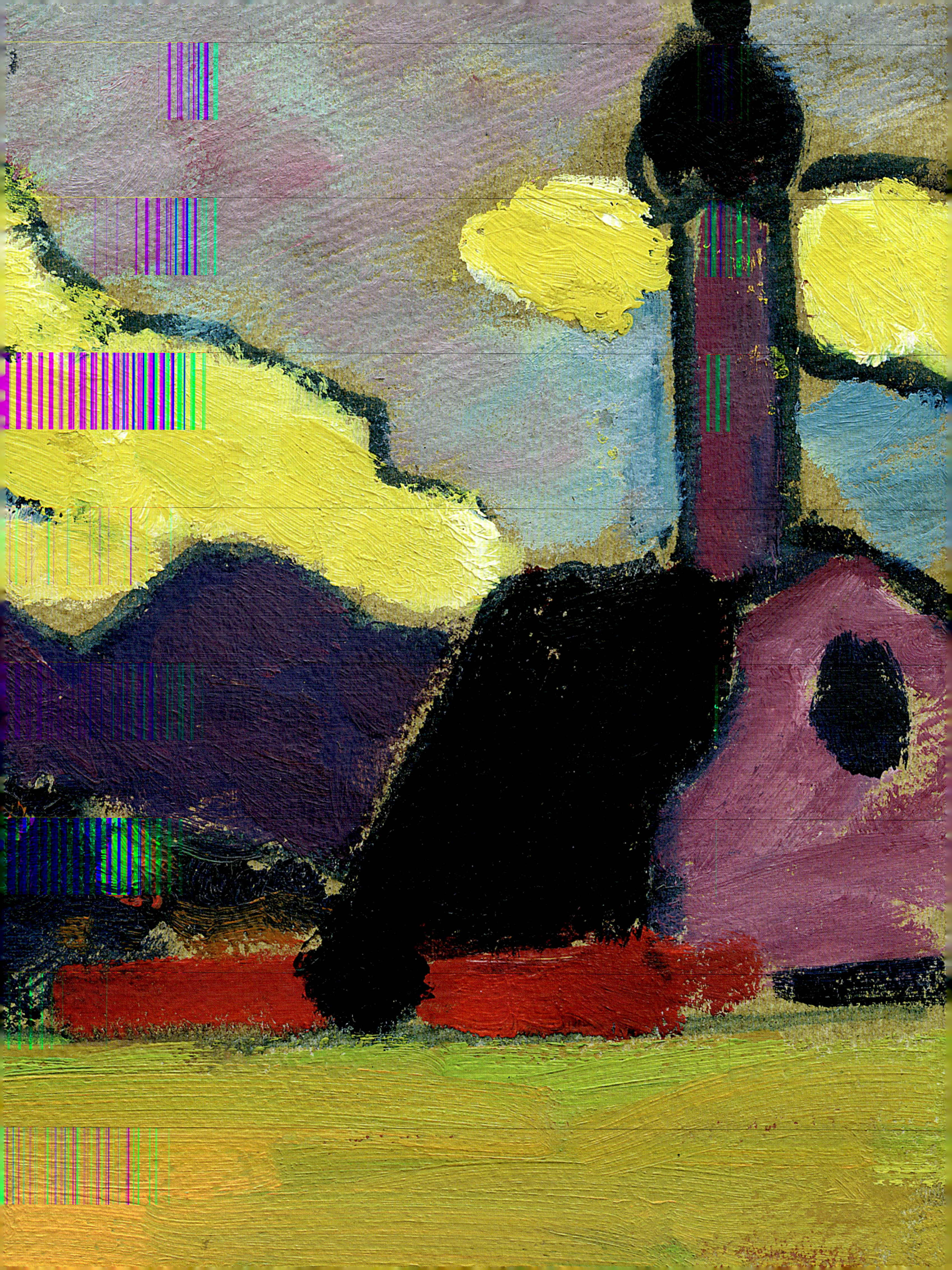

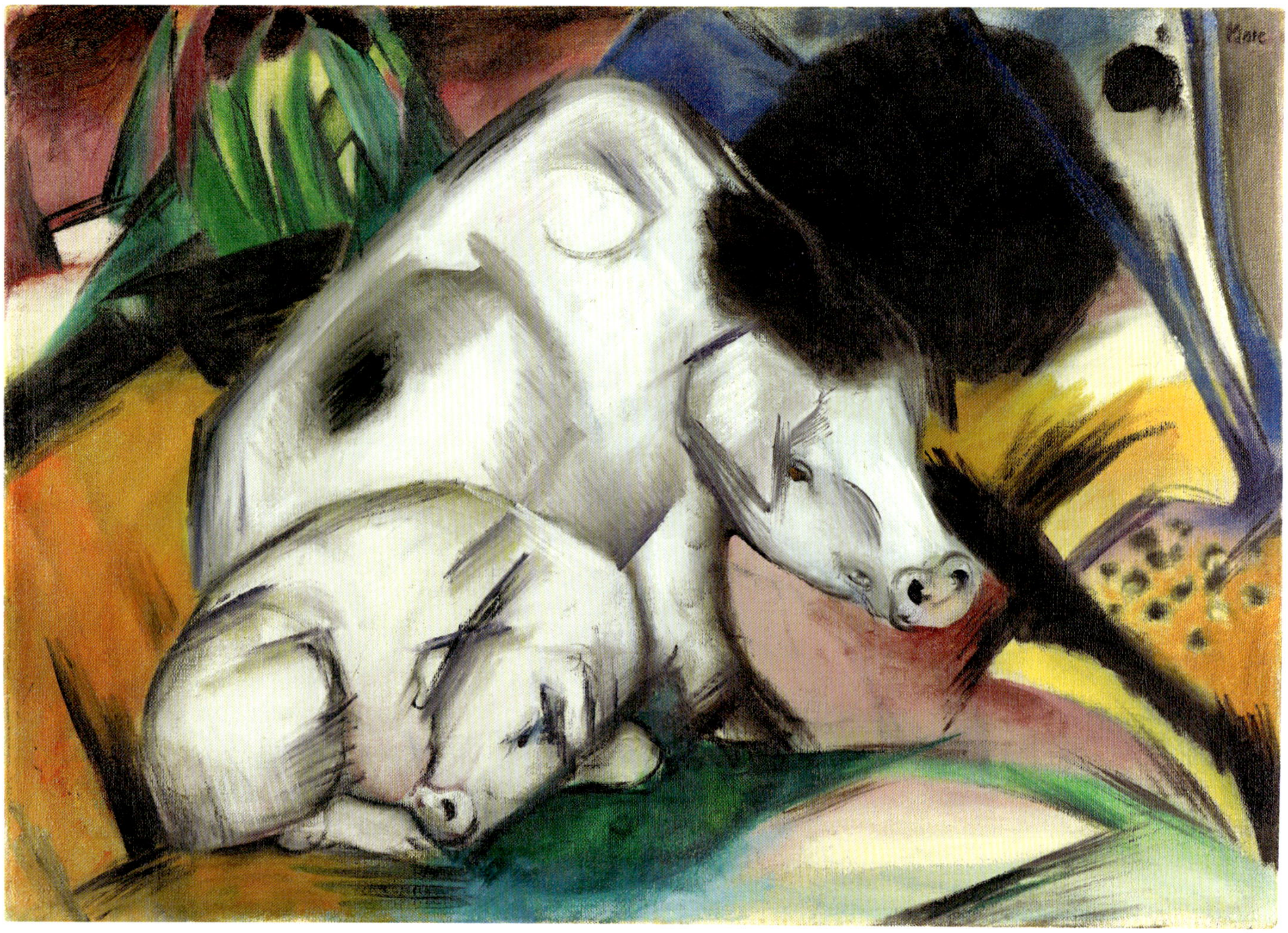

022

Franz Marc
Schweine (Mutterschwein)
1912

Franz Marc
1880 Munich – 1916 Verdun

Oil on canvas
Signed upper right: Marc
58.5 × 84.2 cm

Inv. no. P33T / Acquired 2006

Franz Marc's basically pantheistic worldview was based on the unshakable conviction that all living creatures share a mutual affinity in the constant flow of space and time, and all creation participates in the "organic rhythm" of nature. Since he felt that animals were more beautiful and purer than human beings, since he could "still hear them speak", as the writer Else Lasker-Schüler once said, he devoted his attention to them and their "misunderstood souls". Despite perceiving a certain "anti-sentiment" and "ugliness", the artist felt they were purer because they led more instinctive lives, unlike humans who had been alienated from nature by the applied sciences and technology. Correspondingly, diverse animals populate Marc's paintings, domestic and exotic, above all cats, dogs, cows, swine, horses, and deer but also elephants, tigers, lions, and monkeys. Animals embody the longing for an originary existence in harmony with nature, even when they are a mutual menace. Occasionally, human beings, as if dreaming, become part of the natural creation that inhabits the imagery of this nearly untouched universe.

In visualizing the "animalization" of art as a means of spreading a new spirit, Marc adopted stylistic features of Cubism, Orphism and Futurism to create works of crystalline transparency and radiant colouring. A profound glow marks the palette of *Schweine* (Pigs, 1912); it suffuses the hilly landscape and its vegetation. The sow, painted a pure white, dominates the centre of the composition, while patches of black on her skin and in the background stand in significant contrast. Tenderly, the mother protects her young. Pigs frequently feature in works of art as animals to be hunted, slaughtered and exploited, as useful antagonists or companions of humankind. Marc, in turn, represents them in formal and atmospheric harmony with the open natural environment, emphasizing their original dignity.

1912 marks a highlight in the art of *Blaue Reiter*, a loose association of like-minded artists, initiated by its main exponents, Wassily Kandinsky and Franz Marc, who issued a programmatic almanac that same year. They invoke a "mystical inner construction" of the world and seek to mirror it as a parable in painting – objectives that ultimately led both artists to devote themselves to pure abstraction.

UW

August Macke
Badende Mädchen
1913

August Macke
1887 Meschede – 1914 Perthe-les-Hurlus

Oil on board
Signed lower centre: A Macke 13
23.8 × 18.7 cm

Inv. no. P222M / Acquired 2010

August Macke often spoke of his indebtedness to French painting in the development of his own art. He was drawn to Paris repeatedly between 1907 and 1912 and enthusiastically wrote to his future wife Elisabeth, "When I have been to the Louvre ... and encounter Manet, Degas, Pissarro, and Monet in the Luxembourg, I have the feeling that I am coming out of a crater and into the sunlight." And in 1913, he wrote to the Berlin collector Bernhard Koehler about the Delaunay exhibition in Cologne, "That these pictures, above all others, are capable of showering one with a positively heavenly delight in the sun and in life...."

Macke's treatment of light as a supra-temporal, elementary substance, as the art historian Volker Adolphs observes, and his view of form as a parable of life took their cue from his profound knowledge of Impressionism, the Fauves, Cubism and Orphism. Manet, Monet, Cézanne, Matisse and Picasso were inspiring and indeed seminal models for him. Artistically he was especially close to Robert Delaunay, whom he met in 1912.

Radiant, like stained glass, the *Badende Mädchen* (Girls Bathing) were painted in Hilterfingen on the lake of Thun, where Macke had retired in 1913 after an extremely busy year. Three young women are seen gambolling at the lake under sun-drenched trees, an idyllic scene on a warm summer day. Despite the difference in motif, the subject matter references Manet's *Luncheon on the Grass* (1863), Cézanne's *Bathers* (1899–1906) and Matisse's *Pastorale* (1906). The sense of timelessness, of liberation from the mundanities of life makes one think of Arcadia and nymphs, young and beautiful, though mortal beings who live near waters and in the woods.

The young women are protected by the trees that form an arch of leaves above them. The sun breaks through the foliage, a flickering light that illuminates parts of the trees and the bodies of the girls. The vibrant brushstrokes seem dynamically charged, enabling viewers to trace the act of painting. They invest the picture as a whole with movement that underscores the sense of a captured moment in time. Our gaze wanders back and forth, unable to come to rest. Thus, in spite of the idyllic atmosphere, this wonderful little painting, with no fixed vantage point, is clearly anchored in the twentieth century.

AS

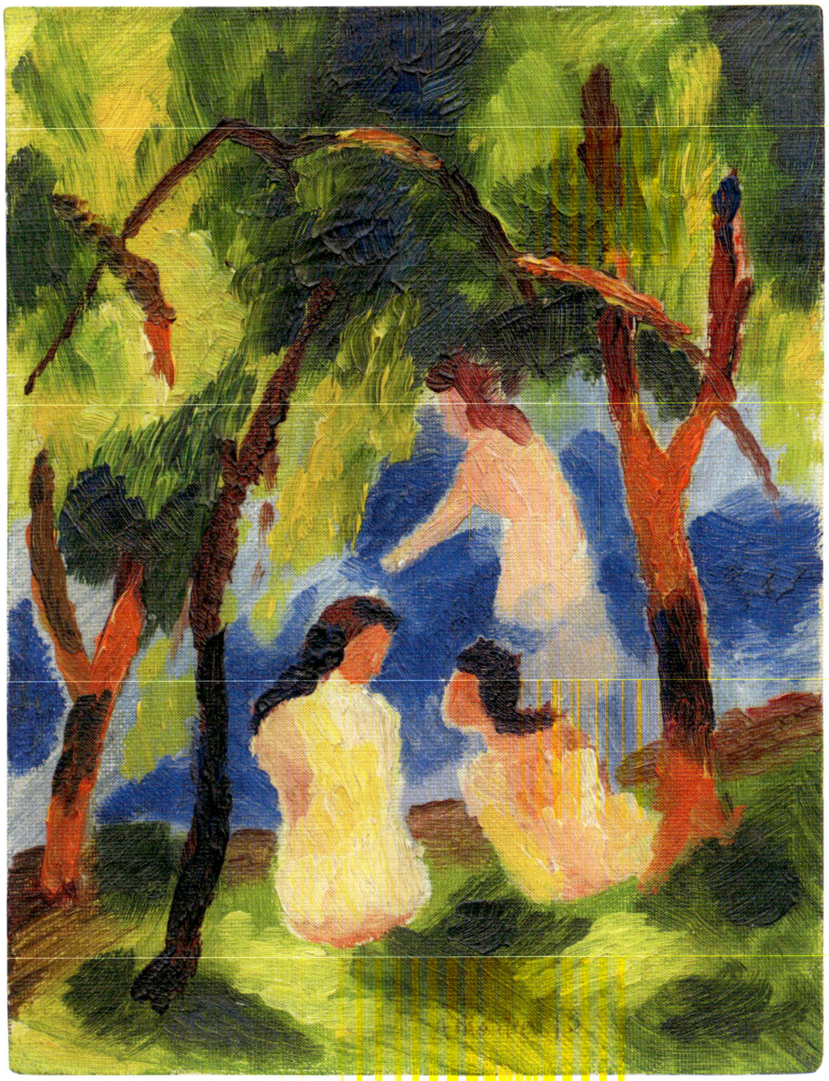

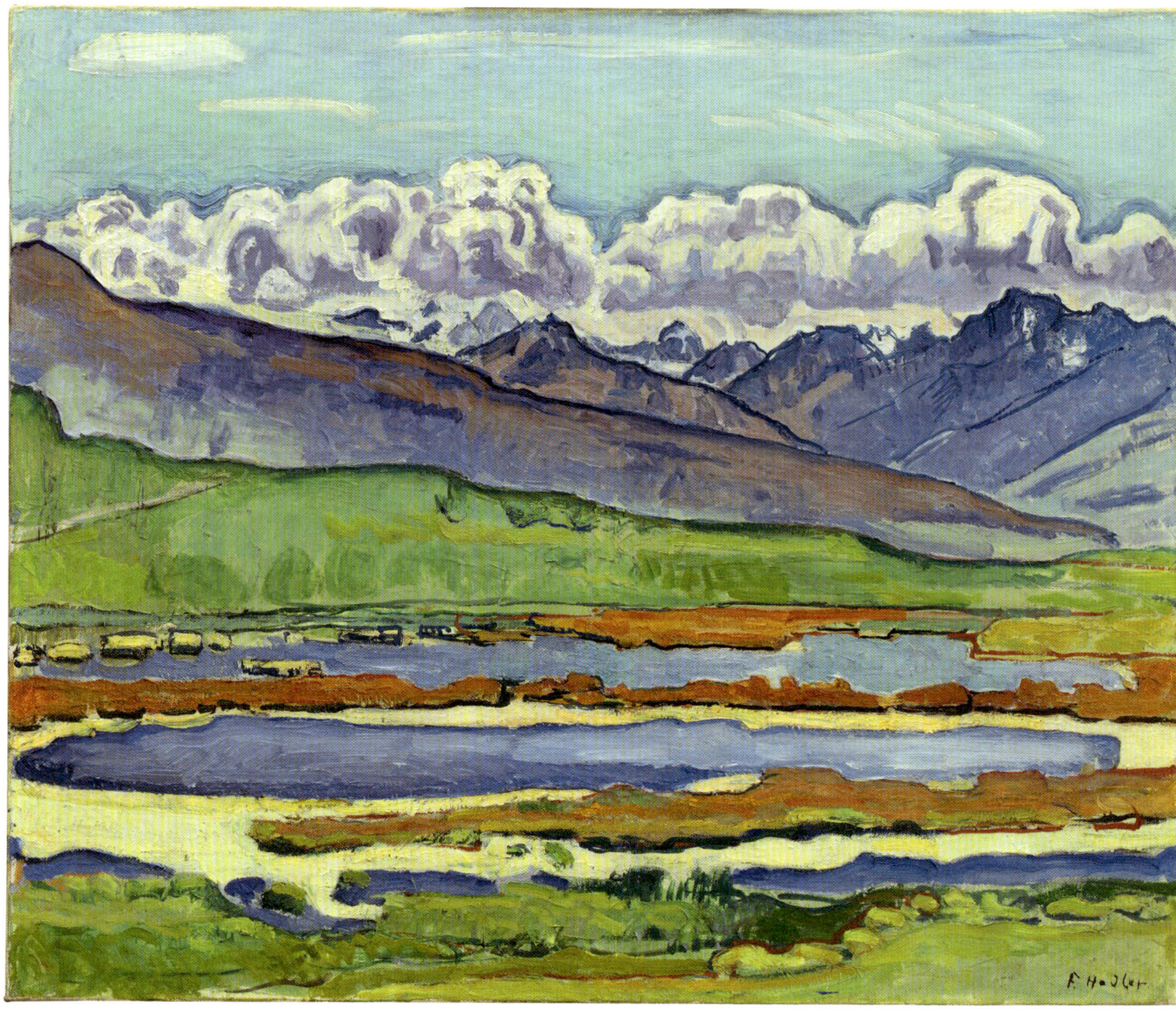
F. Hodler

Ferdinand Hodler
1853 Bern – 1918 Geneva

Oil on canvas
Signed upper right: F. Hodler
65 × 80 cm

Inv. no. P47T / Acquired 2011

Ferdinand Hodler
Les Etangs longs bei Montana
1915

Ferdinand Hodler spent August and September of 1915 in Montana in the Swiss Canton of Valais. During that time he painted a series of five pictures, capturing the marshy ponds near Crans against the southern slopes of the Rhône Valley with the gorges of Val d'Hérens and Val d'Hérémence in the background. Four of the five are identical in format (65 × 80 cm) and the near congruence in the framing of the landscapes is indebted to a grid drawing (Kunsthaus Zürich, Department of Prints and Drawings), showing the same motive on verso, copied from a *Dürerscheibe*, on which Hodler had first sketched the landscape behind it with a paintbrush. He then used this technically produced drawing as the source image to transfer the first picture of the series onto the grid canvas.

The second picture in the series (according to the catalogue raisonné) is accentuated by several pine trees, which also appear in the drawing and therefore presumably in the actual landscape itself. Hodler did not include them in the other versions, thereby emphasizing the horizontal and diagonal features of the landscape. In the present painting, the fourth in the series, our gaze glides from the ponds in the moorlands up to the mountain ranges, sloping down into the composition from the left, and on to the high mountains in the background, a few of them snow-covered and fringed overhead with lush cumulus clouds. Despite the natural depth of the landscape, the picture appears flat, like a stage set. Nor is there any indication of animal or human life, not even botanical life, that would distract from the dominance of the mountainscape. It is as if Hodler had pictured his motif in its original primeval condition. Study of the series as a whole clearly shows that the geological immutability of the landscape is challenged only by variations in weather, lighting and, therefore, the colouring. The depth of perspective in which the valleys and mountains are rendered is dominated by yellow alternating with a strong ochre, alongside greens and blues.

The lakes and Alps of Switzerland appealed greatly to Ferdinand Hodler's artistic imagination and are, in fact, a constant throughout his entire oeuvre. Aside from his large-scale Symbolist paintings of figures set against a landscape, he had done without human staffage since the early 1890s because, as he put it, "figures or anecdotes not only have nothing to contribute but rather weaken the gripping or direct emotional impact." Instead, he devoted himself exclusively to the characteristic features of the landscape itself: trees, brooks, valleys, lakes, single or grouped mountains and mountain ranges reflected in the water. In order to convey mood and atmosphere, the faithful rendition of his subject matter and the realistic treatment of material and topographic details gradually yielded to a visibly purifying and stylized form of expression. Hodler transcended the landscapes that caught his eye, expanding them into cosmic spaces of contemplation, as seen in the late paintings of Lake Geneva with Mont Blanc.

This painting became the source of a colour lithograph in 1917. In 1921 it was reproduced in colour and issued as a print, testifying not only to its popularity in particular but also to Hodler's landscape painting in general.

UW

Alexej Jawlensky
Grosse Variation – Es stürmt
1916

Alexej Jawlensky
1864 Torschok – 1941 Wiesbaden

Oil on canvas
Initialled lower left: A.J.
Inscribed, dated and numbered on verso:
"Es stürmt" 1916 no.14
54.3 × 36.2 cm

Inv. no. P236M / Acquired 2012

When the First World War broke out, Alexej Jawlensky, a native of Russia, was abruptly forced to leave his home in Munich. Rescuing just a few belongings, he escaped into exile in St. Prex, Switzerland on the northern shore of Lake Geneva. A friend of his had arranged for him to move into a small flat there. This untoward change of scenery was tantamount to an artistic caesura. As he said himself, he was no longer able to produce the "forceful, colourful paintings", primarily showing the figures and heads of people, which had characterized his art between 1909 and 1914. Now, an impulse coming entirely from the soul was linked with the view framed, day after day, by the window of his small studio, through which he saw a path, various bushes, trees and, depending on the weather, the mountains in the distance. Between 1914 and 1921, Jawlensky translated what he saw so narrowly framed through that window into an extended series of mostly small-format paintings. These prove to be more a mirror of the artist's inner feelings than a depiction of the ever-changing appearance of the landscape outside. He called them *Variationen über ein landschaftliches Thema* (Variations on the Theme of a Landscape).

It may well be indebted to this window that all of the Variations are vertical in format since he had hitherto shown a preference for the usual horizontal, landscape format (cat. 21). Jawlensky's personal acquaintance with Wassily Kandinsky and Henri Matisse and his knowledge of their works as well as those of Robert Delaunay, in particular his *Windows* series, had taught him to treat colour as a constitutive and autonomous element, that is, as a visual entity in its own right, apart from subject matter. Thus, colour alone marks the composition of his *Variations*, without the *cloisonné* contouring (cat. 21) that often appeared in his earlier work. Although the present work *Grosse Variation – Es stürmt* (Large Variation – Stormy Weather) features an abstract approach, the artist never turned to pure abstraction as Kandinsky did. Applying his thin paint in a range of tender to sturdy strokes of red, purple, blue and green, he created a fabric of rounded forms, primarily representing the vegetation in front of his window. With no indication of a horizon, the shapes occupy the entire plane of the composition, peaking at the top in a tree, resembling a cypress and animated by three ochre-coloured patches. The restless brushstroke persuasively underscores the wind sweeping through bushes and trees.

Jawlensky called these landscapes "Songs without Words", possibly in reference to composer Felix Mendelssohn Bartholdy. How much the landscapes meant to him is demonstrated by the fact that after moving away from St. Prex in 1917, he continued painting them in Zurich and Ascona. He did not end the series of *Variations* until 1921, when he turned to his new series of *Abstrakte Köpfe* (Abstract Heads) and *Meditationen* (Meditations).

UW

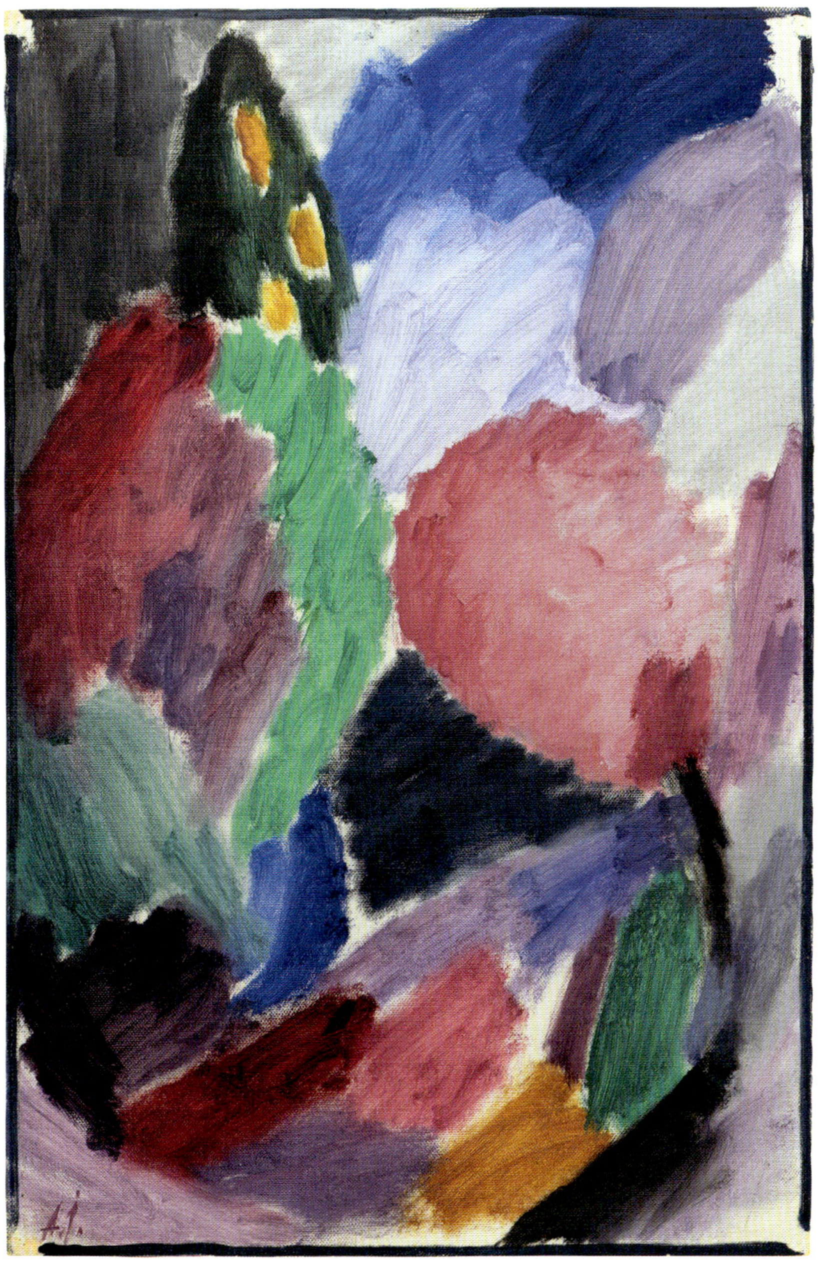

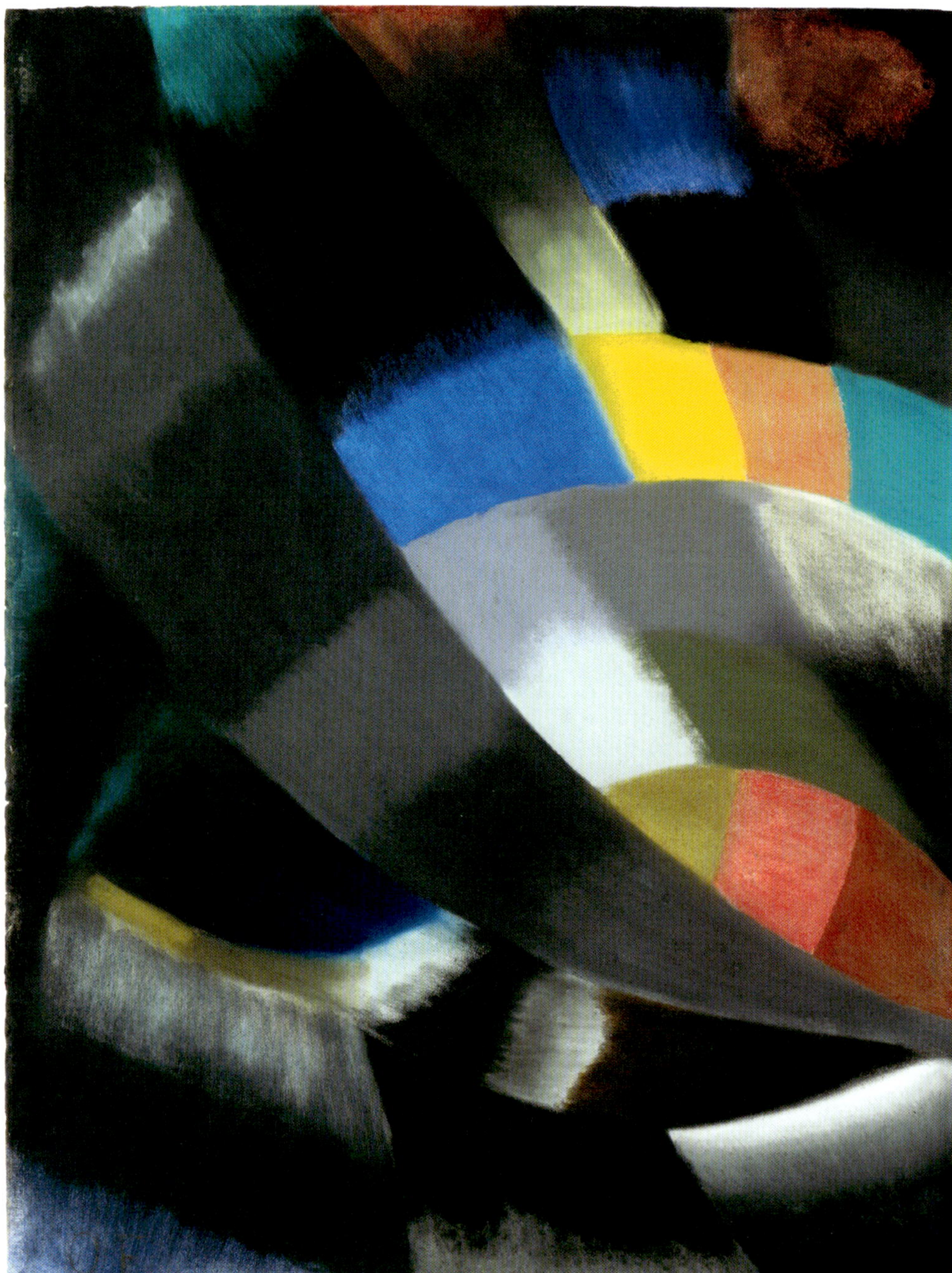

026

Otto Freundlich
1878 Stolp / Pommern–
1943 KZ Sobibor (?) / Majdanek (?)

Pastel on vellum
Initialled upper left: O F
63.5 × 48.5 cm

Inv. no. G45T / Acquired 2011

Otto Freundlich
Schiff im Sturm
1924

As a young artist, Otto Freundlich was influenced by Symbolism and Art Nouveau and showed a tendency towards abstraction, creating an oeuvre, informed from the beginning, with a spiritual component. He spoke of the "cosmic salvation of the finite" and the unboundedness of visible things. Although his studio in Paris (1908) was next door to Picasso's and the two artists were well acquainted, the Spaniard's Cubist style exerted little influence on Freundlich, who explicitly declared that he wanted to explore the pure flatness of painting and therefore chose not to take a Cubist approach. He did, however, appreciate Picasso's "new view of a world apart from appearances". It was not Cubism, but rather Delaunay's Orphism and the deeply moving experience of seeing the mediaeval stained glass windows in the Cathedral of Chartres that ultimately led him to take his subject matter apart, rendering it flattened and expressively heightened by colour. In 1927 he finally crossed the threshold of abstraction and forged a formal idiom in his compositions to which he remained committed until his tragic death in 1943.

Wishing to express the unboundedness of things, which he called their "cosmic self-annulment", Otto Freundlich used no visible outlines. "World dualism", that is, the separation of subject and object, could only be surmounted by liberating the colour plane from lines in order to generate "a pure, spiritual manifestation" beyond solid bodies and fixed perspectives. Freundlich believed that the boundlessness he sought to achieve lay in the human eye itself. He considered it a "cosmic organ", such that vision transcends all constraints and reaches into infinity. In all of this, there lies expressed an almost religious yearning to merge into the universe, whereby things and the ego are still distinct but experience salvation by overcoming their separation.

Freundlich found a formal equivalent for his artistic ideas in "trapezoidal planes" spreading out in all directions and showing no visible lines or sharp-edged points of intersection, instead interrelated only by flowing transitions. These planes are the building blocks of his composition, and like the world's building blocks, they undergo constant change, creating ever new formations.

The title of the pastel, *Schiff im Sturm* (Ship in a Storm), designates a concrete motif in a concrete context, while the composition itself, though turbulent, is entirely non-figurative, characterized particularly by the appealing contrast of a colourful and non-colourful, dark and light, dull and luminous palette. Freundlich pencilled a small-format sketch of this composition (Musées de Pontoise), indicating the colours he intended to use. However, these colours deviate from those in the pastel.

UW

Otto Freundlich
Untitled
1937

027

Otto Freundlich
1878 Stolp / Pommern–
1943 KZ Sobibor (?) / Majdanek (?)

Gouache on paper
Initialled and dated upper right: O.F. 37
21.3 × 19.3 cm

Inv. no. G92M / Acquired 2001

Otto Freundlich's small gouache, almost square in format, shows several clearly delineated planes of colour forming an abstract composition. The configuration of planes does not make a clear distinction between figure and ground, but their contours and the arrangement of the colours do come together to form a shape that dominates the centre of the picture and resembles a human head resting on two shoulders.

The palette is restricted to traditional combinations of yellow, red and blue, both pure and broken, in addition to the achromatic colours of grey and black. The colour composition is uncharacteristic of Freundlich's work as he ordinarily experimented with various combinations of the entire colour spectrum. His use of colour was basically homogeneous and the application of the paint opaque. The colours are not graduated within single planes but the paint does show traces of the brushstroke and occasional differences in the thickness of the application.

UW

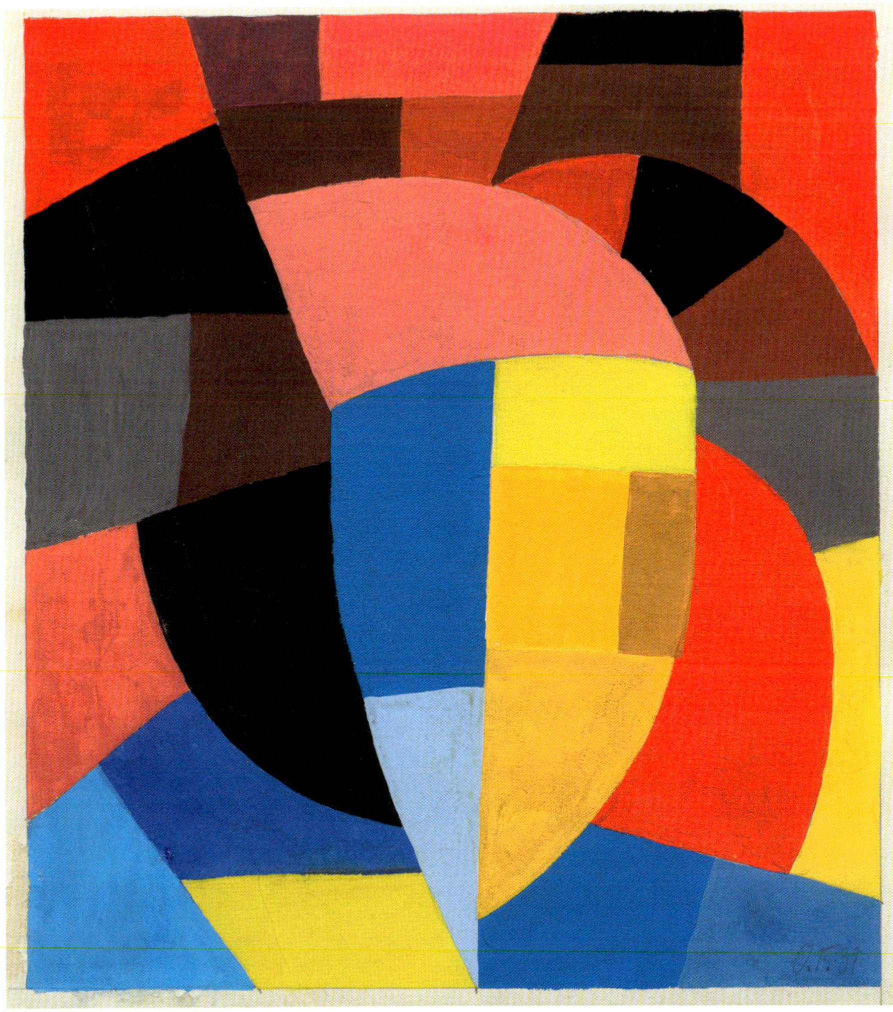

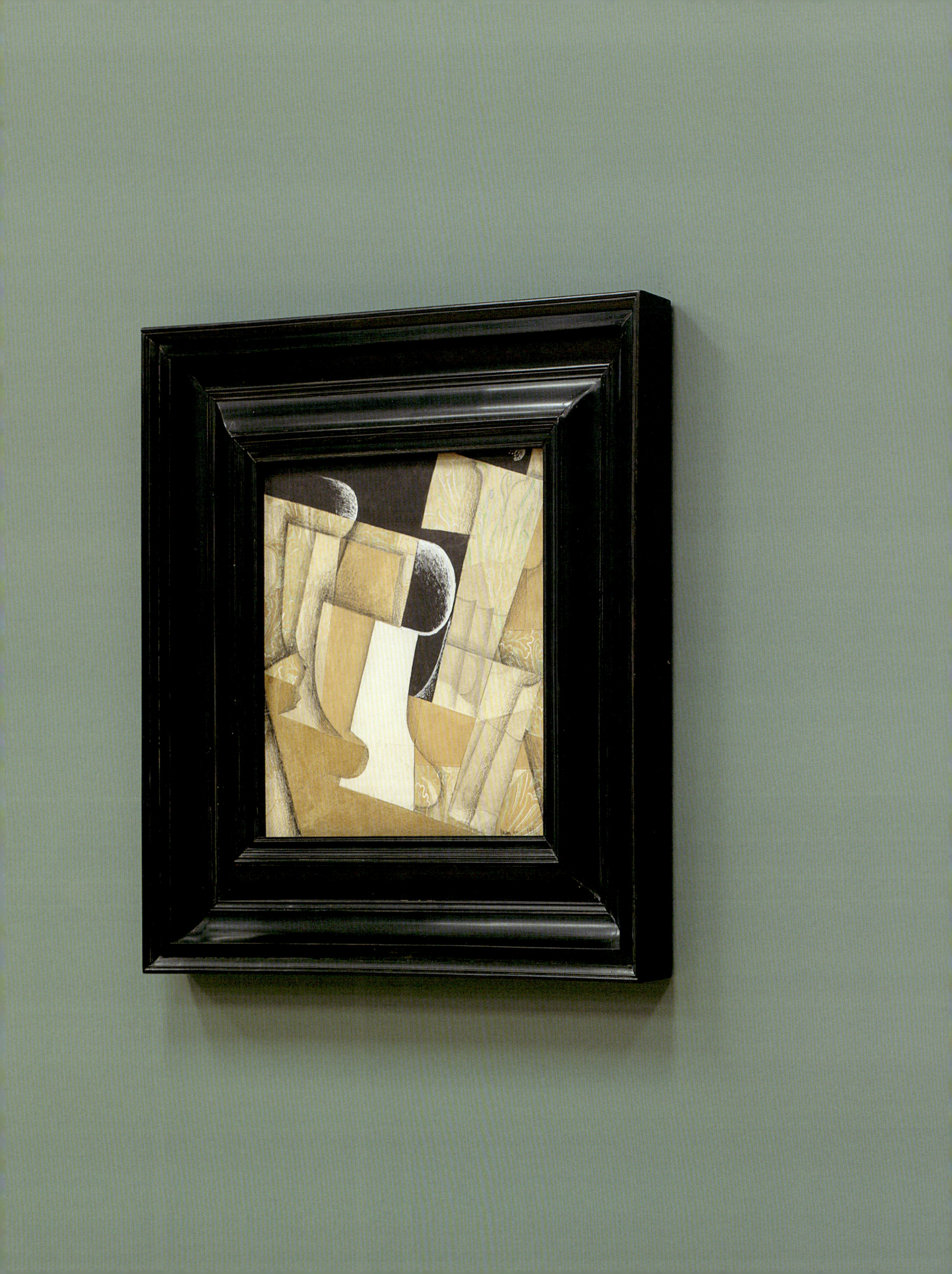

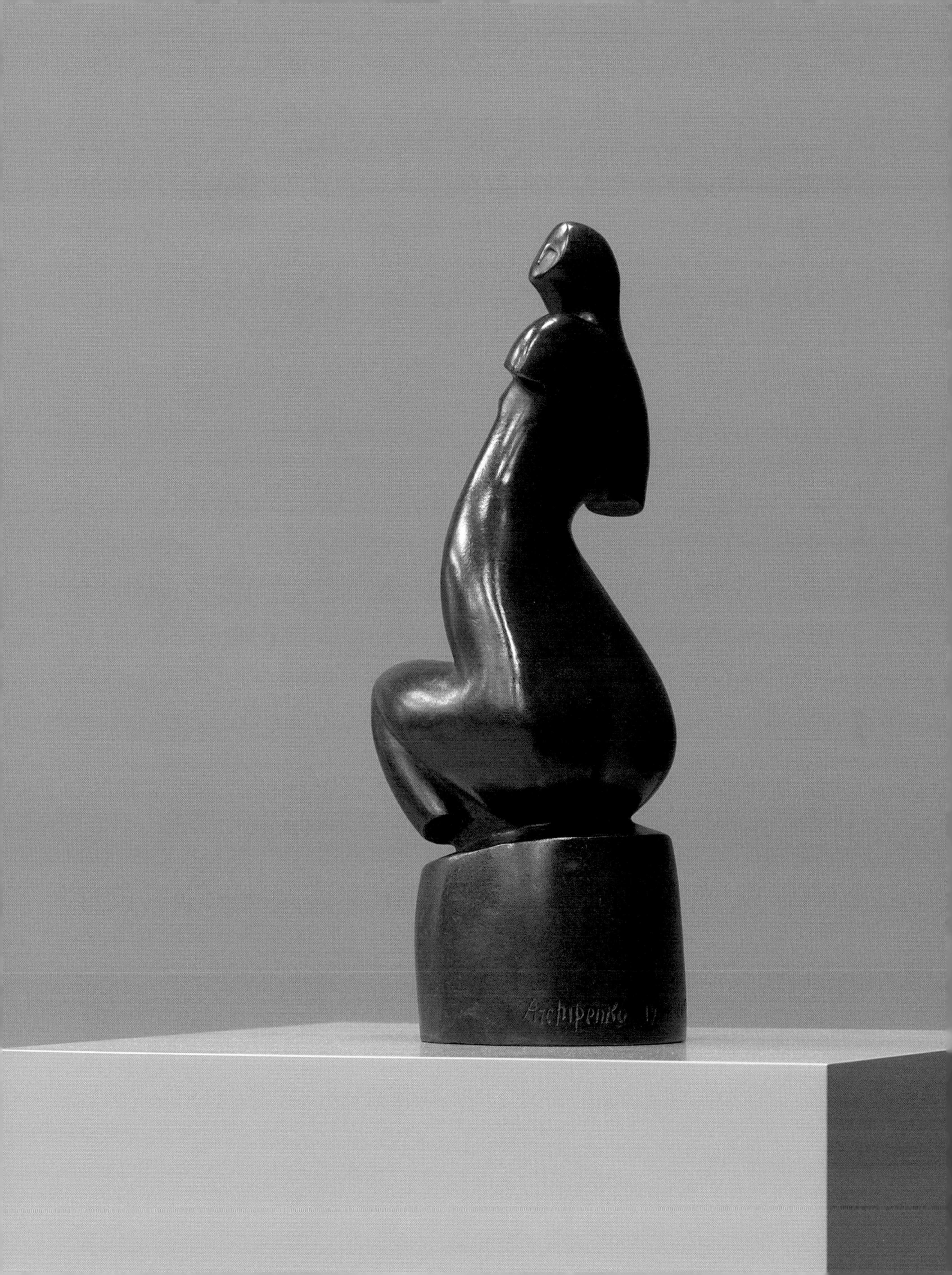
Archipenko

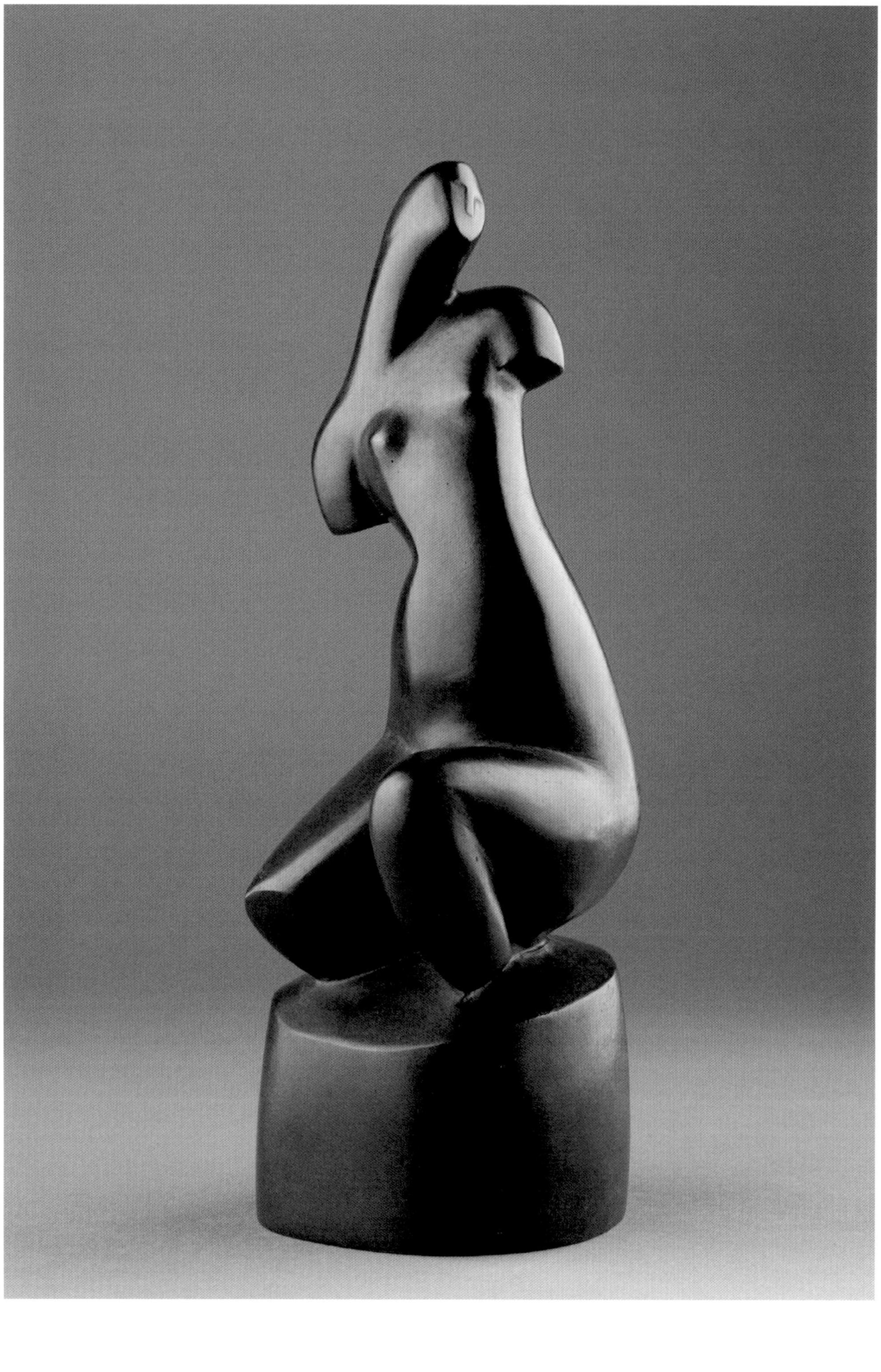

Alexander Archipenko
1887 Kiev – 1964 New York

Bronze
Signed, dated, inscribed (identifying marks) and numbered on the base:
Archipenko 1909. No 5/6
Height: 38 cm

Inv. no. S294M / Acquired 2016

Alexander Archipenko
Black Seated Torso
1909

Archipenko created *Black Seated Torso* (*Femme Assise*), a small bronze, the year after he moved from Moscow to Paris. There, in the European art metropolis, the just 22-year-old artist made the acquaintance of artists and critics who would champion Cubism both practically and theoretically, in particular Delaunay, Léger, Gleizes, Metzinger, Le Fauconnier and the writer Guillaume Apollinaire. Léger was a close friend. When these artists first exhibited at the *Salon des Indépendants* in 1910 (Picasso and Braques, the actual founders of Cubism, were not represented), Archipenko and Raymond Duchamp-Villon also participated as Cubist sculptors, although they were classified as such more because of their friendship with those artists than a shared artistic style. It was, in fact, a label that Archipenko rejected. He certainly appreciated Cézanne's paintings and was well aware of their significance in the development of Cubism, but he himself felt a greater affinity with a different tradition. The pre-Christian stone idol in the garden at the University of Kiev counts among his earliest "sculptural memories". At the Louvre, he took a particular interest in archaic, Byzantine and Gothic works of art. His tendency to simplify shapes and focus on their geometry took its cue from the art of the Incas, North American Indians and African tribes. Drawing on sources of that kind, he did not identify himself with Cubism or Futurism.

Black Seated Torso is Archipenko's first sculpture of art historical standing. The reduced form and serene, smooth surface with its extremely delicate patina stands in clear contrast to the animated modelling of Rodin's and Rosso's Impressionist works (cat. 3 and 4). All of the physical details, the bones and muscles, have been eliminated for the sake of a simple, clear whole with seamless contours. Rodin was the first to render the human figure as a torso, thus creating a new type of model for many artists, but unlike Rodin, Archipenko did not remove the extremities after finishing the figure but instead conceived of the sculpture as a torso to begin with, much like what Constantin Brancusi also did at that time.

The present sculpture rests on an irregular cylindrical pedestal, a clear indication that it is to be appreciated from all sides. The S-shaped sweep of the figure, the small breasts, the curved and deliberately elongated stomach, the voluptuous hips and buttocks evoke female representations of the Late Middle Ages in Europe. The simplicity of the shape, reduced to essentials, lends it a monumentality that belies its actual size.

UW

Raymond Duchamp-Villon
Baudelaire
1911

Raymond Duchamp-Villon
1876 Damville – 1918 Cannes

Cement with terra-cotta patina
Signed, dated and numbered:
R. Duchamp Villon 1911 E/A
Height: 41 cm

Inv. no.: S32T / Acquired 2005

The French art critic, translator, essayist and poet Charles Baudelaire (1821–1867) bestowed upon the world a poetic masterpiece with the publication of *Les Fleurs du Mal* in 1857. Painted in his lifetime by Deroy, Courbet and Manet and photographed by Nadar, Carjat and Neyt, he was honoured once again forty-four years after his death for his trailblazing contribution to modern European literature, especially Symbolism – this time in the form of a sculpture. It was the literary journalist Jacques Crépet, editor and connoisseur of Baudelaire's oeuvre, who commissioned Duchamp-Villon in 1911 to create a monument in honour of the writer. A pencil drawing made by the sculptor gives a vague impression of this unexecuted sculpture, which was to have been crowned by the voluminous head of Baudelaire. Duchamp-Villon produced only this head in plaster, terracotta, bronze, and, as in the present work, in cement. The patina of surface and colour of these versions vary considerably. Raymond and Marcel Duchamp's older brother, Jacques Villon, reproduced the poet's portrait as an etching in 1920, titled *Baudelaire au socle*.

Initially, Duchamp-Villon worked in a style that shows an affinity with Rodin's oeuvre and Art Nouveau, but by 1911 he had taken up the formal idiom of Cubism, eschewing all accidental and anecdotal details. The portrait is pared down to the essential features of Baudelaire's physiognomy and the distinctive shape of the poet's head, drawing attention, perhaps, to the locus of the human intellect. The sculptor worked from a photograph. Nadar (1855), Carjat (1862), and Neyt (1864) equally capture the severity and melancholy of Baudelaire's features, indicative of the existential life crises from which he suffered: narrow, tightly closed lips and eyes focused on the viewer with great intensity. In contrast, the eyes in the sculpture have neither iris nor pupil. The countenance has the austerity of an ancient Egyptian bust, spiritual in appearance and stoically removed from the real world, which Baudelaire famously compared to an "oasis of horror in a desert of boredom". It was with a mixture of curiosity and profound scepticism that the poet perceived modern civilization's march of triumph and, attendant upon it, the global spread of "fuel, steam, and turntable", of industry, photography and advertising. Baudelaire pitted the lifestyle of the dandy against the nauseating tedium and ugliness of bourgeois society, which had led to the loss of spiritual dignity (honorabilité spirituelle) and creativity (imagination). The dandy as the actual hero of Modernism, embodied by himself, renounced utilitarian objectives in order to devote all thought and action exclusively to salvaging beauty through art and poetry as mnemonic devices.

UW

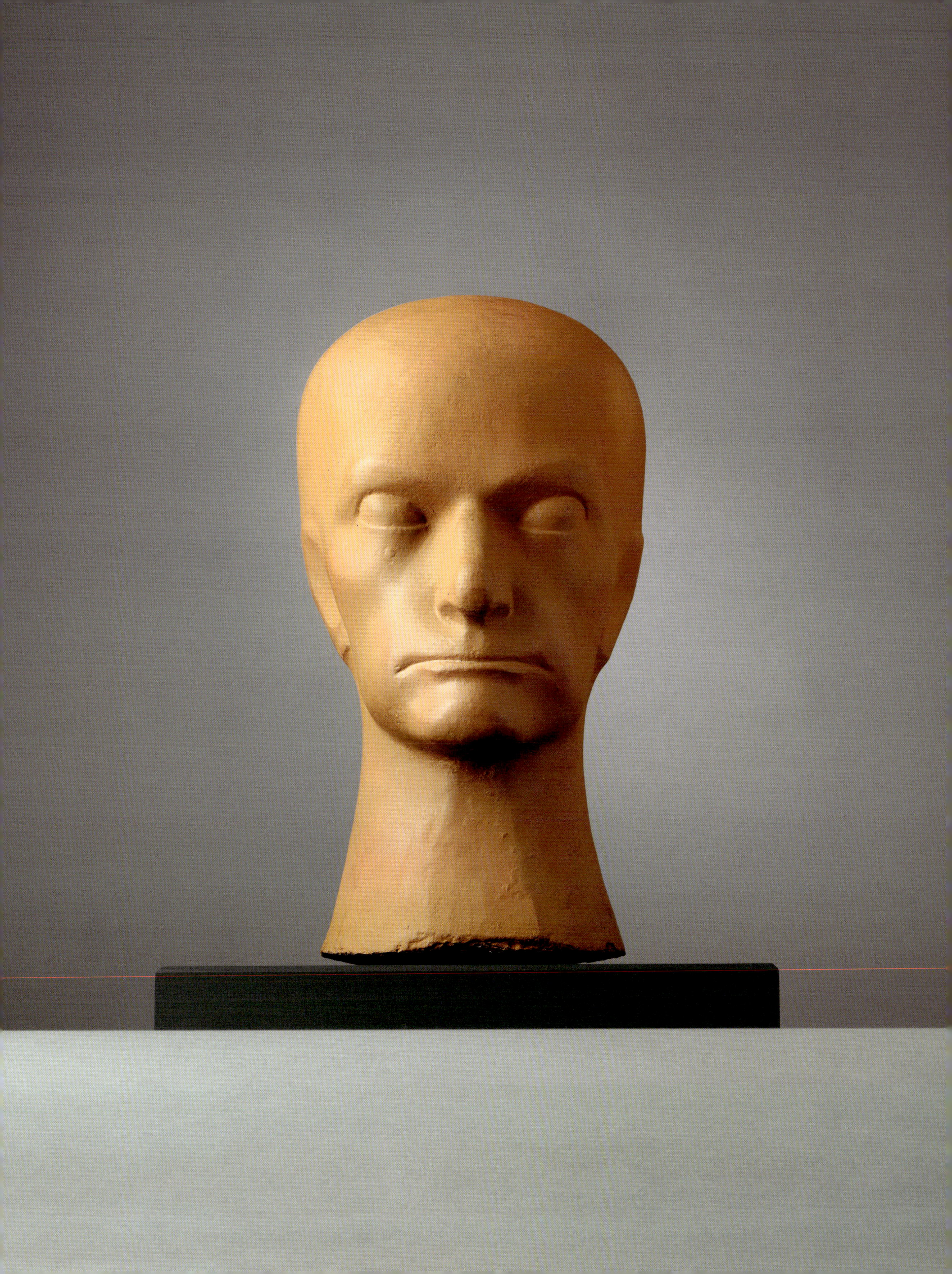

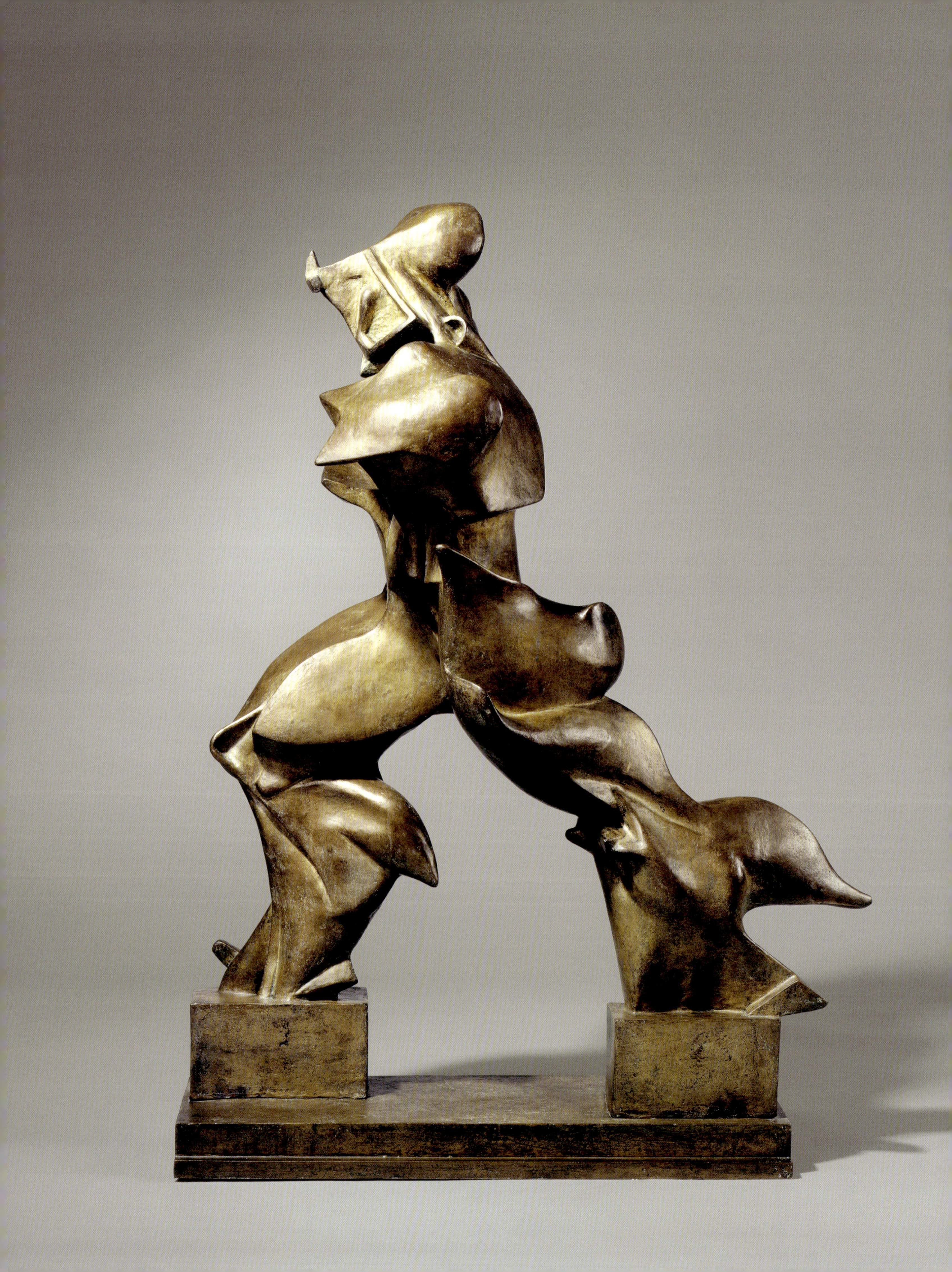

Umberto Boccioni
1882 Reggio di Calabria – 1916 Verona

Bronze
cast of plaster original: 1949
(foundry: Giovanni and Angelo Nicci, Rome)
Height: 120 cm

Inv. no. S7T / Acquired 2000

Umberto Boccioni
Forme uniche della continuità nello spazio
1913

Forme uniche della continuità nello spazio (Unique Forms of Continuity in Space) was created with the objective of making the movements and dynamics of the human body visible in space. Marcel Duchamp, like Umberto Boccioni, explored the same concern around 1912, which Henri Bergson had already attempted to capture in philosophical terms. Duchamp remarked in an interview that no one had ever before thought about introducing actual movement into a work of art. The fact that he and the Futurists had both addressed that potential indicates that the idea was in the air at the time thanks to the invention of the moving picture. He was particularly taken with the idea of capturing the movement of a nude walking down a flight of stairs within the confinement of a static image. Duchamp painted his *Nude Descending a Staircase* (1912) the same year in which Boccioni started working on his sculpture *Forme uniche*. Duchamp had been inspired by chronophotography, a medium he had discovered in physiologist Etienne Jules Marey's textbook *Le Mouvement* (1894). Boccioni was also familiar with the photographic sequences of the human body in movement reproduced in this book. As a sculptural counterpart to Duchamp's *Nude Descending a Staircase*, *Forme uniche* moves into the third dimension but it is still a static visual image. This sculpture is thus unlike all of its art historical precedents inasmuch as it does not merely represent a human body in movement but actually shows the continuum of movement, specifically the way in which it affects and changes the shape of the human body. It is almost as if Boccioni had skinned the body in order to show even more clearly, chronophotographically as it were, how muscles are stretched and elongated by movement. The artist has created the quintessential "futurist image of man" by showing how the body is affected by the "speed of modern life", which was enthusiastically embraced by the Futurists and by Boccioni as one of the movement's main proponents.

To explore the effect of movement on the human body, Boccioni created three other sculptures in 1913, none of which has survived. Ever increasing reduction of his sculptural material ultimately led to *Forme uniche*, which he executed in plaster, as he had the three preceding sculptures. Authorized bronze casts of the original, preserved at the Museu de Arte Contemporânea da Universidade de São Paulo, were not made until after the artist's death.

UW

Lyonel Feininger
Der Raddampfer I
1913

031

Lyonel Feininger
1871 New York – 1956 New York

Oil on canvas
Signed and dated upper left: Feininger 1913
80 × 100 cm

Inv. no. P26T / Acquired 2004

Lyonel Feininger started out as a caricaturist and illustrator and did not take up painting until 1907. Initially, the human figure continued to predominate, often grotesquely elongated and "skewed". Soon however, his paintings would show the influence of Cubism and Orphism, while the new visual syntax that he discovered through his study of Picasso and Delaunay led to a kind of crystalline chromatic Cubism. As a young man, Feininger already felt an affinity for seascapes, not least in consequence of his voyage by ship from New York to Hamburg. Still in his teens, in 1887–88, he made the acquaintance at the Hamburg Kunsthalle of seascapes by the Danish painter Anton Melbye (1818–1875), whose work drew on the tradition of 17th-century Dutch marine painting.

With paddlewheel and sail, the *Raddampfer* (Paddle Steamer) battles the waves of the turbulent waters. Smoke billowing out of the chimney is swallowed up by the agitated winds. Another ship appears on the horizon with sails lowered, taking a course against the wind. Everything is in motion, the raging elements give the eyes no rest. In *Raddampfer*, the contest between nature and technology shows the features of Cubism, or, as Feininger described his style in 1913, of "prisma-ism". Objects, fragmented into facets, yield a crystalline composition of angular, interacting planes. Cubism was motivated more by form than by colour, which explains a spectrum essentially reduced to ochre, brown and shades of grey. This de-sensualisation of painting met with resistance from the Orphists, especially Villon, Delaunay and Kupka, who adopted the structural composition of Cubism but animated it with the vibrant, prismatic colours. However, Feininger was also extremely interested in colour, so much so, in fact, that it would actually become his medium, and fostered his responsiveness to the almost romantically inclined ideas of Orphism. In 1908, he had already made the acquaintance of Robert Delaunay, who experimented with colour to the point of complete abstraction.

The bold colours of the paddle steamer are pitted against the greys and greens of sea and sky. Dark is the hull of the ship, while railing, paddlewheel, sail, chimney, smoke plume and flag are conspicuously rendered in yellow, green, ochre, orange and a reddish purple. Feininger applied dry, rough pigments to his coarse canvas, the white of which shimmers through here and there between the patches of paint. A charcoal drawing that preceded the *Raddampfer* is dated 12 May 1913.

UW

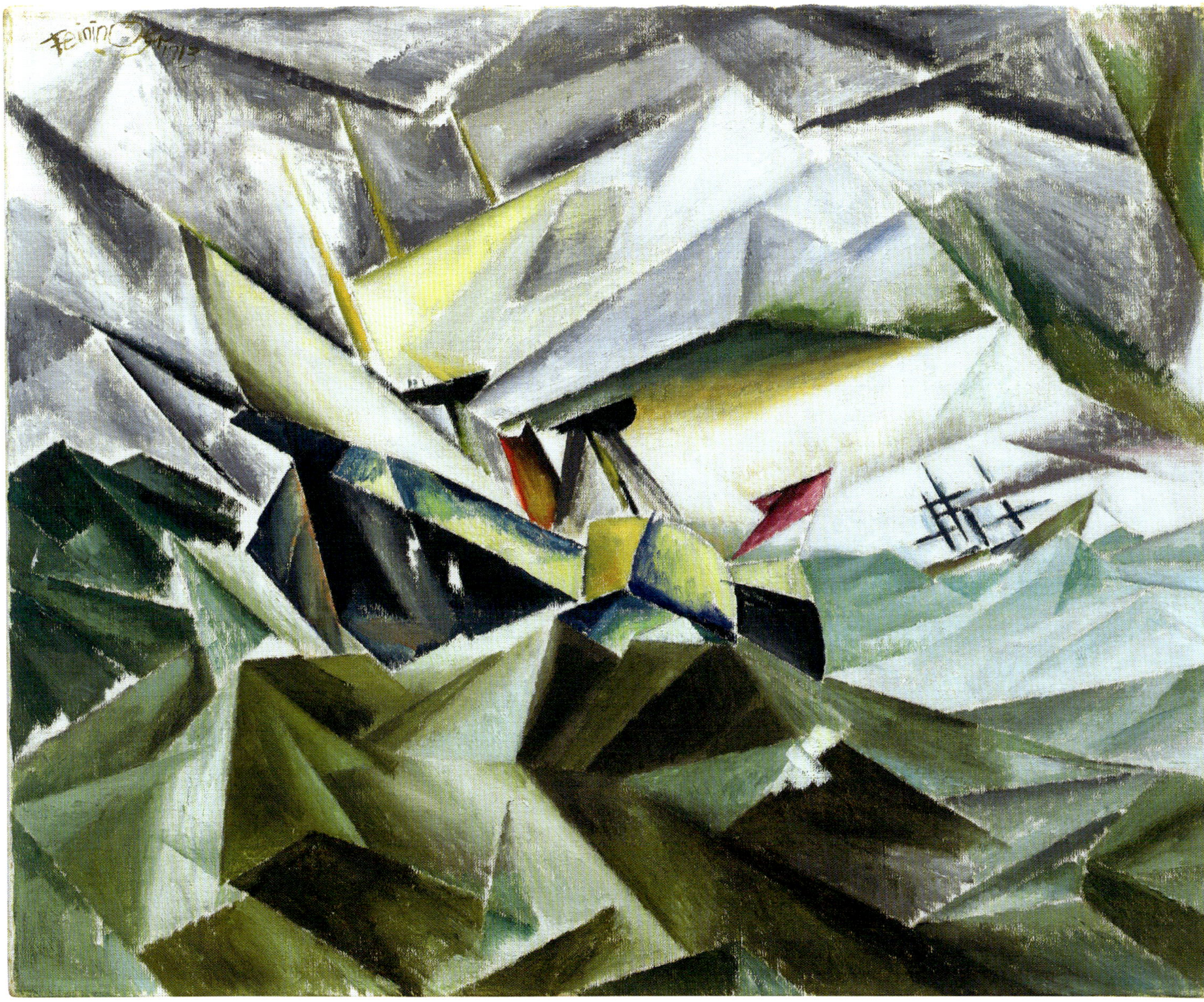

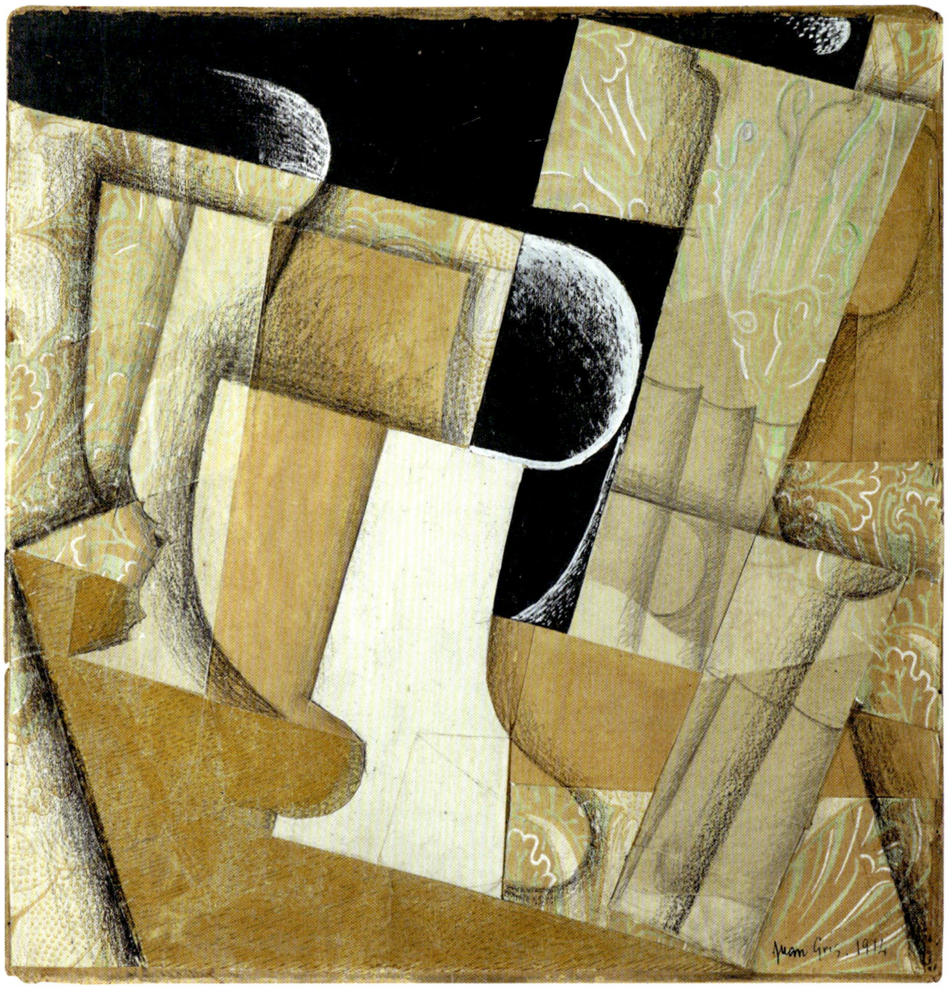

Juan Gris
1887 Madrid – 1927 Boulogne-sur-Seine

Collage, pencil and gouache on cardboard
Signed and dated lower right:
Juan Gris 1914
39.9 × 39.4 cm

Inv. no. G40T / Acquired 2010

Juan Gris
Le verre
1914

While Pablo Picasso and Georges Braque advanced the "analytical" facet of Cubism, it was Juan Gris who contributed substantially to the "synthetic" elaboration of that movement, which has had an enduring influence on painting and sculpture in the twentieth century. When Gris moved to Paris from Madrid in 1906, he immediately sought out his Spanish compatriot. However, by c. 1912–13, he had abandoned the analytic treatment of the world with its uncompromising division into basic geometric shapes and devised a distinctive idiom of his own: synthetic compositions of clearly outlined, abstract planes to which he assigned subject matter and material only afterwards in response to the requirements of the composition as a whole. Gris once commented that Cézanne, whose works and statements were admired by Cubists, had made a cylinder out of a bottle, while he himself had made a bottle out of a cylinder. Working with elements of the imagination rather than empirical perception, he did not proceed inductively from the specific to the general but deductively from the general to the specific, attempting, as he said, to anthropomorphize the general, or rather, the abstract.

The artist's deductive method is quintessentially revealed in the composition of his still life, *La verre* (The Glass, 1914). Out of different types of paper cut into varying shapes, he has created a thoughtfully balanced but purely abstract collage with a reduced palette in which that of "analytical" Cubism still clearly reverberates. In a second, basically intuitive step, Gris drew and painted forms derived from this non-figurative composition, evoking the idea of a drinking glass placed on a wood-grained table against a background of patterned wallpaper and seen from several viewpoints. The use of actual wallpaper as a pictorial element is indebted to the technique of collage, invented in 1912 by Braque and Picasso. Their use of newspaper clippings, labels, tickets, and other real objects did not result in an analytical visual reality but rather a synthetic one in the sense of a higher unity created by the ordering spirit. In contrast to Braque and Picasso, Gris's Platonic spirit surfaces primarily in the guise of a classicism and serenity entirely devoid of subjectivity.

UW

Fernand Léger
Contraste de formes
1914

Fernand Léger
1881 Argentan – 1955 Gif-sur-Yvette

Oil on canvas
Initialled and dated lower right: F.L 14
61 × 50 cm

Inv. no. P11T / Acquired 2000

The paintings and gouaches that Léger titled *Contrastes de formes* were created between 1912 and 1914. In them, the artist made the transition to nonfiguration, or rather to non-imitation inasmuch as the forms in these works are entirely without mimetic ambition. However, they do still resonate with the memory of objects reduced to their elemental shape in the sense of Cézanne – cylinder, sphere and cone. Léger did not actually paint abstract works; instead, he briefly used abstraction as a radical means of coming to terms with the "three basic elements of visual composition, line, shape and colour" and their "simultaneous mutual arrangement" (Léger).

In the present painting, Léger arranged a number of truncated cones of varying sizes as the central figure rising up through a largely vertical structure of lines. Although these truncated cones are interlocked and stacked on top of each other, they are not governed by any structural or perspectival logic. The composition is entirely autonomous – an achievement of Cubism – and obeys only the intent of the artist who is fully aware that the workings of contemplative reason rather than sensual feelings can produce a complete, self-contained image of abstract shapes. In addition to line and shape, this work also makes use of the third "basic element of visual composition" – colour – in order to flesh out the structure. The colouring, clearly a feature that has been added, does not slavishly follow the outlined shapes but rather seems to float in a state of suspension. Yellow, blue and pale purple hues accentuate contrasting reds and dark greens. White highlights on the truncated cones heighten the sense of space and depth, while occasional patches of unpainted, primed white canvas indicate that Léger was not interested in a subtle blend of colours. One might in fact say that his palette is as rudimentary as the shapes into which it is inscribed. The combination yields an image that is both planar and spatial, structural and dynamic, graphic and painterly, robust and fragile – in other words, a composition of many beautifully balanced contrasts.

To Léger, contrast means dissonance. The social and technological upheavals of his time were "dissonant" and he registered the "short-lived, multifarious bustle" of modern life that "shunts us back and forth and threatens to tear us apart" with seismographic sensitivity. Léger's artistic response to such trials, on the eve of the World War I, might almost be read as a parable, for his *Contrastes de formes* are couched in an abstract idiom that reconciles opposites without neutralizing tension.

UW

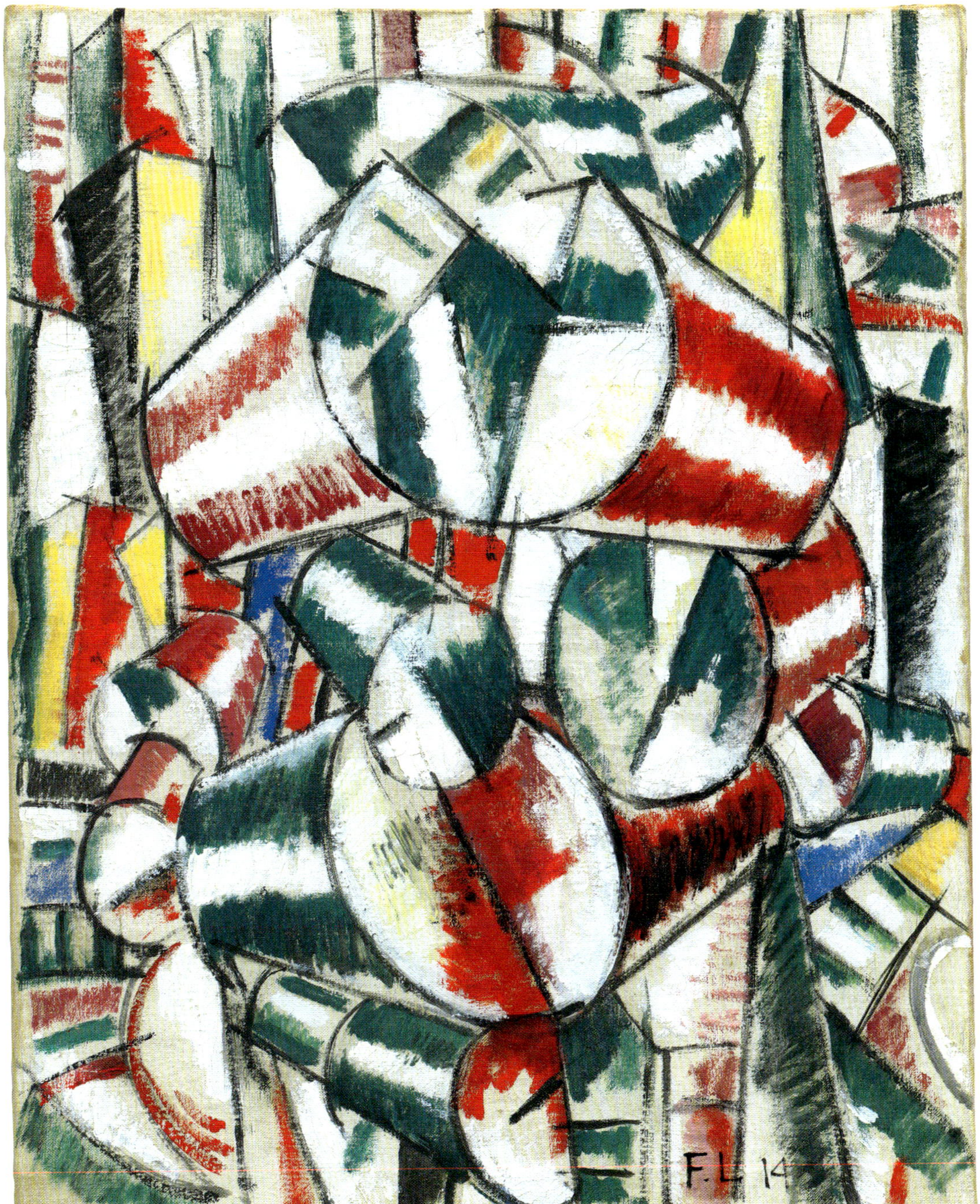
F.L 14

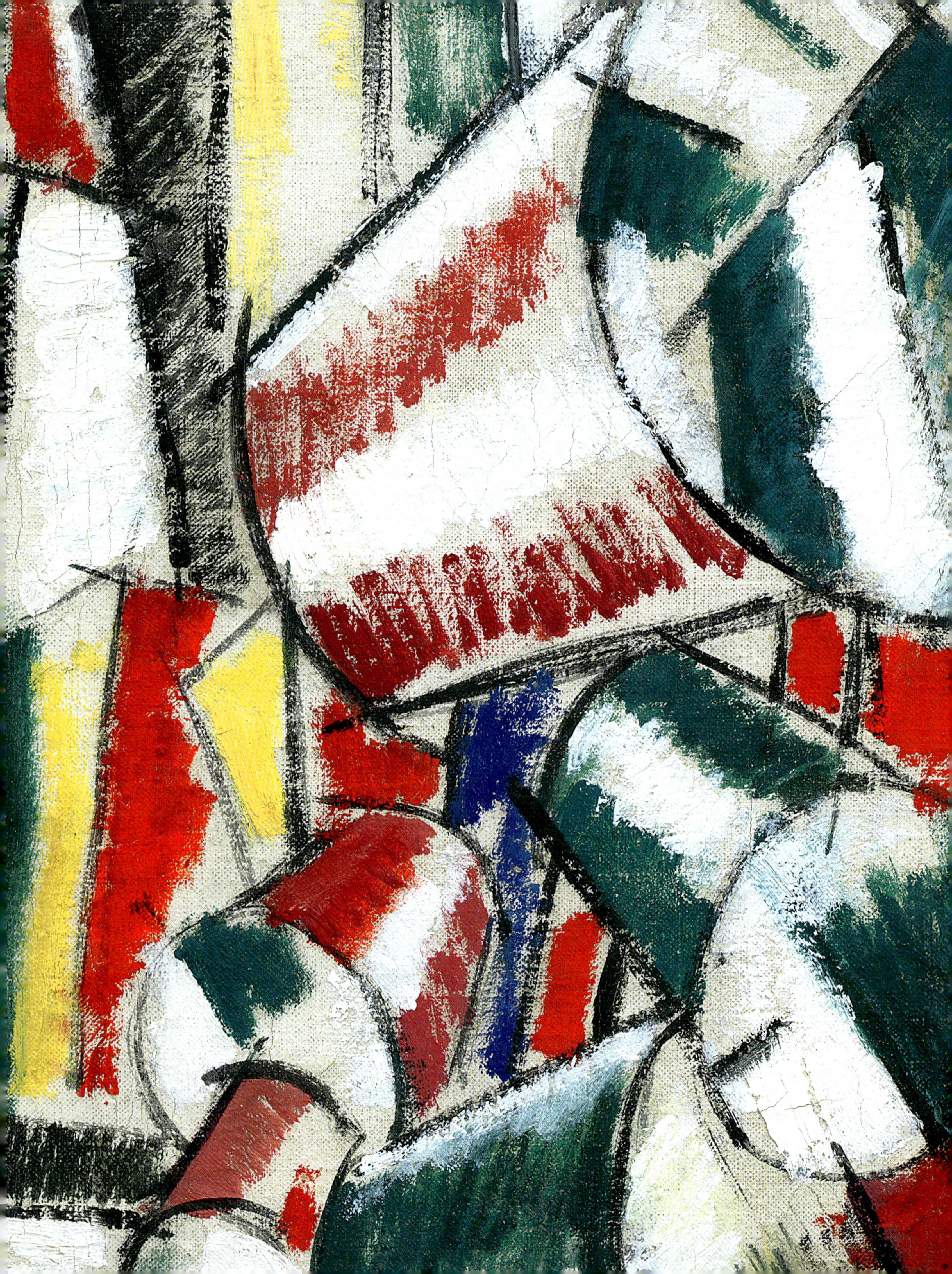

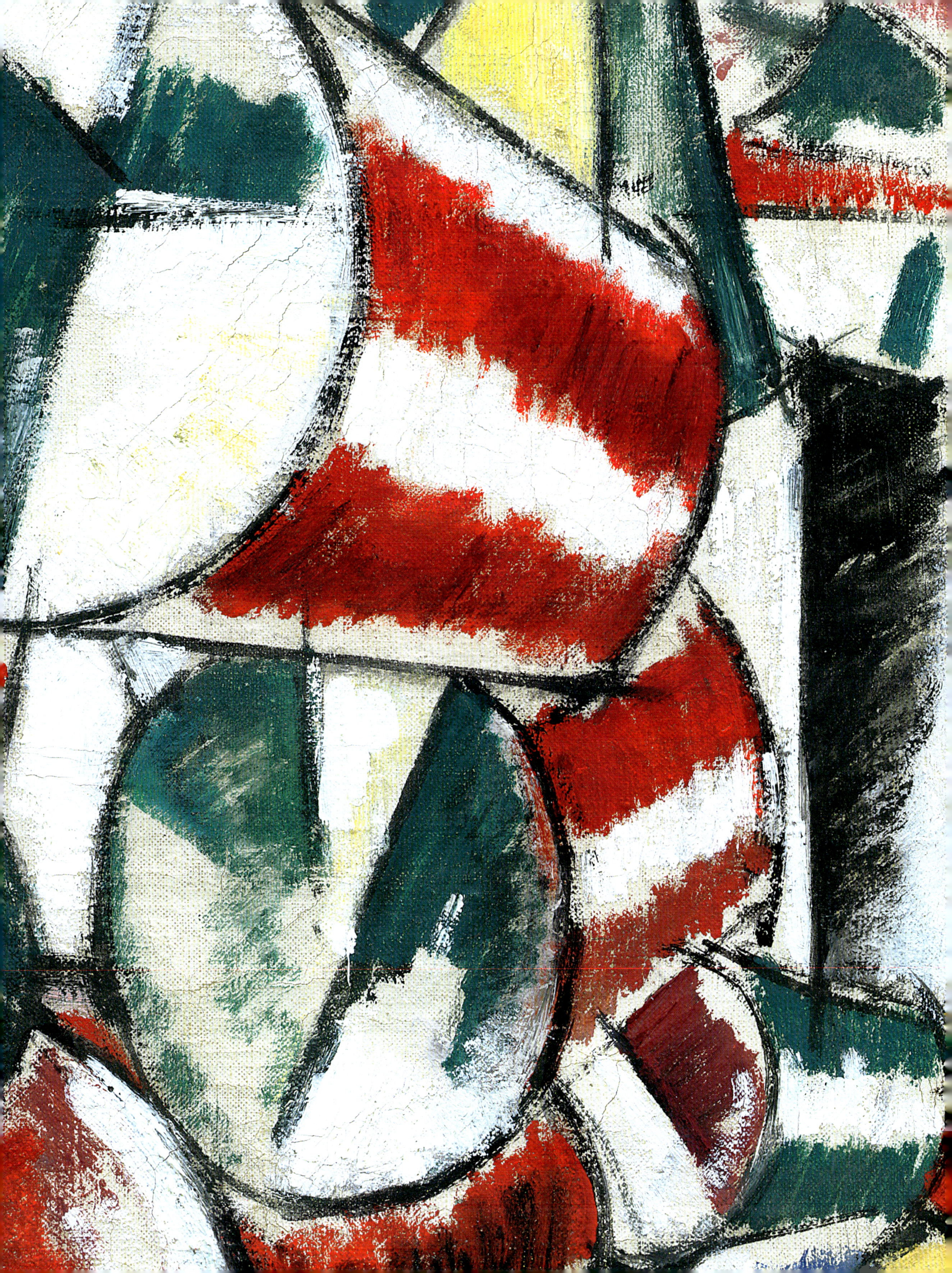

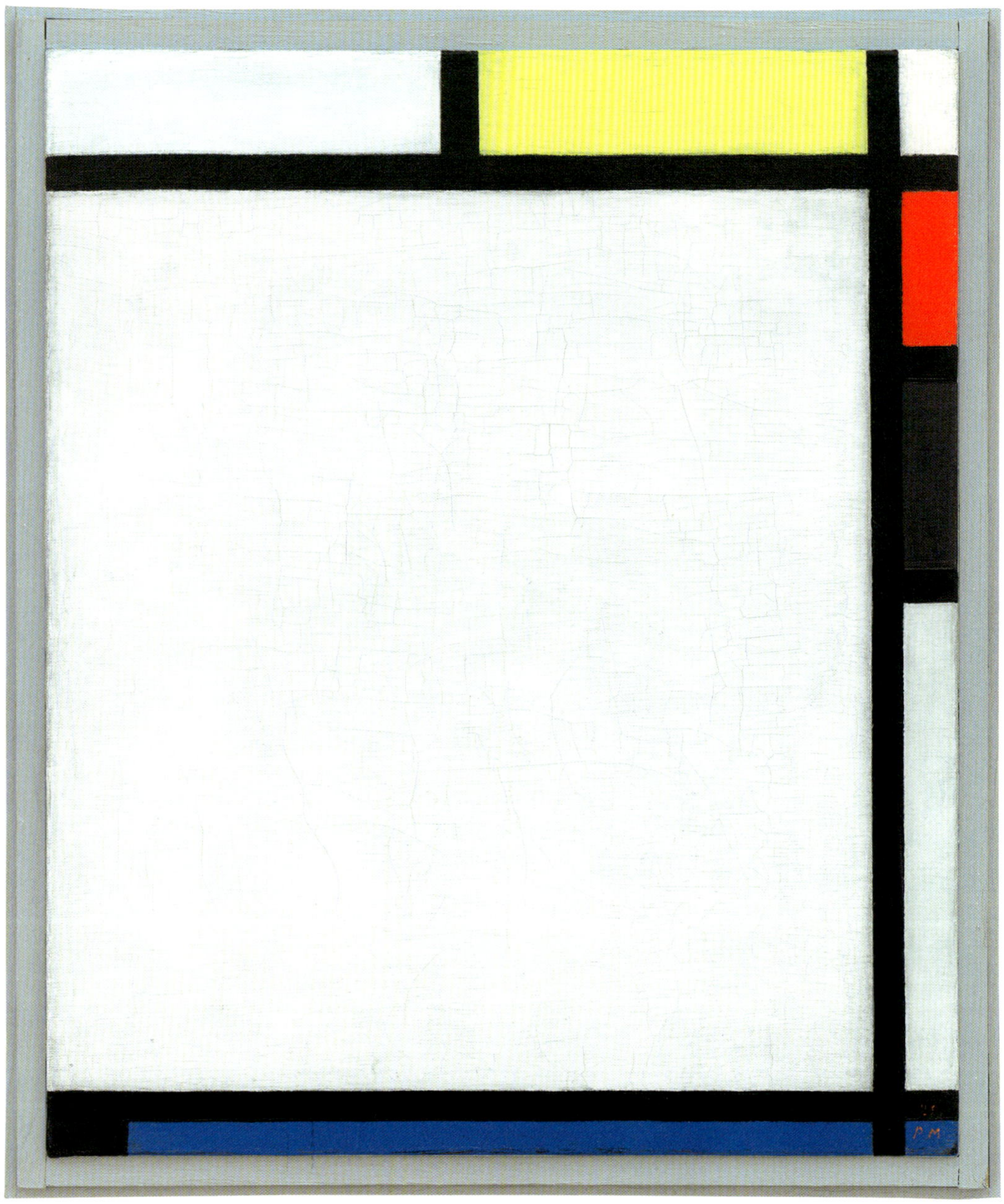

Piet Mondrian
1872 Amersfoort – 1944 New York

Oil on canvas
Initialled and dated lower right: 25 PM
53.2 × 46.2 cm (incl. frame, not original)

Inv. no. P23T / Acquired 2002

Piet Mondrian
Tableau No. VIII with Yellow, Red, Black and Blue
1925

Mondrian wanted to express universals in his art, which he felt were veiled in nature: "Nature reveals everything, truth as well as beauty, but it expresses both under the veil of natural appearances, and this veil that lies in front of the truth is tragic." He came to the conclusion that the universal as the unity of truth and beauty could not be expressed through the illusionist depiction of natural objects but "only through abstract-concrete composition". In consequence, Mondrian reduced his visual vocabulary to line, plane and colour, and he did so with such uncompromising rigour that he allowed for lines only as verticals and horizontals, planes only as rectangles, and colours only as primary colours. On the other hand, he did not aspire to rigid formalism but instead worked to achieve a lively balance of line, plane and colour. Taking his cue from Hegel's dialectics, he was convinced that all being becomes "real" only in connection with its opposite: the universal through the individual, the spiritual through matter, active through passive or masculine through feminine. The liberation of form from accident or chance was to culminate in what he called Nieuwe Beelding (new plastic art or neo-plasticism)– a term that formed the theoretical core of the artists' group *De Stijl*, founded in Leiden in 1917 and to which Mondrian, Theo van Doesburg and others belonged.

Only in small steps did Mondrian achieve his objective of creating compositions that establish a dialectical balance among elements extracted from the diversity of nature's forms and colours. The realization, for instance, that the juxtaposition of yellow, red and blue planes of colour produces an impression of depth contradicted his concept of painting as a strictly two-dimensional phenomenon. To neutralize that impression, he embedded his colours in a strict grid of vertical and horizontal black lines. But since the static structure of this grid undermined his wish to lend the compositions a lively order, he began varying the play of lines, planes and colours, combining them into finely balanced "Compositions".

Tableau no. VIII of 1925, which belongs to Mondrian's "classic" phase (c. 1920–1932), shows all the features of his artistic convictions. It is one of the "peripheral" Compositions, in which a large white rectangle (not a square!) takes up so much room that it pushes the smaller planes of colour to the margins of the painting. All of the colours he permitted himself to use each occur only once. As in all of his paintings, Mondrian avoided centring and symmetry, achieving a balanced composition not by applying mathematical rules but intuitively, through playful combination. By placing the canvas in front of the frame, he additionally gave the painting the status of an object.

UW

Friedrich Vordemberge-Gildewart
Komposition 78
1933

Friedrich Vordemberge-Gildewart
1899 Osnabrück – 1962 Ulm

Oil on canvas
36 × 36 cm

Inv. no. P275M / Acquired 2015

When Friedrich Vordemberge-Gildewart painted this small composition in 1933 following his studies at the Hanover School of Arts and Crafts, he was already closely allied with the international art scene thanks to contacts with Kurt Schwitters, Hans Arp and Theo van Doesburg. In 1925, van Doesburg invited him to become a member of the *De Stijl* artists group in Leiden. In 1927 he and Schwitters founded *die abstrakten hannover*, and in 1932 he joined the *Abstraction-Création* Association of artists founded in Paris by Georges Vantongerloo. All of these groups shared a commitment to abstract, non-figurative forms of architecture, sculpture, painting and design. After fleeing Germany and going into exile in Switzerland and the Netherlands from 1937 to 1955, Vordemberge-Gildewart accepted a position at the Ulm School of Design as head of the Department of Visual Communication.

Between 1922 and 1962, Vordemberge-Gildewart created 223 works, which he numbered consecutively and designated *Komposition* (K) with the exception of the year 1924 when he used the term *Konstruktion*. The constructive and compositional approach that informs his thoughts and drawings goes back to his apprenticeship with a cabinetmaker, and his relationship with the Russian constructivist El Lissitzky, whose studio he took over at the Kestner Gesellschaft in Hanover. He applied his way of thinking not only to painting, but also to typography, furniture, interior decoration and architecture. On his way to abstraction, he managed to do without the academic detour of studying nature because, as he said himself, he derived his forms from material, function and "feeling for design" rather than the objects of nature. The compositions, a body of work comprising close to forty years, take an undogmatic approach to the universal forms of geometry. Their arrangement is basically flat but spatial depth, or rather the character of a relief, is introduced by having them overlap or adding sculptural elements such as wooden frames, hemispheres or little blocks. Vordemberge-Gildewart was equally uninhibited in the treatment of colour, which he did not restrict to the primary colours of yellow, red and blue, as did Piet Mondrian, whose conflicting views led to a severance from the *De Stijl* group in 1925.

The arrangement of the geometrical shapes in *Komposition 78*, though unspectacular and simple, clearly reveals how attuned and sensitive Vordemberge-Gildewart was to matters of composition. A horizontal blue rectangle and a slanting, black rectangular band are "floating" on a white ground. Both correspond to a narrow white triangular plane that runs from the left to the right margin of the picture, its top line generating a "horizon". The blue rectangle can be seen as located above this horizon line and the black one in front of it. The white triangle and the black rectangle are dynamic elements that tend towards the right but their balance is maintained by the blue rectangle, an element at rest. The paint applied to the picture ground and rectangles is smooth and homogeneous while that on the triangle is pastose, the brushstrokes rising relief-like above the picture plane. Vordemberge-Gildewart has created a work of calm and subtle harmony with sparing, concrete means.

UW

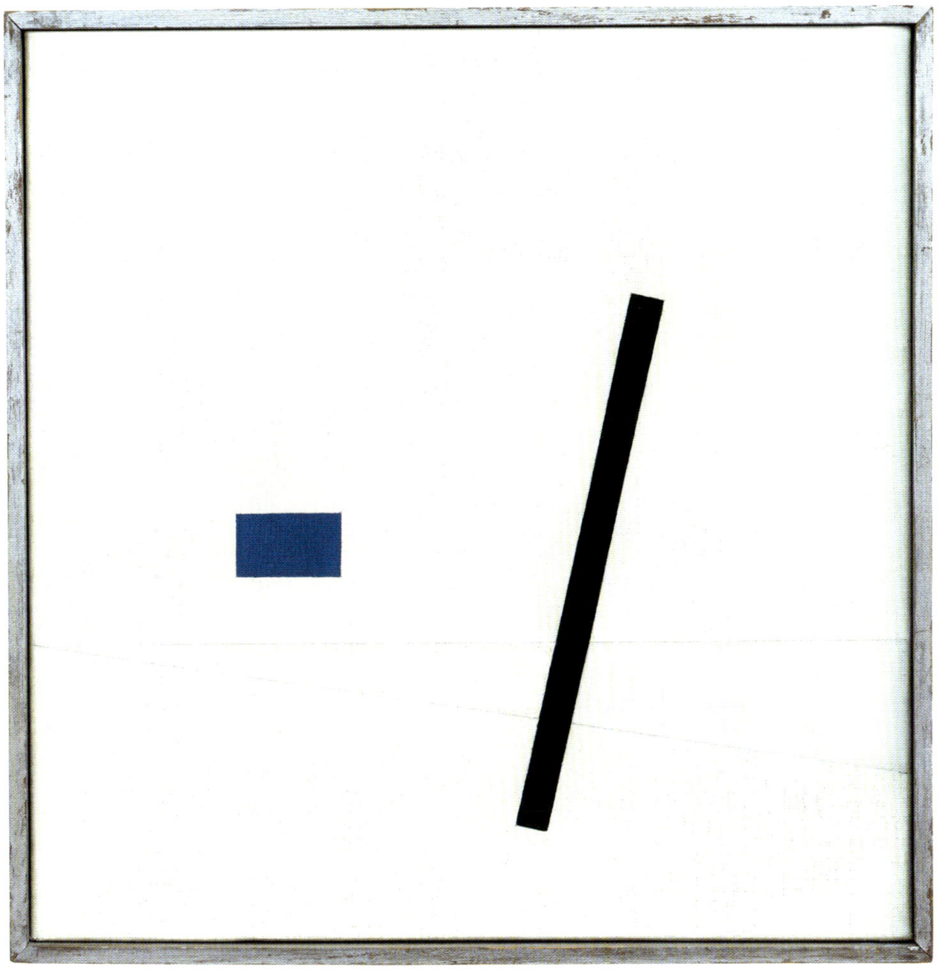

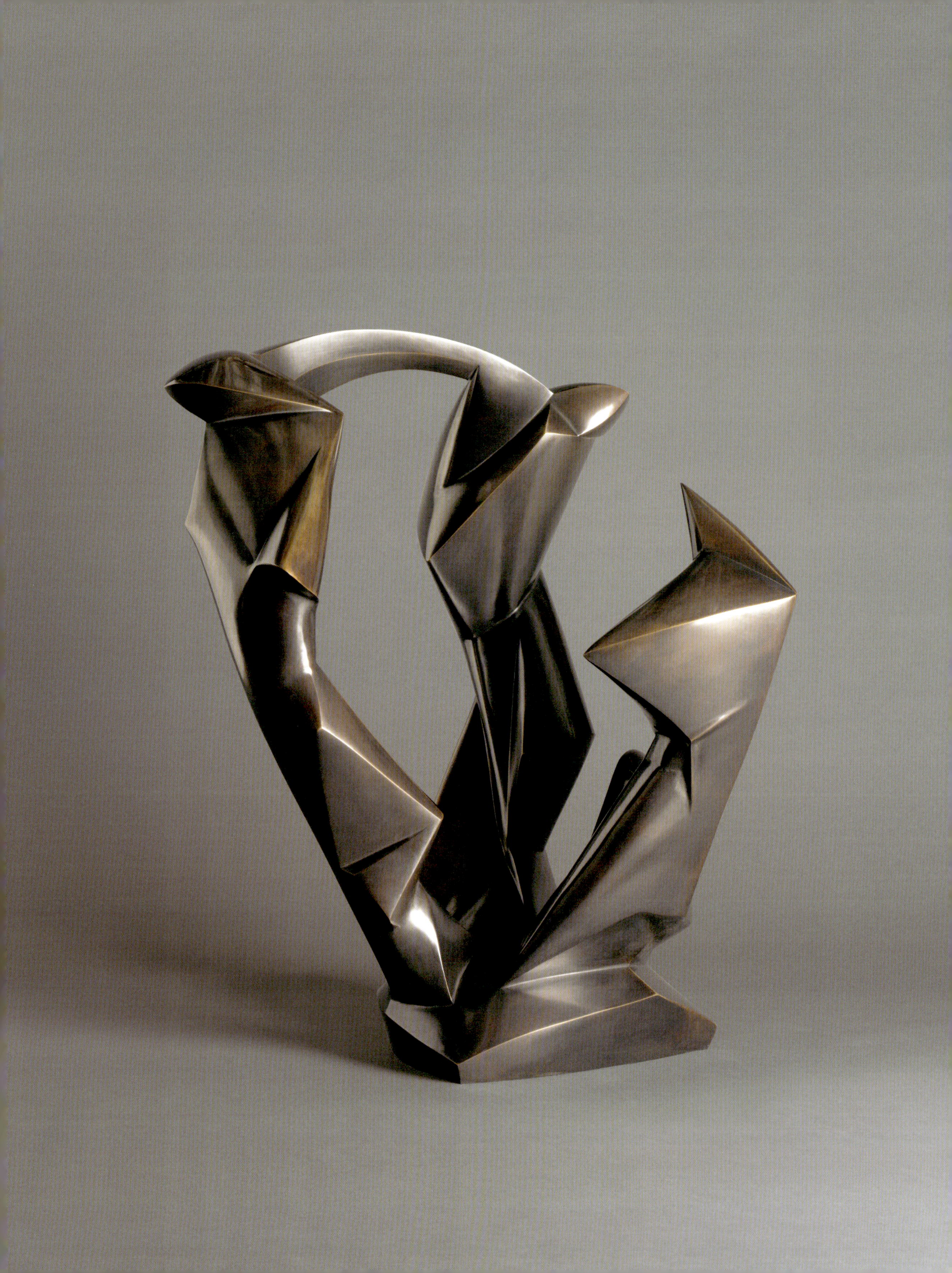

Rudolf Belling
Dreiklang
1919

Rudolg Belling
1886 Berlin – 1972 Krailling

Bronze
(cast: H. Noack, Berlin, 2002–03)
Signed and dated on base: Rudolf Belling 1919
Height: 90,5 cm

Inv. no. S69T / Acquired 2017

Dreiklang (Chord) of 1919 is the first important work by Rudolf Belling, and through it, German sculpture joined the ranks of the international avant-garde. "Sculpture," Belling wrote in 1922, "is the synthesis of sculpture and space! In a consummate sculpture, the sculptural body and the spatial body appear as equivalent values." Born of the spirit of Expressionism and the idea of the Gesamtkunstwerk, *Dreiklang* reconfigures space with its agitated, broken shapes. The artist's study of Cubism reverberates in the connected and overlapping interior and exterior spaces. Three figurations, which have mutated from organic to abstract and adopt the movement of dancers, become an architecturally constituted shape in space, whose theme is the unity of the arts: architecture, sculpture and painting.

Dreiklang was originally the preparatory design of a work that would be 6 metres tall, made out of bricks and stuccoed in colour. The first version was made of plaster, presumably also because there was a shortage of materials after the First World War. In 1924, Ludwig Justi, the then director of the Berlin National Gallery commissioned Belling to build a version out of wood, which is still in the holdings of the Gallery today. A second version out of wood was sent to New York and has been lost since 1931. A third version belongs to the Wilhelm-Lehmbruck-Museum in Duisburg. It was made in 1959 after Belling returned from exile in Istanbul.

Ten bronze casts were produced by Giesserei Noack in Berlin between 1959 and 1972, in other words, still in the artist's lifetime, giving him the opportunity to work the mould himself. This cast, made in 2002–03, is one of three that have been authorized by Belling's heirs.

AS

Rudolf Belling
Erotik
1920

Rudolf Belling
1886 Berlin – 1972 Krailling

Bronze (cast 1970, 1/6)
Signed on base: BELLING
Height: 32 cm

Inv. no. S60T / Acquired 2013

In the 1920s, Rudolf Belling was considered one of the abstract sculptors of the international avant-garde who had abandoned the formal canon of classical sculpture. Belling played a significant role in the art world beyond the borders of Germany. He entertained close contact with representatives of the latest movements in art: dadaism, futurism and constructivism. In 1931 he took part in the exhibition of *German Painting & Sculpture* at the New York Museum of Modern Art. Belling's renown was based at the time on just a few sculptures, of which *Erotik* (1920) is the most interesting. Belling wrote about it in 1935: "The mass is broken up and punctured, intentionally abandoning the solid mass." The sculpture shows a figure that constitutes an oval around an empty space in the middle. The lower half of the complex and artfully linked shapes assumes a female character, while male traits are assigned to the upper half. Single, clearly connoted parts such as breasts and thighs are combined with less specific, geometric shapes.

Belling himself said that he had taken inspiration for the sculpture from observing toads mating in spring. The shape of the sculpture actually does appear to resemble toads with plump thighs, lying on top of each other. Both in terms of content and form, *Erotik* combines Cubist elements with the then budding movement of Surrealism. Belling's visit to Picasso's studio in 1913 also resonates here although Picasso himself did not pursue this combination in his oeuvre until after 1920.

Erotik was originally produced in plaster and in a version of gilded wood, which is now in the National Gallery of Berlin. Belling started having bronze casts made towards the end of his life in the 1970s, restricting their number to a series of 12. He had been declared a degenerate artist in 1937 and emigrated to Istanbul, where he taught and worked. He did not return to Germany until 1966. The present cast is no. 1 in the series and was therefore produced in his lifetime.

AS

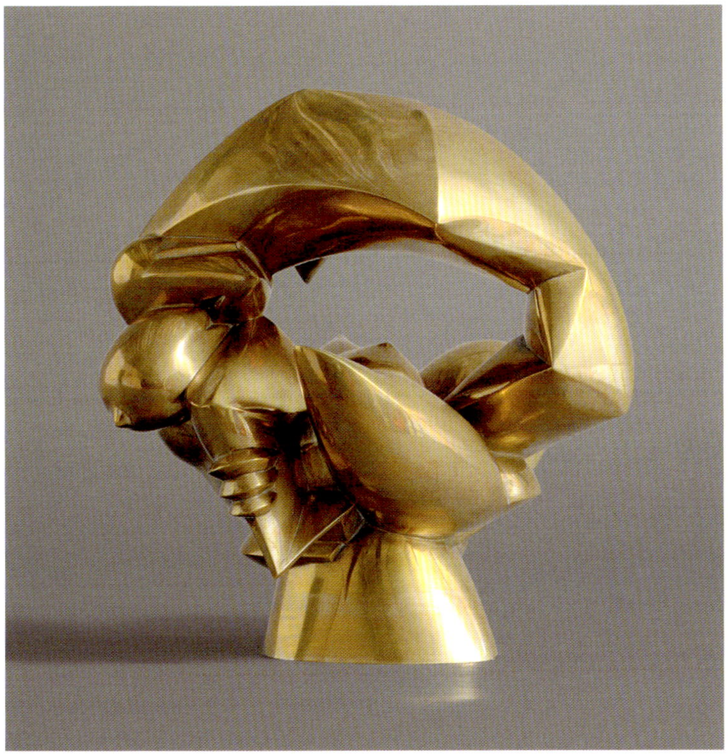

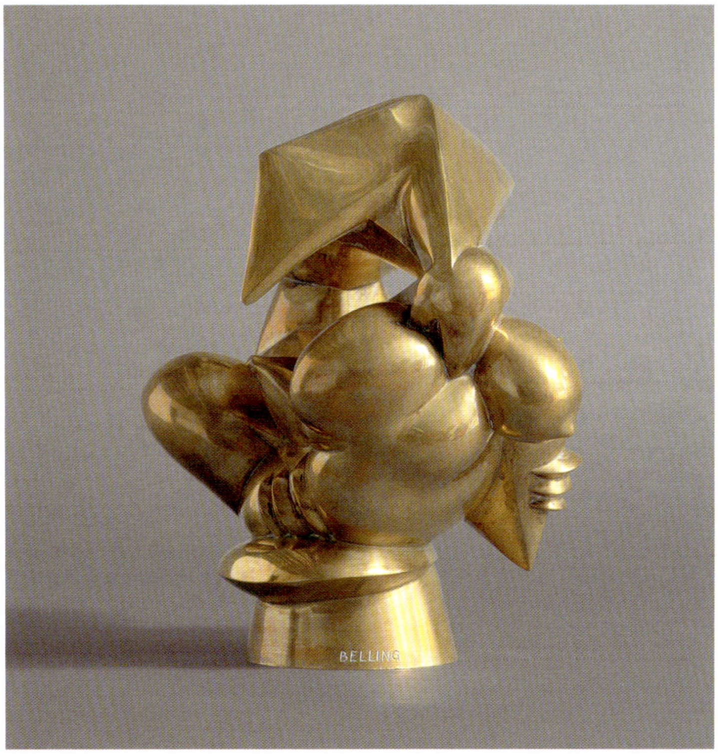
BELLING

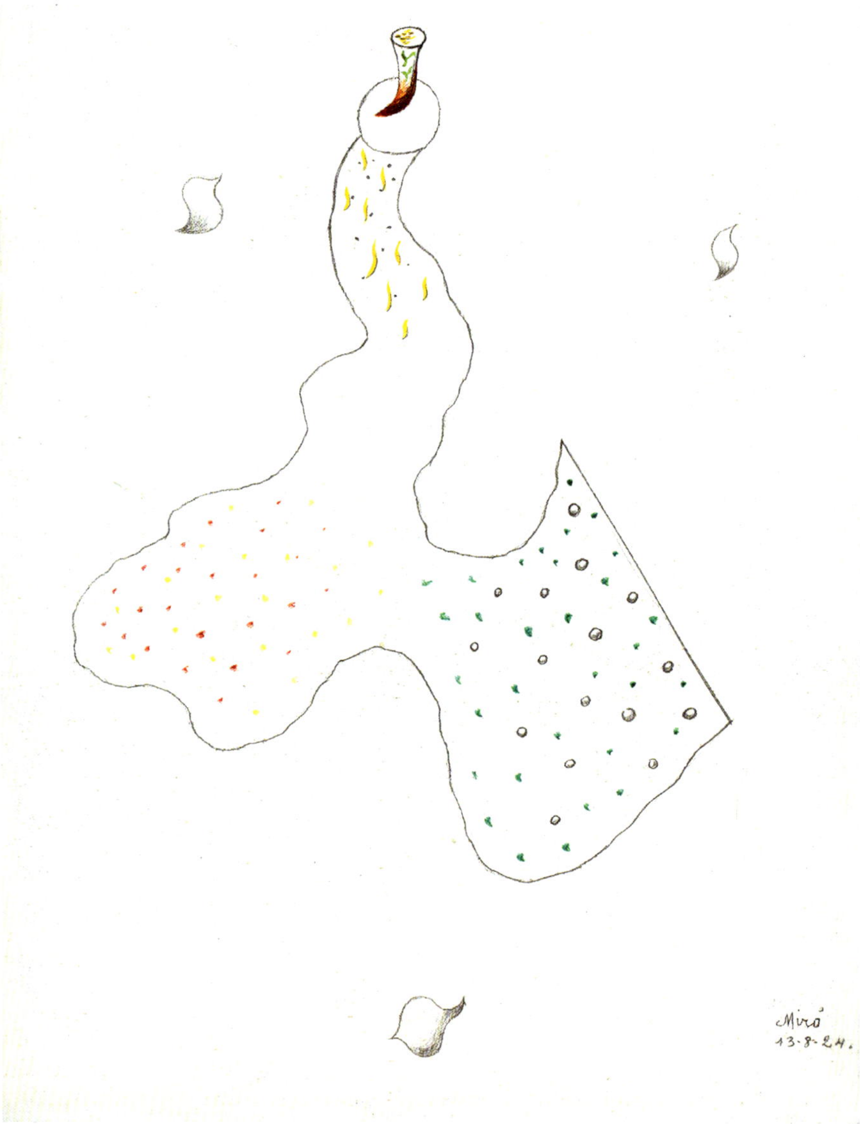
Miró
13·8·24.

Joan Miró
1893 Montroig / Barcelona –
1983 Palma de Mallorca

Pencil, oil and gouache on wood
Signed and dated lower right: Miró 13-8-24.
23.5 × 19 cm

Inv. no. P46T / Acquired 2011

Joan Miró
Untitled
1924

The small, untitled drawing in oil is one of three works Miró created in Montroig on 13 August 1924. The family's farmstead, near Tarragona not far from the sea, appears in a number of Miró's paintings. It was a place of creative retreat, where the artist regularly spent the long summer months in order to work undisturbed. After his first exciting visit to Paris in 1920, he wrote to Ricart, a friend of his youth, "At long last, never back to Barcelona again. Paris and the countryside to the end of my life." The decision may well have been reinforced by Picasso's words, "Believe me, if you want to be a painter, then don't stray far from Paris." And so it was that Paris and Montroig became the focal points in Miró's artistic development.

He set up his studio at Rue Blomet 45 in Montparnasse, where the painter André Masson was his neighbour. The poets Georges Limbour and Robert Desnos as well as the writer and ethnologist Michel Leiris were among his close friends. They would converse, for instance, about Nietzsche's philosophy and spend long nights reading poems to sharpen their appreciation of various poetic forms. Later, Masson was to write in a letter that "poetry in the broadest sense of the term was crucial for Miró and for me". And it did, indeed, exert a seminal influence on Miró's creativity. His work underwent an extraordinary metamorphosis from the post-Cubist, hyperrealistic, and exceptionally disciplined paintings, such as *The Farm* of 1920–21, to the open-ended and fanciful, enigmatic figurations of his *Catalan Landscape* (*The Hunter*) of 1923–24.

The oil drawing of 1924 belongs to this period. The artist has outlined a figure resembling a gourd with three objects, shaped like insects or onions, placed around it as on a coat of arms. The colouring is tenuous. Shown against a white, basically empty ground, the central figure looks like a transparent emblem. The curved contours, drawn with delicacy and ease, describe a biomorphic, supple, almost nimble, and no doubt ambivalent figure. The pipe-shaped horn that crowns it might be interpreted as a stamen, a cornucopia, or a phallus, indicative of a subtle eroticism. The gourd is embellished with yellow, red, green and black dots and lines, resembling siurells, clay whistles from Mallorca in the shape of little devils, farmers, or animals, designed to chase away evil spirits and winds. Probably from Crete or of Phoenician origins, they have become symbols of good luck and omnipresent souvenirs in Mallorca.

Miró had such figurines himself and, like many Surrealists, he was particularly fascinated with their use in magic and ritual. The artist may also have been inspired by Picasso's Cubist works with speckled planes, especially the *Glasses of Absinthe*, painted bronze casts made in 1914.

AS

Joan Miró
Untitled
1924

039

Joan Miró
1893 Montroig / Barcelona –
1983 Palma de Mallorca

Pencil, oil and gouache on wood
Signed and dated lower right: Miró 13-8-24.
24 × 14,5 cm

Inv. no. P41T / Acquired 2010

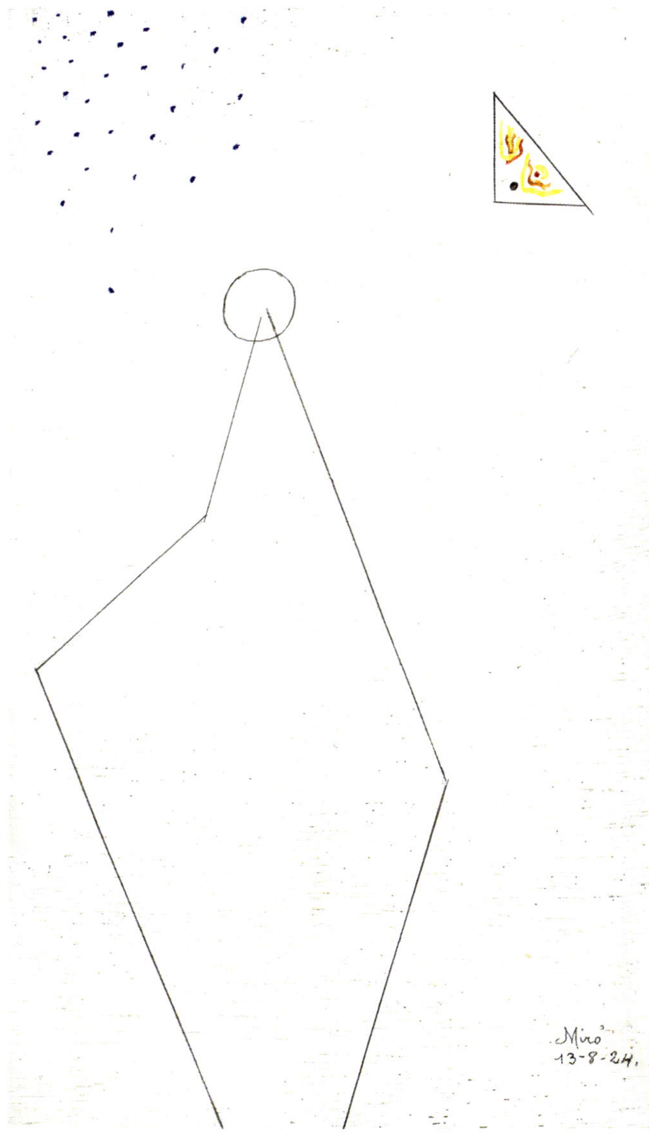
Miró
13-8-24.

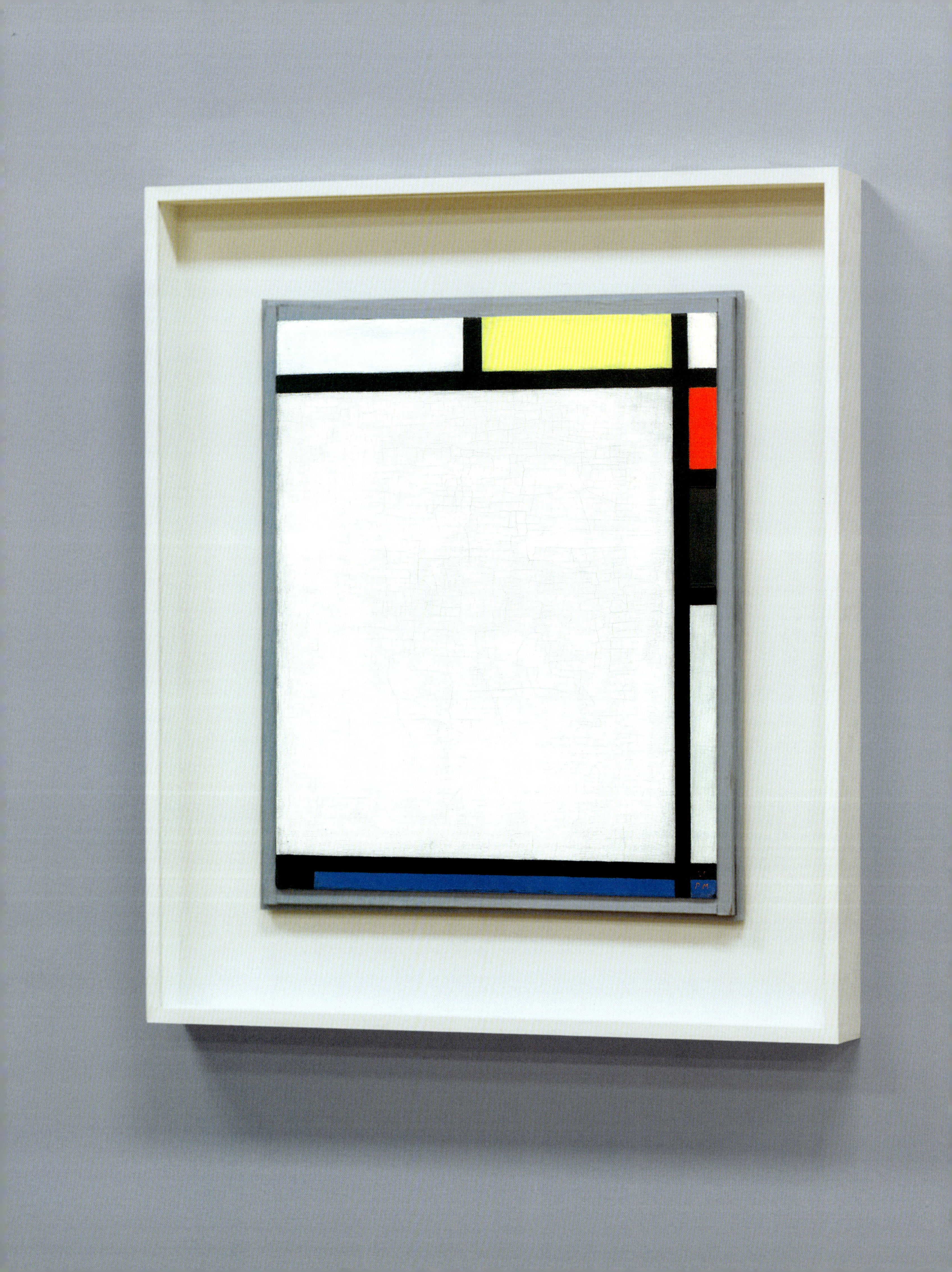

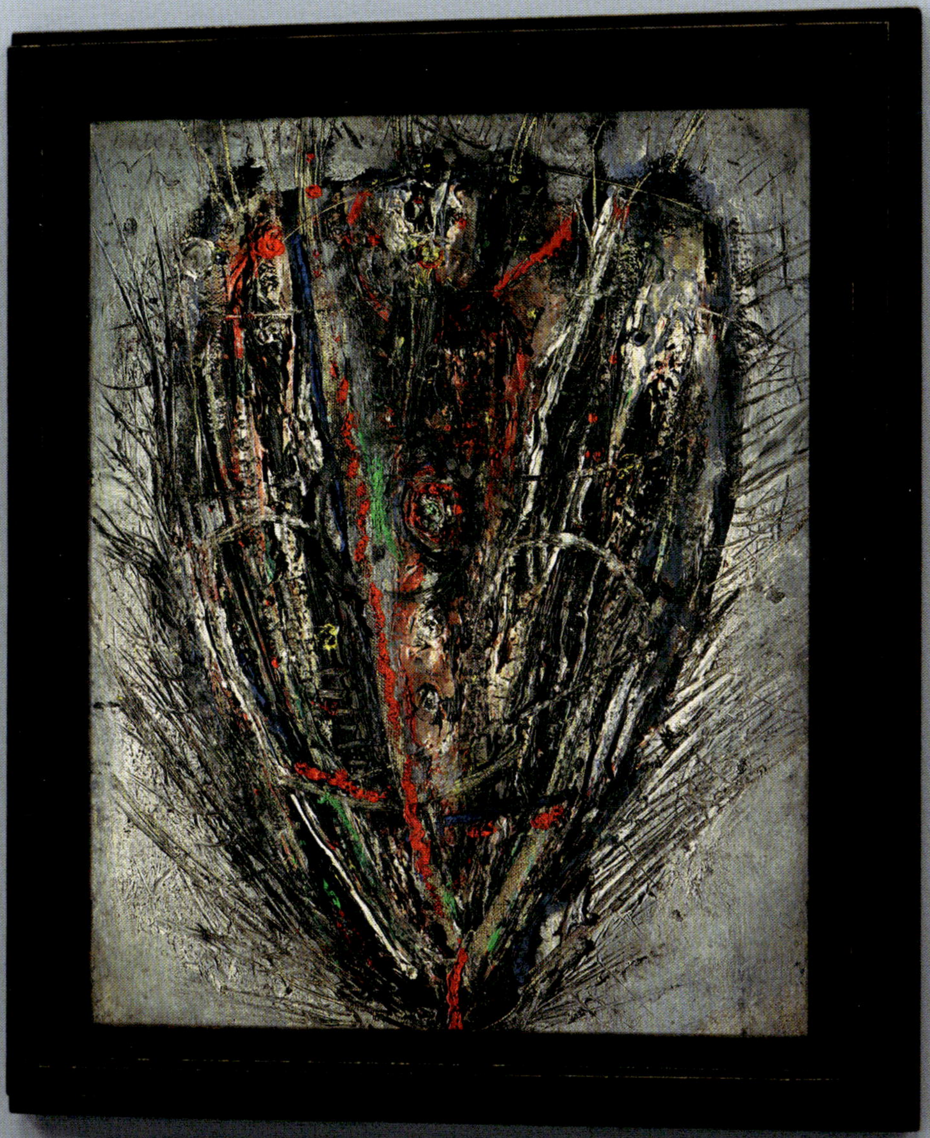

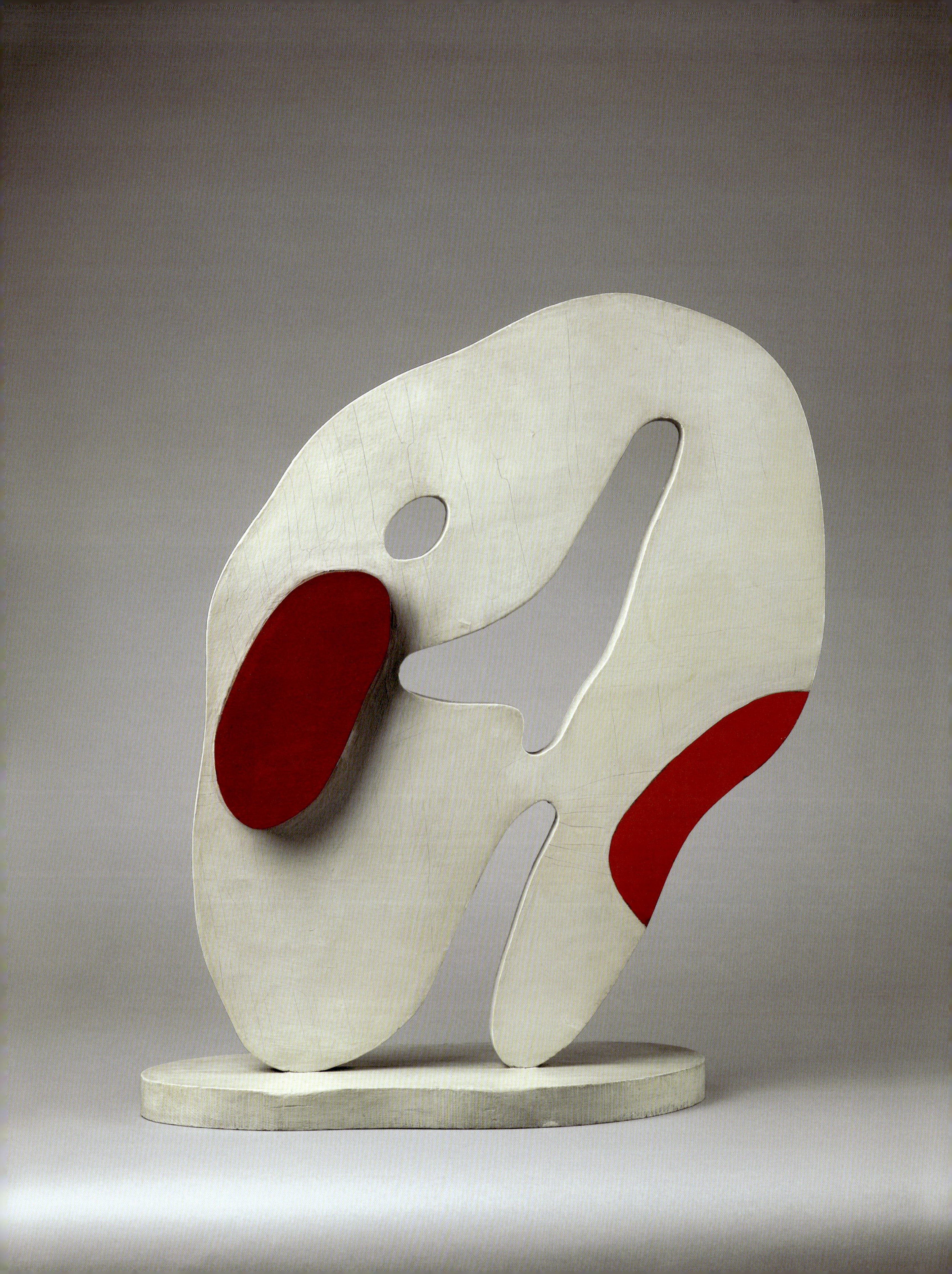

Hans Arp
1887 Strasbourg – 1966 Basel

Painted wood
Height: 61 cm

Inv. no. S43T / Acquired 2010

Hans Arp
Kopf-Stabile
1926

Arp's many talents were recognized and fostered at an early age. His subsequent academic training in Weimar and Paris with a bias for classical mimesis held little interest for him. It was not until he discovered Kandinsky in 1912 and Cubism in 1914 as well as becoming involved with Dada in Zurich in 1916 that his creative powers as a poet and fine artist came to full flower.

Dada did not stand as much for a style as it did for an attitude, for revolt against hierarchy. As Arp wrote in his 1958 essay *Betrachten*, "The Dadaists disdained the conventional notion of art and instead enthroned the entire universe as art: that seems to me to be the essence of Dada." In his poetry, Arp juxtaposed and combined old and new words, creating a seemingly nonsensical universe of infinite semantic potential, a challenge for readers to decode and devise ever new interpretations. Arp's poems are no different from the visual arts in their refusal to be reduced to a single, unequivocal message. This new freedom and emancipation from style gave the artist the impetus to construct small wood reliefs out of found materials and colourful pieces of painted wood. Inspired by the principles of chance and play, these whimsical works act as if they were objects of nature. The study of nature and the structural properties of plants, branches, and pebbles polished by water proved to be an inexhaustible reservoir for Arp's inventive spirit. In time, the "moving oval" emerged as the form that was to beget all other forms.

Arp made *Kopf-Stabile* (Head Stabile) in 1926, the year he left Paris only to return two years later, having acquired French citizenship and moving from Strasbourg to Meudon, southwest of Paris. Measuring sixty-one centimetres in height, Arp's *Kopf-Stabile* is larger than life and the first free-standing relief to interrelate different spatial planes. A smaller oval of wood has been applied to the large, irregularly curved oval of the head, whose significant shapes within – eye, nose and throat – have been cut out of the panel. They are linked to space in keeping with their function: the eye with which we perceive the world, the nose and throat through which we breathe. Art critic and Arp's longtime friend Michel Seuphor remarked in 1966 that the presence of the sky softens the shapes, making everything appear as if it were afloat. The slightly inclined head has been painted white except for the reddish brown oval sections. They could represent the cheeks of an impish yet unfathomable clown face – or a death's mask? The head is seen neither from the front nor in profile, so that our eyes wander back and forth without coming to rest. As Seuphor observed, only Arp can be unmistakably clear and ambiguous at once.

AS

Yves Tanguy
Titre inconnu (noyer indifférent)
1929

Yves Tanguy
1900 Paris – 1955 Woodbury / Connecticut

Oil on canvas
Signed and dated lower right:
Yves Tanguy 29
92.2 × 73.2 cm

Inv. no. P61T / Acquired 2014

According to Yves Tanguy's own legendary testimony, he was so moved on seeing Giorgio de Chirico's paintings in a Parisian gallery at the end of 1923 that he decided to become a painter himself. His early, initially representational work is stylistically indebted to Expressionism, Cubism and the New Objectivity. In 1925 he became closely involved with the Surrealists in Paris, in particular André Breton, who had penned the Surrealist Manifesto in 1924 and spearheaded the international group of writers, painters, photographers, filmmakers and object artists. Inspired by Pierre Janet's and Sigmund Freud's investigations into the human psyche, the group devoted themselves primarily to the workings of the unconscious and to the world of dreams. Tanguy's paintings soon began to show the influence of Max Ernst, Juan Miró, Hans Arp and de Chirico. Increasingly, representation gave way to clearly distinguishable but unidentifiable figurations, suggesting both inorganic and organic origins, coming perhaps from the depths of the oceans, the expanses of the desert, or the infinity of the universe. From now on, these dominate the artist's universe.

Similarly enigmatic, unfamiliar figurations populate *Titre inconnu* (1929), which also dates from Tanguy's early Surrealist phase. The shapes could as easily represent the beginnings of natural history as the catastrophic end of civilization. The four largest of them, casting shadows from an invisible source of light, have congregated around a patch of fog rising in delicate tendrils. Both fog and figurations are seen against a dark ground whose relief-like surface is broken by spectral, white horizontal bands that fade into the immeasurable, pitch-black depths of space. We gaze upon an alien, nonhuman, and yet disconcertingly real universe that is in the process of becoming or of dying away, buffeted by the primeval clash between light and dark. The art of Max Ernst, for instance, *Der Nordpol* (The North Pole, 1922), resonates in this painting as well as the work of Hieronymus Bosch and, as Reinhard Hohl has observed, other Dutch masters of the early sixteenth century.

The Swiss psychiatrist C. G. Jung, who acquired Tanguy's painting the year it was created, discusses it in detail in his book *Flying Saucers: A Modern Myth of Things Seen in the Sky* (1979, first published in German in 1958). He associates it with bleakness, coldness and human detachment, with cosmic inhumanity and endless abandonment, additionally interpreting it as an example of the loss of beauty and meaning in contemporary art, which has thrown human beings back on themselves as viewing subjects. However, the absence of explicit meaning, as demonstrated by *Titre inconnu*, can also lead to associations and reactions that yield illuminating insights into the world of darkness, very much in the spirit of Surrealism.
UW

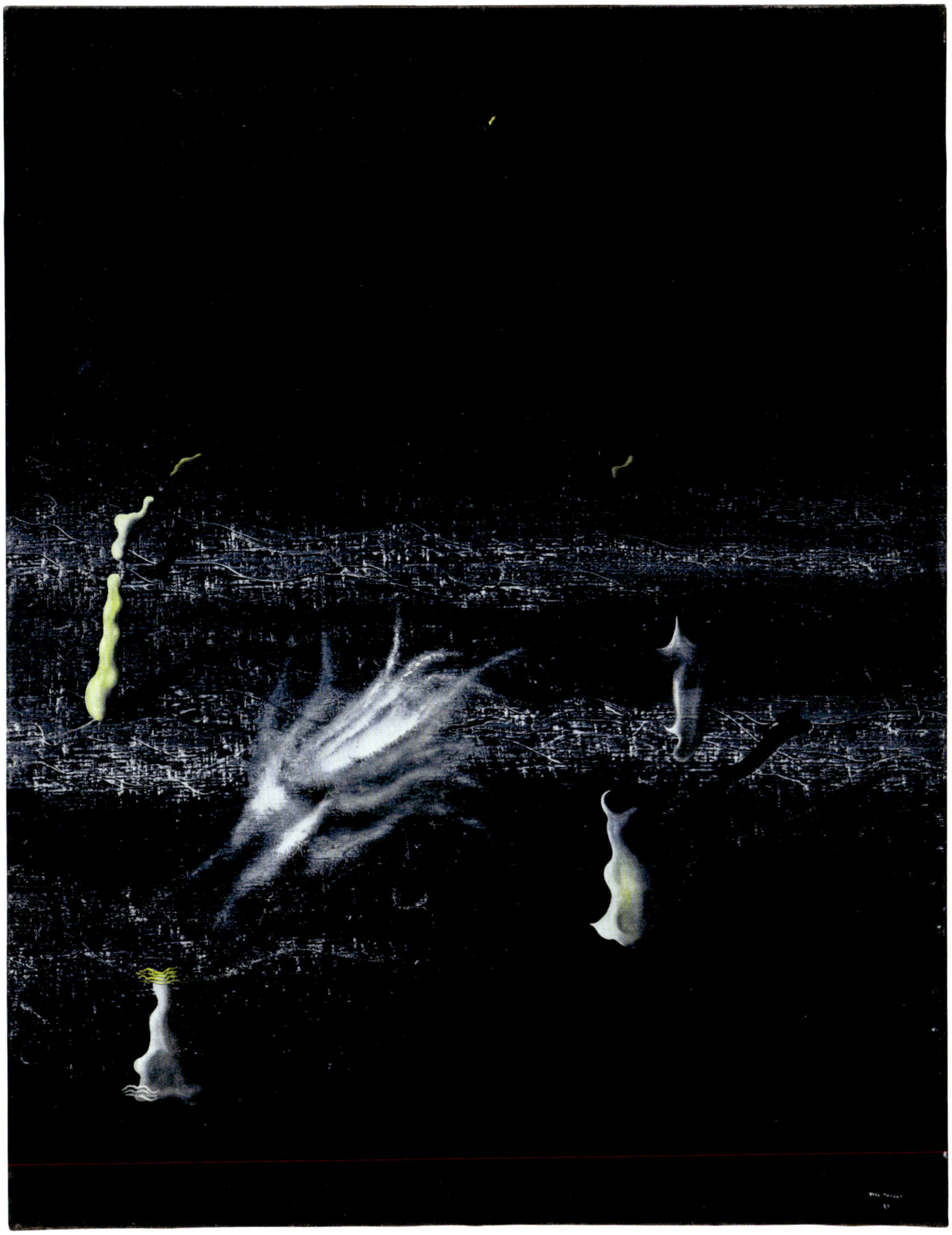

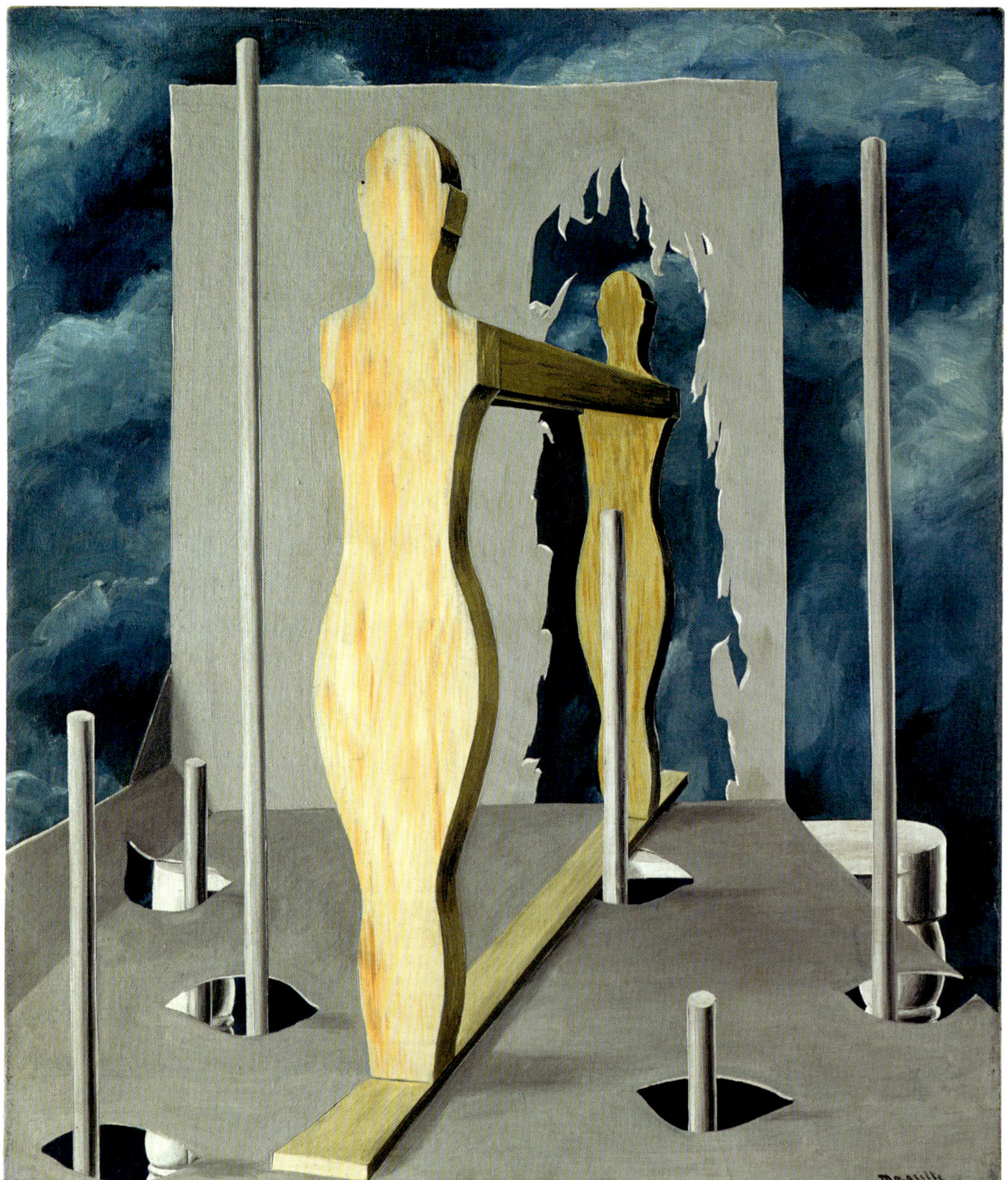
magritte

042

René Magritte
La chambre du devin
1926

René Magritte
1898 Lessines / Hainaut – 1967 Brussels

Oil on canvas
Signed lower right: Magritte
74 × 65 cm

Inv. no.: P57T / Acquired 2013

Magritte painted *La chambre du devin* (The Seer's Chamber) in 1926. The year is significant, for it was then that the artist joined the musician and poet Édouard Leon Théodore Mesens, the art dealer Camille Goemans, and the biochemist and photographer Paul Nougé to found the Surrealist group in Belgium. The work is an early example of the Surrealist universe that began to evolve as of 1925, particularly through the inspiration of the Italian artist Giorgio de Chirico. Magritte was fascinated by Chirico's "pittura metafisica" and his notion of a "complete break with the mental routine of artists".

In 1927 *La chambre du devin* was on view at Le Centaure Galilean Brussels along with forty-eight other paintings and twelve papiers collés, a group of works by the then twenty-eight-year-old artist that was to form the foundations of his entire oeuvre. The exhibition, which opened on April 23, was Magritte's first solo presentation. *La chambre du devin* already shows salient features of Surrealist painting: the form and content of its subject matter, though painted illusionistically, defies the logic of everyday experience. Oscillating between reality and appearance, causality and absurdity, conscious and unconscious, Surrealism equally features a delight in metamorphosis, eroticism, spiciness, play, and originality. Duplication, another common characteristic of the movement, is also typical of Magritte's early work. The present painting shows two largely identical flat figures carved out of wood, standing opposite one another and immovably affixed to a long board. One single pair of shared, straight, stiff arms connects them but also keeps them at a distance. They are placed on a platform that rests on a balustrade with a rear wall, somewhat like a stage, behind which clouds dramatically fill the sky. Rods protrude through the irregular holes in the platform. The figure in the rear stands in a flame-shaped opening cut out of the wall, providing an additional view of the turbulent skies and lending the figure a flickering "aura". Are these two people, possibly a woman and a man, condemned to face one another for all eternity in their raw state, inseparable and yet irrevocably separate? Or is it humankind per se with its alter ego? Or the body of the soul, the substance of the spiritual, the "ether body" or "astral body" on uncertain ground above the yawning abyss of space? The painting is inescapably enigmatic, in the spirit of Surrealism, and its title, more confounding than clarifying, follows suit. This, too, is a strategy that Magritte enlists to subvert the logic of everyday life.

UW

Max Ernst
Le paradis
1927

Max Ernst
1891 Brühl – 1976 Paris

Oil on canvas
Signed lower right: max ernst
60.2 × 92 cm

Inv. no.: P9T / Acquired 2000

The title of the painting, *Le paradis*, draws attention to the fundamental discrepancy between meaning and representation, between word and image, that is one of many bewildering constants in the oeuvre of Max Ernst. When we hear the word "paradise", we are unlikely to envision anything resembling this painting. As if privy to absurd theatre, we are confronted with a frightening, life-threatening scene of animalistic, sexual violence and bondage. The figures we see clearly embody the central themes of Surrealism.

The terrified animal arrested in flight in the centre of the picture might be a cow or a mare. It has been brutally overpowered by a monster almost twice its size that could be anything from a dinosaur to a hyena. As André Breton reports, the Parisian Surrealists used to entertain themselves of an evening by inventing animals and producing unexpected images. The head of the soft, white domestic creature, delineated with the charm of a picture-book illustration, is thrown back to the sky in a desperate plea for help, although it is already in the stranglehold of its tormentor and about to be raped. The demonic figurations sprouting out of the skeletal, snaky body of the bloodthirsty beast also appear in the crowd paintings Ernst made during the same period. The encounter between the two animals takes place at eye level, as it were, their visages converging into a horrific image of abject fright, terror, and animalistic violence. This turbulent scene, which also applies to its formal execution, is the centrepiece of the composition while off to the right a white barn owl, the traditional symbol of wisdom, is perched in a compact, box-shaped cage. Although it is not clearly behind bars, it has been apprehended and robbed of its effectiveness.

The fluid painting style and the bright, quasi-enlightened atmosphere, underscored by a colourful palette of red, yellow, green, blue, brown and purple, stands in stark contrast to the dismal subject matter of the composition. The luminous green meadow and the light-blue sky are flooded with light. The fine black lines would seem to be fragments of constellations, implying a universe out of joint. The complexity of Ernst's enigmatic imagery is a consequence not only of his intellectual inventiveness but also of his curiosity and mastery in devising new painting techniques. Taking inspiration from the accidental "natural" shapes that emerge when using frottage and grattage, he follows their trail without surrendering control over his compositions.

The title *Le Paradis* is not primarily ironic but rather a description of our paradise on earth. It is also an example of "convulsive beauty", in the words of Breton, who invited Max Ernst to mount his first exhibition in Paris in 1921, shortly after the devastating war. In his foreword to the catalogue, Breton expressed his admiration of Ernst's ability to achieve different realities without abandoning the realm of experience.

AS

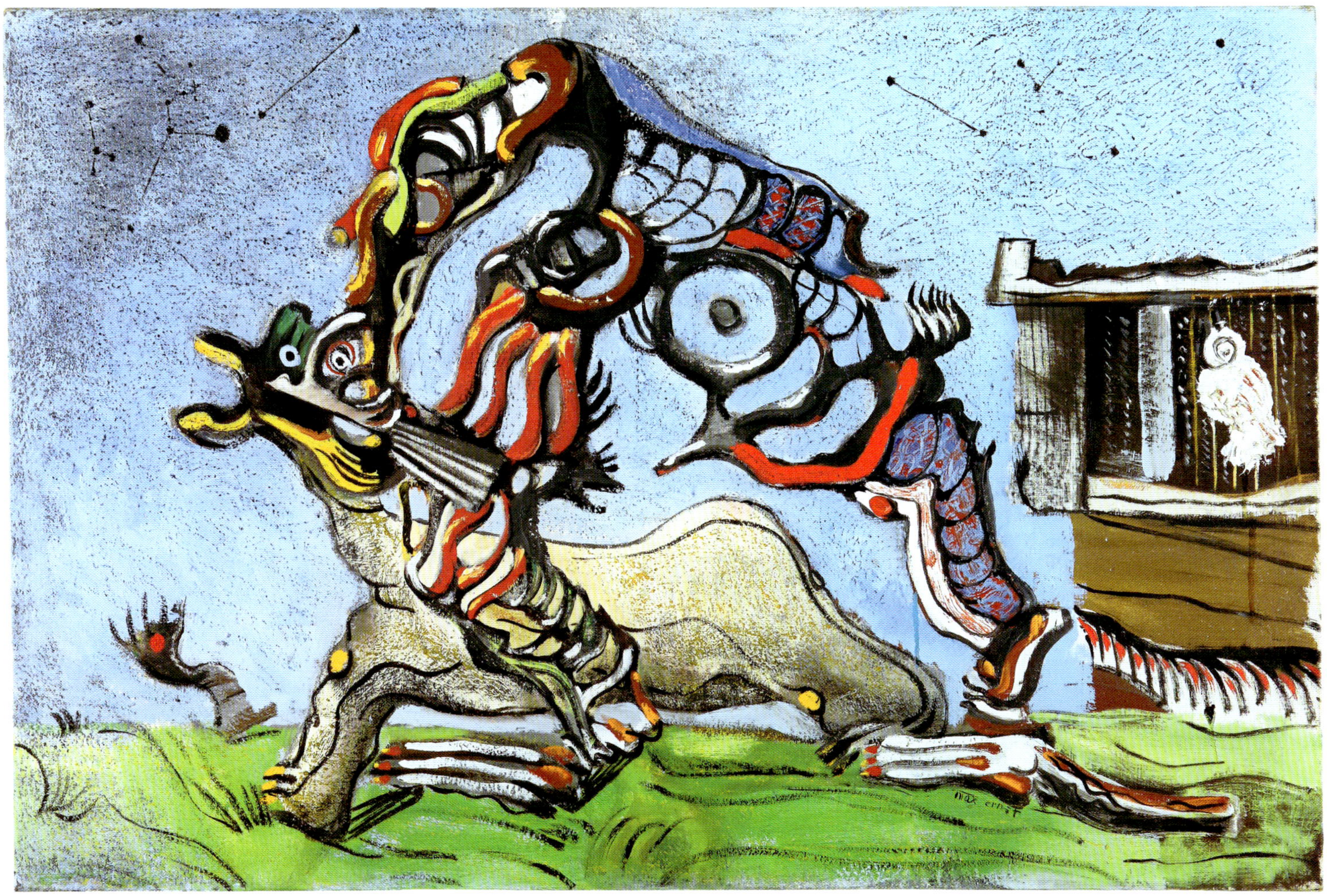

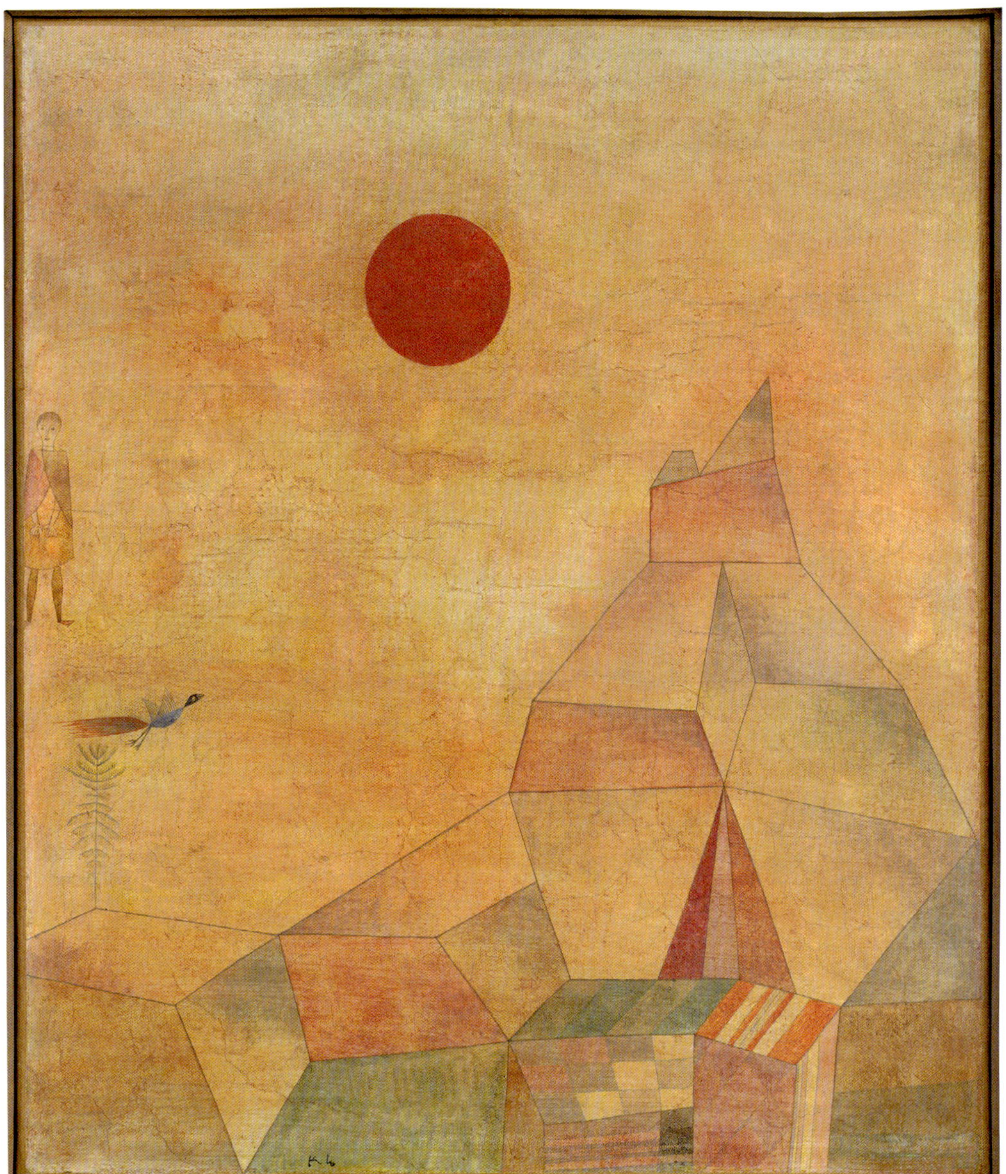

Paul Klee
1879 Münchenbuchsee / Bern –
1940 Muralto-Locarno

Gouache on primed paper on canvas
Signed lower centre: Klee
50.1 × 42.5 cm

Inv. no. P76M / Acquired 2000

Paul Klee
Märchen
1929

In the winter of 1928–29, Klee had the opportunity to spend 18 days in Egypt on a holiday financed by the Klee Society in honour of his upcoming 50th birthday. Since his youth, Klee had always been enthusiastic about the Orient. His wife Lily speaks in her memoirs of "Klee's eternal yearning for Africa". When the artist journeyed to Kairouan in 1914 with his friends August Macke and Louis Moilliet, he noted the discovery of colour in his diary: "Colour and I are one. I am a painter." In Egypt, he was enthralled by the light and the landscape, by the sky and the water. Followingthe Nile, he visited ancient sites, travelling from Cairo to Luxor, Karnak, Aswan and the island of Elephantine. "My husband was extremely enthusiastic and artistically inspired after his journey to Egypt. He saw wonderful things...."

In contrast to other works like *Monument im Fruchtland* (Monument in Fertile Country), *Architektur im Orient* (Architecture in the Orient) or *Nekropolis* (Necropolis), all painted after his return in 1929, the title of *Märchen* (Fairy Tale) does not refer specifically to Egypt. However, the all-pervasive sunlight of the desert resonates in the luminous watercolours of saturated, almost golden yellow, bright red and pale tones of brown and green. The glowing red sun is the crucial feature in the centre of the painting with its perfect geometrical shape and densely applied paint. Subordinate to it and bathed in its light is a crystalline shape compiled of various interlocking and irregular rectangles that might be interpreted as a mountain, a piece of architecture or a tent. Despite its transparency, it is impenetrable and establishes a presence in space. It evokes the tombs of the caliphs in Cairo that Klee described with such enthusiasm in his letters, "I saw something wonderful today: the tombs of the caliphs, also a kind of Valley of Kings, entirely in the desert but close to the city; not only caliphs but also commoners are buried there in a metropolis of the dead of exquisitely pure Arabian style. Not only the tombs but also the buildings for relatives to stay in." The details of Klee's fragile architecture are geometrically complex. They do not reveal their secret despite the blurred hint of a corpse in the bottom right-hand compartment.

Nor does Klee tell us which fairy tale the painting commemorates although the boy in the left margin of the painting and the little bird could refer to *The Shepherd Boy* by the Brothers Grimm (as kindly pointed out by C. Hopfengart). The little boy was known throughout the land for the wisdom of his answers and so the King asked for his advice. In the third question that he posed, the king wanted to know how many seconds there are in eternity. The boy answered, "Every hundred years a little bird comes and sharpens its beak on the peak of the mountain and when the whole mountain is worn away by this, then the first second of eternity will be over."

The near immeasurable span between moment and eternity, demonstrated in the fairy tale, adds a semantic dimension to Klee's work that is related to the representation and opens avenues to further associations. The almost sacred golden ground of the painting and the bright red celestial body stand for notions of eternal permanence and rest but also for the universe. The small bird flying through the air, reminiscent of the black raven released from Noah's Ark, lends movement and vibrancy to the hieratic scene.

AS

Paul Klee
Gemüsegarten
1925

Paul Klee
1879 Münchenbuchsee / Bern –
1940 Muralto-Locarno

Oil on cardboard
Signed and inscribed upper left:
Klee 1925 K4
36 × 53 cm

Inv. no. P70T / Acquired 2000

"Art is related to creation like a parable. It is always an example, similar to the way the earthly is a cosmic example." In this sentence from his *Creative Confession*, written in 1918 and published in 1920, Klee describes where he stands as an artist. The first sentence reads, "Art does not reproduce the visible; rather, it makes visible." Throughout his career and the extraordinarily diverse oeuvre that originated from it, the artist repeatedly embarked on new exchanges with the forces of the universe. This explains the exceptional extent of his reach. But despite the diversity of his output, we do gain an insight into his stylistic development and certain thematic highlights on studying his diaries, talks, essays, and even his poetry.

Nature was always a crucial concern, to which Klee testifies in an essay on his Bauhaus teachings, *Wege des Naturstudiums* (Paths of Nature Study, 1923): "The dialogue with nature is a sine qua non for the artist." Walking and hiking gave Klee the opportunity to cultivate his meticulous observation of the things of this world. On those occasions, he would gather leaves and blossoms, moss and lichen, stones and butterflies, which he preserved in a cabinet of nature in his studio. With great empathy and scientific acumen, he examined all the minute details and fundamental structural givens of each object.

Klee painted *Gemüsegarten* (Vegetable Garden) in 1925, the year he moved from Weimar to Dessau with the Bauhaus. It is a memory of all the gardens, beds and patches of forest, translated into an abstract form and presented in a tableau that resembles a type case. The view from above is combined with a view from the front, establishing a symbiosis between depth and plane. On the densely painted ground, divided into a host of individual fields that look like soil or moss or grass, we see stick figures of plants, flowers and trees. They stretch and bend, demonstrating movement. Klee's repertoire of forms concentrates on a basic but variable pattern of verticals, horizontals and diagonals as well as curved and circling lines that sustain movement on the picture plane. "Movement underlies all becoming," Klee wrote. Movement and depth are also generated by a lightness and transparency of colour alternating with a dark, almost impenetrable palette, emerging among subtle tones of green, single dabs of orange and brown sections. They might be read as part of a "natural" palette, ranging from spring to fall as the expression of passing time.

Like other paintings done in those years, *Gemüsegarten* can also be seen as a panel with indecipherable data, secret messages from another world, whose code remains undisclosed.

AS

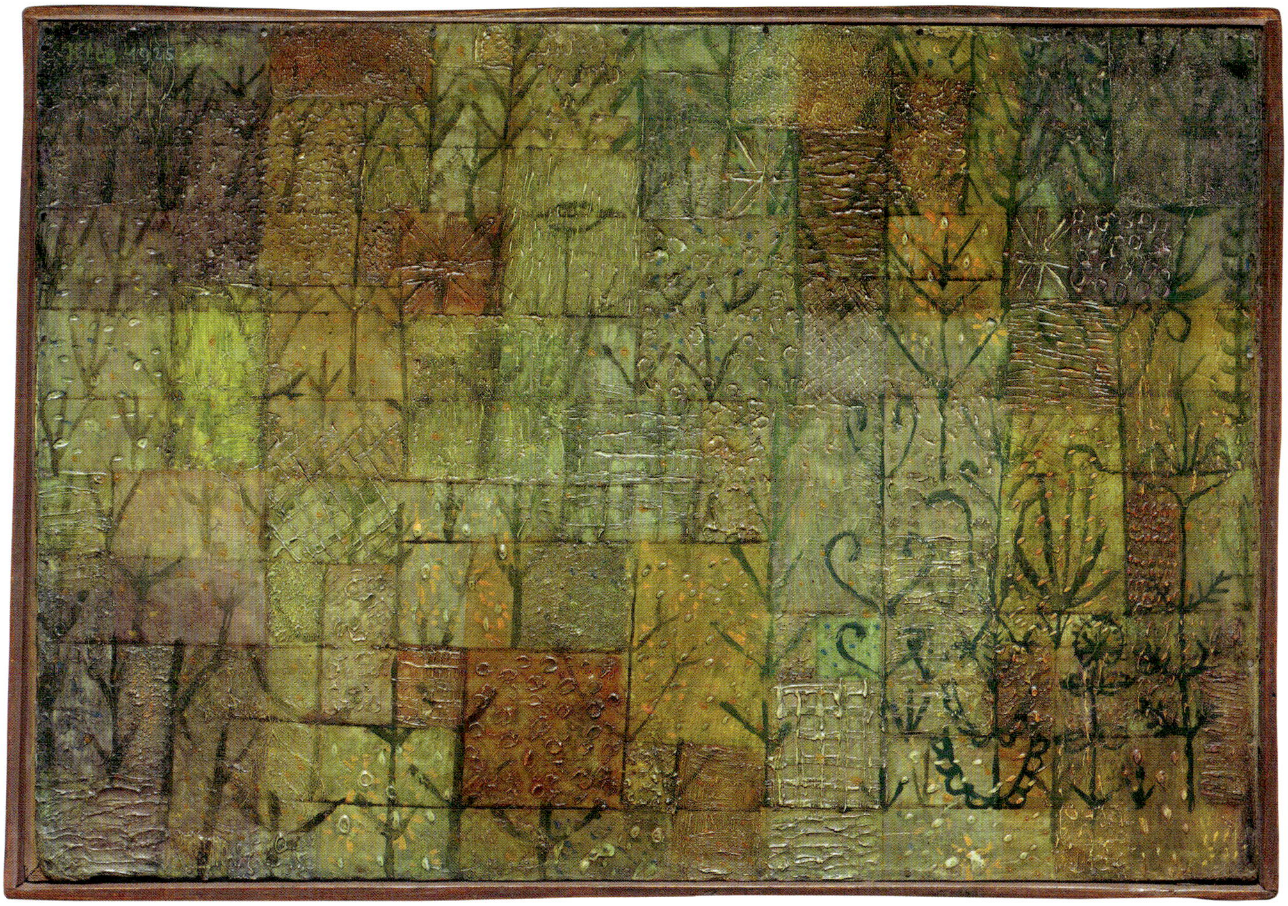

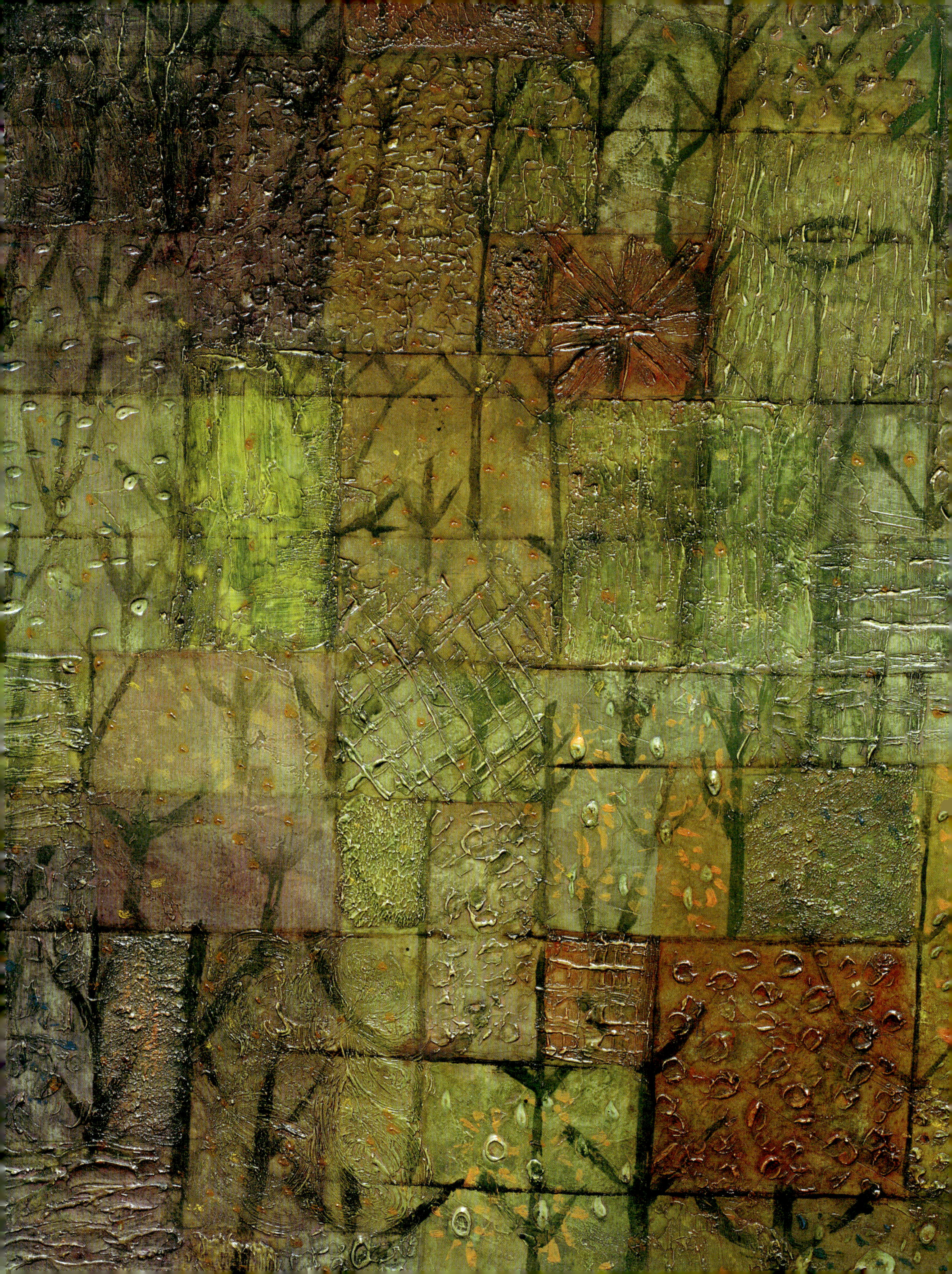

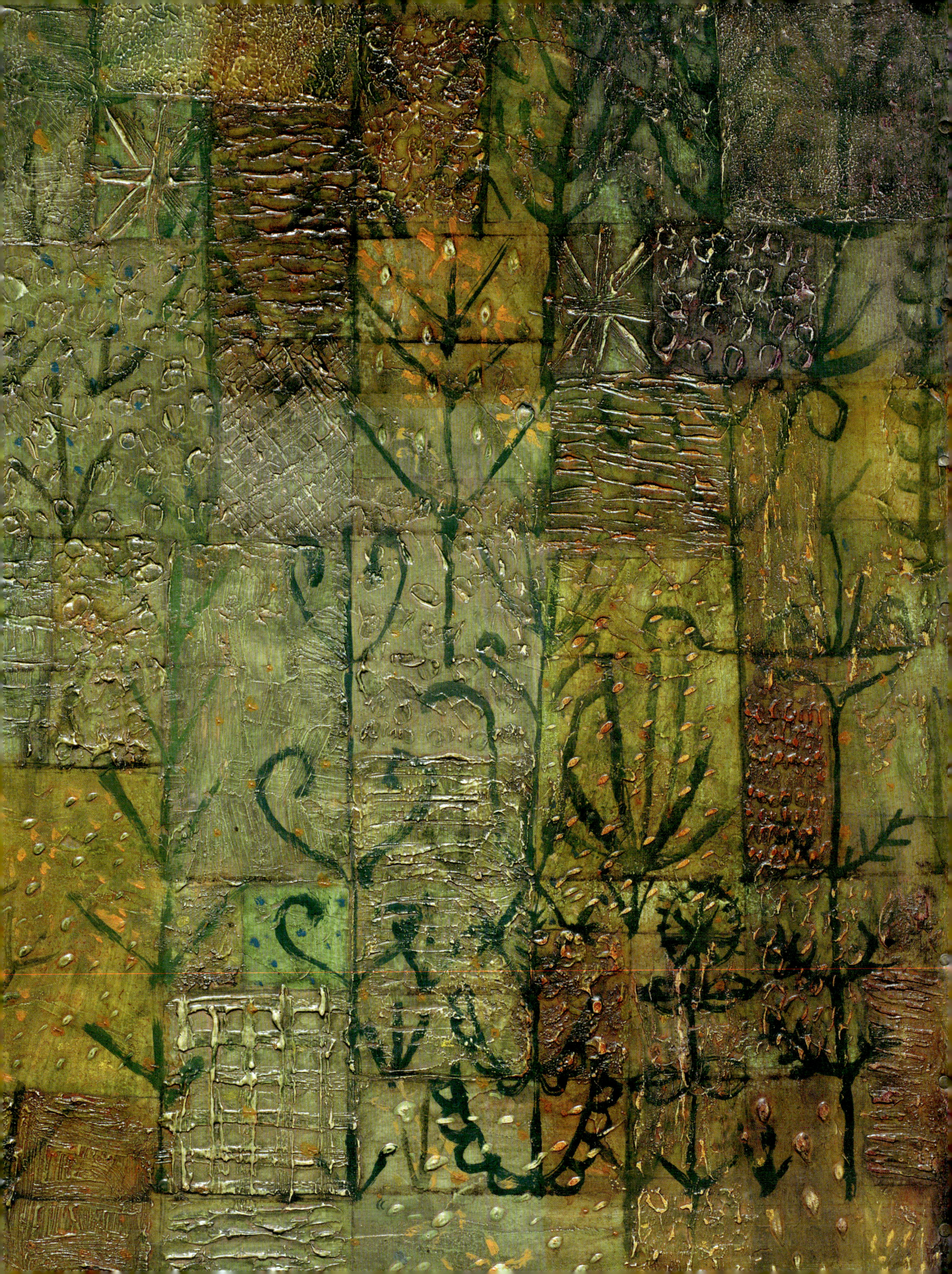

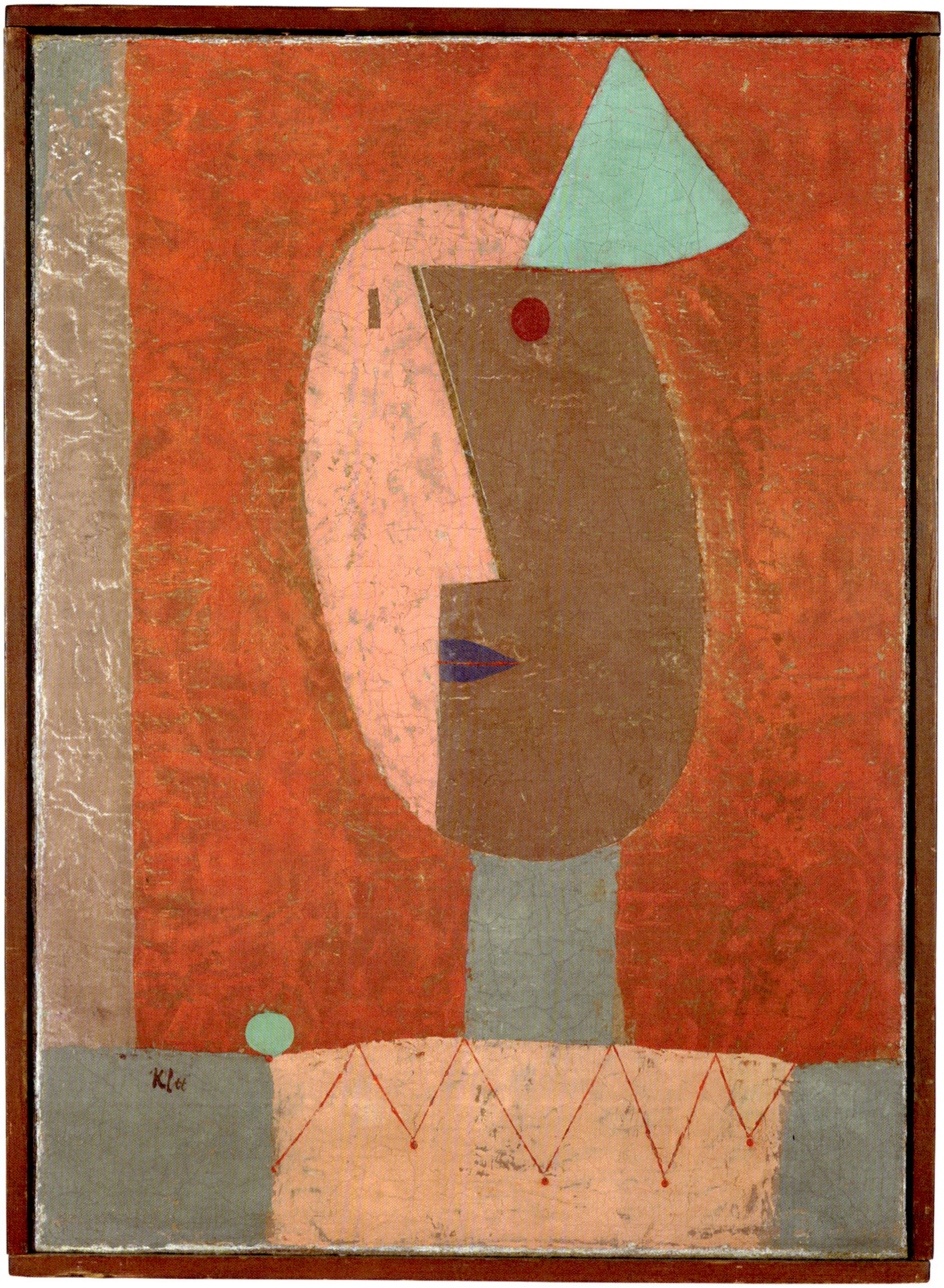

Paul Klee
1879 Münchenbuchsee / Bern –
1940 Muralto-Locarno

Oil on canvas
Signed lower right: Klee
68 × 50.5 cm (including original frame)

Inv. no. P5T / Acquired 2002

Paul Klee
Clown
1929

The medium of the stage, particularly the theatre and opera, but the circus and puppetry as well, fascinated Klee all his life. Frightening masks, grotesque comedians, tightrope walkers and fools, fairground musicians and clowns appear in his drawings and paintings since his early years in Munich. As society's outsiders, they populate a motley universe, comic at times, at times ironic, that occasionally seems to be thrown entirely out of joint. *Clown* – Klee always titled his pictures himself and kept a meticulous record of them – was painted in 1929 when he was teaching at the Bauhaus in Dessau. Offered a position by Gropius in 1920, he had essentially outgrown the Bauhaus by 1929 and was looking for an occupation that would give him more time for his painting. In 1931 he took up a position at the Art Academy in Düsseldorf, from which he was dismissed as a degenerate artist in April 1933 shortly after the Nazis came to power.

Clown is a statuesque work and relatively large in comparison to most of the paintings from the Bauhaus period. The matt layers of paint almost give the expansive and clearly structured composition the appearance of a fresco. Although so very different in content and form, the inner monumentality and the regal gaze of the bust bring to mind likenesses of the early Italian Renaissance. This impression is reinforced by the framing, which is part of the composition and firmly anchors the clown's egg-shaped head within the picture plane. Instead of the inscriptions used in the Italian likenesses to provide information about the sitter, Klee has drawn a zigzag line that might be interpreted as an extremely sparing indication of the clown's ruffle or perhaps as the ups-and-downs that mark the life of a clown. The clown's head is like the "manichini", the jointed dolls from which Carlo Carrà and Giorgio de Chirico drew inspiration in creating their mechanical figures. Above all, however, Klee's oeuvre itself contains a diversity of clearly structured egg-shaped heads or moon faces, articulating another demonized, desperate, and driven aspect of humankind. Examples include *Köpfe* (Heads, 1913), *Selbstporträt* (Self-Portrait, 1919), *Wissen, Schweigen, Vorübergehen* (Knowledge, Science, Passing, 1921) and *Orientierter Mensch* (Oriented Man, 1927).

The clown's head, boldly filling the picture plane, shows a countenance that links profile and frontal view, as in many paintings by Picasso, whose work Klee had studied with great intensity. The face consists of two halves that are distinct in colour and form, with the left side resembling a child's drawing of a moon. The little turquoise hat and ball still reference the attributes of a clown, but the eyes gazing into the distance, one of which resembles an embrasure, suggest that the portrait might also be read as a seer, shown against a fiery, blood-red background from which he looks out at a world that remains hidden from us.

AS

Paul Klee
Zank=Duett
1938

Paul Klee
1879 Münchenbuchsee / Bern –
1940 Muralto-Locarno

Oil on jute
Signed lower left: Klee
Dated, inscribed, titled and signed on stretcher: 1938 K8. "Zank=Duett" Klee
71 × 102 cm

Inv. no. P77T / Acquired 2017

Klee painted *Zank=Duett* (Quarrel=Duet) in 1938 in Bern, having retreated to his native country after active years at the Bauhaus in Weimar and Dessau as well as the Düsseldorf Academy. Discredited as a "degenerate artist", he had been forced to flee Germany in the wake of Hitler's rise to power. In spite of the circumstances and an increasingly debilitating illness (scleroderma) contracted in 1934, the year 1938 was, as Werner Haftmann writes, a "golden year, full of fruit", which saw the creation of 489 works.

Zank=Duett is typical of Klee's mature style, which generally features larger formats, a rigorously reduced linear and formal syntax, striking ciphers and, as Klee put it himself, "secret signs" as distillations of extremely personal and, at the same time, generalized, supra-individual experiences of life and suffering.

Two beings, presumably a man and a woman, confront one another in *Zank=Duett*. In the process of quarrelling they have worked themselves into such a rage that they have undergone a bestial metamorphosis. They are arguing not in words but in gestures and have reached a point of no return, having become spirally entangled and almost inseparably wedged into one another. The dark, severe composition of the linear figures is embedded in a dynamic overall structure of nervous white hatching on a reddish-brown ground, as if to lend visibility to the flow of energy released by the quarrel. At the top of the painting, two horizontal arrows point in opposite directions, vectors of physical and mental energy. The hand raised beneath them, in the central axis of the composition, signals supplication, or perhaps defence.

Zigzagging, or rather angular spiralling shapes as ciphers of the human figure often appear in the works Klee created in 1938, not seldom in connection with negatively connoted titles (e.g. *Timider Brutaler* [Timid One Brutal One], *Im Deckmantel* [Under Cover], *Cunctator* [Cunctator], *Will weg, muss weinen* [Want to Go, Have to Cry]. In *Beiträge zur bildnerischen Form- und Gestaltungslehre* (Contributions to a Pictorial Theory of Form, 1921–22) and his *Pädagogisches Skizzenbuch* (Pedagogical Sketchbook, 1925), Klee associates the expanded spiral with life and the contracting spiral with death. Two arrows determine the direction of movement, either this way or that, either life or death. *Zank=Duett* does not tell us what the outcome is, whether it is conciliatory or devastating.

With devices as simple as they are incisive, Paul Klee's painting encapsulates the existential moment of conflict between two people. Considering Klee's musical expertise in theory and practice as well as his humour in word and image, one might attribute an ironic, or at least positive connotation to *Zank=Duett*. Sadly, the artist's grievous circumstances at the time are hardly conducive to such an interpretation.

UW

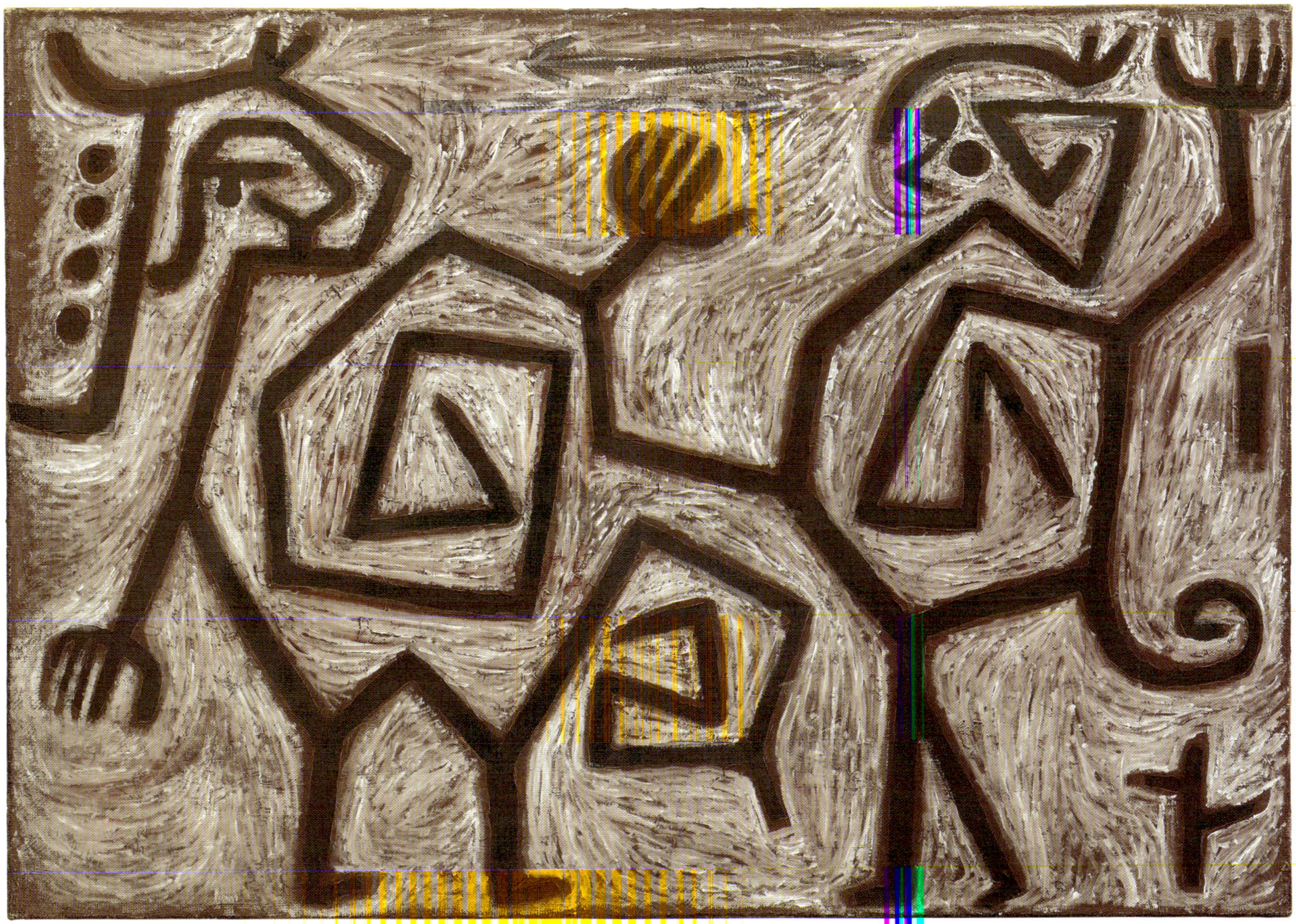

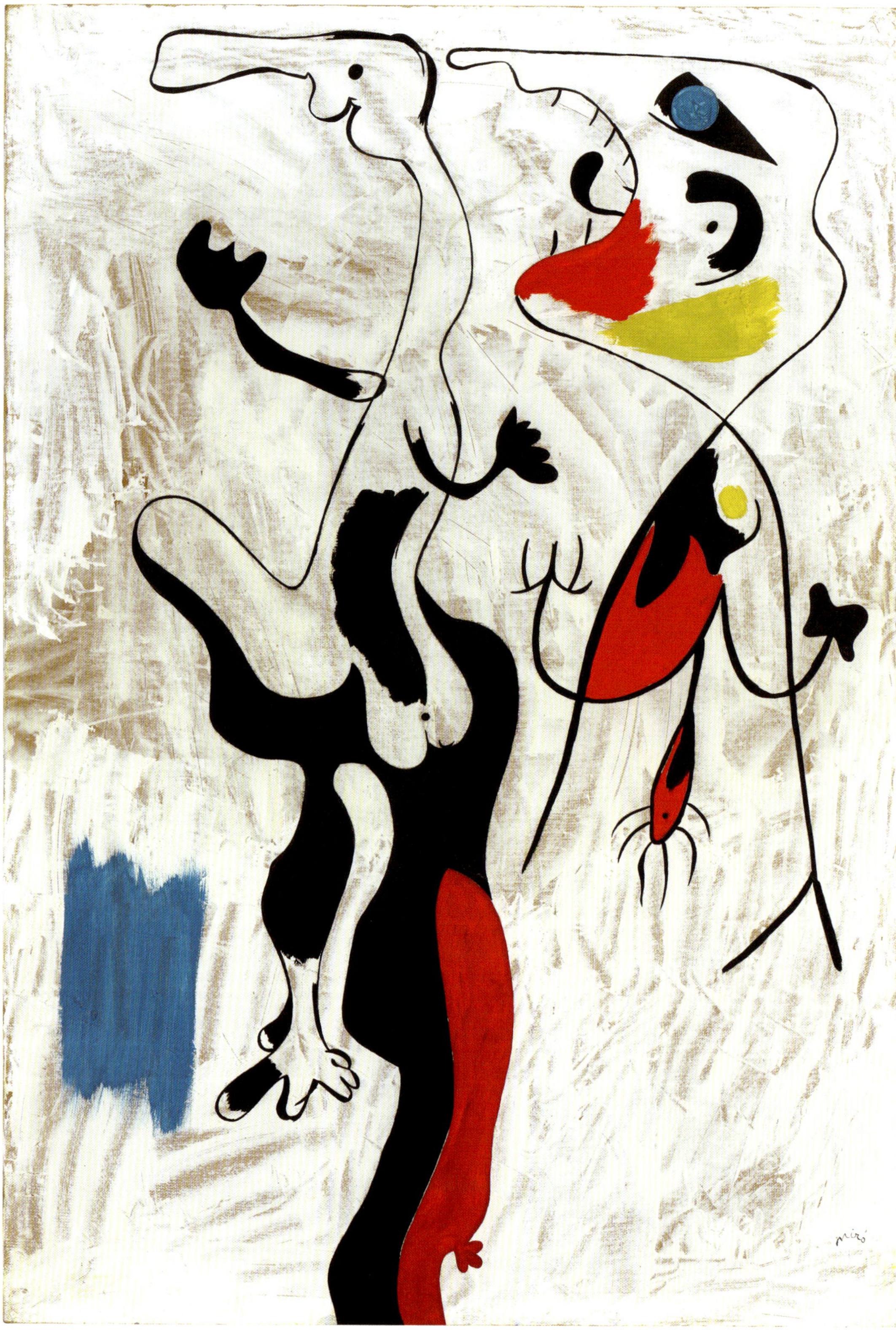

Joan Miró
1893 Montroig / Barcelona –
1983 Palma de Mallorca

Casein / gouache on painter's cardboard
Signed lower right: Miró
Signed, dated and inscribed on verso:
Joan Miró. 26-4-35 "Homme et Femme."
104.8 × 74.6 cm

Inv. no. P64T / Acquired 2016

Joan Miró
Homme et femme
1935

In 1923, after Fauvist and Cubist beginnings, the Catalan Joan Miró turned to a symbolic formal idiom and soon joined the group of Surrealists in Paris, where he was living at the time. He animates both earthly and cosmic spaces with largely floating geometric and biomorphic shapes. According to Miró, nothing in his universe of forms is invented. Everything exists. Even in the guise of playful poetry, his is a universe that aims at existential essences: on earth, heaven and stars, at life, work and play, in eros, dream and violence. Works of the 1930s, like *Homme et femme*, show an increasingly pessimistic and aggressive tenor that echoes the artist's experiences in times scarred by political and social upheaval on the eve of the Spanish Civil War. Miró lived in Barcelona between 1932 and 1936. When the war broke out, he left the city and returned to Paris.

In *Homme et femme*, Miró returns once again to the age-old theme of the erotic relationship between the sexes. To the left, an extremely aroused male figure is pictured with his back turned to a woman standing behind him to the right, from whom he seems to be fleeing. She in turn follows him, equally aroused, with her mouth wide open. Miró has arrested this event at a moment of acute, unresolved tension. The lack of resolution between the sexes was repeatedly addressed throughout Modernism often taking a misogynist turn, not only in the fine arts but also in literature, theatre and music. On occasion, the Surrealists portrayed the female figure as a praying mantis; they were intrigued by the insect's sexual behaviour of occasionally devouring the male after or even while mating. In reference to psychoanalytical theory, the female praying mantis was perceived as symbolizing the latent – and threatening – aggression of female Eros. Study of *Homme et femme* also suggests comparison with traditional representations in European art history of the biblical story of Joseph and Potiphar's wife (1 Genesis 39: 7–19), in which Joseph seeks to resist her attempt to seduce him. The loss of his robe, a loss that also characterizes Miró's male figure seen in naked vulnerability, becomes his downfall.

Entirely in the spirit of Surrealism, *Homme et femme* not only depicts human beings under the yoke of unbridled instinct but also refers to the changeability of the material world through physical metamorphosis, in particular of men. The physical and emotional drama of the subject matter in this work is formally embodied in the animated lines of the drawing and the artist's uninhibited application and treatment of colour. The figures are rendered in sparse outlines, their features and gestures marked by a humorous touch despite the drama of the subject matter. The "crude manner" of the painting exemplifies Miró's anti-academic approach to painting and his pursuit of creative immediacy and freedom.

UW

Louis Soutter
Vierges cruel / Pur novice
1937–1942

049

Louis Soutter
1871 Morges – 1942 Ballaigues

Finger painting, oil on paper
Inscribed on upper margin:
vier Ges cruel puR noviceE
44 × 58 cm

Inv. no. G228M / Acquired 2011

Louis Soutter long remained an outsider in the history of art. It was only twenty years after he died, around 1960, that the importance of his oeuvre was discovered. Soutter first studied the violin with the well-known Belgian composer and violinist Eugène Ysaÿe, and subsequently painting in Geneva with Charles Koella and in Paris with Benjamin Constant. After several ultimately unsuccessful years in Colorado, he left the United States in 1903. Upon his return to Switzerland, he was unable to find a footing as a painter or musician despite good connections through Ysaÿe, the painter René Auberjonois and his maternal cousin Le Corbusier.

After years of instability, his family sent him to a hospice in Ballaigues in the Swiss Jura. He was only 52 years old at the time, but he stayed there for the rest of his life. Largely isolated, he produced the frenzied drawings and finger paintings that would later make him famous. Soutter's art addressed such themes as loneliness, anxiety, religious delusion and the desperate dance of life. He wrote "catastrophe" on one of his drawings.

Vierges cruel – Pur novice belongs to the last phase of his oeuvre from 1937 to 1942; like all of the work made during that period, it has no date. Deprived of traditional painting materials, Soutter resorted to printer's ink, shoe polish and even car paint, smearing the materials directly onto wallpaper with his fingers and creating expressively vibrant figures with brilliant verve. At first sight, the seemingly grotesque scenes resemble the silhouettes that illustrate books of fairy tales. Three "villains", looking as if they had come straight out of hell, are attacking a boy who attempts to defend himself, but in vain, for he has already been deprived of his freedom by one of the devils, who has wrapped his skinny tail around one of the boy's legs.

Soutter may have taken inspiration for the ritual character of these demonic figures, all of them male, from early cave painting or the black-figure vase painting of ancient Attica. Movement and expressiveness as signs of enhanced vitality may well refer to the dancing figures of Expressionism, to Matisse, Kirchner and Klee, but also, beyond Europe, to the art of Africa and India. Their vitality captivated and seminally influenced artists in the early 20th century, profoundly changing their work. Soutter's figures, surrounded by numerous fingerprints, their hands oversized, like branches growing out of their thin arms, similarly conjure up the timelessness of vital life energies.

AS

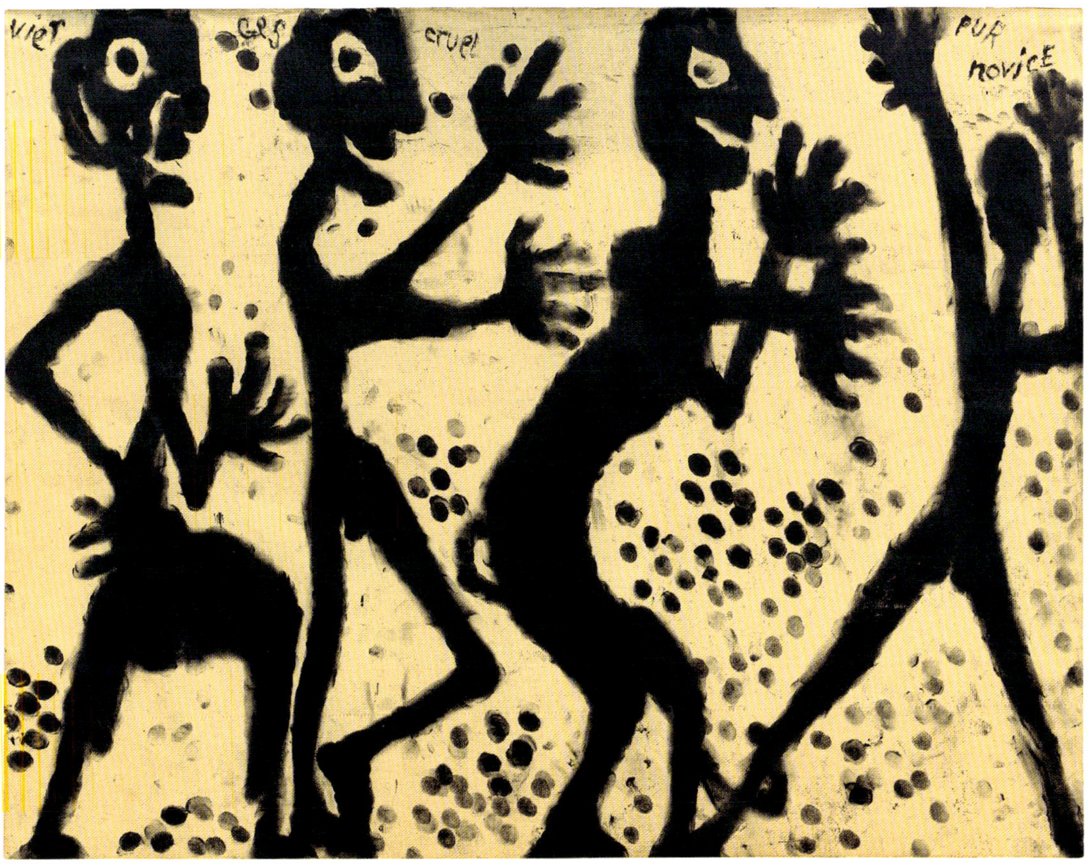
vieT
GES
cruel
PUR
noviCE

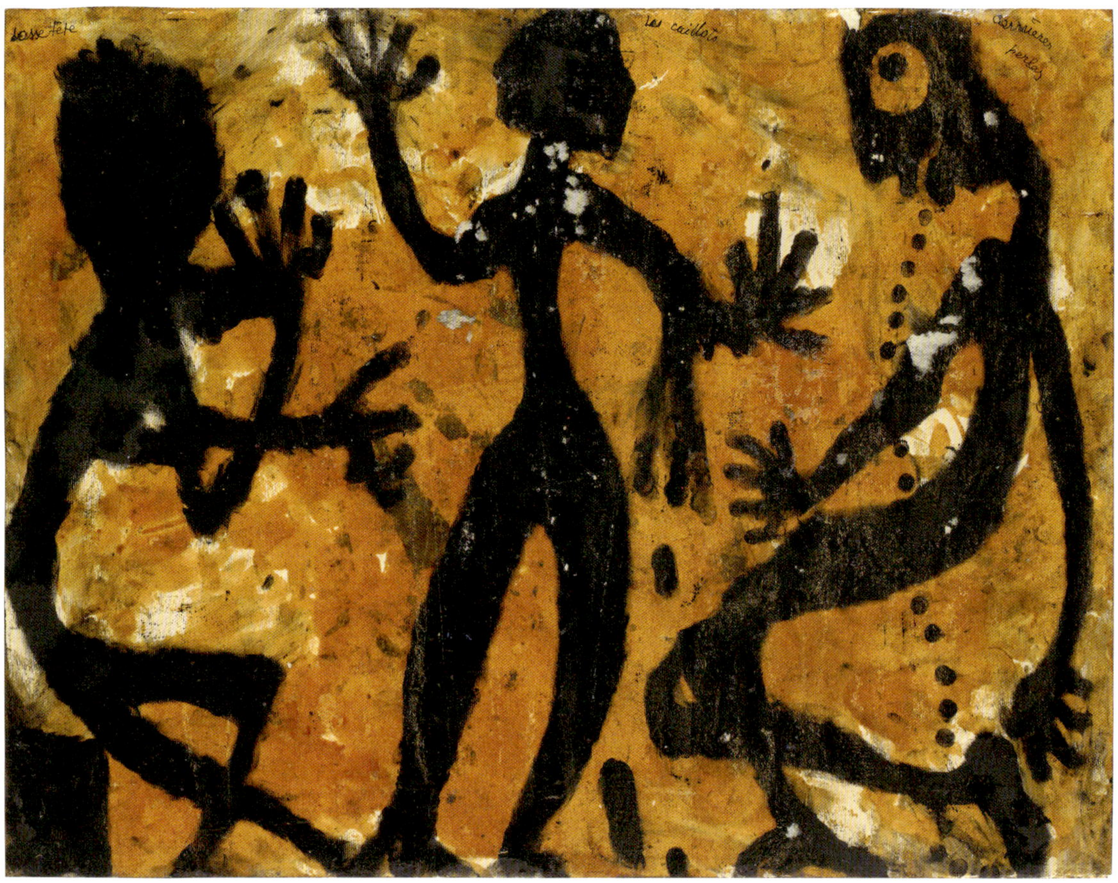
basse tête

050

Louis Soutter
1871 Morges – 1942 Ballaigues

Linseed oil lacquer, ink, paper
inscribed on upper margin:
Lasse tête Les caillots Dernières perles
44 × 58 cm

Inv. no. G312M / Acquired 2018

Louis Soutter

Lasse tête / Les caillots / Dernières perles

1937–1942

Lasse tête / Les caillots / Dernières perles was a gift for the painter Marcel Poncet (1894–1953 Lausanne), known in French-speaking Switzerland primarily for his religious subject matter. He occasionally supplied Soutter with painting materials. Like *Vierges cruel / Pur novice* (cat. 49), it is one of the undated finger paintings made between 1937 and 1942. The three figures, painted on the paper with fingers and ink, show transparent patches and are drawn in diffuse, fragile outlines. The linseed oil has darkened the paper over time. The ground of the painting, structured in varying browns, recalls rock cliffs and sand, linking the scene, despite its contemporaneity, to prehistoric painting. The symmetrical arrangement, with the figure in the middle facing front and flanked by two figures in profile, recalls prehistoric cultures. Its hieratic character prevails even in this vibrant, enigmatic scene.

The hands of the black silhouette in the middle are expressively extended in space like the dancers in Mary Wigman's performances. The magical gesture propels the flow of energy, forcing the two assisting figures onto their knees. The figure on the left attempts to protect itself, perhaps even with a teasing retort, while the one to the right is already bowing in humility, eye gazing vacantly into nothingness, a long chain of pearls dangling from mouth to foot.

When Soutter added words to his paintings, they were not intended as precise titles but rather as explanations. They represent fragments of the artist's mental universe, which is not always identical with the painted figures, although their tenor, as in this case, is undoubtedly gloomy. *Lasse tête* might be translated as an exhausted or wearied head. *Les caillots* or blood clots are seen dripping onto the floor out of the figure's arm, possibly out of the artery, and *Dernières perles*, the last pearls, might be interpreted as a chain that prevents the skeletal snake man from falling apart, a motif found in other works of the same period. In a much-cited poem about Soutter, Herman Hesse writes, "Nicht korrekt, nicht schön, sondern richtig. / Mal ich mit Tinte und Blut, male wahr. Wahrheit ist schrecklich." (Not correct, not beautiful, but right. / If I paint with ink and blood, I paint true. Truth is dreadful.)

AS

Julio González
Le rêve / Le baiser
c. 1934

Julio González
1876 Barcelona – 1942 Paris

Bronze
(cast: F. Godard Fondeur, Paris)
Signed and numbered: J. Gonzales 0/0 ©
Height: 65.5 cm

Inv. no. S66T / Acquired 2016

The sculptor Julio González from Catalonia trained in his father's art foundry in Barcelona, where he was schooled primarily in forging and hammering techniques. His inimitable contribution to 20th century art as the "inventor of iron sculpture" is closely associated with Pablo Picasso, whose acquaintance he already made at the end of the 19th century. They enjoyed a fruitful relationship of give-and-take and remained friends for the rest of their lives.

Initially interested in both painting and sculpting, González decided to devote himself exclusively to sculpture at the end of 1920s, after having spent two years in Paris as an assistant to Brancusi. González's experience with welding and the use of iron motivated Picasso to seek his advice in working with a material that had not yet been of significance in the history of sculpture. Picasso commissioned González to cast his welded iron sculpture *La femme au jardin* (1929–30) in bronze, benefiting from his technical expertise. González, in turn, benefited artistically from Picasso, having asked him for permission to make use of his method of montage and assemblage, that is, combining separate, in part found, in part self-made single parts into a single artistic whole. It is in this way that González created his first iron version of *Le rêve / Le baiser* (MNAM, Paris).

González often referred to his sculpture as "drawing in space", indicating that he treated the medium of sculpture with the same immediacy and associative thinking ordinarily applied to working in pencil on paper. A colour drawing (1933) for *Le rêve / Le baiser* shows the basic elements of the sculpture although the latter follows its own formal requirements rather than slavishly following the preliminary sketch.

It was important to González that his work enabled one to trace the process, to see the forging, welding and the seams between the parts. These traces have been retained in the bronze cast that his daughter Roberta commissioned in accordance with her father's wishes after his death. Roberta also recalls that her father referred to this work both as *Le rêve* and as *Le baiser*. The titles associate the sculpture with Surrealism, with dream and Eros. In fact, the same year that González made *Le rêve / Le baiser* (1934), he participated in the important surrealist exhibition at Kunsthaus Zürich, which also showcased such artists as Hans Arp, Max Ernst, Joan Miró and Alberto Giacometti.

Le rêve / Le baiser embodies the idea of a male-female encounter although it shows few features indicative of figuration: waving hair or the hollow shape as a womb penetrated by a pointed conical shape. This detail suggests comparison with Giacometti's bronze *Man and Woman* created in 1928–29. In González's sculpture a kiss takes place in a dream, and even more, an erotic encounter and indeed, an erotic union, revealing on close study that the woman seems to be playing an active part. Only on walking around the work, do we discover the tension, in both form and content, with which González informed this sculpture, dating from the most important years of his artistic career.

UW

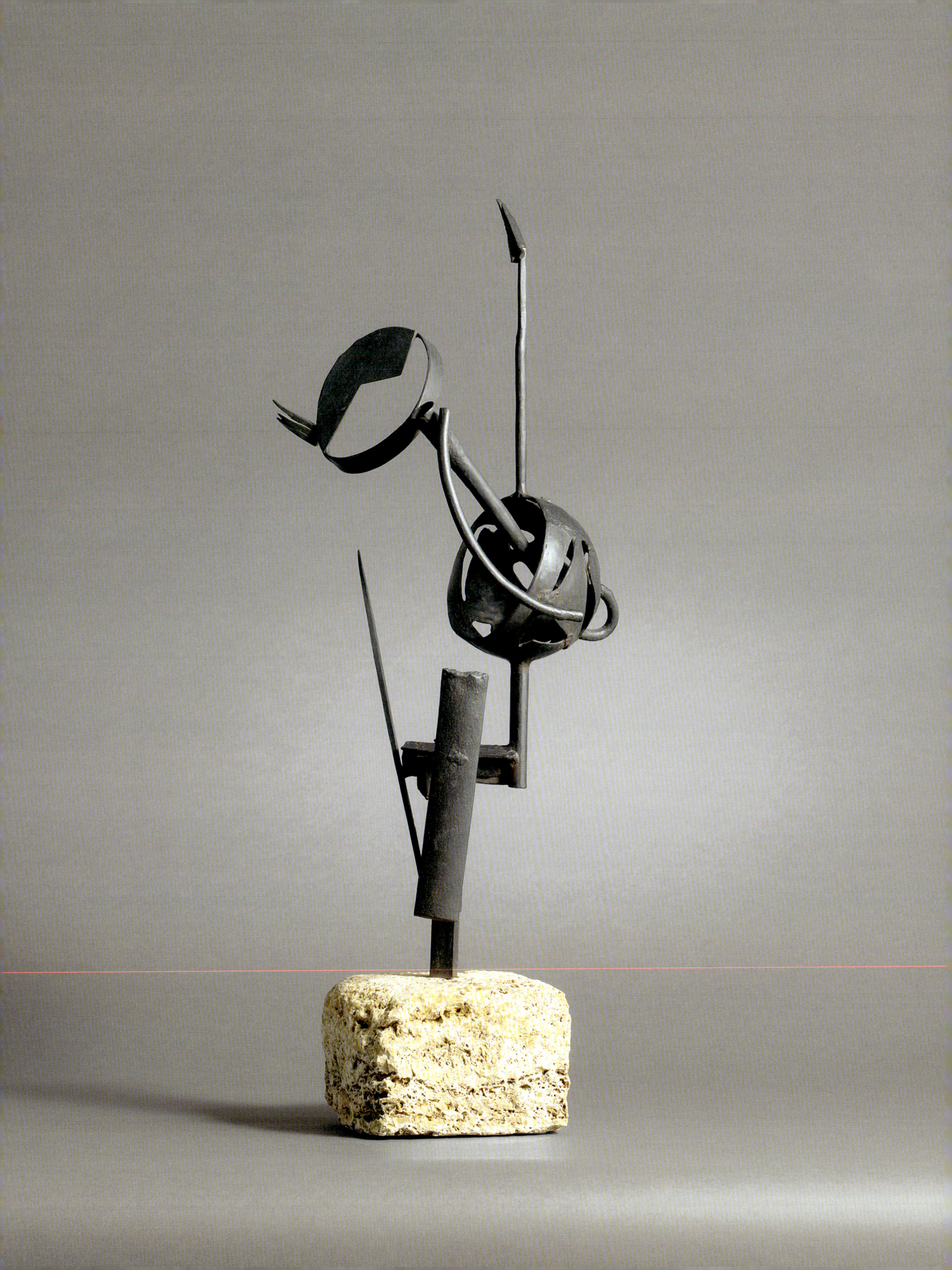

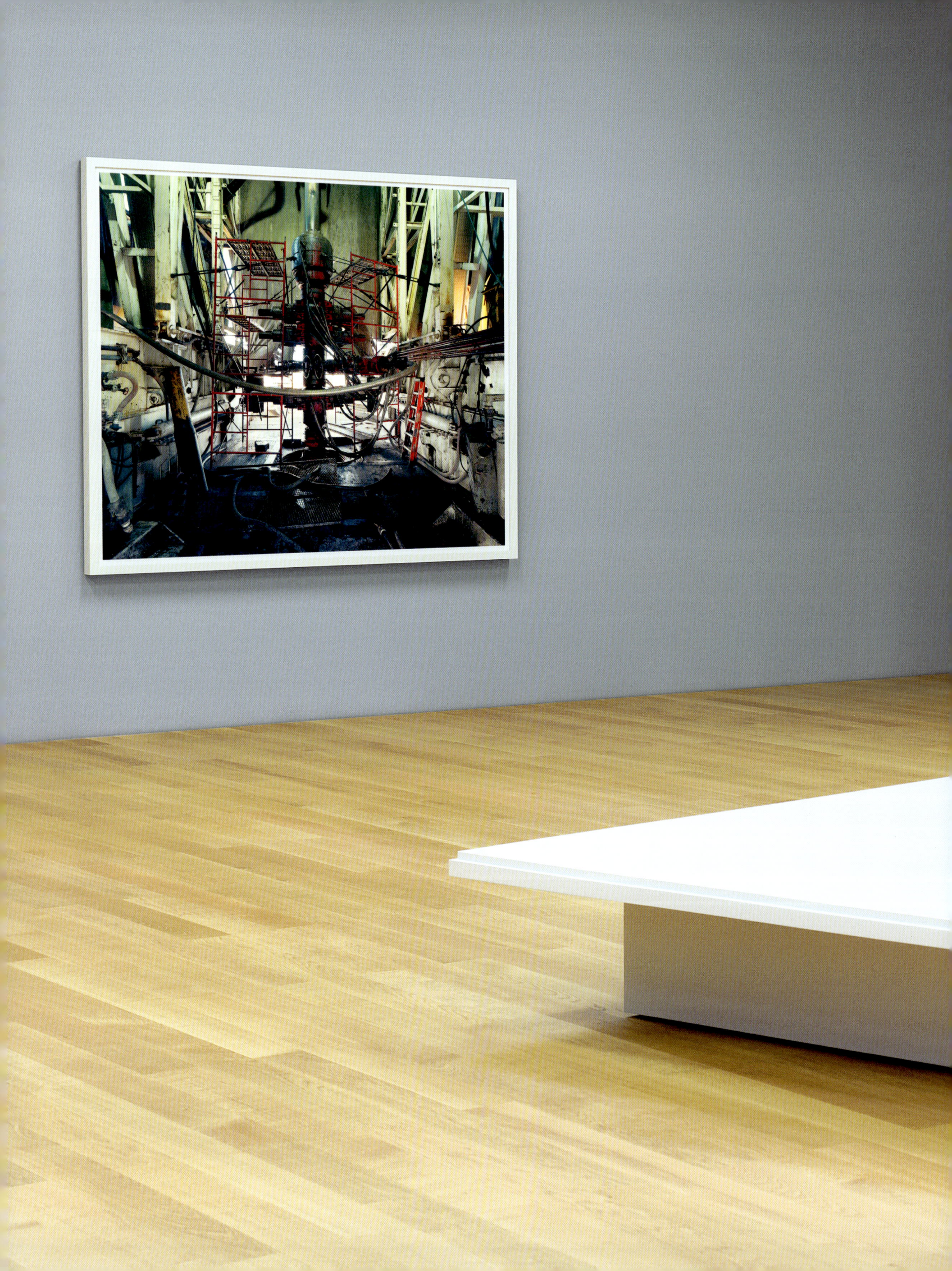

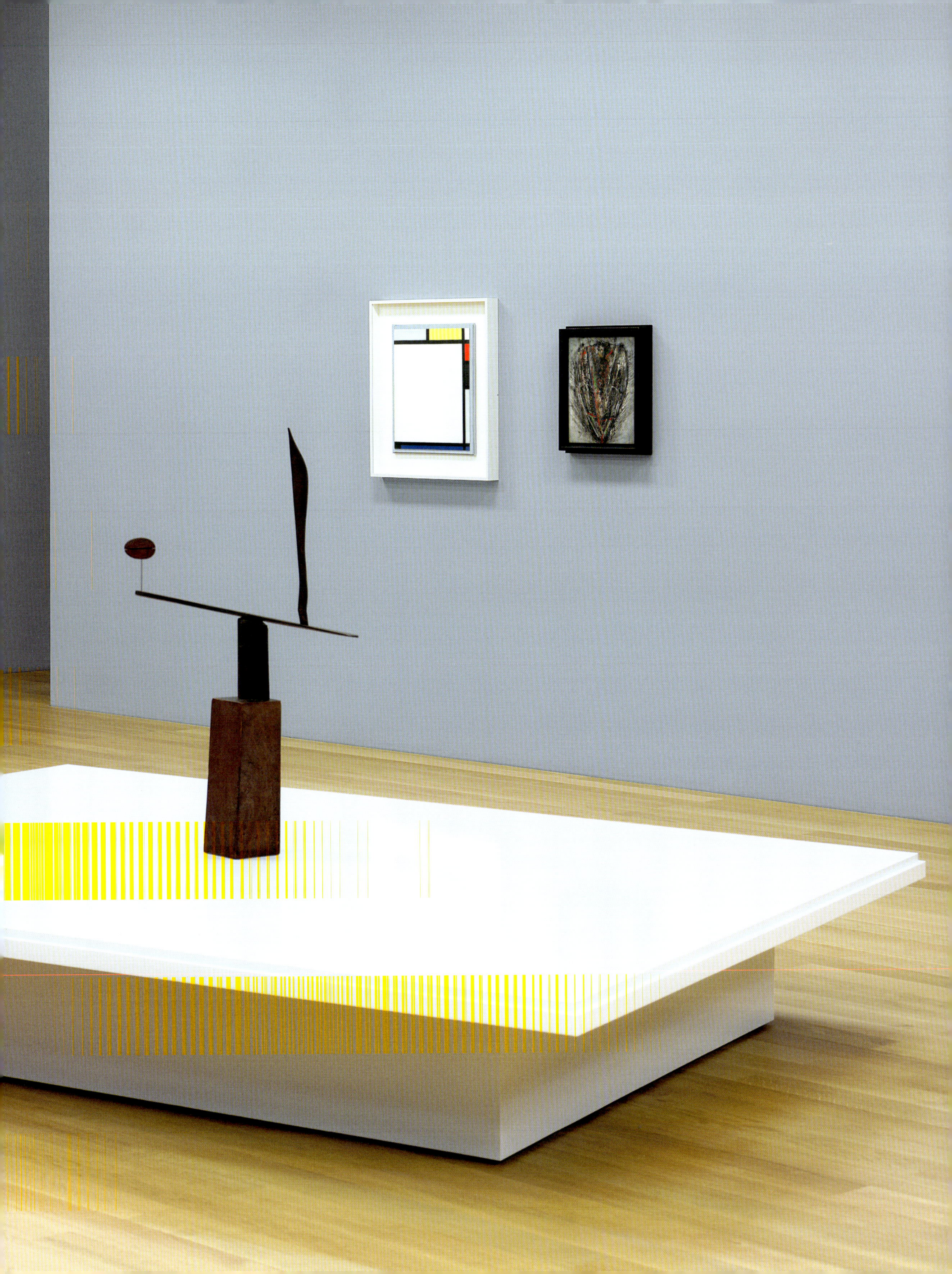

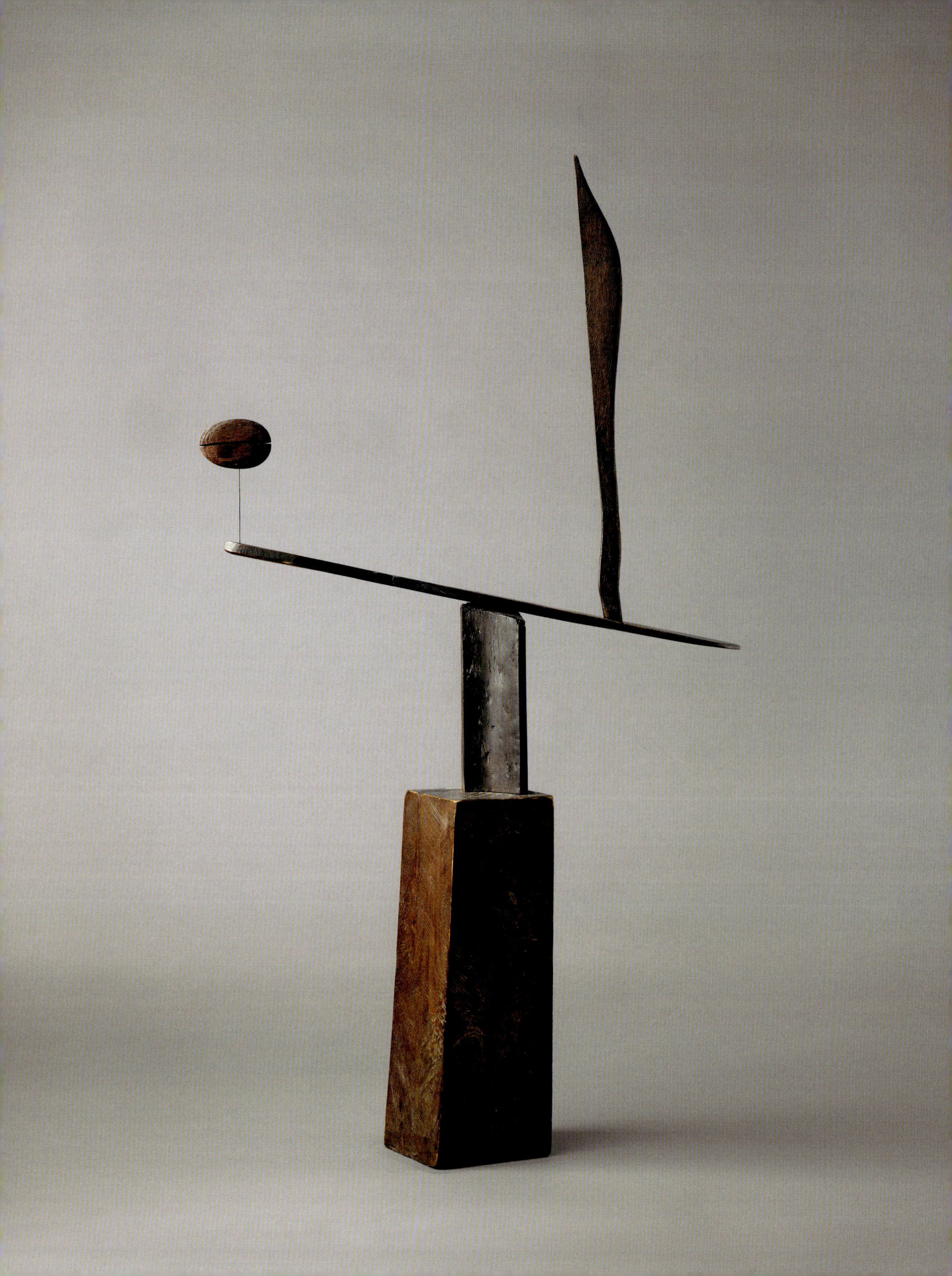

Alexander Calder
1898 Lawnton / Pennsylvania – 1976 New York

Wood and wire
Signed and dated on stand: Calder 1935
Height: 102.4 cm

Inv. no. S53T / Acquired 2012

Alexander Calder
Untitled
1935

We associate the art of Alexander Calder primarily with large and small mobiles that playfully keep forming new configurations and in turn reconfigure space and time. He is equally well known for the towering, imposing stabiles that have invested numerous public spaces with life since the 1950s.

With the exception of his famous *Cirque Calder* (1926–1931), the works that he made in the days of Surrealism are not as well known although they are seminal to his subsequent oeuvre. While living in Paris in the early 1930s, Calder frequently met with such artists as Joan Miró, Hans Arp, Fernand Léger, Piet Mondrian, and the uncompromising head of the Surrealists, André Breton, though without ever joining the group himself. Chance, play, magic and eroticism were not only of interest to the Surrealists; they also feature significantly in Calder's work. It was Marcel Duchamp who coined the term "mobile" for the kinetic sculptures, and Hans Arp who in turn came up with the term "stabile" for the stationary ones.

In 1933, Calder returned to the United States for a few years, where he purchased a small farmhouse in Roxbury, Connecticut, some 100 kilometres north of New York. He later built a studio extension to the farmhouse. The present work from 1935 was made during this period, using items that happened to be in his studio at the time. The pieces of wood in different colours have not been worked in any way but were left instead in their original, raw state. Such objets trouvés, which first appeared in the Cubist collages made by Braque and Picasso, establish a link between art and real life. They are relics of daily life, testifying to unknown stories now embodied in the work of art.

The present work consists of a precarious wood construction placed on a slender square pedestal. A board lies at a slant on a narrow, semi-circular piece of wood, possibly from the back of a chair or an armchair. On the board, Calder has balanced an undulating piece of wood tapered to a point at one end and an oval wooden shape mounted on a metal wire at the other. The two objects are related and communicate with each other; they resemble parts of a plant. The leaf growing upwards and the nut-shaped fruit represent the cycle of nature, in visual tribute to processes of growth and transience. The phallic shape of the board and the female, ovular shape of the wood represent in turn the male and female elements and the fragile balance between them, for it seems that they could collapse at any moment.

AS

Wassily Kandinsky
Entre Deux
1934

Wassily Kandinsky
1866 Moscow – 1944 Neuilly-sur-Seine

Oil, tempera on canvas
Initialled and dated lower left: K 34
Initialled, numbered, inscribed and dated on verso: K//N° 601 „Entre Deux"//1934
130 × 95 cm

Inv. no. P20T / Acquired 1998

The painting *Entre Deux* belongs to Kandinsky's late work. The painter had the privilege of looking back on many years of fruitful and successful endeavour. He was a professor at the University of Moscow, at the Bauhaus in Weimar and later in Dessau. He had numerous collectors and artist friends, had published acclaimed theoretical writings on art (*Über das Geistige in der Kunst* [Concerning the Spiritual in Art], 1910; *Punkt und Linie zur Fläche* [Point and Line to Plane], 1926) and had shown many of his paintings in international exhibitions. As co-founder and one of the foremost representatives of abstract painting, he contributed substantially to the genre's art historical breakthrough from 1913 onwards. Then, in 1933, the National Socialists shut down the Bauhaus in Dessau and Berlin, whereupon Kandinsky, who had acquired German citizenship in 1928, decided to emigrate to Paris.

Despite financial straits in his new environs, where his art initially met with somewhat cool detachment, Kandinsky soon began producing work that featured a positively oriental voluptuousness of colour and form. The geometric tectonics of the Bauhaus years gave way to canvases displaying largely biomorphic, free-floating configurations. Matisse and Miró may have had a stimulating influence, but Kandinsky is also known to have taken inspiration from illustrations in biological and zoological publications. He gave a new materiality to his pictorial elements, for the first time mixing sand into his paints. Seven of fifteen works that he painted in 1934 show this additive. One of them, *Entre Deux*, seems to give us an insight into both micro- and macrocosmic universes.

The division of the motif into two parts is notable. Also found in other works made at the same time, these "twin forms" unite and divide, complement each other dialectically and may perhaps be interpreted as feminine and masculine, spirit and matter, or becoming and passing.

Kandinsky speaks of "inner necessity" as the driving force that gives form to his abstract art. That inner necessity or "inner imperative", as he later describes it, did not yield work that required an objectified something beyond the painting for its justification. But in the 1930s, he felt the abstract relied too much on the object, from which it still appeared to be "abstracted". Like Theo van Doesburg just a few years earlier, Kandinsky pondered and wrote about the concrete in art which refers to nothing but itself. Given these premises, one must be wary of reading symbolic interpretations into his later work.

UW

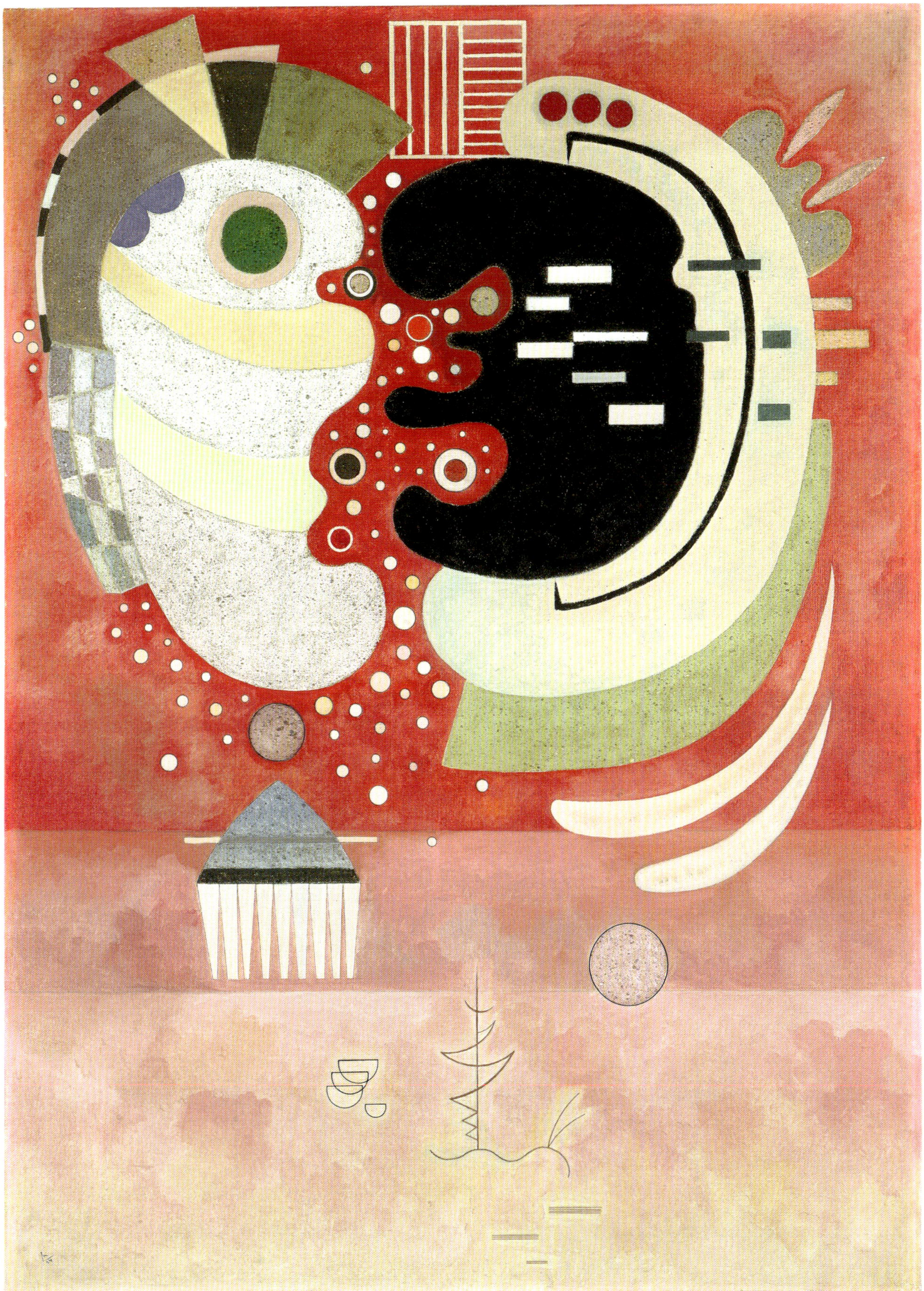

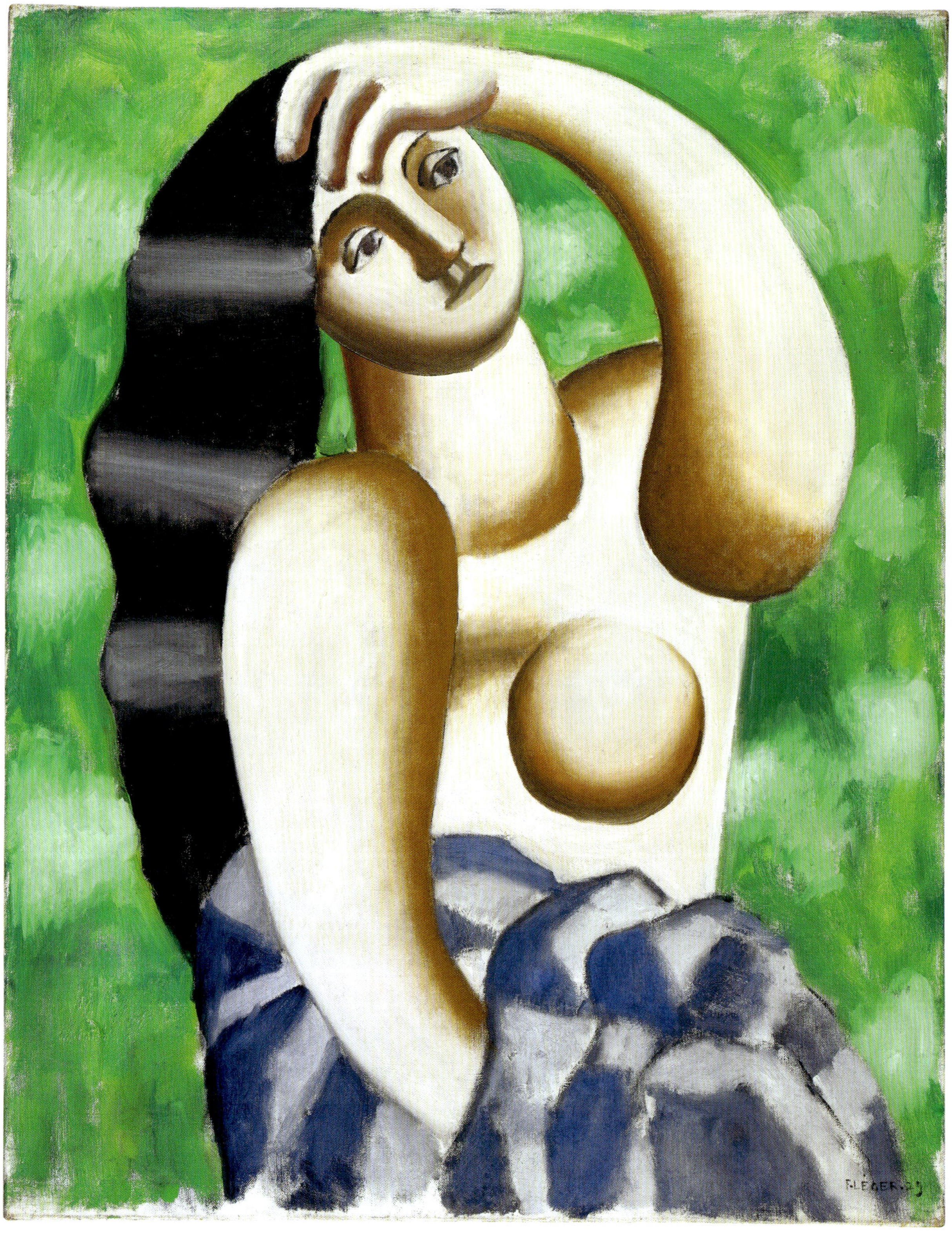
F.LEGER

Fernand Léger
La danseuse
1929

Fernand Léger
1881 Argentan – 1955 Gif-sur-Yvette

Oil on canvas
Signed and dated lower right:
F. LEGER. 29
92 × 73 cm

Inv. no. P10T / Acquired 2001

In a review of the *Salon d'Automne* written in 1911, the critic Louis Vauxcelles characterised Léger's work as "tubistic". His neologism pinpointed an essential distinction from the Cubist approach to subject matter, which no doubt influenced, though it did not really accord with Léger's artistic ideas. Unlike the manner in which analytical Cubism broke down its subject matter into surfaces and planes, Léger had consistently gravitated toward cylindrical, three-dimensional representation, accompanied by a certain planarity of detail. The "tubist" idea of representation basically informed all of his subject matter, which was drawn from classical themes and included the representation of the human body.

Léger was both fascinated and threatened by the technological and mechanical invasion of modern life. Human beings held sway over gigantic machines, yet they were nothing but machines themselves, whose parts obeyed mechanical laws. Despite the destructive violence of mechanized warfare introduced in the First World War, Léger did not abandon his open-minded approach to technology and mechanics. Such developments did, after all, testify to human progress. What's more, they were compatible with a de-individualized image of humankind inspired by the idea of equality and could easily be brought to bear on "tubist" notions of form.

Women as the sole subject matter of a painting appear in Léger's oeuvre as early as 1912–13. The artist increasingly pared down his formal vocabulary in the course of the 1920s, rendering his figures in archaic "blockiness". As in *La danseuse* (The Dancer), he depicted women alone or in pairs against a single colour background. The half portrait of the dancer is set apart as if in relief against the vibrant shading of green mixed with white and yellow, generating an impression of limpid nature. Her limbs are clearly distinguished through contrasting ochre and white. Her black hair cascades in large undulating waves over her shoulder and back. A cloth, striped blue and white in beautiful contrast to the green and ochre, is draped across the lower part of her otherwise unclothed body. Her right hand reaches into the cloth; her left hand is resting on her forehead. Leaning back with her head slightly inclined to the left, she gazes gravely but impersonally as if lost in reverie, in disinterested appreciation of an object. One might imagine her sitting rather than standing, but certainly not dancing. Léger has undoubtedly taken inspiration from Picasso, as demonstrated by the latter's drawing of *Three Dancers* (Musée Picasso, Paris, Zervos XXIX, 432, 1919–20), whose voluptuous limbs lend a somewhat ponderous feel to their ballet poses. The attitude of head and arms in particular prompts direct comparison with Léger's figure. For poses of this kind, Picasso in turn found inspiration in press photographs for Ballets Russes.

La danseuse could also be called "Buste de femme" (Bust of a Woman), as in the pencil drawing of 1931 in which Léger placed the same figure at the corner of an interior. The bared left breast in the painting has become an apple that she holds in her right hand – both versions equally symbolize seductive femininity. The main theme of the painting, however, is no doubt the sculptural presence of the human body as a synthesis of line, form and colour.

UW

Henri Laurens
Flora
1939

Henri Laurens
1885 Paris – 1954 Paris

Fired clay
With monogram and numbered on base: HL 4
Height: 27 cm

Inv. no. S172M / Acquired 2006

The small sculpture belongs to a group of squatting and sitting female figures created by Henri Laurens in a return to figuration in the late 1920s, following a period of Cubist experimentation. The figure, sitting on the ground, is a mere 27 cm in height but her sensuous full-bodied limbs, her slender torso, round breasts and head thrown back lend her a compelling dynamic. "Even when rendering movement," Laurens told Yves Taillandier in a 1951 interview, "I seek stability. Movement does not interfere with the sense of rest that my sculptures should convey. The strongest impression ... is not that of disintegration because these statues do not represent movement so much as they do a composition of forms. The harmony, the sculptural laws by which they are defined, the system of their mutually generated volumes, the fact that empty space counts just as much as space that is filled – all of this aims to lend them stability."

The sculpture is firmly rooted in the tradition of French art. The motif of the seated figure recalls Charles Despiau's *La Bacchante* of 1909, Auguste Rodin's *Squatting Woman* of 1882 and also Aristide Maillol's nudes, despite differences in the content of the messages they each convey. Laurens studied Rodin intensely in his early years, but the older artist's "will to create form" as "expressed in transitory physical configurations in space" (Werner Hofmann) was of significance to him in his later work as well. In addition, the artistic message that informs the sculpture shows the inspiration of paintings. The soft, full-bodied, "natural" woman with her gently curved legs reverberates in Ingres' *Turkish Bath* of 1867, in Picasso's paintings of the 1920s and 30s, and in the paintings Fernand Léger made in the 1930s.

However, the voluptuous character of the figure also evokes associations with plants, exotic flowers and forked trees. According to his wife Marthe, Laurens used to take walks every morning and loved studying the trees. When he returned to the studio, he would try to render the impressions of what he had perceived in his sculptures. "But whatever I try to picture in my sculpture," Laurens says in the above-quoted interview, "remains a sculptural reality or, to be more precise, a consequence of sculptural events ... I choose the title at the end."

Flora takes us back to Roman antiquity, to a figure that was commemorated as the goddess of flowers and gardens, of youth and fertility. In paintings of the Renaissance and classicism, we see *Flora* as a beautiful young woman decked out in blossoms. The facial features of Laurens' small statue recall the Greek idols of the Cyclades, and although her seductive body resembles early idols of fertility, she is still a very contemporary, 20th century piece of art. In the words of Henri Laurens himself, "What characterises the quest of modern art is precisely its yearning to restore the continuity lost through the departure from the Renaissance and classicism by embracing primitive forms of art, the archaic and the Romanesque."

AS

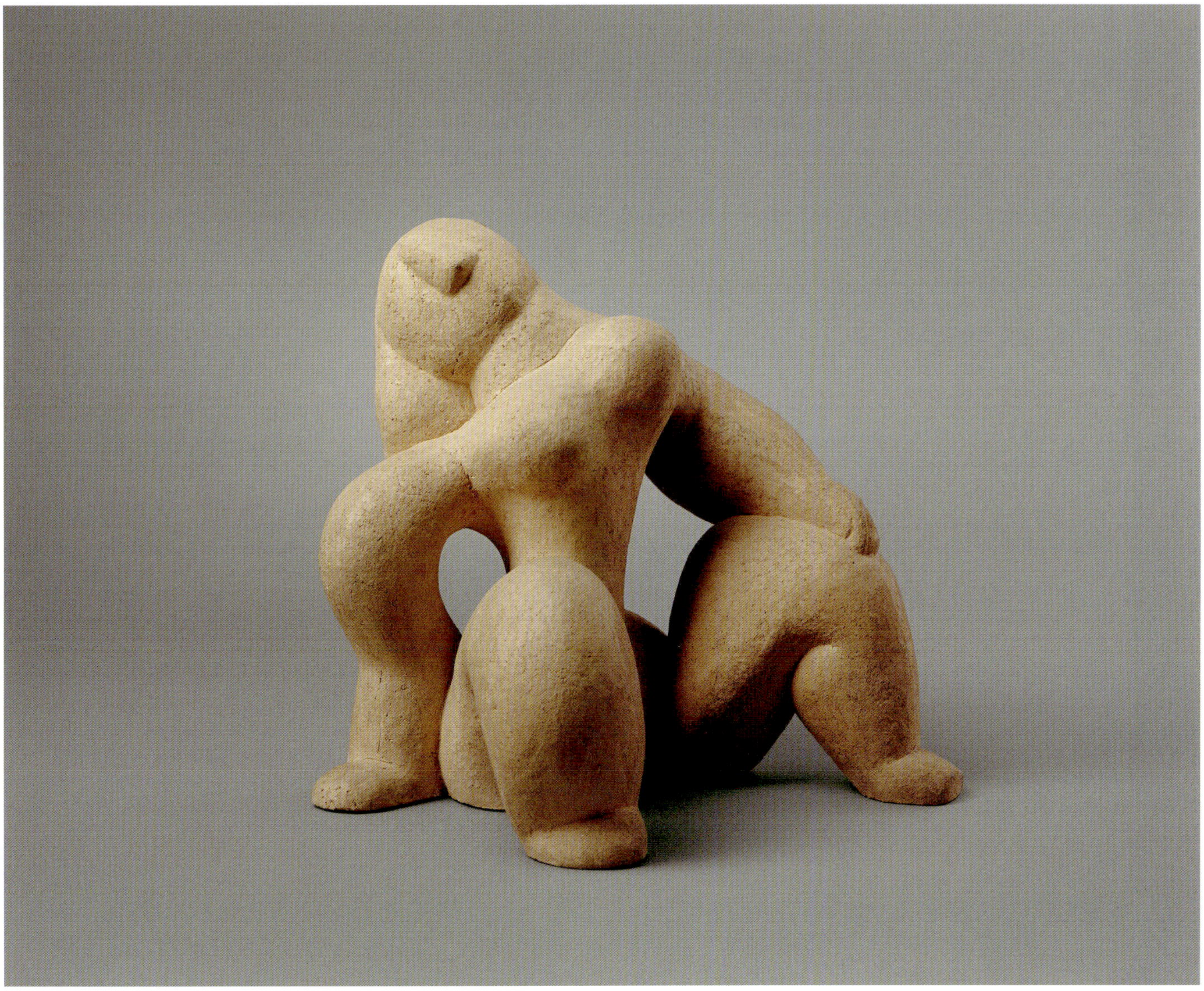

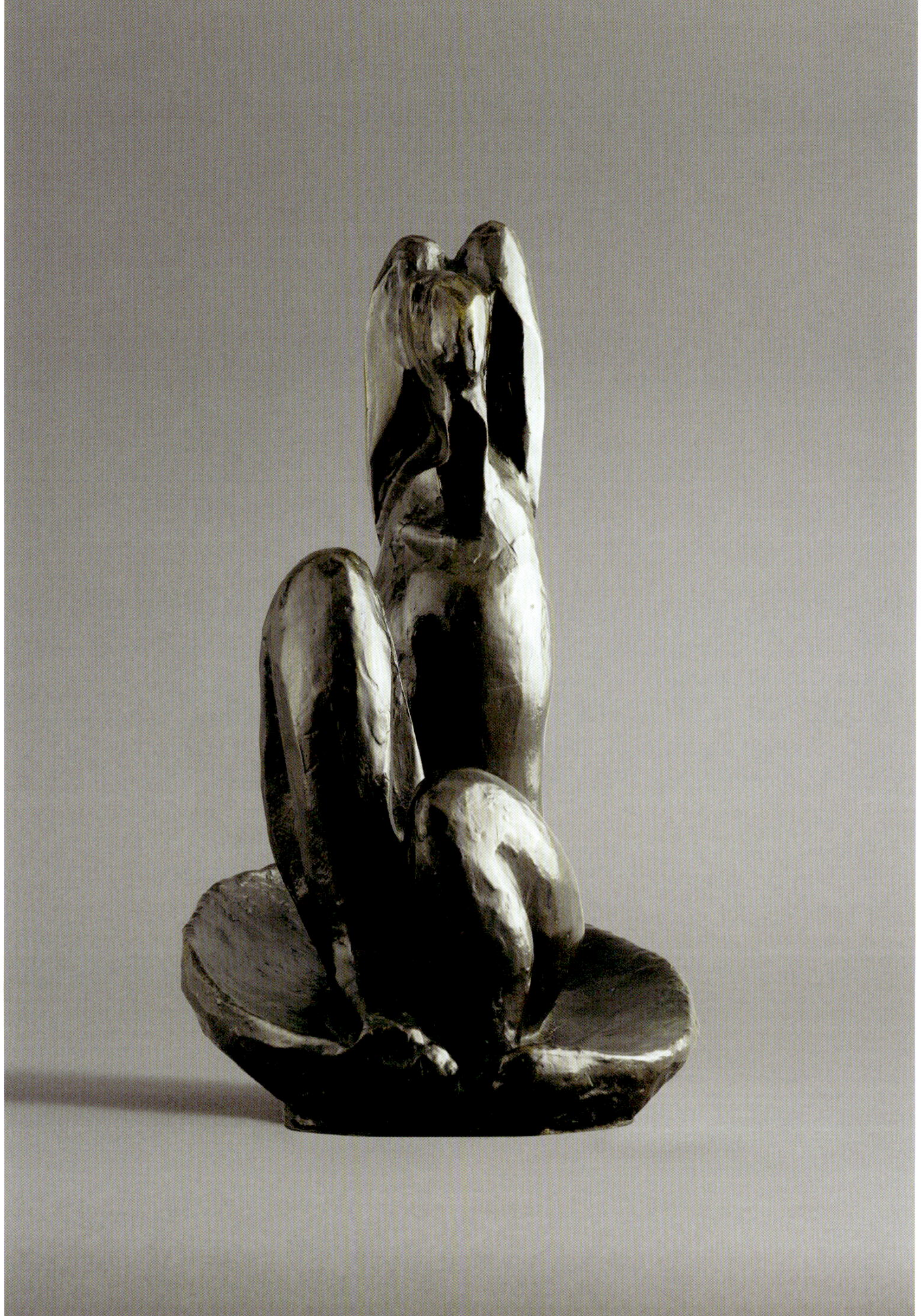

Henri Matisse
Vénus à la coquille I
1930

Henri Matisse
1869 Le Cateau-Cambrésis –
1954 Cimiez / Nice

Bronze (cast: Valsuani, 1954)
Initialled and numbered on the base: HM 7/10
Height: 31 cm

Inv. no. S174M / Acquired 2006

Alongside his work in two dimensions, Matisse soon turned to sculpture in order to recover from painting and tidy up his brain, as he put it. He was already an experienced sculptor when he created *Vénus à la coquille* (Venus in a Shell), a motif frequently addressed in the fine arts since antiquity and ultimately going back to ancient Greek literature, to Hesiod's *Theogony* (c. 700 BC). According to this narrative of the origins of the world and the workings of the gods, Venus (Greek: Aphrodite), the goddess of love, was born of the foam that had formed when Cronus castrated his father Uranos with a sickle and cast his genitals into the sea. Venus, a child of Uranos like her brother Cronus, is pictured adrift in a shell, driven towards Kythera until she finally reaches terra firma in Cyprus.

More familiar art historical versions of this motif generally show Venus lying or standing in a shell, as in works by Sandro Botticelli, Peter Paul Rubens, Bertel Thorvaldsen or Odilon Redon. She is also seen crouching or sitting. In 1926, four years before Matisse's *Vénus à la coquille*, Antoine Bourdelle sculpted a sitting Venus, knees pulled up and arms spread wide. In particular, however, study of Matisse's figure suggests comparison with *The Tub* (c. 1886) by Edgar Degas, a painting that shows the profane motif of a woman at her ablutions. Although Matisse may well have been familiar with these works, he himself refers to an equally profane but entirely different source image. During his sojourn in Tahiti in 1930, he saw a cloud formation that resembled a woman emerging out of the water. This image was the inspiration that same year of his first version of *Vénus à la coquille*, followed in 1932 by a second one.

Sitting erect in the shell, Venus has her legs pulled up, as in Bourdelle's work, the right leg more than the left, while her arms, raised behind her head, are sharply bent at the elbows, lending her a severe and yet aspiring attitude. The overall impression of the work takes precedence over the details, testifying to Matisse's overriding interest in the whole of his figures. However, his point of departure was not the displacement of space through mass but rather, as he often reiterated, the arabesque, that is, a linear, decorative motif, which enabled him to render a harmony of volume and space, form and rhythm. Already underpinning his early sculptures, the arabesque also figured prominently in the works of the 1930s, albeit in a form that was more abstract and compact.

Although *Vénus à la coquille* refurs to a mythological motif of antiquity, Matisse took a thoroughly modern approach to his iteration. As he declared in a conversation of 1912 with Clara T. MacChesney, "We of today are trying to express ourselves today – now – in the twentieth century – and not to copy what the Greeks saw and felt in art over two thousand years ago."

UW

Henri Matisse
Presages
1937

Henri Matisse
1869 Le Cateau-Cambrésis – 1954 Cimiez / Nice

Gouache and ink on paper, cut and pasted
Maquette for magazine cover of *Verve I*, no. 1, 1937
Inscribed on lower right margin: PRESAGES
36.5 × 55.5 cm

Inv. no. G31T / Acquired 2005

The Greek publisher E. Tériade and Matisse met in Paris in the late 1920s. In 1932 they issued their first publication together in the publishing house of Albert Skira. In 1937 Tériade launched the art magazine *Verve* with the backing of Coco Chanel and the American publisher David Smart. *Verve* was to be an intellectually ambitious and luxuriously designed magazine, containing original lithographs by the great artists of the day, like Picasso, Chagall, Matisse, Giacometti and Masson; texts by Jean-Paul Sartre, André Gide, Albert Camus, Ernest Hemingway and James Joyce; photographs by Henri Cartier-Bresson, Man Ray and Brassai; and also contributions on the art of the Middle Ages and antiquity. Tériade asked Henri Matisse to create a cover for the first issue. Matisse's design for the front and back of the cover took the shape of cut-outs intended for subsequent printing. These papiers découpés are collages made out of pieces of paper in vibrant colours. Matisse cut the shapes freehand with great mastery, initially using industrial paper. Later, his assistants would paint the paper from which he cut his shapes. "Instead of drawing and then applying paint," Matisse wrote, "I draw directly with the paint."

The colouring for the cover of *Verve* I features a harmony of saturated red and an intense dark blue, combined with black and white; red, blue and black provide the basic geometric structure, which is then playfully varied. White is used for the superimposed figurative arabesques but also for the background of a drawing depicting a dancer.

Dance is a central concern in Matisse's oeuvre. In 1909–10, he painted *La danse* (The Dance) a large-format panel of five figures orgiastically dancing in the flat, open space of the painting, where the abstract bodies are reduced to their expressive potential.
In combination with its counterpart *La musique* (The Music) of 1910, this painting has written art history; both works are now in the collection of the Hermitage in St. Petersburg. In 1932 Matisse painted his frieze of acrobatic dancers for the American collector Albert C. Barnes, which is now part of the Barnes Foundation in Philadelphia.

Matisse took inspiration both from contemporary dance and the art of antiquity, in particular the representations of athletes on vase paintings from Attica of the 5th century BC. The dancer in *Verve* I also brings to mind a rider in the Parthenon frieze; the figure seems rapidly painted, almost like a torso, and unites movement with harmony and balance. Framing white lines echo the movement, expanding the space of the figure. Matisse wrote the name of the magazine in black ink down the right margin, *présages*, but it was subsequently changed to the catchier *Verve*.

The back cover shows an arum lily or calla and two tulips, both originally exotic flowers. Calla lilies come from Africa and tulips are native to Central Asia. Many works by Matisse revealed his interest in exotic cultures and their flora. He travelled to northern Africa several times and also to Tahiti. The calla lily with its sensual, porcelain-like calyx has been charged with meaning ever since antiquity; the flower stands for beauty, elegance and luxury and, in Christianity, above all for purity. In ancient Rome it was a symbol of the summer solstice.

AS

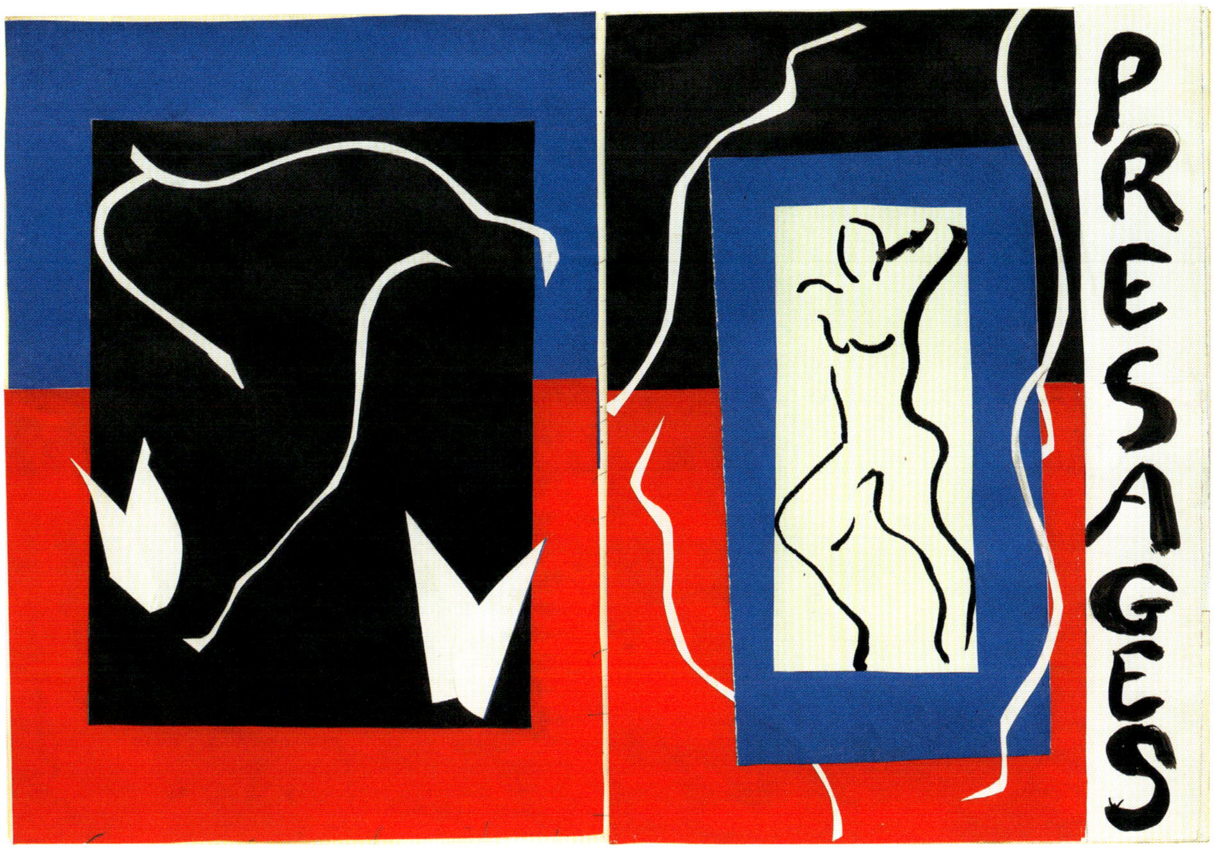
PRESAGES

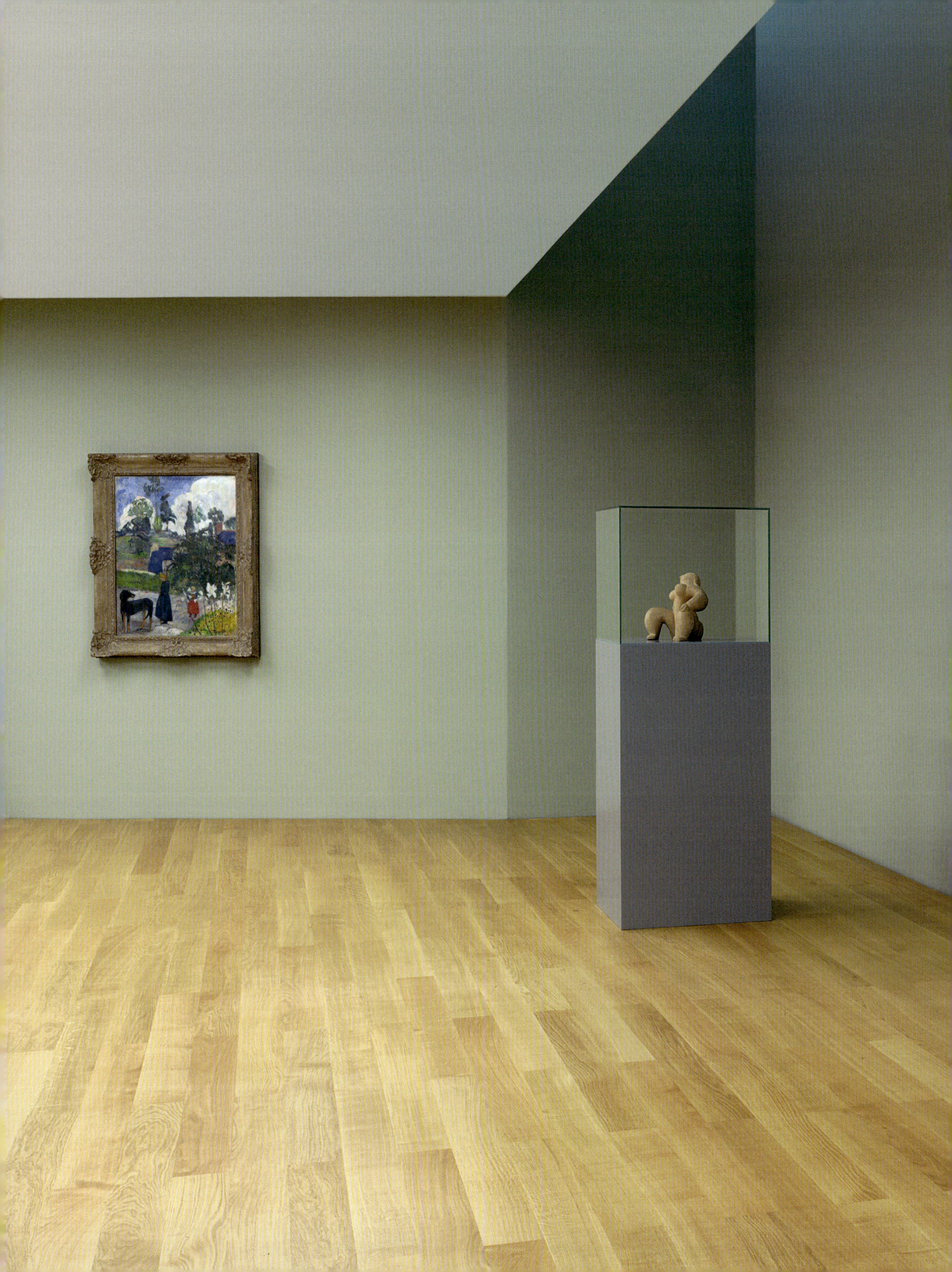

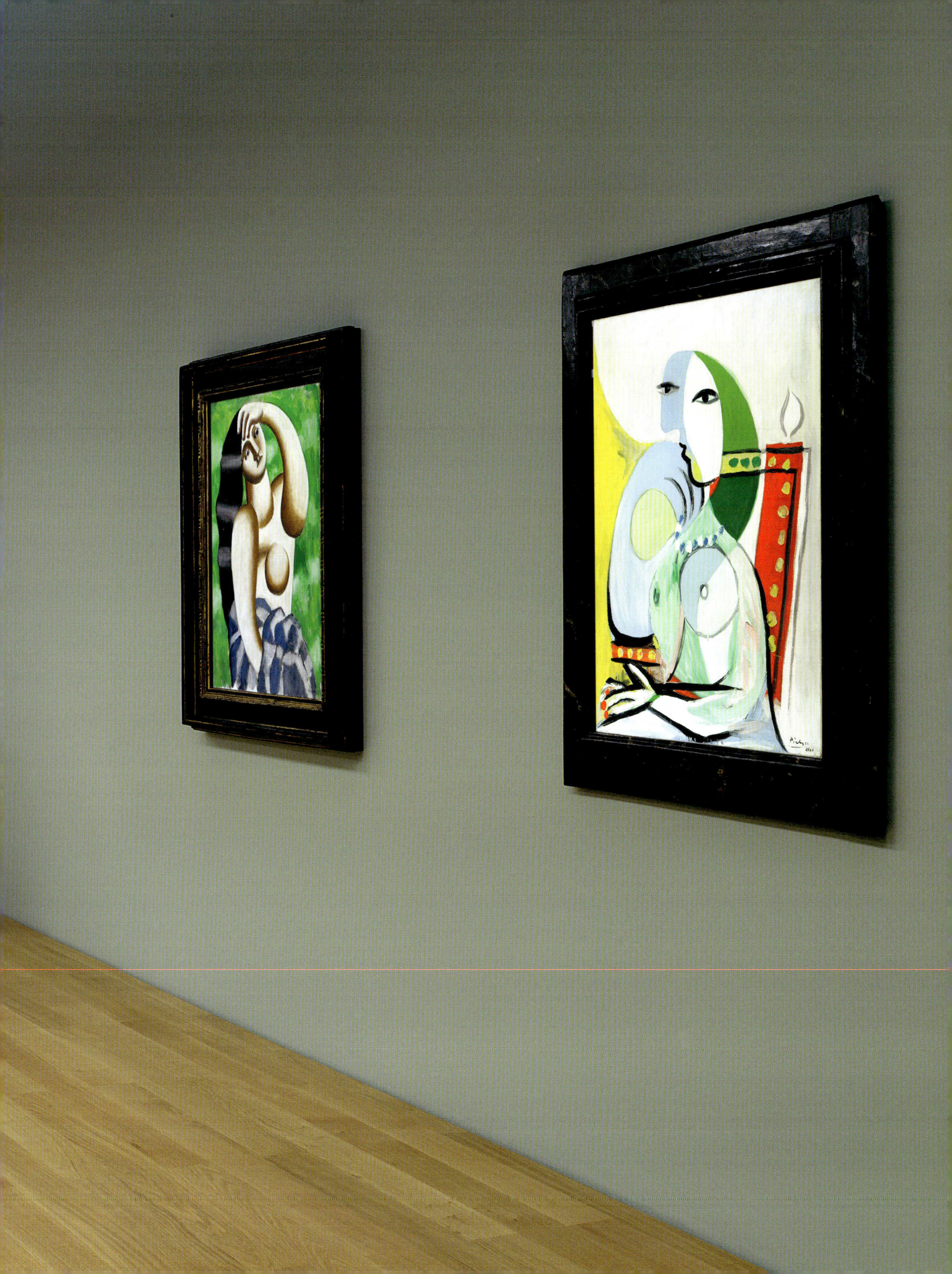

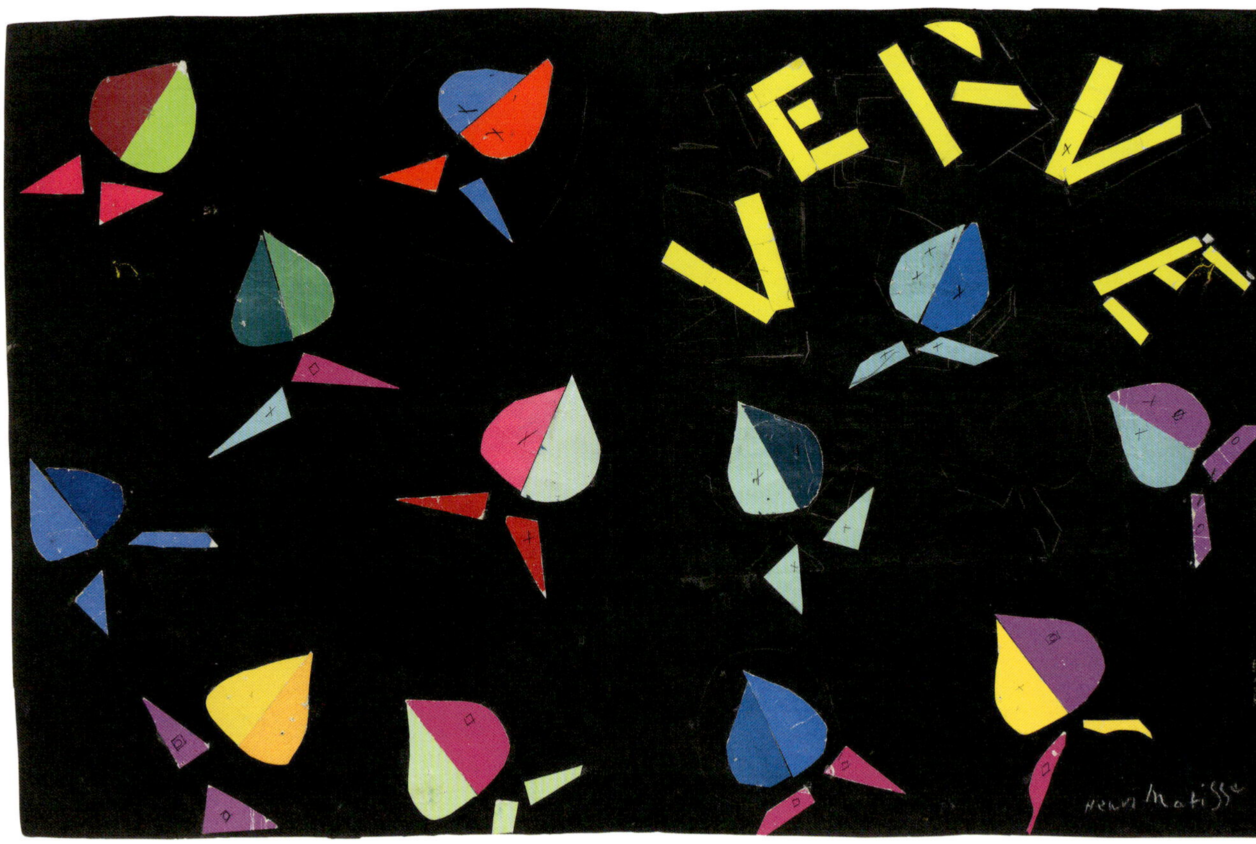
VERVE
Henri Matisse

Henri Matisse
1869 Le Cateau-Cambrésis –
1954 Cimiez / Nice

Coloured paper, cut and pasted
Maquette for magazine cover of *Verve II*, no. 8, 1940
Signed lower right: Henri Matisse
35.2 × 55.3 cm

Inv. no. G34T / Acquired 2012

Henri Matisse
Symphonie chromatique
1939

Matisse created the maquette for the cover of *Verve II*, no. 8 in August 1939, on the eve of the Second World War. In contrast to his first, traditional design (cat. 57), Matisse has scattered the colourful heart-shaped leaves on the cover, as if blown about by the wind. The motif is explained in the American edition: the artist had previously been interested primarily in the tree and its branches while now he is concerned with the artistic potential of the different leaves. Formally simplified, the shape of the leaves resembles those of linden, beech or fruit trees. Each of the leaves is unique. Made of differently coloured paper and divided down the middle, they present a colourful array on the black ground of the whole.

Matisse titled this design *Symphonie chromatique* in reference to the relationship between sound (in music) and colour (in art). The mutually stimulating relationship of music and painting was a popular phenomenon in the art of those times, as demonstrated not only by Matisse but also by Van Gogh, Signac, Gauguin, Kandinsky and many more. The colours in *Symphonie chromatique* form a whole comparable to the structure of serial music and also to that of J. S. Bach. "All of my colours," in the words of Matisse, "are sounds that come together like music."

AS

Henri Matisse
Composition, Jaune, Bleu et Noir
1947

059

Henri Matisse
1869 Le Cateau-Cambrésis –
1954 Cimiez / Nice

Gouache on paper, cut and pasted
Signed lower left: H Matisse
Verso: drawing in pencil of a reclining nude
47 × 34 cm

Inv. no. G65T / Acquired 2016

Matisse initially used cut-outs as an aid in designing stage sets, wall paintings and covers but they gradually outgrew their secondary, applied function and became part of his oeuvre as an independent genre. Thanks to its perfected development, the result of prolonged experience and, according to the artist, a perfect synthesis of drawing, painting and sculpture, the technique constitutes a late work that is incomparable in the history of 20th century art. In this genre, Matisse unites classical form with a decorative and indeed light-hearted, cheerful approach.

Composition, Jaune, Bleu et Noir is an autonomous, non-figurative work. The shape in the middle of the picture does suggest something vegetable, like most of the forms in the cut-outs that Matisse mounted on the wall of the Villa le Rêve in Vence, where he lived and worked from 1943 to 1948. They are a reflection not only of the lush flora that the artist encountered on a trip to Polynesia in 1930, but of his relationship to nature in general. In his cut-outs, he was always seeking aesthetically simplified equivalents for nature's diversity and rhythm.

As shown in a photograph of 1948, Matisse had originally included this work in the numerous, densely arrayed cut-outs mounted on the wall of a room in the Villa le Rêve. But a year later, as indicated in another photograph, he had already separated and framed them for the exhibition *Henri Matisse: Œuvres Récentes, 1947–48* at the Musée National d'Art Moderne in Paris. This cut-out also appears in a third photograph taken at Galerie Berggruen in Paris in 1953. Heinz Berggruen was the first and only dealer to exhibit Matisse's cut-outs in his lifetime.

UW

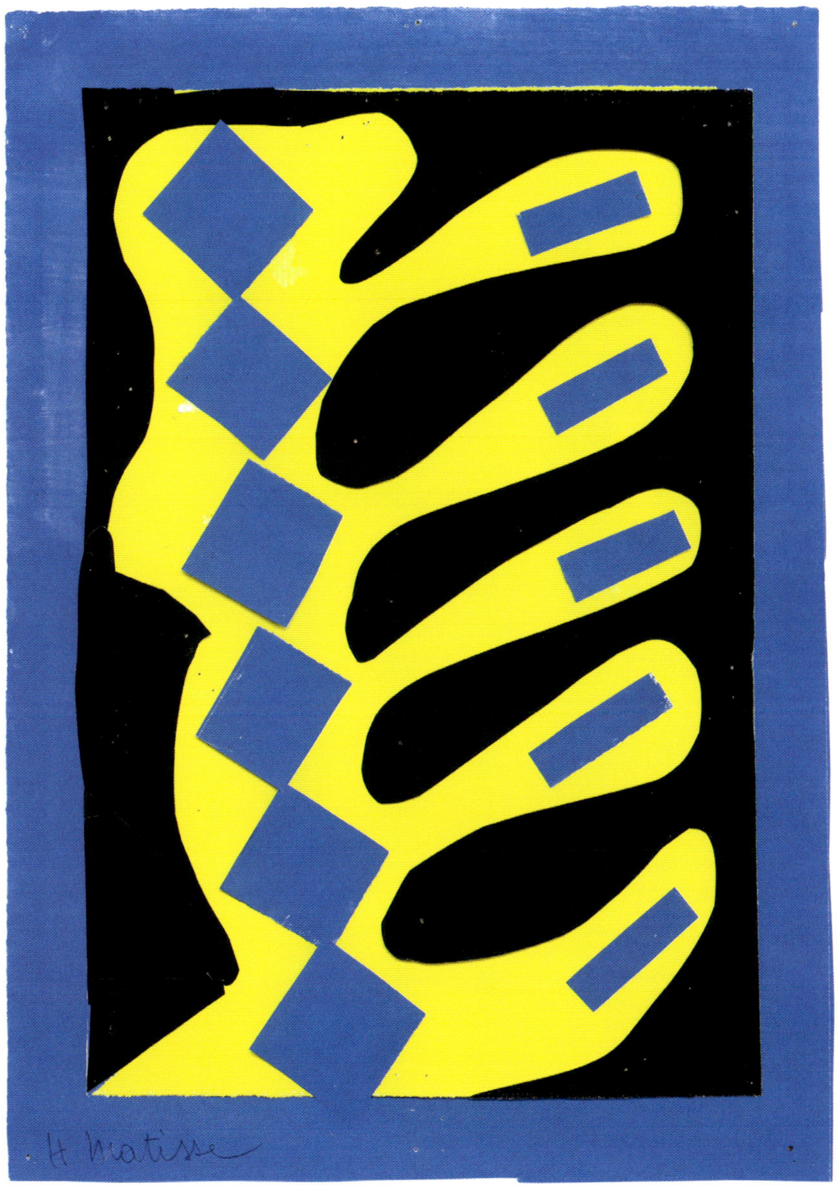
H. Matisse

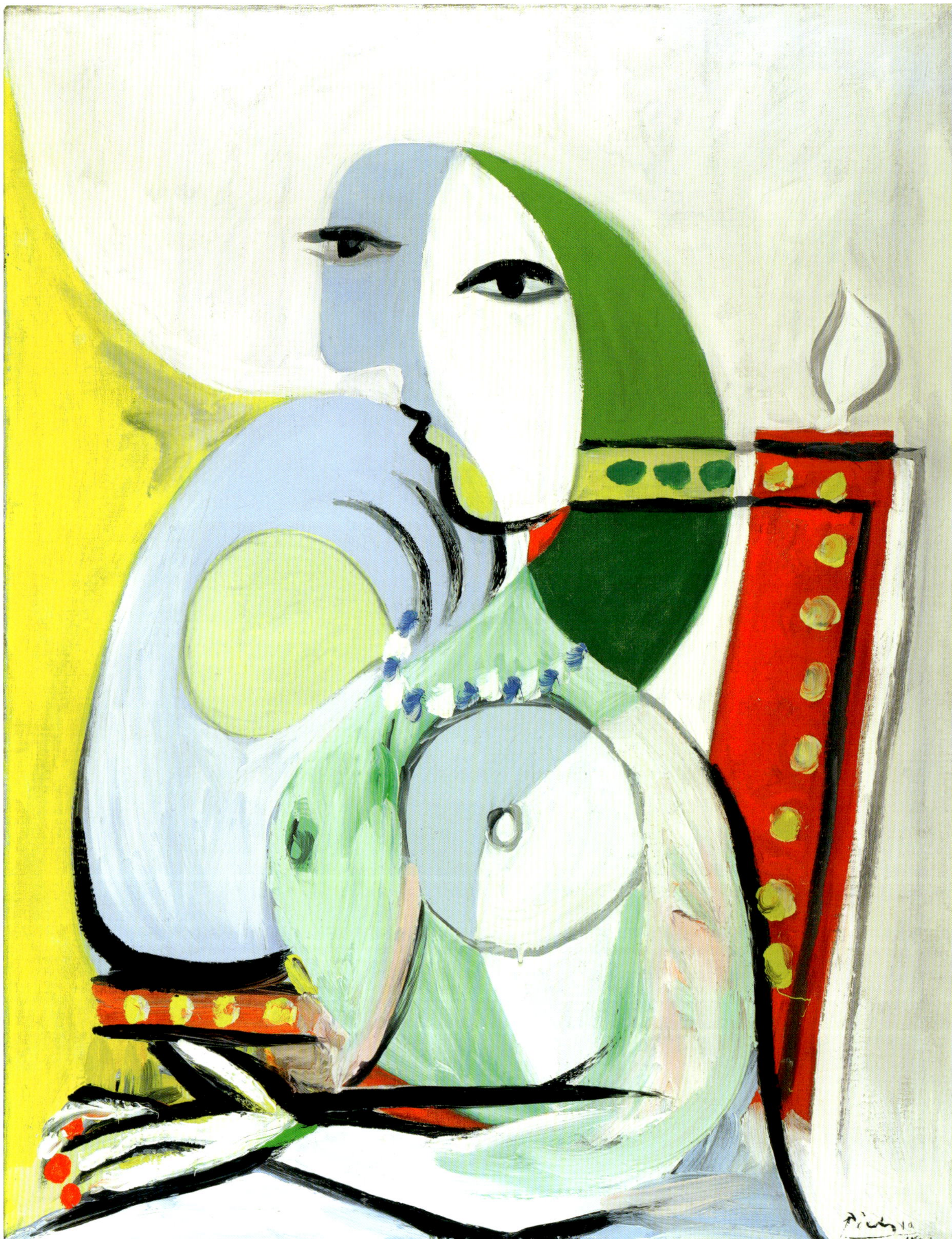

060

Pablo Picasso
1881 Málaga – 1973 Mougins / Cannes

Oil on canvas
Signed and dated lower right: Picasso XXXII
Inscribed and dated on verso:
Boisgeloup, 14 Août XXXII
92.1 × 73 cm

Inv. no. P25T / Acquired 2003

Pablo Picasso
Femme dans un fauteuil
1932

In 1931–32 Picasso painted several pictures of a young blonde woman, usually seen sitting and in some cases sleeping. In some of these paintings, the model that inspired Picasso can clearly be identified as Marie-Thérèse Walter. Her perfectly aquiline nose, giving her the look of an ancient Greek sculpture, made a profound impact on Picasso at their initial and now legendary encounter in front of the Lafayette department store in January 1927. Her youthful face first appeared in a few drawings, and her entire figure came to dominate many paintings in the years that followed. Through the hand of the artist, Marie-Thérèse's body undergoes virtuoso transformations from a blossoming Venus and a sleeping saint to an archaic sculpture.

Picasso painted this work, dated 14 August 1932, in Boisgeloup, the castle near Gisors northwest of Paris that he had purchased the year before. Marie-Thérèse is sitting in the nude in a Spanish armchair against a light yellow and off-white background, as if the wall were bathed in sunlight. The sitter, and in fact everything in the painting with the exception of the chair, is rendered in soft, rounded, and at times biomorphic shapes. The essentially static motif of a seated figure is animated by sweeping curves, obviously connoting femininity, in explicit contrast to the angular, "masculine" linearity of the chair. The movement is generated by the arrangement of the interrelated circular shapes and is heightened by the additional movement within the picture of the overlapping colours and shapes that mark the sitter's head and torso. Variations in painterly composition are seen, for instance, in the patches of spontaneous and expressive brushstrokes that alternate with "cool" smoothly painted sections. Subtle differences between top and bottom, distance and closeness, intellect and eros are combined with formal details, testifying to the artist's relationship to his model. The Spanish armchair, which may well mark the presence of the painter himself, shows a motif of upholstery tacks that is echoed in the pearl necklace and the red fingernails.

The yellow, green and mauve palette that typifies paintings of Marie-Thérèse alludes to her "natural" complexion, her blonde hair and blue eyes. The pertinent literature has also drawn attention to an artistic predecessor, Paul Gauguin's painting *Spirit of the Dead Watching* of 1892, which Picasso had seen in 1901 at the gallery of his Parisian dealer Ambroise Vollard. As in Picasso's *Femme dans un fauteuil*, the ghostly ancestor sitting next to the bed is pictured in profile with both eyes facing front. Despite her unmistakably erotic presence, Marie-Thérèse's "magic" eyes ultimately give her an aura of unattainability, characteristic of many other paintings by Picasso as well.

AS

Pablo Picasso
Figure, Femme de trois-quarts gauche
1934

Pablo Picasso
1881 Málaga – 1973 Mougins / Cannes

Oil on canvas
Inscribed and dated upper centre:
Boisgeloup 12 juillet XXXIV
55 × 33 cm

Inv. no. P51M / Acquired 1998

As in *Femme dans un fauteuil* (cat. 60), Marie-Thérèse Walter can also be identified as the model in *Figure, Femme de trois-quarts gauche*. Similarly painted in Boisgeloup, but almost 2 years later in July 1934, the composition is somewhat tighter. The bust, narrowly framed in vertical format, resembles a cameo. The head is rendered en face against a striped background, though shifted slightly into a three-quarter profile. Another profile has been inserted in the oval of the face. At first sight, it depicts the classical profile of Marie-Thérèse Walter, so famously, pointedly and repeatedly rendered by Picasso.

If we adopt the thesis proposed by Rubin and Rosenblum that Picasso is always personally present in his paintings, particularly in those of family and friends, the Hellenic profile could also represent the artist himself. This might be confirmed, for instance, by the painting *Les modistes* (Zervos VII, 2) of January 1926. But in the studio painting (Musée Picasso 111) of 1928–29, the artist also appears with a comparable classical profile. The interpretation of two superimposed "views" of model and painter is further reinforced by the gimlet and magic eyes, so characteristic of Picasso and not least the indication of a Harlequin pattern that is reiterated in head, neck and collar – the figure of the Harlequin was the artist's classical alter ego.

However, with the exception of the stripes in the background, the colours belong entirely to Marie-Thérèse. Purple and yellow dominate alongside green and blue as in many other portraits of Marie-Thérèse. On the other hand, the yellow stripes on the red and black ground take up the national colours of Spain and refer in turn to the artist, while the motif of stripes itself occasionally crops up in the pattern of Marie-Thérèse's clothing, for instance, in the famous *Portrait de Marie-Thérèse* (Zervos VIII, 324) of January 1927 at the Musée Picasso.

AS

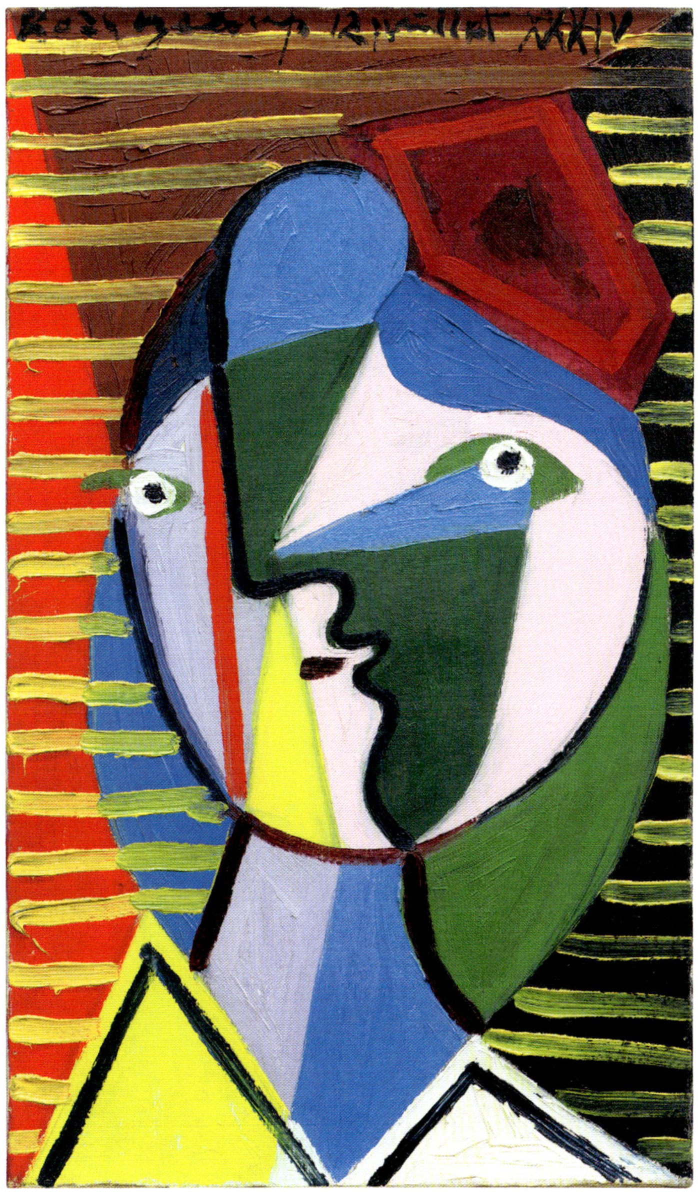

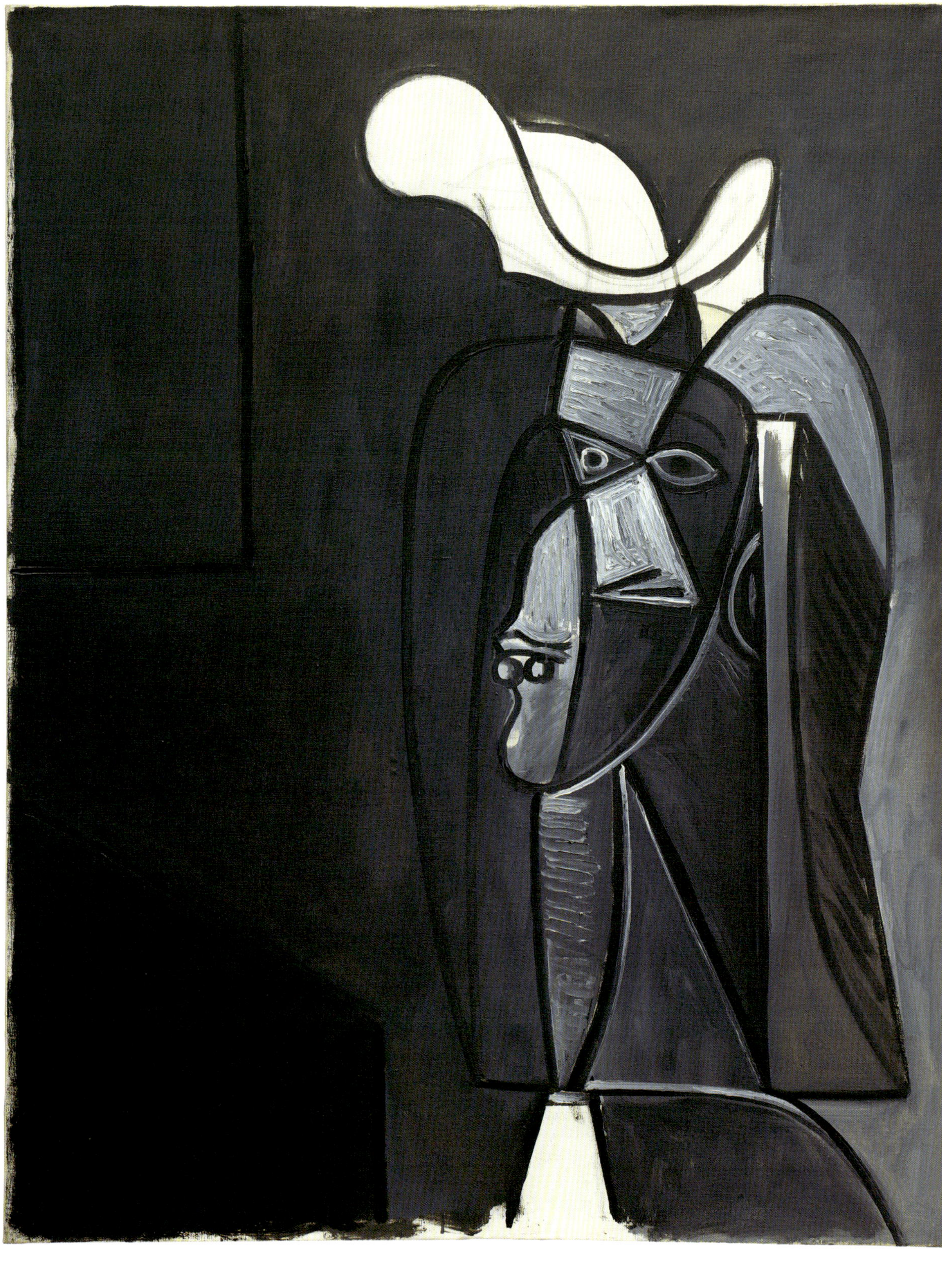

Pablo Picasso
1881 Málaga – 1973 Mougins / Cannes

Oil on canvas
Dated and inscribed on verso: 12.4.47. / II
92 × 73 cm

Inv. no. P76T / Acquired 2017

Pablo Picasso
Visage gris foncé au chapeau blanc
1947

Picasso painted *Visage gris foncé au chapeau blanc* (*Femme au chapeau*) during his approximately ten-year partnership (1943–1953) with Françoise Gilot. She was pregnant at the time and gave birth to their son Claude just a few weeks later on 15 May 1947.

Unlike the war years in the early 1940s, which meant occupation and constrained living and working conditions in Paris, the post-war years meant political optimism, flourishing artistic endeavour and new personal relationships. Nonetheless, Picasso was repeatedly the target of criticism from a nationalistic French press and art scene, which took umbrage with his style and his depiction of the human body. Untold variations on the human body and the head testify to Picasso's creative energy, described by Werner Spies as trying out "every conceivable modality of deformation". In portraying and characterising specific individuals, the artist was not necessarily bent on achieving a discernible likeness.

In contrast to the vibrant colours seen in the two portraits of Marie-Thérèse Walter in the collection of the Hilti Art Foundation (cat. 60 and 61), *Visage gris foncé au chapeau blanc* is restricted to a dark palette in black and white. Picasso pictures a woman with a white hat saucily perched on her head, setting a strong accent against the almost black ground of the painting. The artist had a penchant for painting his models with extravagant headgear, a liking fostered particularly by Dora Maar, his mistress from 1936 until 1943, when he met Françoise Gilot. Maar much enjoyed sporting the great variety of hats made by her mother, a fashion designer.

Visage gris takes both a linear and sculptural turn while the colouring clearly follows a painterly trajectory. In keeping with the multiple views of Cubism, eyes, nose and profile point in entirely different directions. The mouth features conspicuously, taking the shape of two circles, a device first introduced in a portrait of Marie-Thérèse Walter (1932). More explicitly accentuated in the portraits of Françoise Gilot after 1944, circles begin to appear as delicate parts of the lower lip and as highlights, before gradually acquiring a life of their own and finally representing the lower lip altogether, without any additional contours.

The pictorial space is cryptically implied by the mere hint of a window, a mirror or a picture frame, as well as a piece of square furniture. It communicates an atmosphere of silence without resonance. Unlike Renaissance and Baroque portraits, the composition does not lead to a unity of figure, space and outside world. Quite the opposite: the sitter, isolated in stark, hermetic darkness, is thrown back on herself. This ultimately existential situation, at an infinite remove from time, acts as a stark foil for the coquettish and short-lived trendiness of the hat. The artist's delight in extravagant shapes applies not only to the hat but, in playful irony, to the deformed physiognomy of the face as well. Although this face brooks no psychological reading and is, in fact, open to any interpretation, it is clearly informed with an expression of alert existential awareness.

UW

Pablo Picasso
Hibou sur une chaise
1947

063

Pablo Picasso
1881 Málaga – 1973 Mougins / Cannes

Oil on canvas
Signed upper left: Picasso
Dated on verso: 20.1.47
73 × 60.4 cm

Inv. no. P28T / Acquired 2004

"Pablo loved to surround himself with birds and animals. In general, they were exempt from the suspicion with which he regarded his other friends." Thus does Françoise Gilot, Picasso's one-time partner, write about him in her book *Life with Picasso* (1964). She immediately follows up that remark with a description of photographer Michel Sima, who lived and worked at Château Grimaldi in Antibes from July to December 1946. While there, he brought the artist an injured owl that he had found in a corner of the premises. Picasso and Gilot bandaged the bird and ended up taking it along to Paris. Looking after the bird gradually led to a mutual rapport. While Sima recorded the encounter in photographs, Picasso produced numerous paintings, lithographs and drawings of the owl, testifying to his deep affection for the animal.

Hibou sur une chaise (Owl on a Chair, 20 January 1947) pictures the bird, now recovered, in Picasso's flat on Rue des Grands Augustins in Paris. It is perched on the back of a chair, presumably in front of a window or a door that is ajar. In other variations on the theme, it seems to be a mirror. The owl, in deep blue, is set off against the lighter hues of the multi-angular background, which echoes the constructions of Cubism and obscures the perspective of the space. Viewers are drawn above all to the owl's eyes, its black pupils surrounded by a luminous white. Picasso may have seen in them an affinity with his own eyes, to which has been ascribed not only a sharpness of vision but a positively magical impact on others. Ten years later, in 1957, on the occasion of the American photographer David Douglas Duncan's visit, Picasso drew a picture of an owl on a piece of paper, cut out the eyes and held the paper up to his face like a mask. By looking at the photographer through the mask, it is as if he were presenting a portrait of himself as an owl. Duncan placed the photograph he took at that time on the cover of his book *Goodbye Picasso*, published in 1974, a year after the artist passed away.

Over the years, Picasso paid tribute to the owl in a variety of genres – painting, lithography, drawing, sculpture and ceramics. In addition to this painting, the collection of the Hilti Art Foundation holds two prints (lithographs) by Picasso on the same subject.
UW

064

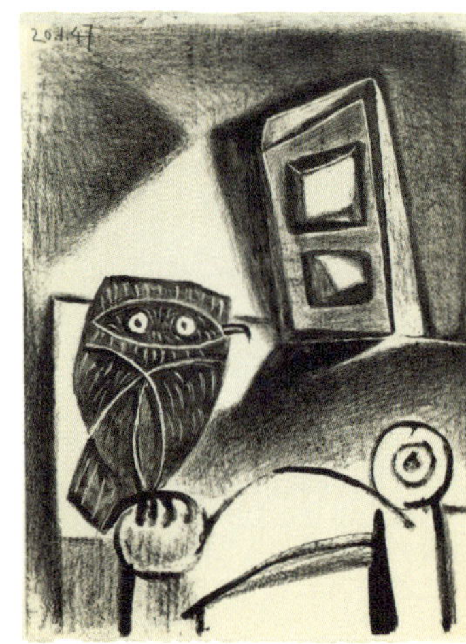

065

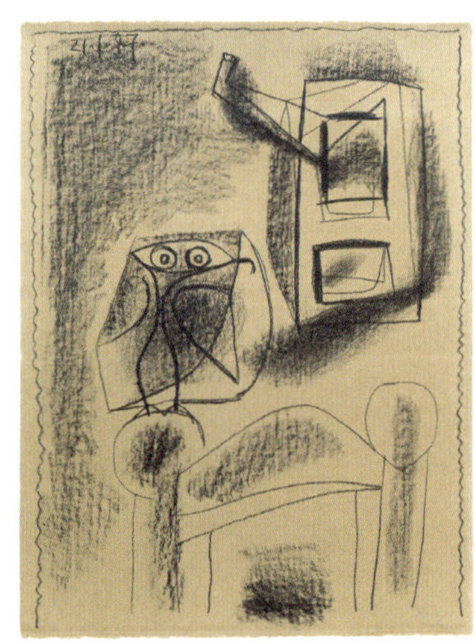

For details, see p.227

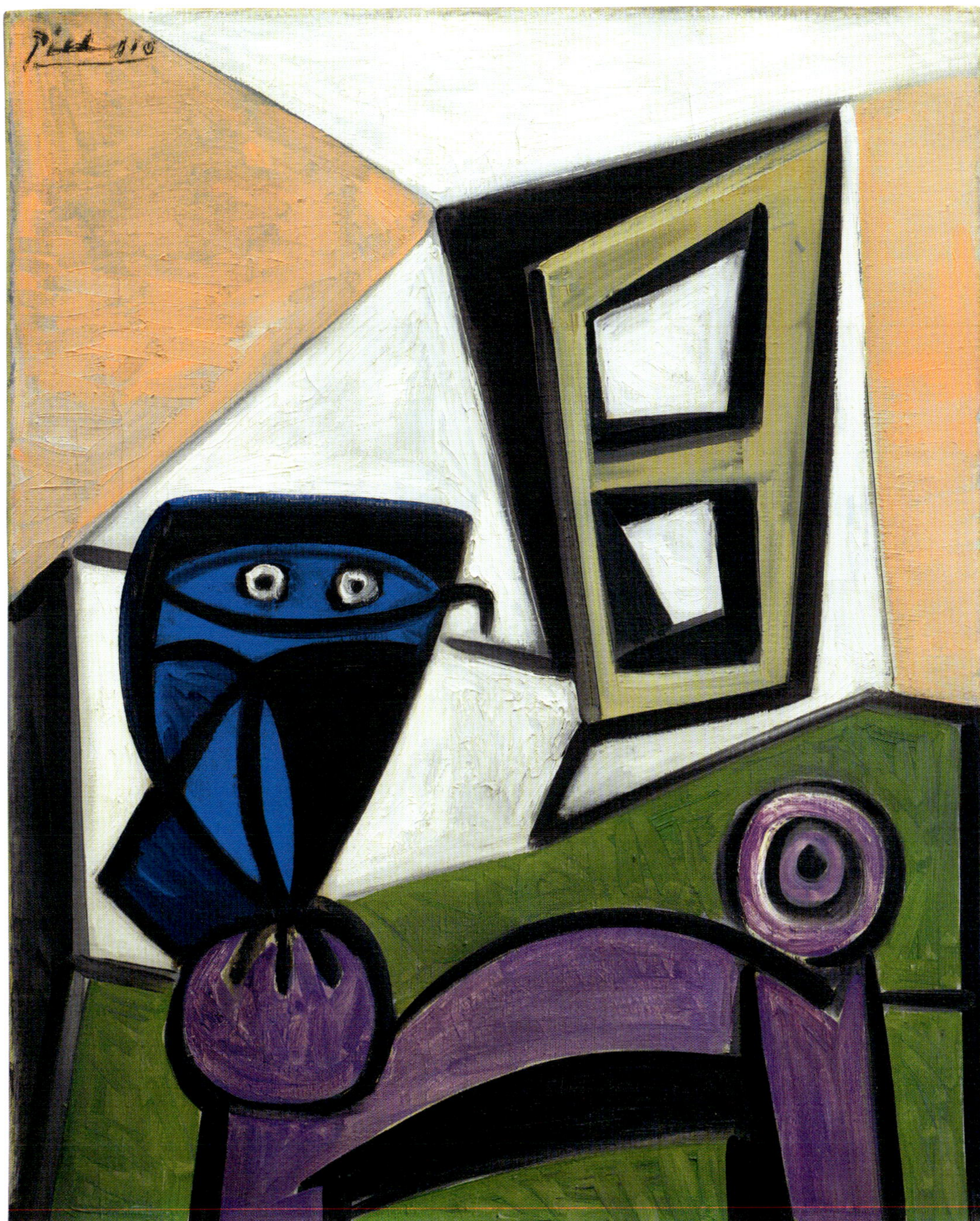

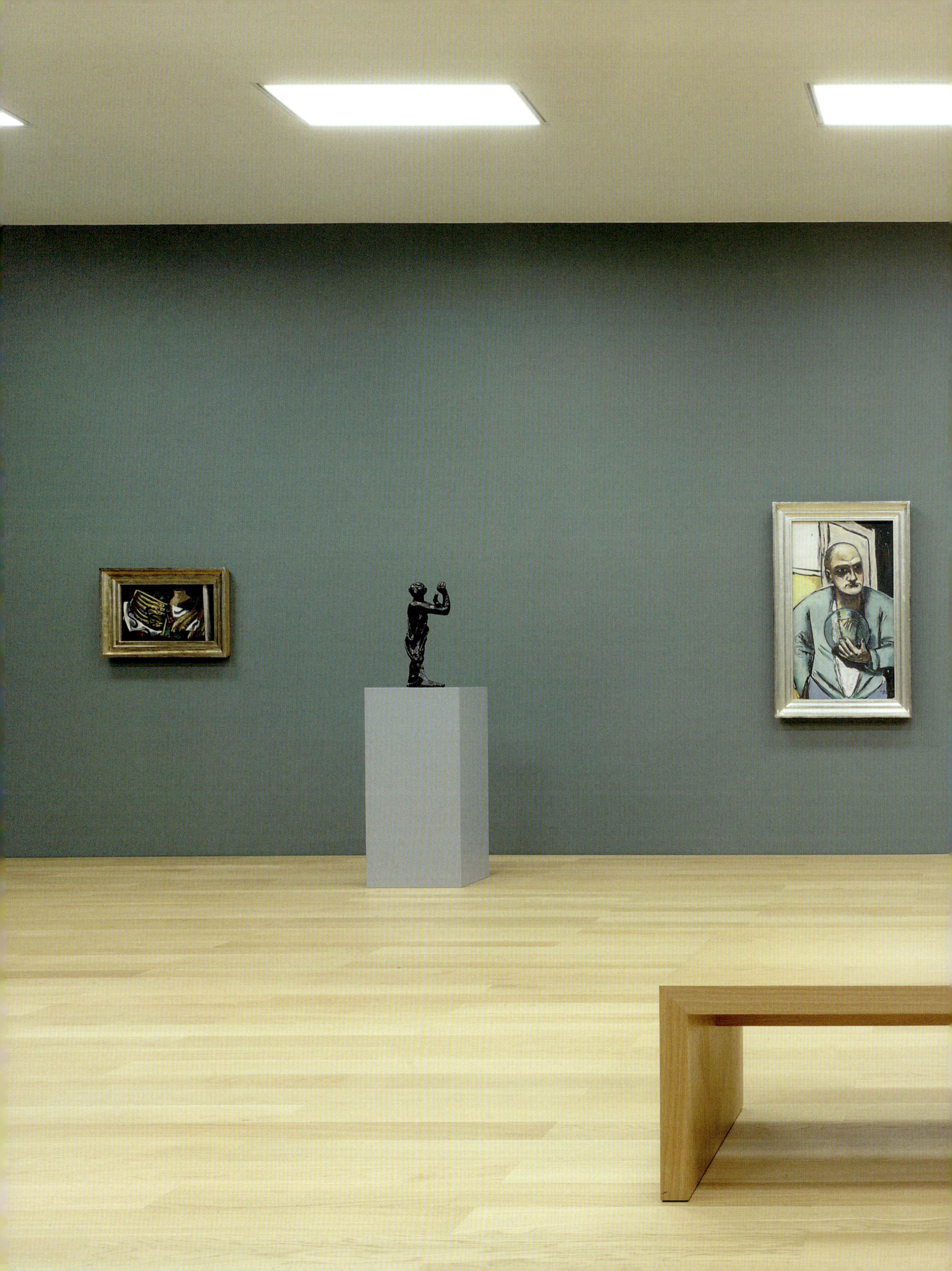

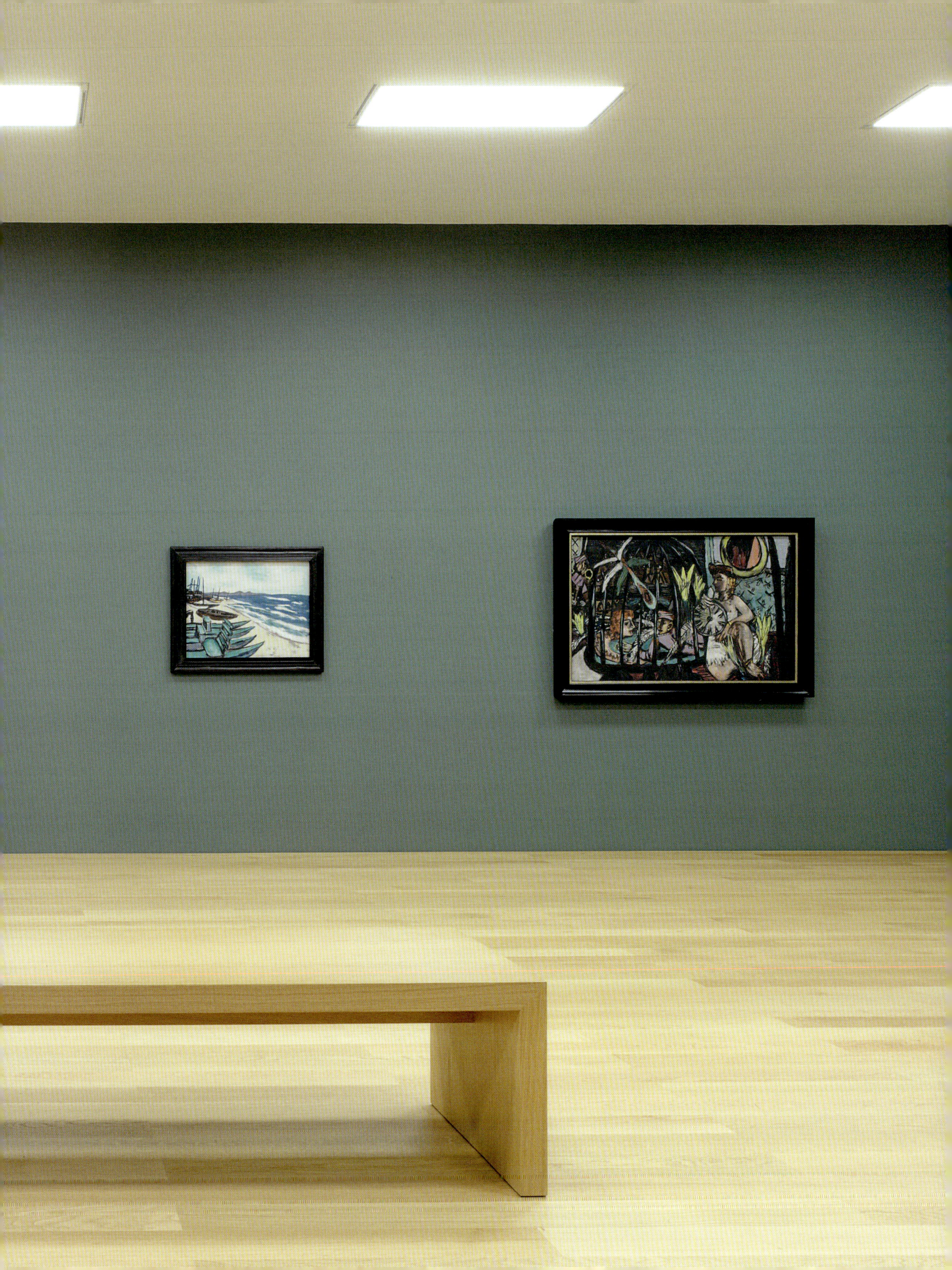

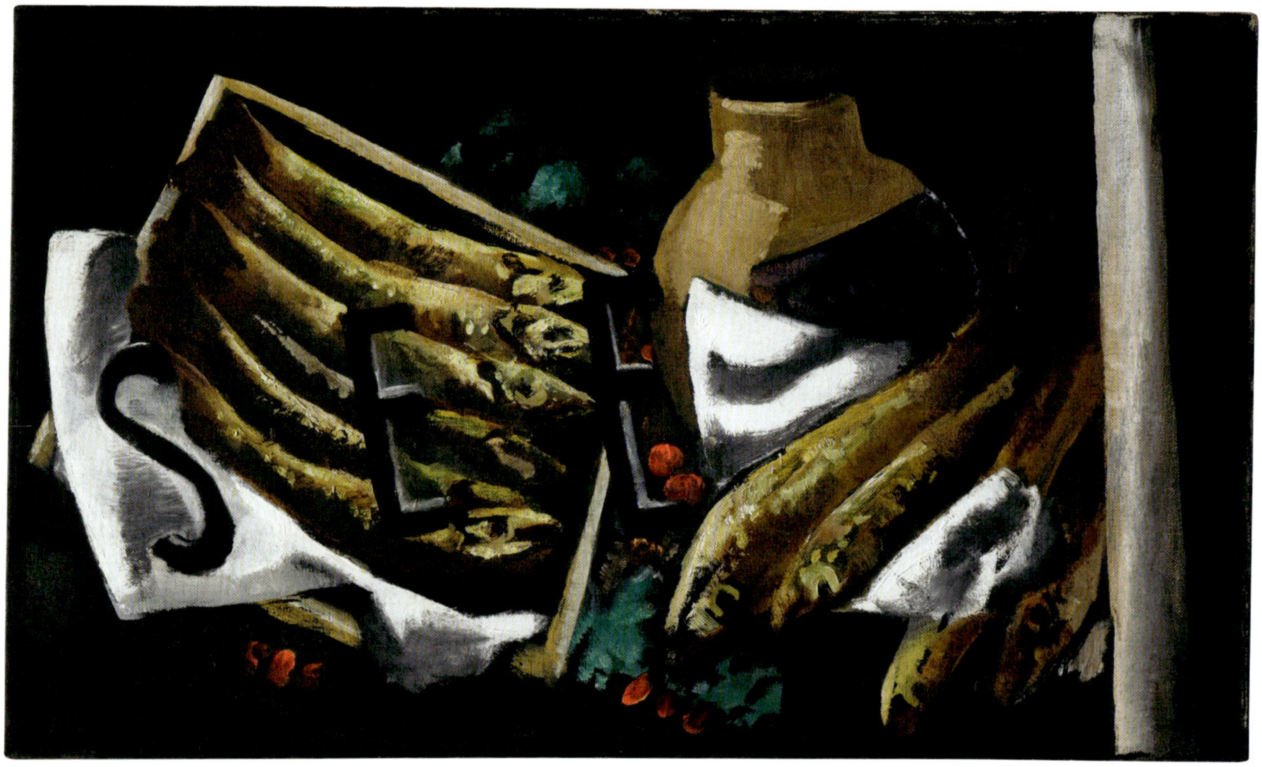

066

Max Beckmann
Bücklinge
1928

Max Beckmann
1884 Leipzig – 1950 New York

Oil on canvas
34 × 59 cm

Inv. no. P58T / Acquired 2013

In memory of the former owner of this painting, the German art collector, art dealer and journalist Alfred Flechtheim (1878–1937), who was forced to leave his country in 1933.

Max Beckmann painted the still life *Bücklinge* (Kippers) in Frankfurt am Main, where he settled in 1915 and, after marrying Mathilde (Quappi) von Kaulbach in 1925, took over a master class at the Städelsches Kunstinstitut. Beckmann had his first major retrospective at the Städtische Kunsthalle in Mannheim in 1928, the same year that he made this painting.

It was not until 1926 and after years of experience that he turned to the genre of the still life in addition to his long-standing interest in figure painting. He invested the tangible objects of reality depicted in his paintings with meanings that transcend their visible appearance and allude to the great themes of life: eros, passion, happiness, knowledge, faith, fear and death. The small format painting *Bücklinge* is no exception.

Beckmann's expressive formal idiom in this work combines the achievements of Cézanne's art with synthetic Cubism. The lettering S E E, which runs at a slant across the picture from left to right, not only draws attention to the fundamental distinction between image and word, but also to two levels of spatial perception: we see a still life composition of fish along with the cloth, the jug and scattered cherries, as well as the fictional window of a fishmonger with the lettered advertising. Fish and cherries can be interpreted as food for use but also as an allusion to the masculine and feminine, the latter reinforced by the jug that contains cherry brandy and thus refers to the spiritualization (or evaporation?) of matter. The Vanitas notion underlies this composition and, in fact, the still life in general, for all things earthly are transient.

The strictly serial arrangement of the kippers, squeezed side-by-side into a wooden box with their heads facing the stoneware jug, lends the image a hint of aggression that is heightened by the strong contrast of light and dark colours. Red, green, ochre and purple accents enliven the composition and underscore the exceptional, painterly quality of the work as a whole.
UW

Max Beckmann
Mann im Dunkeln
1934

067

Max Beckmann
1884 Leipzig – 1950 New York

Bronze
(cast between 1958 and 1968)
Height: 56.7 cm

Inv. no. S179M / Acquired 2007

In the spring of 1933, the Nazis relieved Beckmann of his post as professor at the Städelschule in Frankfurt although he had already moved to Berlin in January, hoping that the large, anonymous city would enable him to work undisturbed and in peace. From 1933 to 1937, he created a number of important paintings, including the triptych *Abfahrt* (Departure, 1932–33), *Versuchung des Heiligen Antonius* (Temptation of St. Anthony, 1936–37) and *Selbstbildnis mit Glaskugel* (Self-Portrait with Crystal Ball, cat. 68), as well as six of the eight sculptures that he made during his lifetime. Beckmann may have turned to sculpture for several reasons. His lifelong interest in people and in the philosophical implications of space – its darkness, uncertainty and infinitude but also the home of the gods – may well have played a role. In addition, the physical reality of sculpture lends itself more easily to rendering a message than the complexity of paintings. The artist created *Mann im Dunkeln* (Man in the Dark) in 1934, the year he turned fifty. It is the first of the sculptures that he fashioned in a small room adjoining his studio in Berlin. His landlord, a trained caster, made the plaster mould for him. The bronze cast was produced posthumously (between 1958 and 1968) at the Roman Bronze Works, a foundry in New York. Measuring fifty-eight centimetres in height, it stands in contrast to the over life-sized, pseudo-heroic figures of official Nazi art. Friedhelm Fischer writes, "Once you have seen *Mann im Dunkeln*, you will not forget him." The entire energy of the sculpture is concentrated in the figure's extremities, in the oversized feet and the expressive hands. Although clothed in a toga-like garment, the figure does not evoke antiquity. Holding his hands in front of him, he is protecting himself against the menace of the unknown, which he cannot consciously perceive for his face is turned away and his eyes are closed. Even so, we feel as if the wandering man is looking into an abyss, a sleepwalker, unable or unwilling to confront what he divines.

We know that Beckmann did not think of himself as a political artist but his letters and the entries in his diary clearly indicate that he was acutely aware of the terrible menace of events looming around him. In this context, *Mann im Dunkeln* becomes a devastatingly prophetic commentary on what has now become history. However, Beckmann's interests were larger: transcending the specific historical moment, he sought to represent the invisible forces that beleaguer humankind. In Amsterdam, in a diary entry from 1940, the artist noted, "One thing is certain, pride and defiance in the face of invisible forces shall prevail regardless of the worst to come."

AS

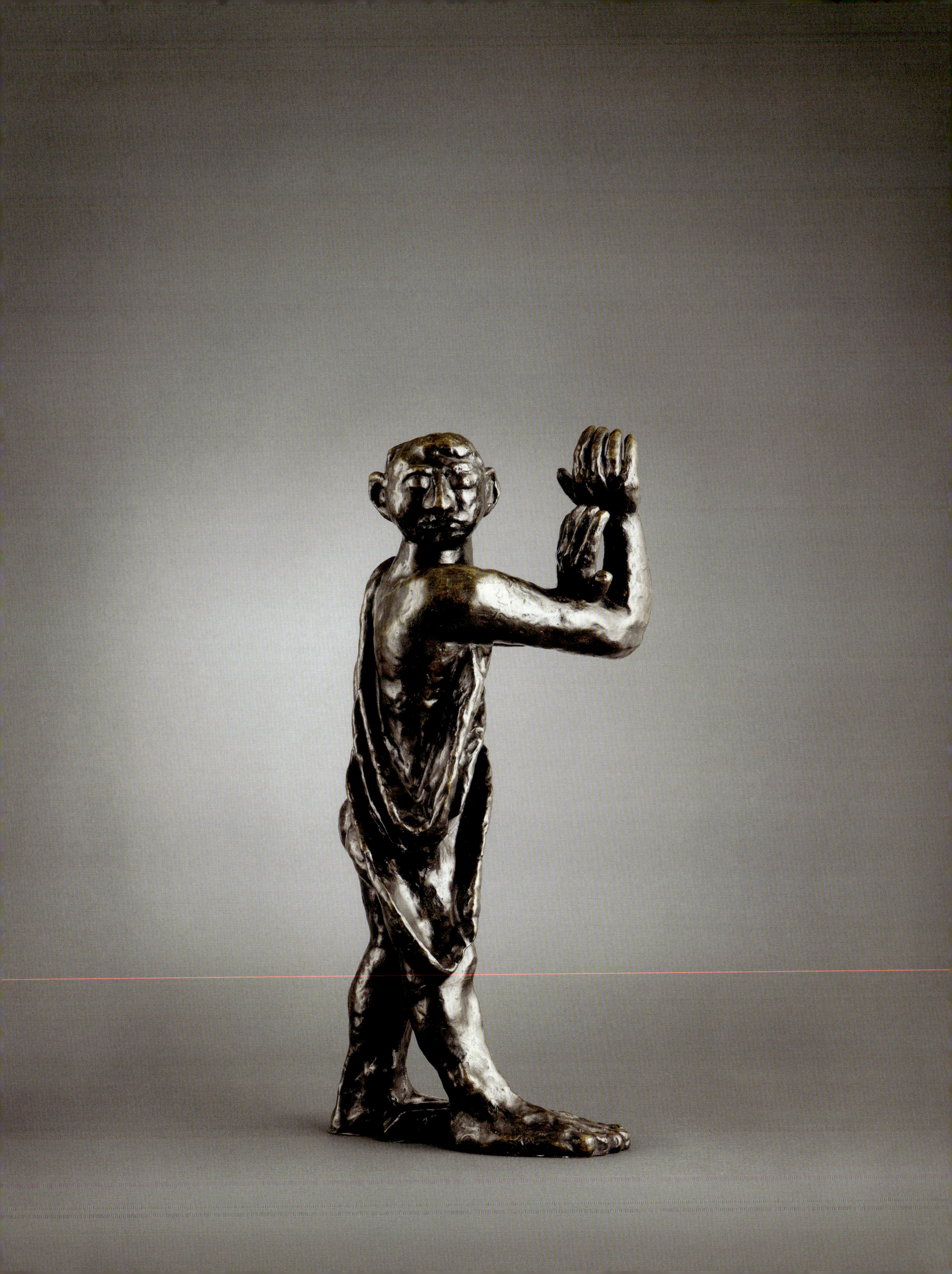

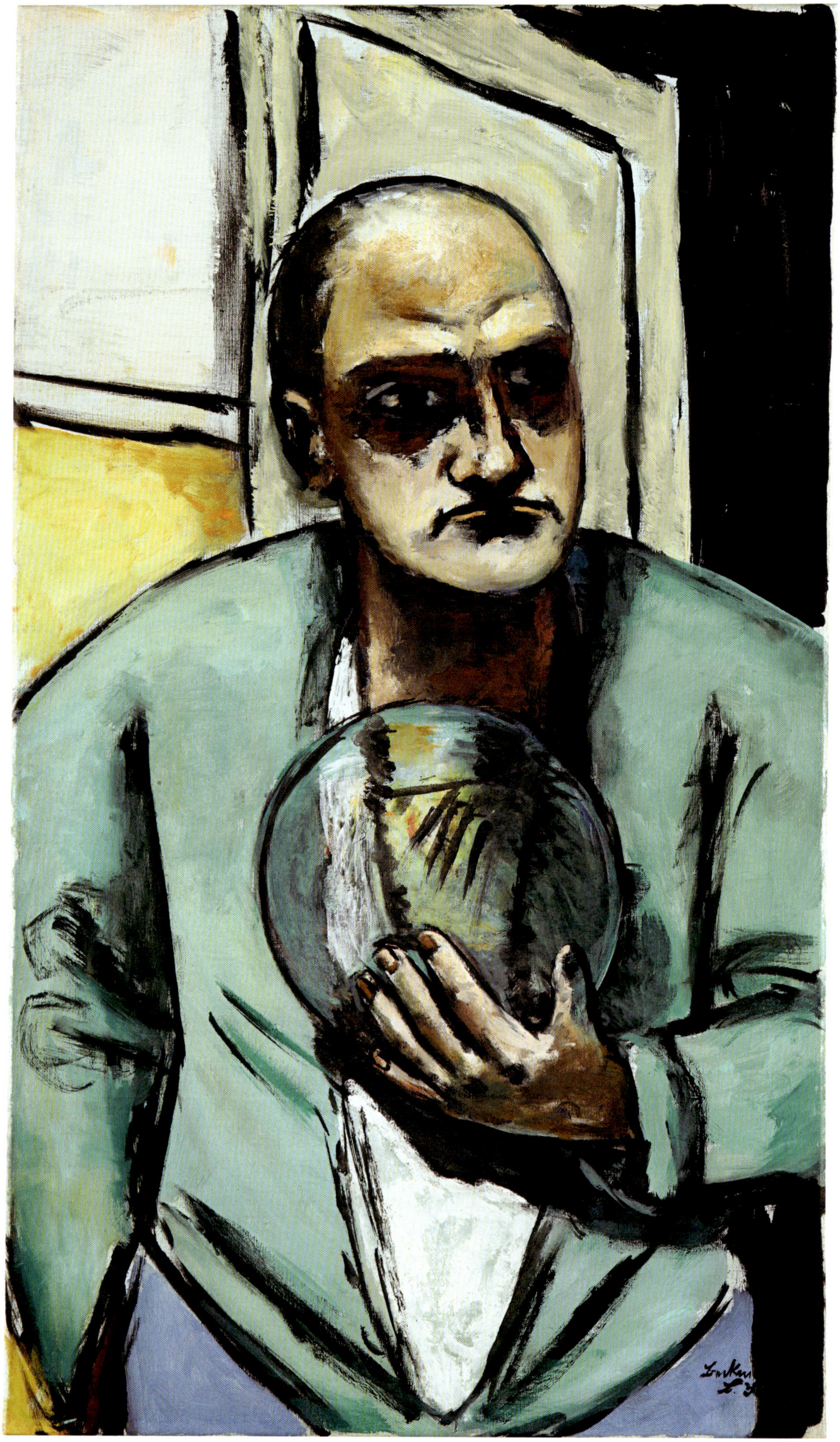

Max Beckmann
Selbstbildnis mit Glaskugel
1936

Max Beckmann
1884 Leipzig – 1950 New York

Oil on canvas
Inscribed lower right in German script:
Beckmann B. 36
110.2 × 64.4 cm

Inv. no. P62T / Acquired 2014

In the course of his artistic career, from his youth until his death, Max Beckmann repeatedly portrayed himself in drawings, prints, paintings and sculptures. Like the self-portraits of other great artists, these works bear witness to the physical appearance and mental state of a creative person within the context of ever-changing life circumstances. Reflecting these circumstances, marked by artistic success as well as private and social recognition, but even more so by two world wars, professional banishment, exile and emigration, Beckmann depicts himself in a diversity of attitudes: self-confident or vulnerable, sublime or devastated, argumentative or melancholic, clear-sighted or gloomy. But no matter how he related to the "Lord's great, eternally changing world theatre" with all its passions and longings, conflicts and miseries, his interest in the "mystery of being", which always included himself, never waned.

When he painted his *Selbstbildnis mit Glaskugel* (Self-Portrait with Crystal Ball) in 1936, Beckmann was still living in Berlin but considering emigration to the United States. Three years earlier, shortly after the Nazi party had come to power in Germany, he had been relieved of his teaching post at the Städelschule in Frankfurt. He was slandered in the press for his "degenerate" art, and his paintings were removed from the walls of Berlin's Kronprinzenpalais, a section of the National Gallery of Modern and Contemporary Art.

He did not succeed in immigrating to the United States. But in 1937, immediately after Hitler's radio speech in Munich on the opening of the *Grosse Deutsche Kunstausstellung*, Beckmann and his wife fled Berlin and settled in Amsterdam, which was occupied by German troops in 1940. After ten years of oppressive exile, they finally immigrated to the United States on 19 August 1947.

This brief biographical sketch reveals the circumstances under which Max Beckmann painted his *Selbstbildnis mit Glaskugel*. What would follow the extremely bleak present? To investigate the future the artist uses a crystal ball, an instrument of divination, turning himself into a seer and a soothsayer. Max Beckmann had always been responsive, across eras and cultures, to anything that would further knowledge and insight into the various guises of reality. His reading encompassed religion, philosophy, mythology and belles lettres. Esotericism and occultism captivated him. Anything of significance could become the subject matter of his art.

The crystal ball quietly rests in his hand, gently pressed against his chest. Light falls on his face and on his high forehead, but his eyes are deep in shadow. His grave, pensive gaze looks both inwards and out into the dark room that fades into infinity and uncertainty beyond the looming figure of the artist and the open door behind him, which frames his head like a nimbus. By eliminating all narrative detail, Beckmann, seen only with the attribute of a seer and soothsayer, appears suspended from the reality of the times. He has devoted his painting to the timeless subject matter of the unswerving recognition of truth with both mind and eye. This challenging work of art lends the artist a near prophetic aura. Hölderlin, one of the many writers in Beckmann's library, once wrote, "Yet in the man a god has his dwelling, too, so that he sees what is past and to come." This thought reverberates in Max Beckmann's paintings.

UW

Max Beckmann
Strand mit Booten an der Riviera
1938

069

Max Beckmann
1884 Leipzig – 1950 New York

Oil on canvas
Signed lower right in German script:
Beckmann A. 38
60.5 × 80 cm

Inv. no: P38T / Acquired 2008

When Max Beckmann painted *Strand mit Booten an der Riviera* (Beach with Boats on the Riviera) in 1938, he did not work en plein air but in the solitude of his studio in Amsterdam, as indicated by the "A. 38" that follows his signature in the lower right-hand margin of the picture. The artist and his wife Quappi had already fled Nazi Germany the year before and were living in exile in the Netherlands (see also cat. nos. 67 and 68). They took several trips from there within Europe, including a trip to France, until their travels came to an abrupt halt for eight years with the outbreak of the Second World War in September 1939.

In August 1938 Beckmann travelled with his friend, collector and patron Stephan Lackner to the French Mediterranean. In the course of their journey they came across the scene pictured in this painting. The exact location is not known but a black-and-white photograph found among the papers of Quappi Beckmann testifies to the fact that the subject matter was not artistic invention but a real site. Beckmann had in fact based his painting on the photograph. In addition to photographs he would occasionally use postcards as source material for his work in the studio. In comparison to the photograph, his composition and subject matter heighten the drama of the scene. Turquoise blue pedal boats are pulled up at the shore, their pointed hulls facing the breakers of an equally turquoise blue sea. Other boats line the shore, among them four sailing boats with masts, as well as buildings and cranes that may be part of a boatyard or a harbour. A few people can be distinguished in the middle distance, and the range of hills marking the horizon line slopes gently down to the sea where the smoke of two steamers billows up into the cloudy, overcast skies.

Beckmann's paintings of the French Riviera between Bandol and Cap Martin give an insight into the sensual and spiritual impressions the exiled artist retained through his encounter with life and landscape on the Mediterranean. They are images of memory, fulfilment and anticipation. In 1939, following his last trip before the war erupted, he wrote to Lackner that the colouring of all his "nerves and ideas" had changed, so much so that he had quite enough to do in his studio for the next 20 years. Beckmann's reaction to the sea was particularly intense; it was both a real and symbolic space of physical and spiritual unboundedness. In *My Theory of Painting*, a speech that he gave in London on 21 July 1938 shortly before making this picture, he remarked, "Often, very often, I am alone. My studio in Amsterdam, an enormous old tobacco store-room, is again filled in my imagination with figures from the old days and from the new, like an ocean by storm and sun and always present in my thoughts. Then shapes become beings and seem comprehensible to me in the great void and uncertainty of the space which I call God."

On his first journey after the war with his wife Quappi in March 1947, Max Beckmann immediately went to Nice on the French Riviera again. In August of that year, they left Europe for good, boarding a ship for the United States, a journey the artist had already wanted to undertake in 1936. He died there in 1950.

UW

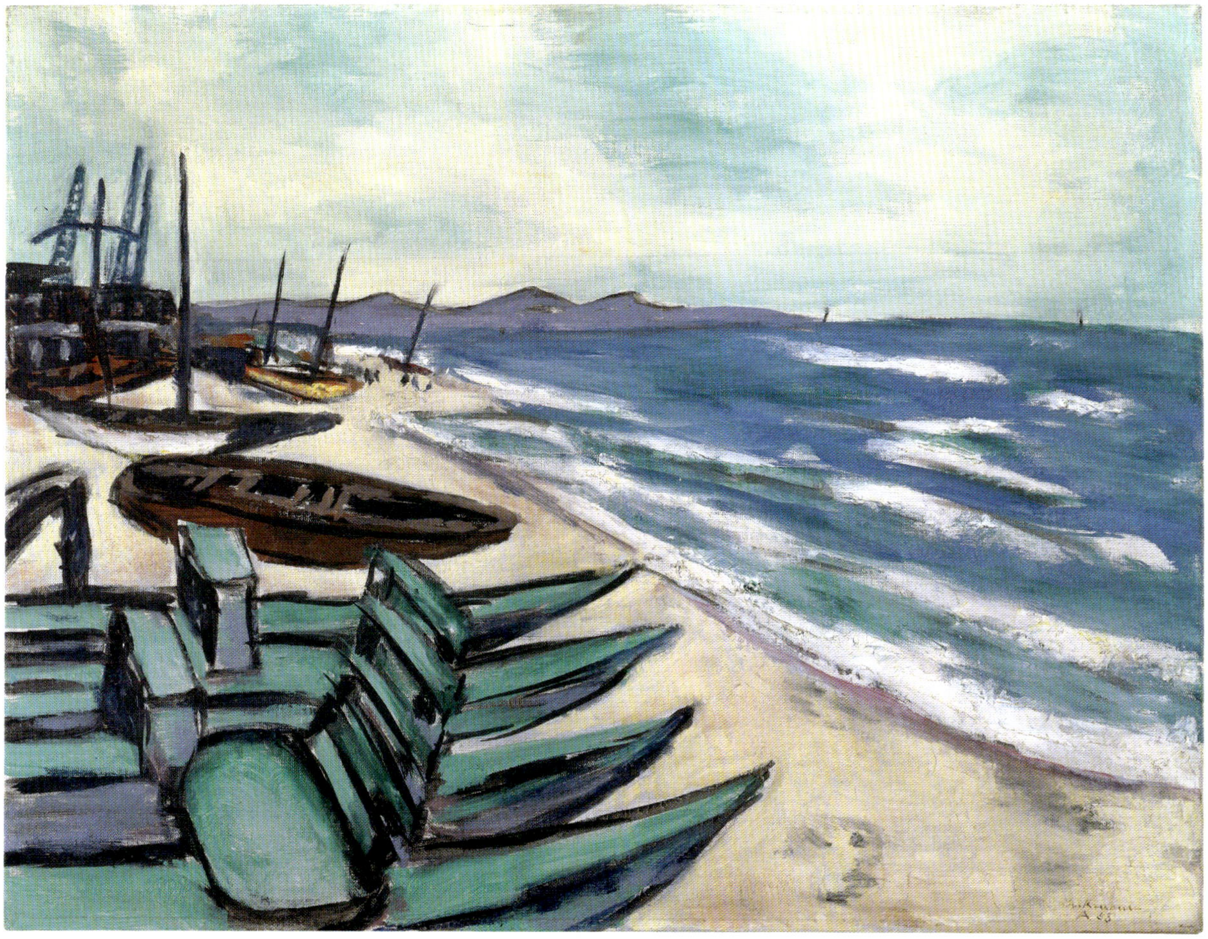

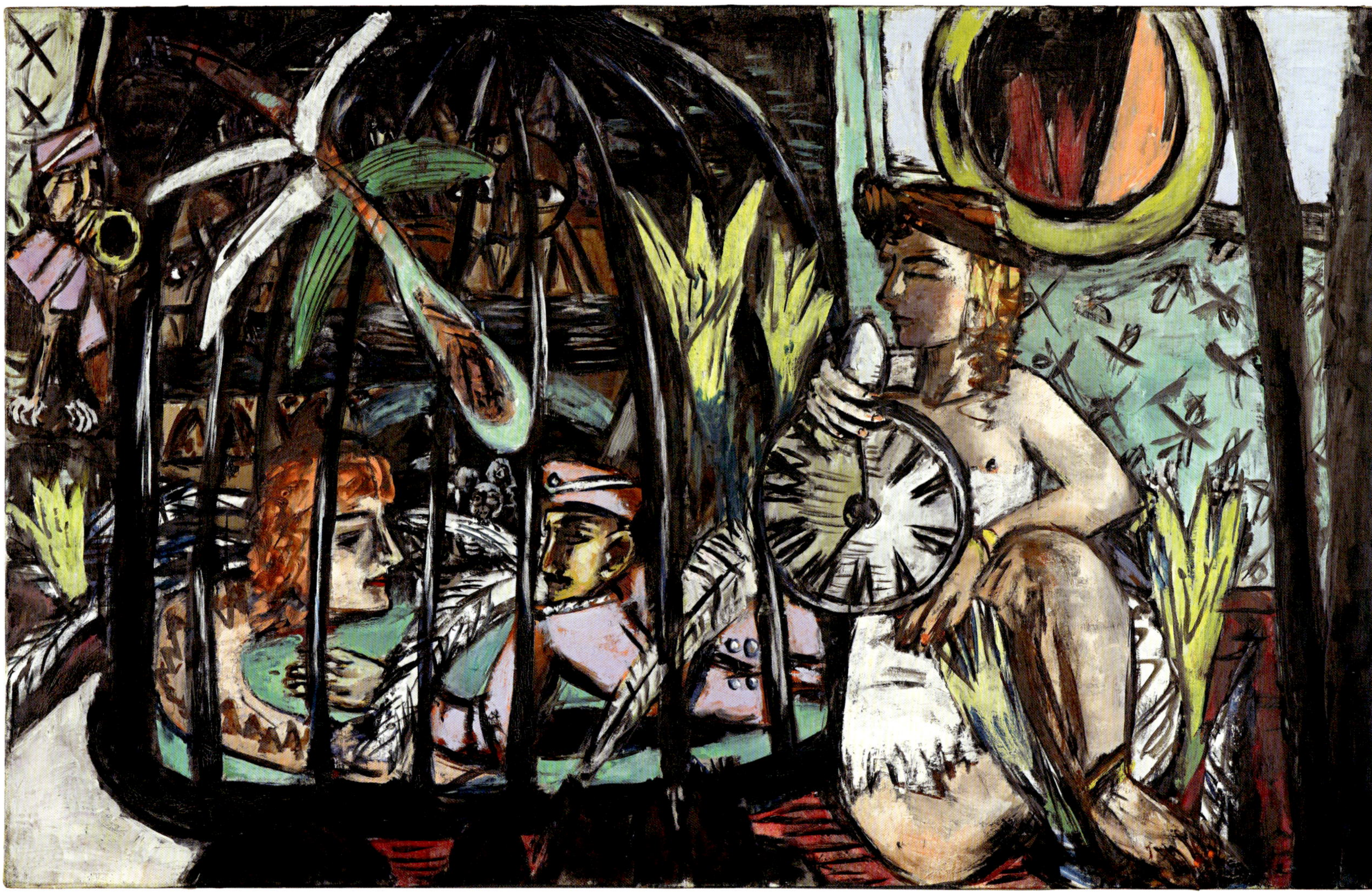

Max Beckmann
1884 Leipzig – 1950 New York

Oil on canvas
Signed, inscribed and dated on the bottom, right of centre, in German script:
Beckmann A 43
90 × 145 cm

Inv. no. P36T / Acquired 2007

Max Beckmann
Traum des Soldaten
1942–43

On 19 July 1937, the day after Hitler had given his speech to open the *Grosse Deutsche Kunstausstellung* in Munich, Max Beckmann left Germany to go into exile in Amsterdam. What was meant to be a temporary measure proved to be a ten-year stay, and he did not move on to the United States until 1947. In spite of the war and German occupation, the years in Amsterdam were extraordinarily fruitful. Beckmann painted six triptychs, two major cycles of illustrations of the Apocalypse and Goethe's *Faust*, and a number of iconographically and stylistically important pictures.

Traum des Soldaten (Soldier's Dream) was painted in 1942 (dated 1943) when the murderous war of Nazi dictatorship had swept across Europe. By speaking of a soldier's dream in his title, Beckmann refers to the war. But a dream also implies the discontinuity of space and time, the fragmentation and displacement of memory, images of desires and fears and ultimately a description of the world that was in many ways visually crucial to Beckmann's compositions.

The dark subject matter of the painting unfolds like a drama. The trim young soldier, his uniform resembling that of a page, is almost wedged in between two seductive and disconcerting beauties. Both attracted and repelled, he is lying down next to the snake-like redhead in a birdcage, onto which a plant is falling like a heavenly missile as if targeting three shrunken heads. The extremely attractive blonde, sitting on the floor next to the cage in the same attitude as the figure to the right in Delacroix's *Women of Algiers*, has a touch of Marlene Dietrich about her; she is scantily attired in white lingerie that reveals her left breast. Her enamel-white skin is radiant in the bright light; the yellow lilies, traditionally symbols of vanity and pomposity, enhance her enchanting allure. She demonstratively holds up a large clock, its hands set at shortly after 11:30. Resembling a wheel, it shows time running out. Thus, in addition to her role as an allegory of time, the seductive young woman can also be seen as Fortuna, the fickle goddess of fate.

This unusually fragile and ambivalent idyll is surrounded by harbingers of doom: the small, birdlike man with eagle's claws, presaging calamity with his bugle, his clothing marking him as the soldier's alter ego; the horned, apocalyptic monsters rising up out of the sea under a moonlit night; the dark, beaverlike animals in the foreground, desperately gasping for air at the bottom of the painting. In counterpart to this apocalyptic scenario, presumably taking place on a ship, a mirror is seen, in which the planks of the ship fade into the infinite blackness of space. It is the "Ein Sof", a Kabbalistic sign, whose circular shape is divided in half, symbolizing the horizon of infinity in the sense of the absolute, the divine, the infinite, and the highest form of knowledge. Its impact transcends the great "theatrum mundi" of humankind.

AS

Max Beckmann
Frau mit Zigarette in Blauviolett
1944

Max Beckmann
1884 Leipzig – 1950 New York

Oil on canvas
95 × 56 cm

Inv. no. P27T / Acquired 2004

In 1937 Beckmann left Nazi Germany and emigrated to Amsterdam, arriving there with his wife Mathilde (Quappi) von Kaulbach on July 19. When German troops invaded the Netherlands in 1940, he burnt the diaries he had kept since 1925. Not until more than 10 years later, on 29 August 1947, did Beckmann's exile in Amsterdam come to an end. Instead of returning to Germany, he went to New York, where he died three years later. Despite the occupation and bombing, the hunger and illness that Beckmann suffered in exile, he was extremely productive. He created approximately a third of his entire oeuvre in Amsterdam, including *Frau mit Zigarette in Blauviolett* (Woman in Purple with Cigarette), which he painted before the end of the war in September 1944.

Max Beckmann was especially interested in figure painting. Feelings of ambivalence prevailed in his relationship to women; he found them both attractive and repelling. Their eros expressed in his paintings is as subtle and muted as it is lascivious and threatening, as detached and blasé as it is seductive and alluring; at other times they appear tender, serene and at rest. However, whatever the case, Beckmann's women are at peace with themselves and have an unbroken relationship to their bodies – not only in the presence of a man but also when they are alone, like the young woman in this painting, whom Beckmann had met in a locale that he frequented in Amsterdam, the Caliente Bar on Lijnbaansgracht.

She seems to be taking a rest, perhaps from dancing, in a room where she is protected from covetous gazes or advances that she spurns, while not entirely averse to reciprocating them. She is entirely at one with herself, leaning against the wall with her legs bent, hugging her knees and holding a cigarette in her left hand. Her low-slung purple dress reveals her shoulders, décolleté and thigh. She is wearing black stockings and yellow shoes. The warm, soft and sensual pastose rendering of her skin is set off against her clothing. Beckmann has framed her tightly within the format of his painting as if toemphasize the moment of withdrawal. The distinctive features of her young face are outlined in sharp profile against the dark blue window. The colour accents in the background are grouped around a shape that has been interpreted as a flower. A black, feathered hat is lying next to the young woman – the prop of her seductive performance at a locale of iridescent pleasure and fleeting distraction in the midst of the war.

On 27 September 1944, Max Beckmann wrote in his new diary: "Have finished pinkish purple resting 'Caliente girl'." Another entry reveals his state of mind: "Bad mood, heading for the abyss after all. Moving – heading into it – though slowly. Cold bombs, the destruction of five years of work – all that stands in rosy clarity for the future – and a totally devastated Europe." Here, in a small room of the Caliente Bar, there is peace and rest, if only for the length of a cigarette.

UW

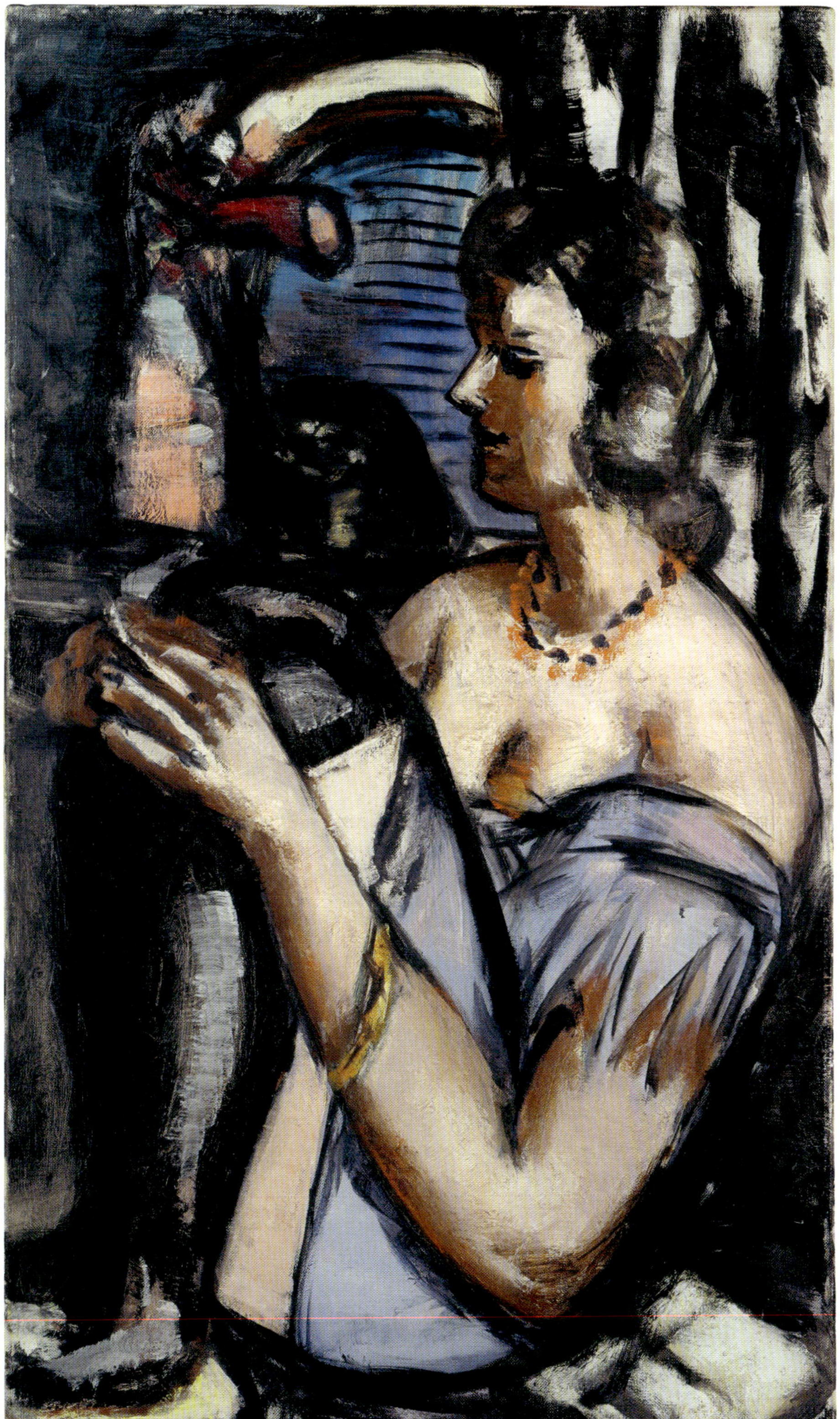

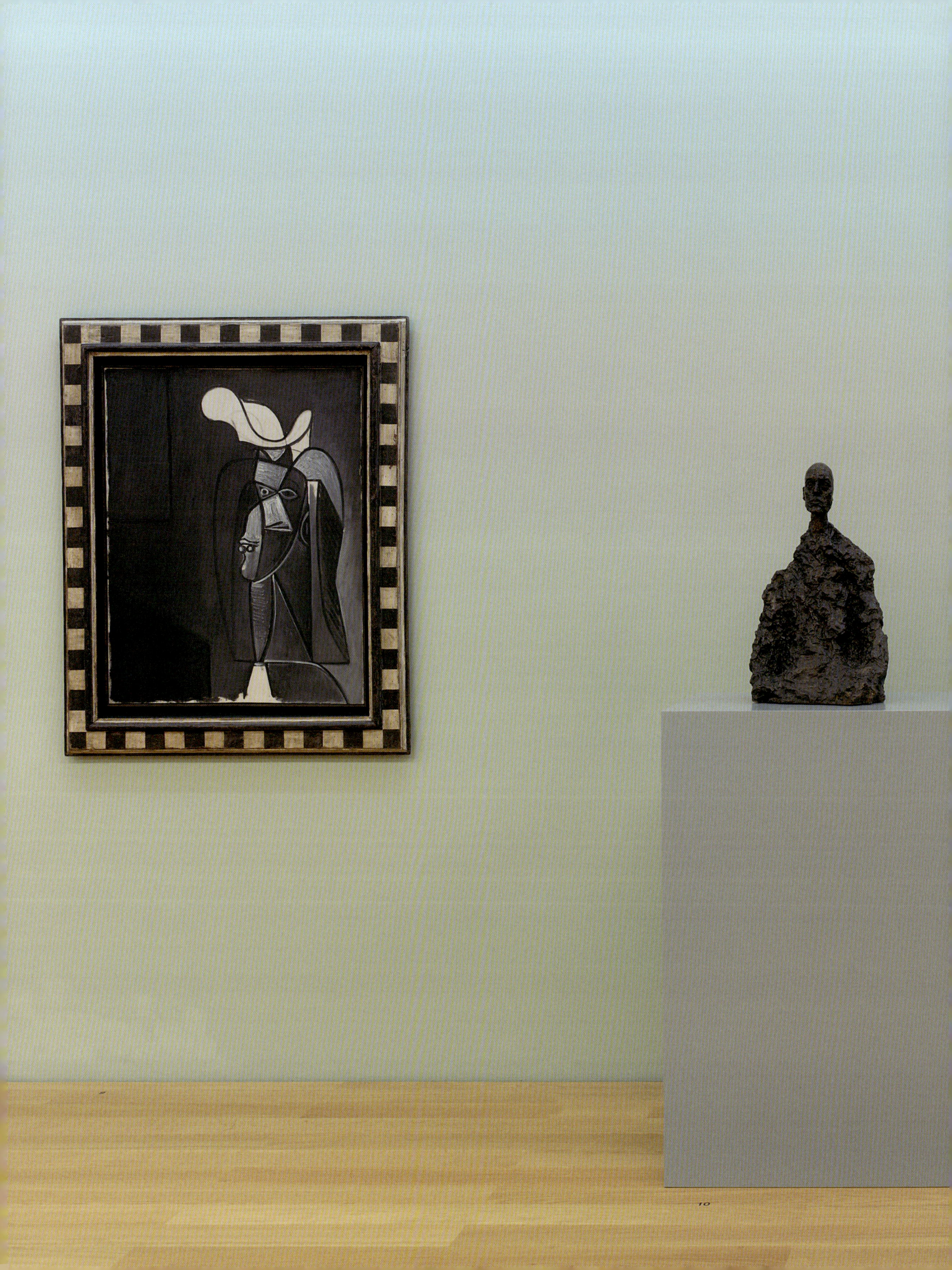

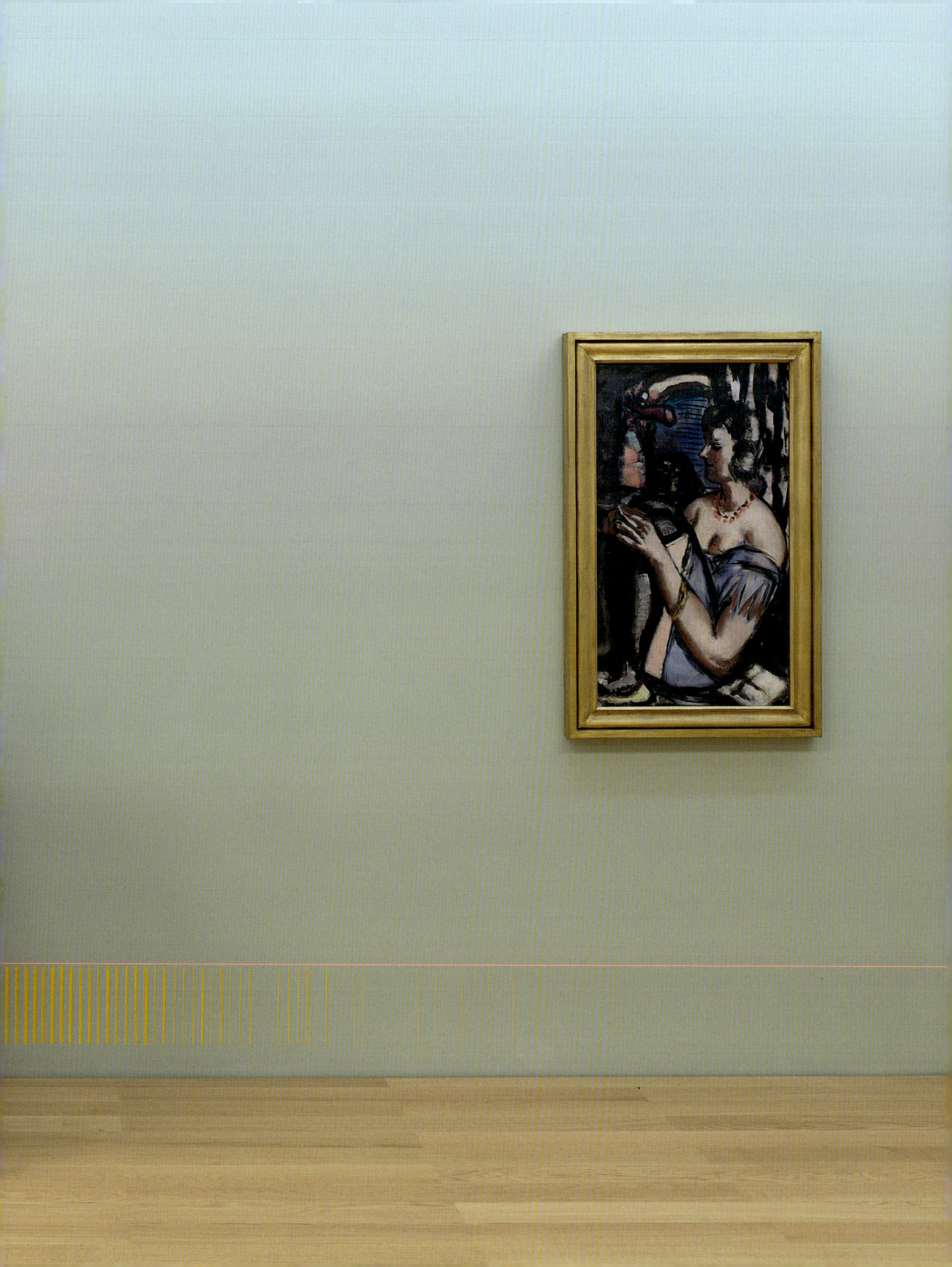

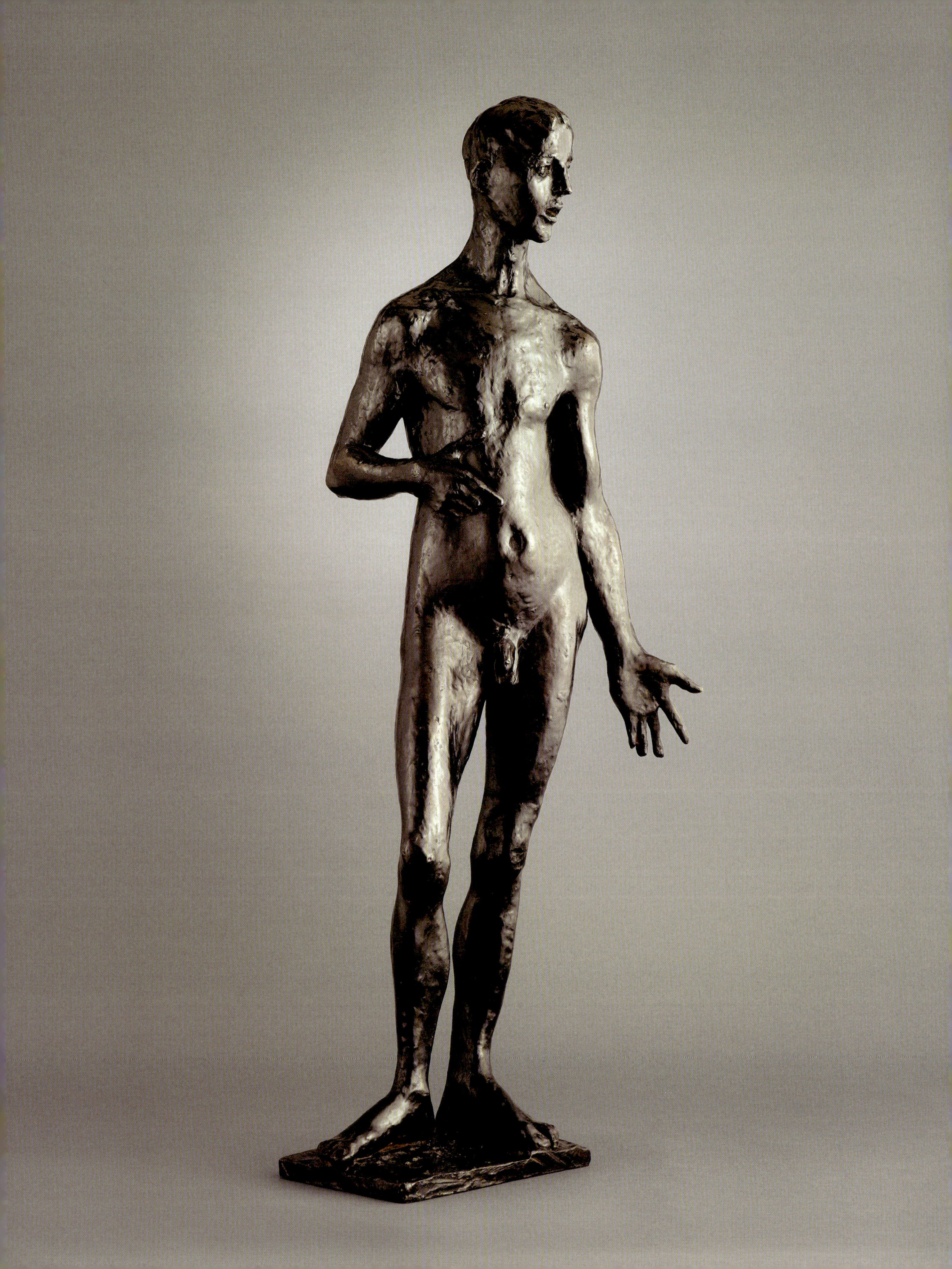

Germaine Richier
1902 Grans / Arles – 1959 Montpellier

Bronze
(cast: K. Stutz, Kunstgiesserei, Zurich)
Signed on the plinth: G. Richier
Height: 89.9 cm

Inv. no. S35T / Acquired 2006

Germaine Richier
Juin 40
1940

World War II broke out in September 1939 while Germaine Richier was on holiday in Switzerland with her husband Otto Charles Bänninger, a sculptor from Zurich. As a result, they decided to settle down in Zurich. The following June the German Wehrmacht occupied Paris, where Richier had been living and working. Devastated by these events, the artist created *Juin 40*, a figure of a nude boy cast in bronze. Between 1920 and 1929, Richier had worked with Louis-Jacques Guigues in Montpellier and later Antoine Bourdelle in Paris, experiences that resonate in the making of her sculpture. Both men had studied with Auguste Rodin, so one might say that Richier was a "granddaughter" of this great master of modern sculpture.

Richier's statue invites comparison with Rodin's *Age of Bronze*, which he created in the wake of the Franco-Prussian war of 1870–71. However, the pathos of Rodin's young man is entirely internalized while Richier's boy looks out at the world in anguish with eyes and mouth wide open. His nudity is an expression of his helplessness and vulnerability; the attitude of his arms and hands of suffering and surrender. In contrast to Rodin's young man, the legs of this statue in contrapposto do not offer stable support. As an allegorical figure, *Juin 40* symbolizes human agony and embodies a primal denunciation of the ravages of war.

Initially, Germaine Richier devoted herself primarily to sculptural depictions of the female body. Increasing intensity of expression and figurative deformation led, as of the mid-1940s, to the bizarre hybrids, half-animal half-human, characteristic of the artist's late work, in which she raised essential questions regarding life between nature and civilization, between fate and freedom, between barbarism and humanity.

UW

Alberto Giacometti
Quatre femmes sur socle
1950

Alberto Giacometti
1901 Borgonovo / Stampa – 1966 Chur

Bronze
Signed and numbered on verso:
Alberto Giacometti 6/6
Height: 75.5 cm

Inv. no. S6T / Acquired 1999

After the war, between 1947 and 1950, Giacometti, now in Paris again, created a series of sculptures that focus on compositions of several small figures. These include model-like arrangements of striding men and standing women. The pattern of the questing man in full stride and the woman standing as she always does was to remain a recurring feature of his oeuvre. Giacometti created *Quatre femmes sur socle* (Four Women on a Base) 1950 in his studio in Montparnasse. He made six bronze casts of this work, two of which he painted.

Delicate figures seen at a great distance: this is the first impression of these vulnerable, fragile statuettes. Their large, triangular feet stand firmly grounded on a relatively high base. They radiate an energy that flows through slender elongated legs, up into skeletal bodies, through shrugged shoulders and small heads that sit tight as if they had been screwed on. Explicitly frontal in composition, the hieratic figures create the impression of people perceived from a distance, complete and whole and alien, but with features blurred. On taking a closer look, we lose our way in the crannied surfaces.

The figurines elude any clear-cut visual interpretation; their flat bodies evoke tree trunks. Giacometti venerated trees, so much so that they could become alter egos. Looking at the autumn acacias on the Rue d'Alésia, he once remarked to his American biographer, James Lord, "one ought to be a tree." The resemblance of these female statuettes to gristly tree trunks underscores their affinity with nature.

Memories of the artist's frequent attendance at brothels resonate in *Quatre femmes sur socle.* The formal rigour of the statuettes, their arms held close to their bodies and the large base, refur to the Egyptian and archaic sculptures that had always seemed so "lifelike" to Giacometti and that frequently figured in his drawings. The bodies formed by countless fingerprints bear traces of human warmth and proximity coupled with a subtle eroticism.

Giacometti commented on the sculptures in the second letter he wrote in 1950 to Pierre Matisse, a friend from his days as a student and later his dealer: "I saw them (the prostitutes) often, very close and menacing, especially one evening in a small room in the Rue de l'Echaudé." And speaking to the writer Jean Genet, he remarked, "When I walk down the street and see a fully clothed whore, I see a whore. When she stands naked before me in a room, I see a goddess."

AS

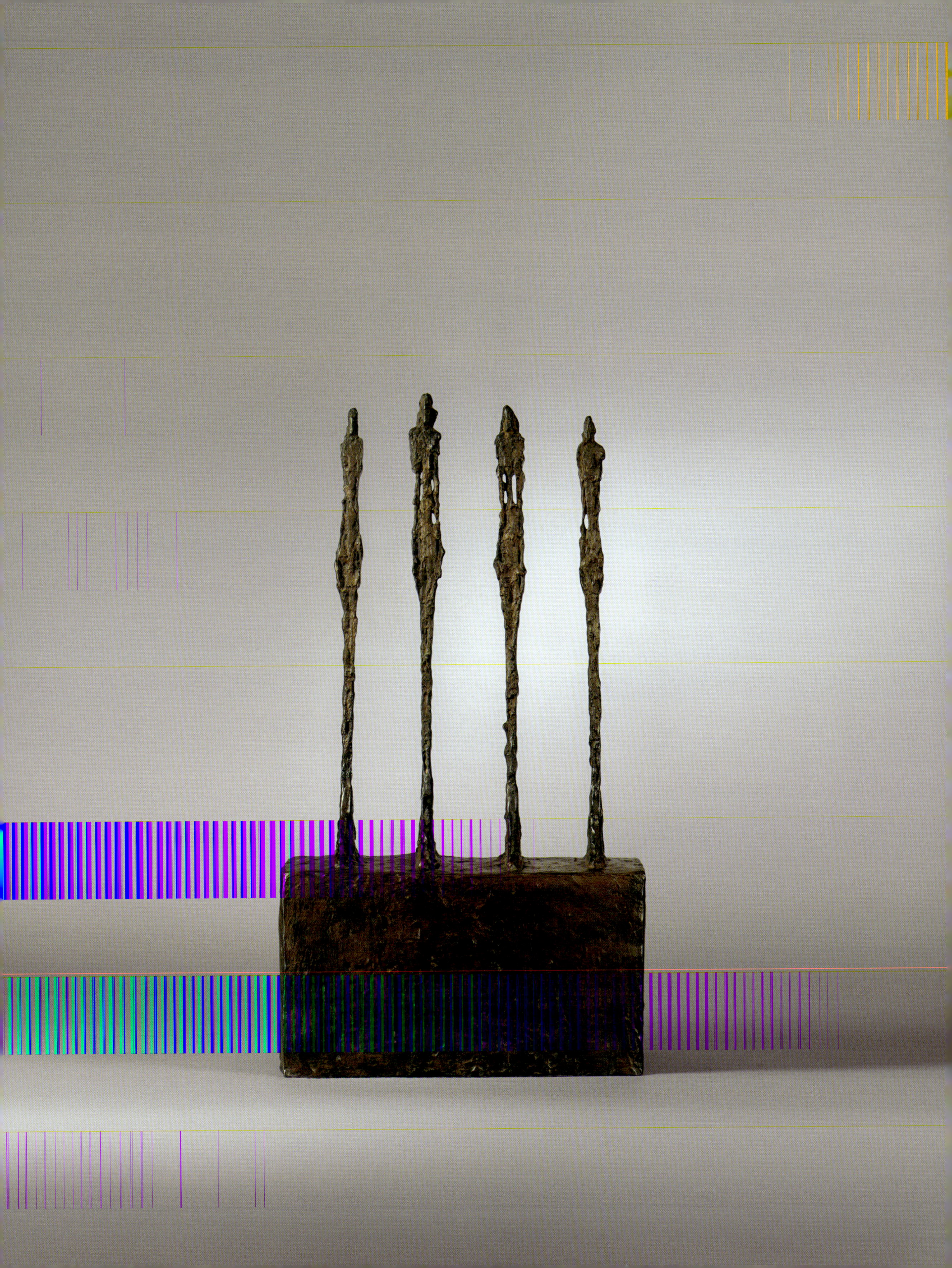

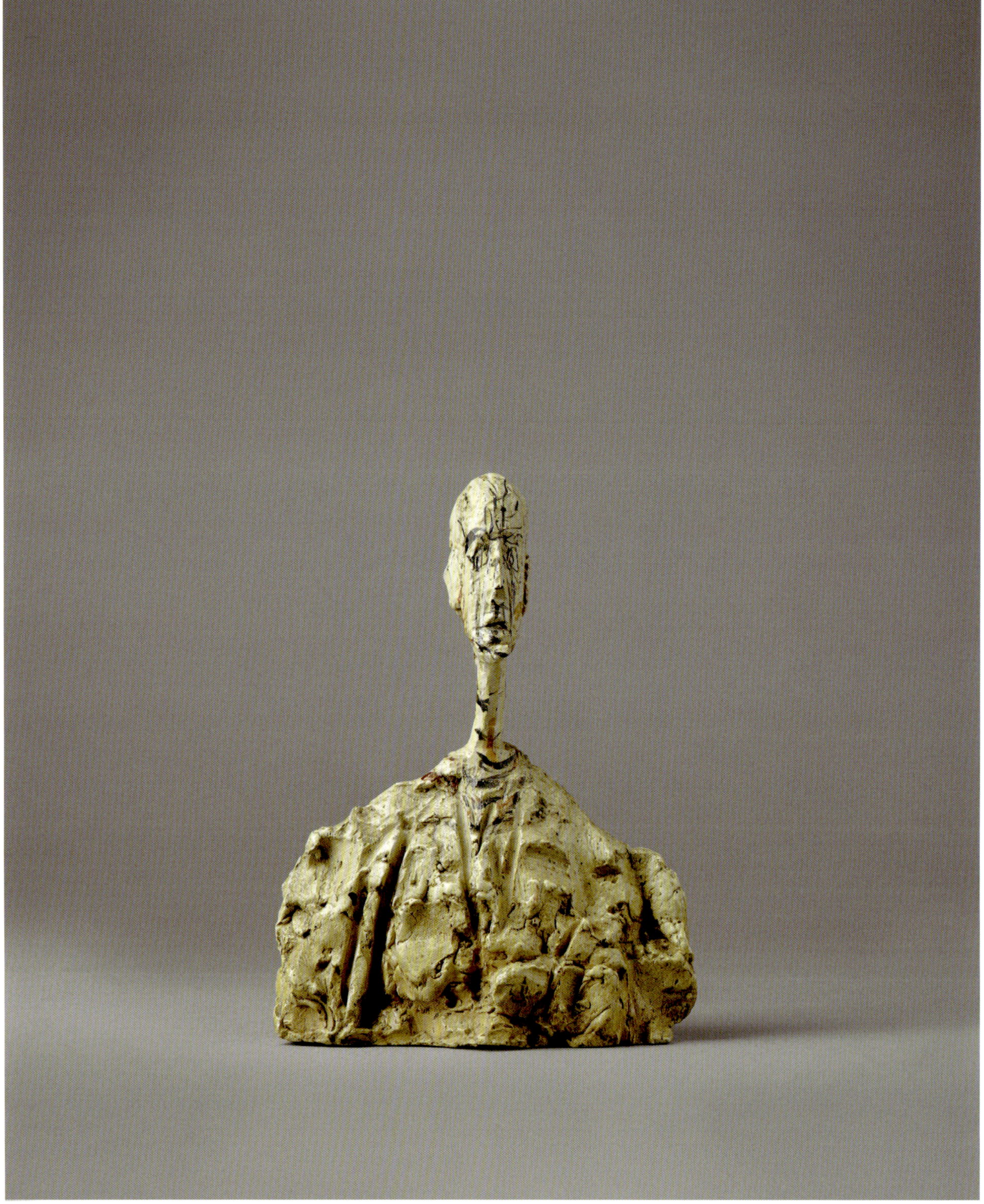

Alberto Giacometti
1901 Borgonovo / Stampa – 1966 Chur

Painted plaster
Height: 21 cm

Inv. no. S30T / Acquired 2005

Alberto Giacometti
Petit buste d'homme
1950–51

When Giacometti left Geneva in September 1945 to return to his Montparnasse studio in Paris, his sculptures were so small that they fit into a matchbox. They had progressively shrunk in size as a consequence of his desire to render the figures as he had seen them in the distance, together with the space around them. However, gradually his sculptures began to grow again, turning into slender, elongated, sometimes even skeleton-like figures, standing uncertainly on their large feet. The heads of his busts, sometimes placed on a pole, evoke skulls and war.

Another change made an appearance in 1949. Giacometti was now working almost exclusively with models, primarily with his brother Diego and his wife Annette. With renewed intensity, he had returned to the old question of what a head actually is and how it might be formed "as an equivalent of life". *Petite buste d'homme* (Small Bust of a Man)cannot be attributed to any of Giacometti's usual models. The torso and, in fact, the entire figure are shown facing the artist head on, as he saw his model sitting opposite him. The jacket and sleeves, looking slightly padded, are clearly distinguishable, despite the glacier-like furrows and gouges in the structure of the plaster. On the long stem of a neck sits a narrow elongated head, resembling a sad clown or a philosopher of antiquity plagued by doubts.

Before coating the entire plaster figure with shellac, Giacometti painted a web of black and red lines onto certain portions with a pointed brush, the currents of energy rising up to the head and converging in the face. Among other things, they mark the large, blank eyes that gaze neither inwards nor outwards but instead appear as if paralyzed, looking at something that remains hidden from us. According to Giacometti, it was reality that had abruptly metamorphosed into the shock of the unknown. Something never before seen, utterly unknown, something wonderful, he later explained in a 1961 interview with Pierre Schneider.
AS

Alberto Giacometti
Diego dans un intérieur
1949–50

Alberto Giacometti
1901 Borgonovo / Stampa – 1966 Chur

Oil on canvas, mounted on wood
Signed lower right:
Alberto Giacometti 1949–50
74 × 44 cm

Inv. no. P2T / Acquired 2002

Although Giacometti considered himself primarily a sculptor, he essentially treated the paintings he made from 1946 until his death in 1966 as equivalent to his sculptural output. Sympathetic to the achievements of Modernism, his father Giovanni had already introduced him to painting as a child. Giacometti began his career with a paintbrush in his hand. He painted his first picture in oils when he was twelve years old and his first sculpture followed a year later.

Early on in his career, Alberto Giacometti found himself embroiled in the conflict between the perception of visible reality on one hand and its artistic representation on the other. Understanding something as a whole and simultaneously perceiving its countless details was terribly difficult for him. He therefore distanced himself from his subject matter only to the extent that he could see it in its totality, while rendering its overall appearance in untold quantities of the finest brushstrokes. The resulting texture creates the impression of a wealth of detail seen in extreme close-up and converging into the shape of a human body.

Diego dans un Intérieur (Diego in an Interior, 1949–50) shows Giacometti's brother in his studio in Paris. We see only sparing hints of the room itself: a few lines mark a shelf, possibly a couch, and behind it an unembellished wall. Diego, sitting on a chair in the exact centre of the composition, faces the viewer head-on in an attitude of aloof detachment. The picture is more like a drawing than a painting. Using a pointed paintbrush, Giacometti has rendered the contours and shape of the body in black, adding white highlights to the overall grey of the whole so that we seem to perceive light and shadow but barely any colour. The figure looks oddly unfinished like a provisional wire construction – as if flesh and bodily warmth had been mislaid by the simultaneous distance and closeness of Giacometti's gaze, as if in the emptiness of the room Diego were only permitted a fleeting existence between the void out of which he has come and the void into which he will go. Sartre, existentialist and Giacometti's friend, writes that in every one of his images the artist raises the age-old metaphysical question of why anything, rather than nothing, even exists at all.

Giacometti's artistic oeuvre explores single, concrete individuals and at the same time human existence per se. For decades, he made do with very few people as models for his paintings and sculptures: his wife Annette, his brother Diego, friends and others who were close to him. His sitters can always be identified and named, and yet ultimately they are generalized representations of the human species in all its complexity and unfathomability.

UW

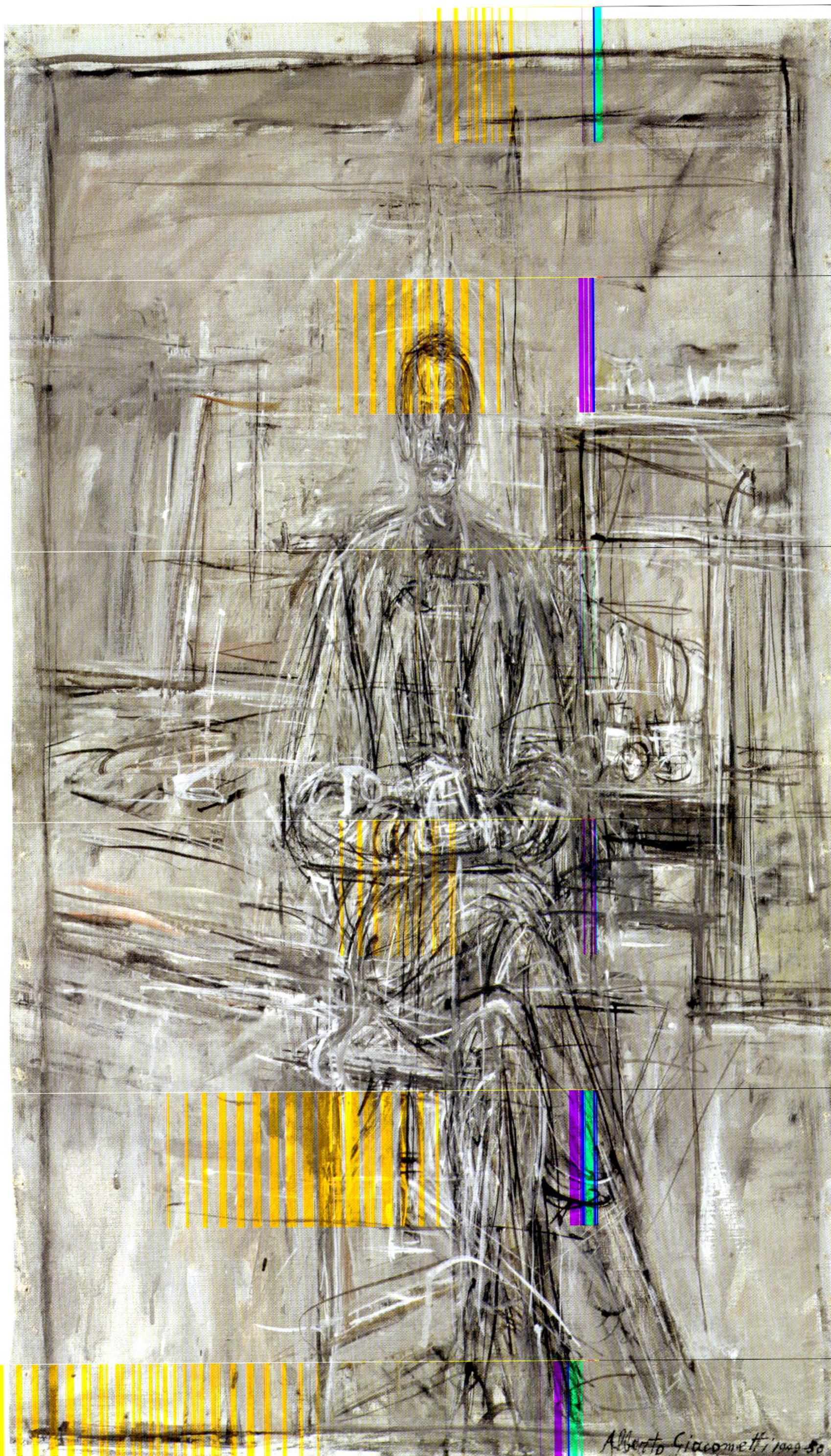
Alberto Giacometti 1949-50

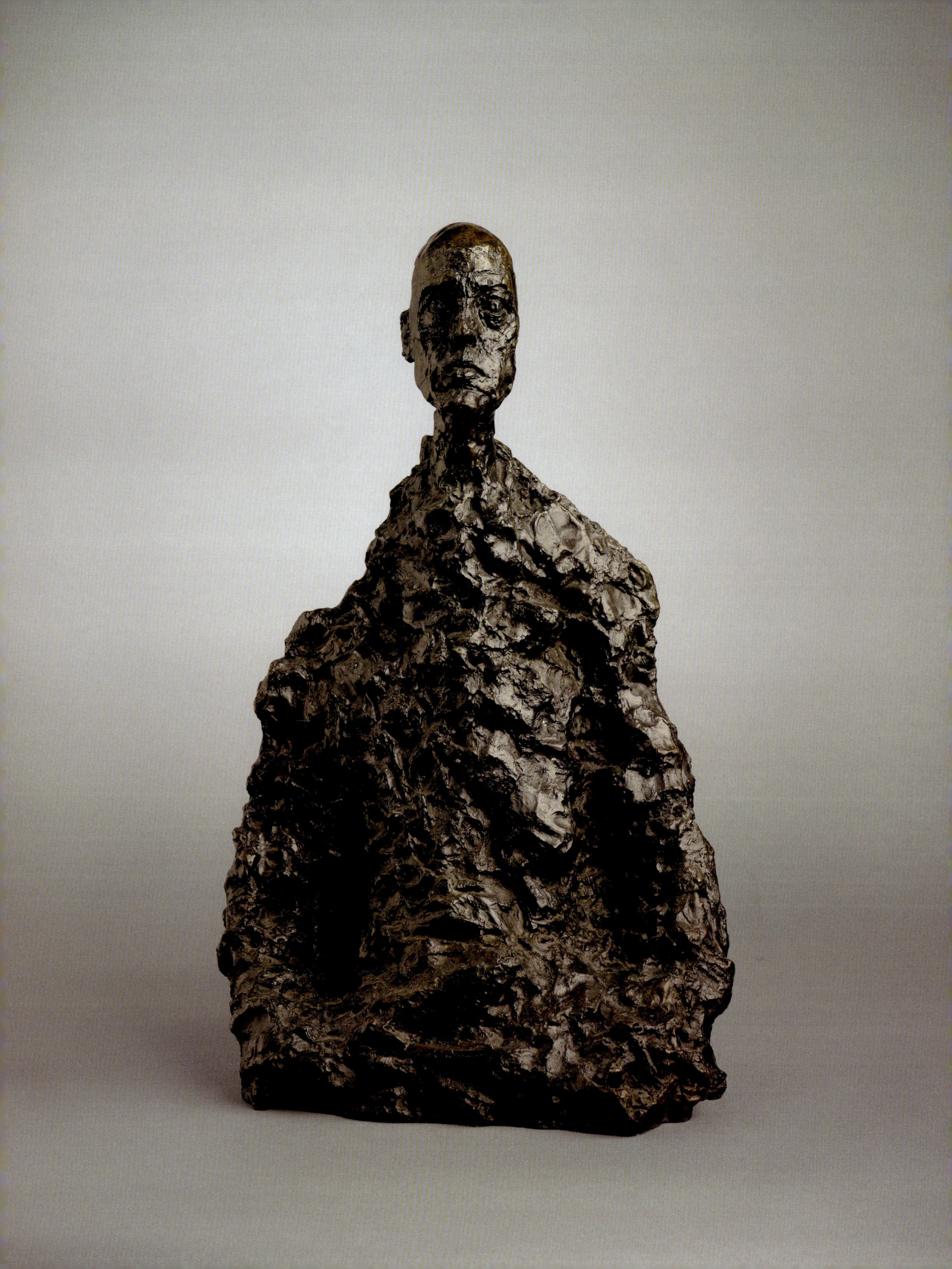

Alberto Giacometti
1901 Borgonovo / Stampa – 1966 Chur

Bronze
(cast: Susse Fondeur, Paris 1973)
Signed and numbered on reverse:
Alberto Giacometti 6/8
Height: 57.7 cm

Inv. no. S54T / Acquired 2012

Alberto Giacometti

Buste d'homme (Eli Lotar II)

1964–65

In 1964–65, the last two years of his life, Giacometti fashioned three sculptures of the photographer and filmmaker Eli Lotar. When he died in 1966, the last one, *Eli Lotar III*, was still propped up in his Montparnasse studio. He had completed plaster versions of the first two, *Eli Lotar I* and *Eli Lotar II*, in 1965. All of the bronze casts were produced posthumously between 1968 and 1981.

Giacometti had met Lotar in the milieu of Parisian nightlife. The talented son of a Romanian poet, Lotar wasted his time as an habitué of the bars in Montparnasse, a quintessential example, according to Giacometti's biographer, James Lord, of artistic failure and of the inability to work – issues that always troubled Giacometti as well.

Photographs taken in the studio by Giorgio Soavi show the intensity of Giacometti's relationship to his sitter. He spent the entire year in 1964 working almost daily on the two busts, which took excruciatingly slow and laborious shape in countless sittings. Giacometti wanted to capture every single vibrant moment, every single aspect of his model – an insuperable undertaking.

The bust of *Eli Lotar II*, measuring 57.7 centimetres in height, culminates in a clearly detailed head, pitted against the amorphous mass of the torso with sloping shoulders and arms hanging slack, resembling flowing lava or a craggy mountainside. It bears traces of Giacometti's modelling, of his powerful hands that have animated the inert matter. The sitter's head rises out of this mass like a piece of fruit. All the energy of the work is distilled here, in Lotar's mouth, nose, and above all in his eyes. His gaze pierces reality, peering into the distance with utmost concentration, focusing on an infinitely remote, unnameable goal. In contrast to the transient body, which returns to pure matter, the seeing spirit, physically embodied in this head, survives.

AS

Wols
La flamme
1946–47

Wols
1913 Berlin – 1951 Paris

Oil on canvas
41 × 33 cm

Inv. no. P48T / Acquired 2011

Wols – his real name was Wolfgang Schulze – created some 1800 photographs, 2000 drawings and watercolours, and approximately 80 to 100 paintings. Much of his oeuvre was lost in the brief thirty-eight years of the artist's turbulent life. The first paintings, made shortly after the war in 1946 and 1947, were exhibited in the upscale René Drouin gallery at Place Vendôme in Paris. Drouin also supplied him with oil paints and canvases. The works did not attract much attention at the time, becoming more widely known only later in the wake of art historical interest in Art Informel and Tachism. They were preceded by fifteen years of personal artistic development with no classical training, although no doubt with a knowledge of Surrealism. Having emigrated from Germany to Paris in 1932, Wols initially worked as a photographer and later concentrated on drawing, watercolours, etching, and finally painting. In addition to his delight in telling and inventing stories, one can detect stylistic similarities between the photographs and watercolours, especially an intense interest in the small and delicate structures of a wide variety of organisms that often remain hidden from the naked eye.

Wols mit der Lupe (Wols with His Magnifying Glass): thus the title of philosopher Bernard Collin's aphorisms in which he conducted an ongoing conversation with the artist. It is through Collin, who was still a student when he probably acquired *La flamme* from Drouin in 1948, that the work is now held by the Hilti Art Foundation. Wols ordinarily left his work untitled to protect it from premature and facile interpretation. *La flamme*, like the second title *Le bouquet*, presumably stems from Olga Drouin.

The small, unsigned picture shows a shape with a complex inner structure placed against a light-grey ground mixed with white. The shape, basically symmetrical in composition, acquires a slant through the red lines that form a slightly tilting cross. The turbulence in the centre is accentuated by round shapes of different sizes made by the imprint of tubes of paint; they might be interpreted as eddies or drops or eyes. Fragile, partially broken contours delimit strands of paint left and right that Wols structured like the bark of the tree. He used the handle of his paintbrush to make scratches in the bundles of thin, swaying lines, sprouting out of the edges. They resemble magnetic field lines but also evoke a variety of associations: trees, underbrush, a seed, a piece of sliced-open fruit, and, of course, body parts. In his own undated aphorism, the artist wrote, "But Wols honestly loves / the matter that surrounds us."

Wols pencilled CACCA into the top left corner. This is not only an ironic commentary, like the much-quoted words that Wols attributed to his dog Rip, "Your painting is idiotic." More importantly, Collin refers in his aphorisms to Antonin Artaud, whom Wols knew and greatly admired. Collin writes, "Caca, here the cry of Artaud / Is God leaving or staying?"

AS

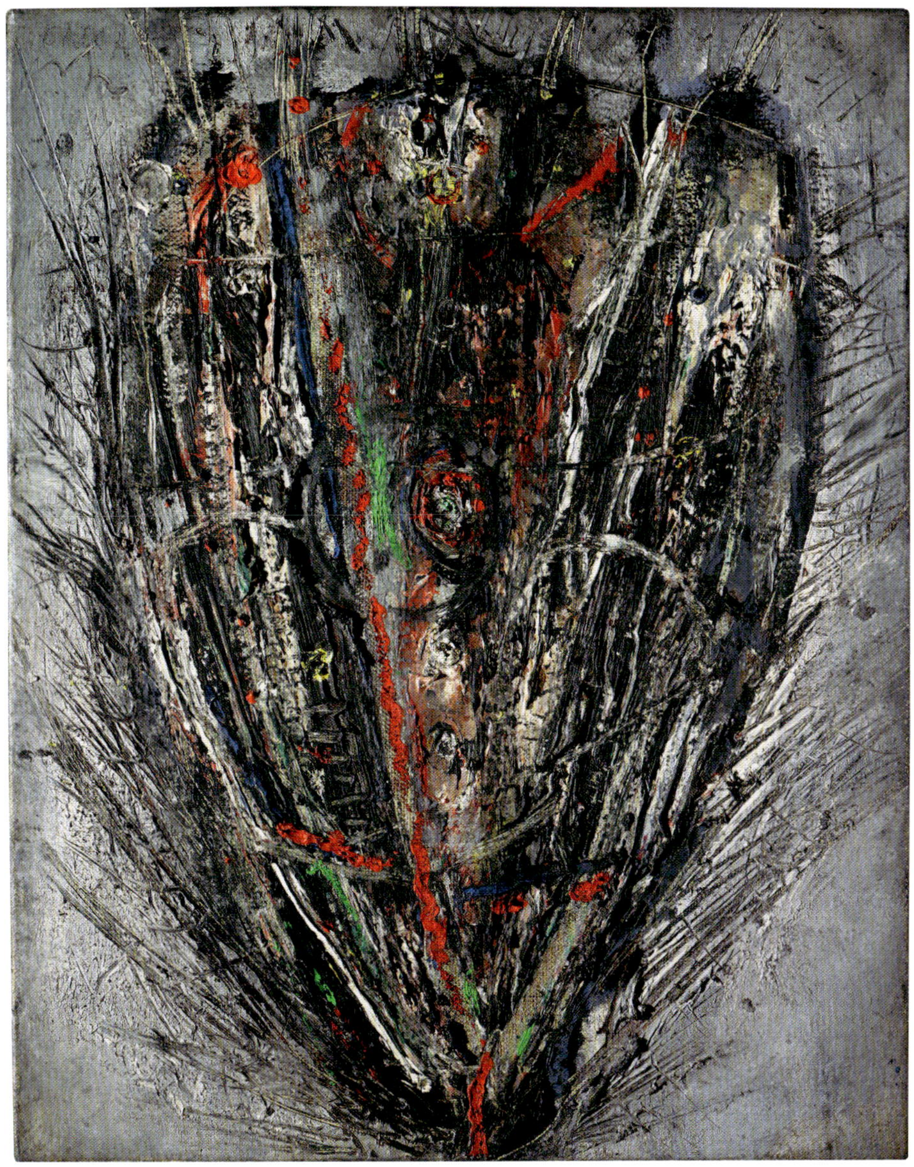

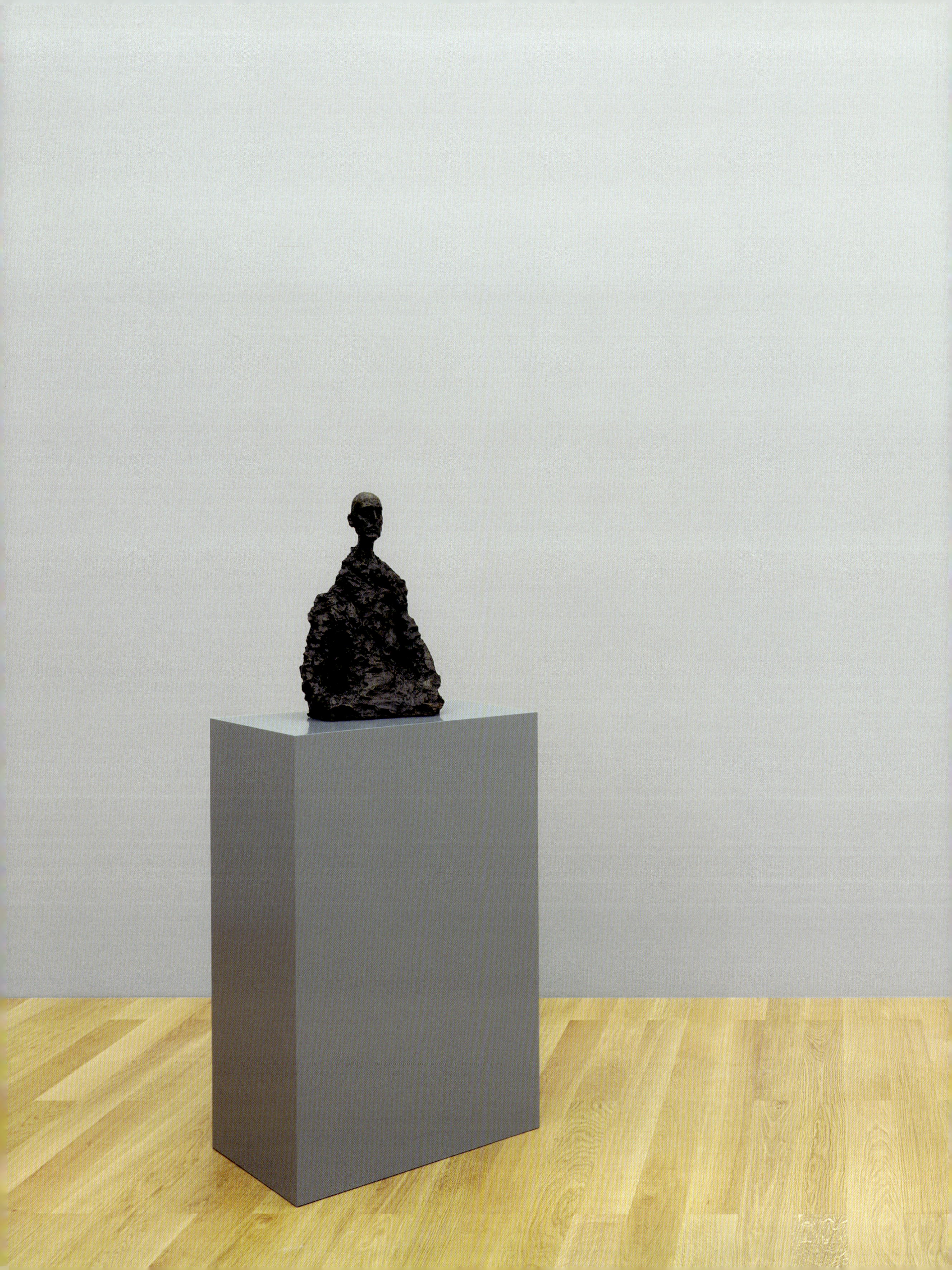

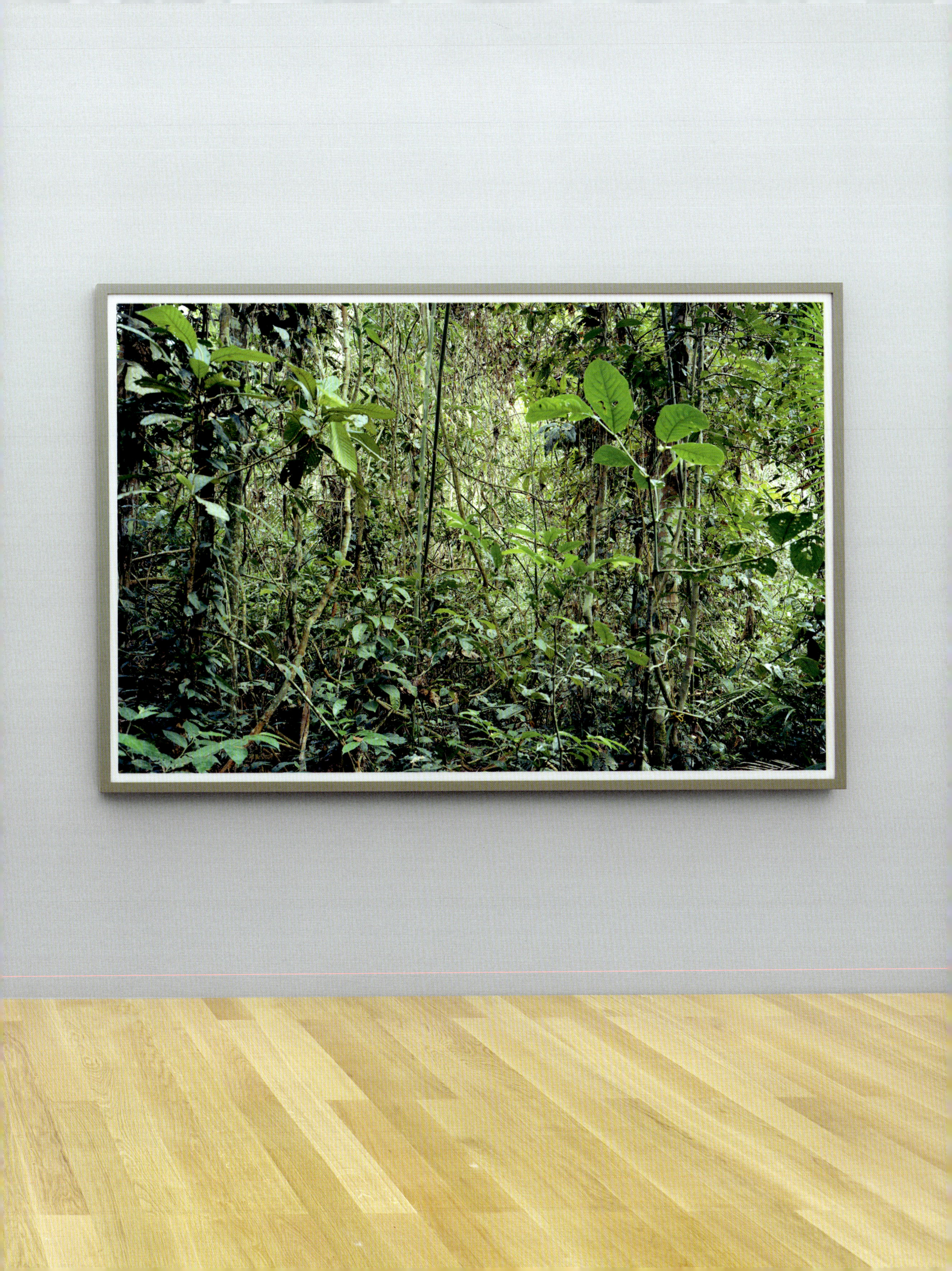

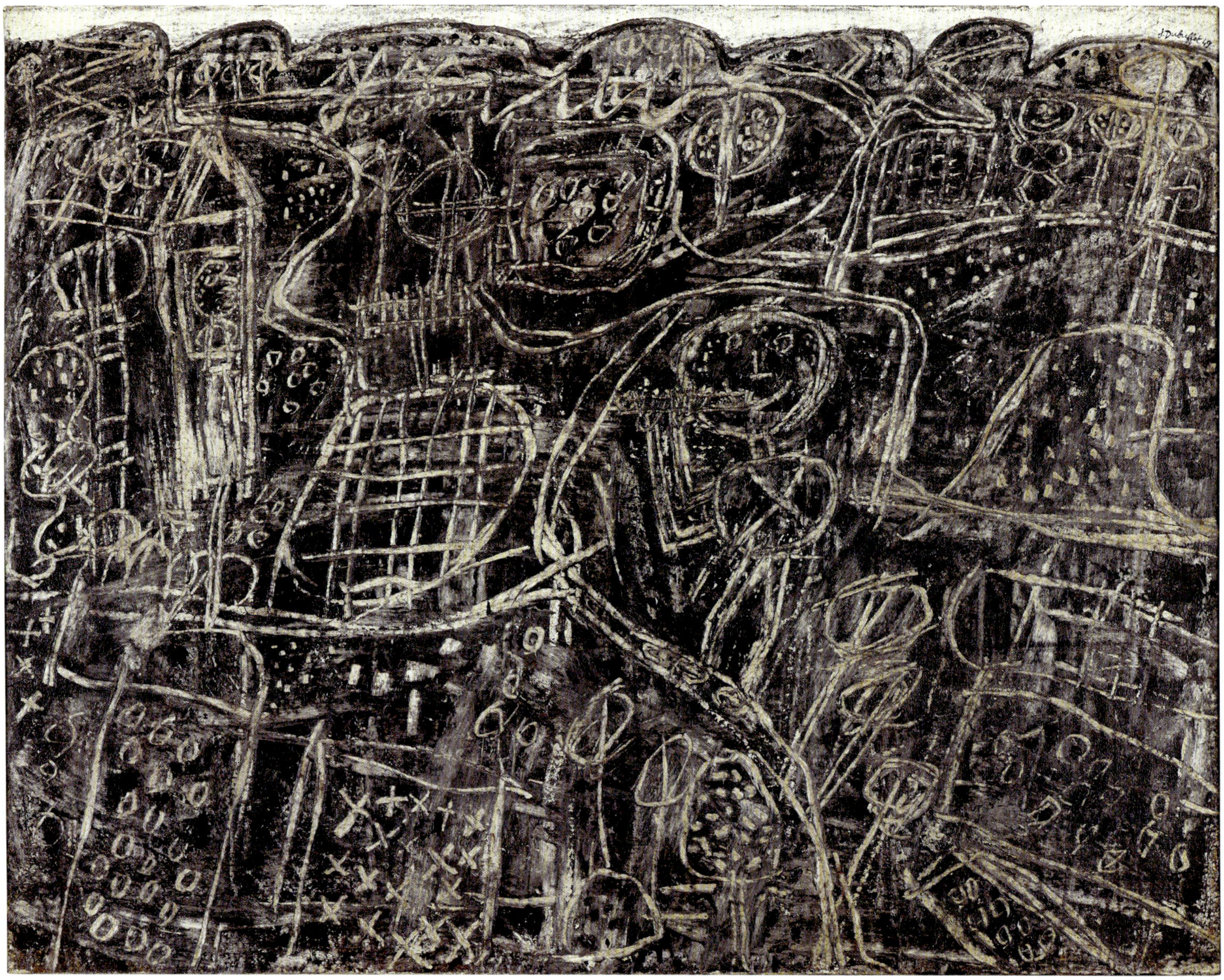

Jean Dubuffet
1901 Le Havre – 1985 Paris

Oil on canvas
Signed and dated upper right:
J. Dubuffet 49
89.5 × 116.5 cm

Inv. no. P42T / Acquired 2010

Jean Dubuffet
Paysage noir avec joueur de fifre
1949

It was not until 1942, at the age of forty-one, that Jean Dubuffet finally gave up his wine business altogether to devote himself entirely to painting. Previous attempts to work exclusively as an artist had failed, particularly since he was not interested in classical painting, an attitude reinforced by the Surrealists with whom he became acquainted in Paris in the 1920s and 1930s. He clearly shared their interest in children's drawings, the art of the mentally ill and in "primitive" art, and had read Hans Prinzhorn's book *Artistry of the Mentally* Ill with great enthusiasm in 1924. In the 1940s, he began collecting outsider art, for which he coined the term Art Brut, literally "raw art". He started painting his first series of pictures, such as *Métro*, in 1943. A year later, Dubuffet made a suite of lithographs titled *Matières et Mémoires* (Materials and Memories), a revealing title that could easily apply to his entire oeuvre.

Paysage noir avec joueur de fifre (Black Landscape with Piper) is one of the *Paysages grotesques* (Grotesque Landscapes), a series of works painted in 1949. The series reflects Dubuffet's experiences during visits to the Algerian oasis El Goléa in 1947, 1948, and 1949. Painted on a coarse canvas, the work pictures a scene of this oasis, one of the most beautiful and exceptionally fertile in the Sahara, known for its palm trees, orchards, and vegetable gardens. Dubuffet scratched the images out of the dark ground of thick but unevenly applied layers of paint – as if the desert wind were blowing through the picture. Orange trees, palm trees, beds of vegetables, buildings, people and paths look like washed out graffiti. The circles, dots, and many variations of hatching recall Paul Klee's depictions of landscapes and cities. The artist has superimposed his motifs with no regard for perspective. Somewhat childlike, but drawn with great fluidity, the figures cover the entire picture plane like a carpet except for a narrow strip at the top marking the sky above the mountains in the distance.

In an essay published by Gallimard in 1946, Dubuffet wrote that he refused to bow to the constraints of optical perspective because that would curtail the freedom he required to picture all of the objects that he imagined. He elaborated his critique of civilization in a lecture given in Chicago in 1951: "Western man despises trees and streams. He hates the very thought of being like them. The 'primitive' however loves and admires trees and streams. ... These 'primitive' societies certainly have a greater respect than western man for all the creatures on the earth. They do not see humankind as the lord of other creatures but merely as one of them." This is indeed the mood conveyed in Dubuffet's landscape.

The title alludes to Manet's famous painting *Le fifre* (The Fifer, 1866), rejected in its day for being too simple and modern, but nonetheless admired by Emile Zola. The *Images d'Épinal*, prints of popular subjects sold in France in the nineteenth century, no doubt reverberate in the motif of the flautist.

AS

Jean Dubuffet
Riant été
1954

Jean Dubuffet
1901 Le Havre – 1985 Paris

Oil on canvas
Signed and dated upper right: J. Dubuffet 54
inscribed, signed and dated on verso:
Riant été J. Dubuffet dic. 54
89.5 × 116.5 cm

Inv. no. P219M / Acquired 2010

Dubuffet always thought of himself as an anti-classical artist. The sources that he drew on for inspiration – and there were many – did not come from the Occidental heritage of antiquity, but rather from such varied traditions as the then much admired "primitive" art, prehistoric cave paintings, the grotesque and absurd theatre of Antonin Artaud and even the scriptural paintings of the Surrealists.

In *Anti-Cultural Positions*, a talk he gave in 1951 at the Arts Club of Chicago, Dubuffet explained his convictions: "...my own art, and my own philosophy, lean entirely on stages more underground. I try always to catch the mental process at the deeper point of its roots, where, I am sure, the sap is much richer."

Dubuffet cultivated a view of the world that did not dissect an object, a tree, for instance, into its constituent parts but treated it as a vibrant whole that is bound up with its surroundings and the world. In his own words, "I think the wind that blows through its leaves is absolutely necessary for the knowledge of the tree and cannot be separated from it."

When Dubuffet took up art at the age of 41 years, he organized his output into series that each had titles above and beyond the individual works. He painted *Riant été* (Laughing Summer) in Auvergne in 1954 as part of the *Vaches* (Cows) series. In 1967 he wrote about a small house he had purchased in July 1954 not far from Clermont-Ferrand, where he set up his studio. He describes watching the cows for a long time, as he used to do, and then drawing them afterwards from memory. Occasionally, though much more rarely, he would also draw them after nature.

At first sight *Riant été* appears to be a furrowed, very green summer landscape, with cool turquoise highlights: a picture of meadows lined with trees. The artist describes the green as comforting and calming. A narrow strip of blue sky fills the top margin of the composition that is seen both from below and from the top. Only after examining the confusion of lines and meticulously studying the scratches scored in the paint with a spatula or the handle of a paintbrush can figures be distinguished, both clear-cut and vague. In the foreground, the silhouettes of two young cows and a dog can be made out despite their irregular and repeatedly broken contours. Here and there, the figures sink into the paint again, cropping up as if out of collective cultural memory, only to become part and parcel again of the overall scriptural fabric of lines.

AS

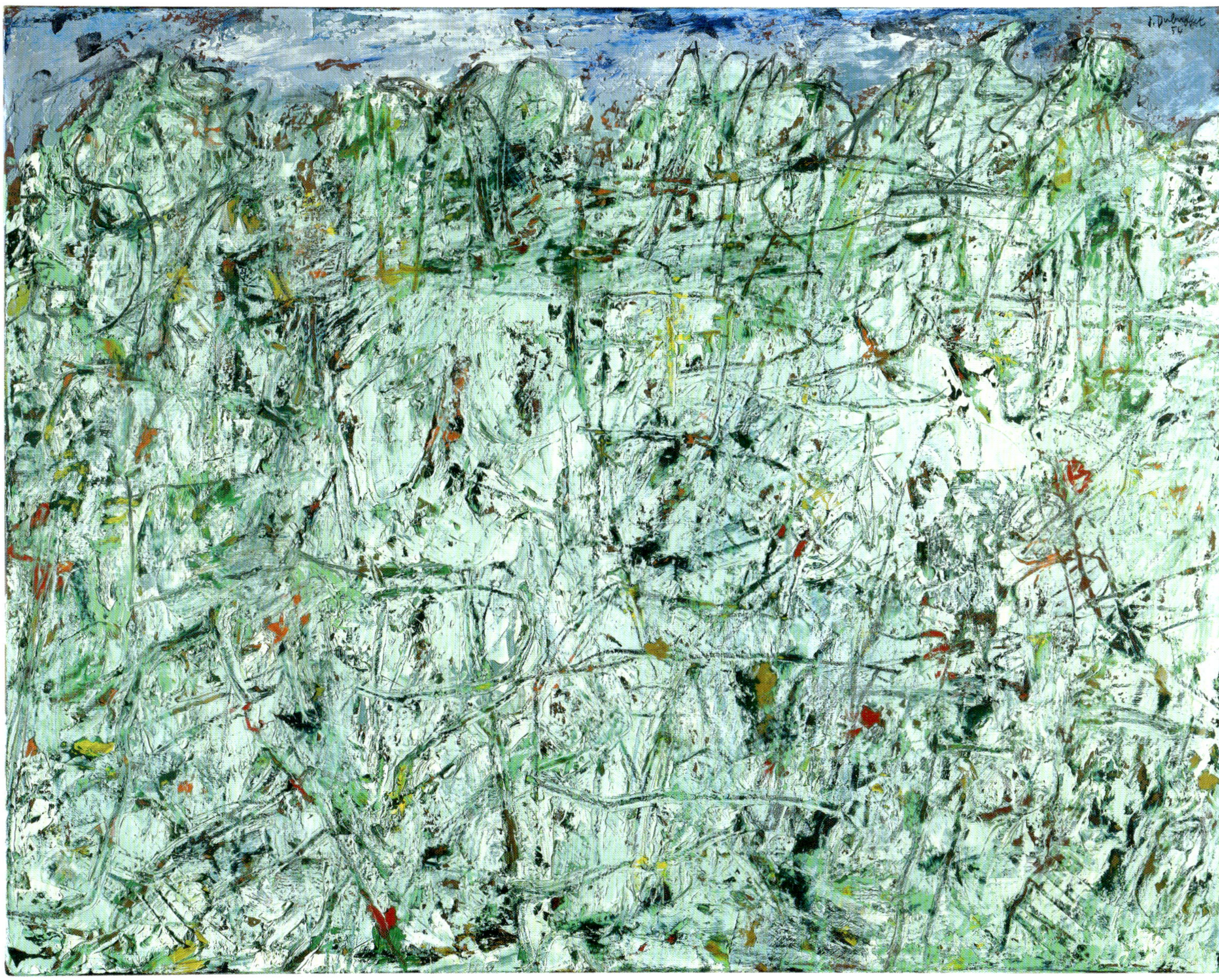

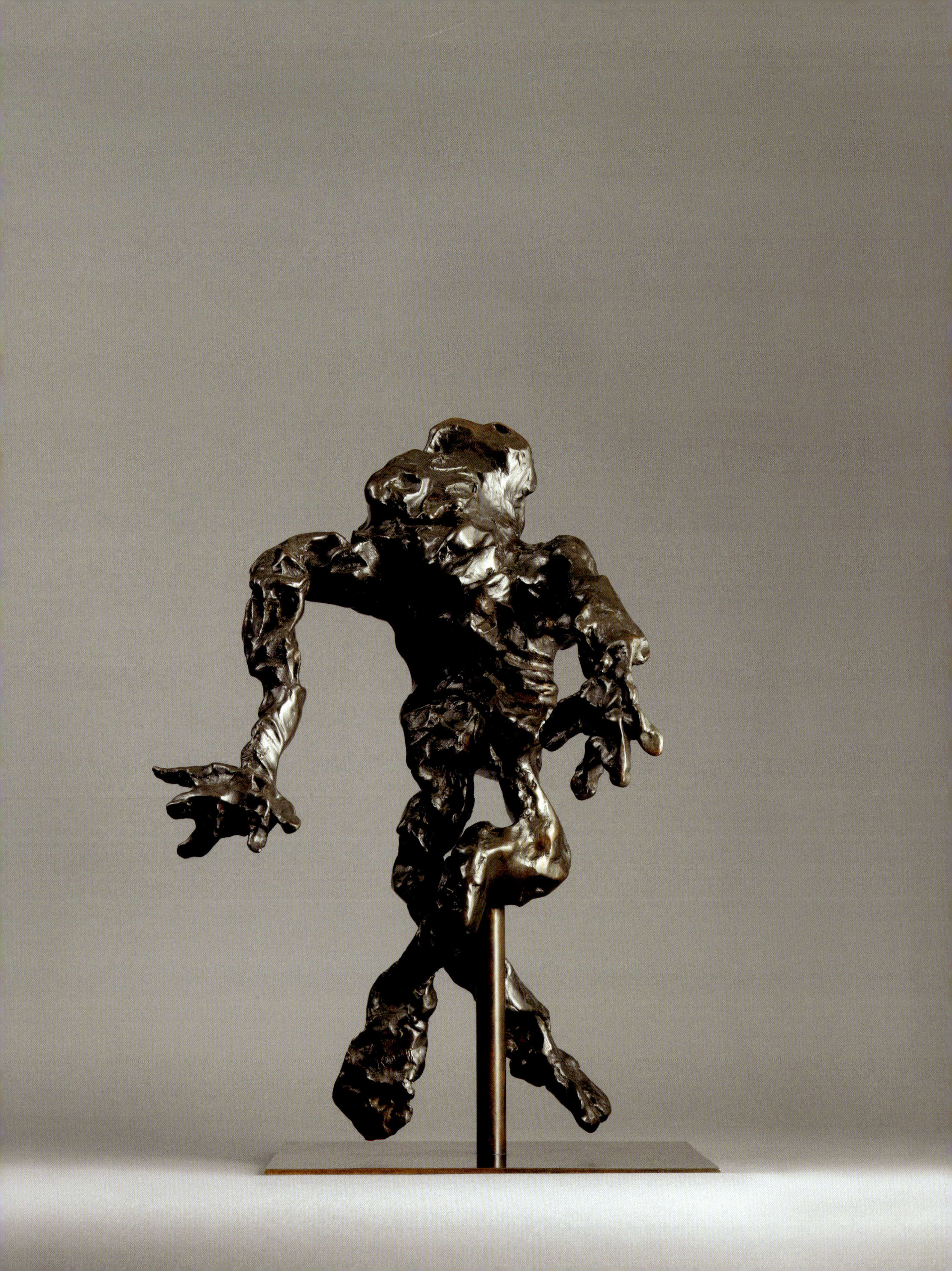

Willem de Kooning
Cross-Legged-Figure
1972

Willem de Kooning
1904 Rotterdam – 1997 Long Island / New York

Bronze
(cast: Modern Art Foundry, New York)
Signed and numbered on right leg:
W. Kooning A/P I
Height: 62.2 cm

Inv. no. S59T / Acquired 2013

In comparison to his paintings, the twenty sculptures that Willem de Kooning created in the short period between 1969 and 1974 play a relatively subordinate role within his oeuvre as a whole. Nonetheless, the artist, who was deeply interested in the human figure, gave this body of work a compelling shape that is as self-contained as it is significant.

In 1969, de Kooning took advantage of a chance encounter in Rome with a friend, the sculptor Herzl Emanuel, who gave him the use of his workshop and foundry in Rome where he playfully worked in clay and then cast the results in bronze. He started out making small objects almost like amulets, before moving on to medium-sized and later monumental sculptures, which were basically anthropomorphic in appearance. The striking way in which de Kooning treated his materials led to figures that do not appear to have been worked from inside out in the traditional fashion, starting with a sturdy skeleton and gradually fleshing it out. Instead, they trace the action of the hands, working from outside in: we do not see the hands following the logic of the figure, but rather the figure following the logic of the hands and their direct impact on the clay. Often shaped with his eyes closed, the works quite literally incorporate the flow of the artist's movements and sensations, yielding results that are analogous to the iridescent nature of de Kooning's expressive painting between figuration and non-figuration.

Structurally, some of the sculptures, like *Cross-Legged-Figure* of 1972, cannot stand on their own; they are presented lying down or require a support to appear more or less stably suspended in space. The works draw attention to primary, fundamental aspects of sculpture, to the initial creative impulse in handling materials. This impulse, which relies primarily on the sense of touch, is motivated by the artist's search for origins, immediacy and vitality. The floating dynamics of this particular sculpture evoke a dancing figure, for instance, the Indian god Shiva, a medieval Morris dancer, or early modern dance, indeed, dance in general with its both standardized and ecstatic forms of movement. *Cross-Legged-Figure* inspires other associations as well, its raw existence possibly representing an early stage of natural history, a creature that embodies all the immanent potential of the development of matter and spirit, or, quite the opposite, an end state of civilization, in which catastrophe has exhausted that potential, leaving behind nothing but deformed, lifeless matter.
UW

Provenance
Exhibitions
Literature

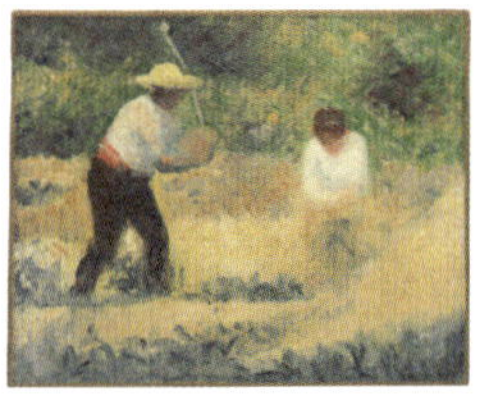

001

Georges Seurat
Le tas de pierres
c. 1882–1884

Provenance
Paul Signac, Paris
Berthe Signac, St. Tropez
Léon Salavin, Paris, c. 1957
Wildenstein & Co., Paris
Mr. & Mrs. Sidney R. Barlow, London
Sotheby's, London, 2 April 1979, lot 9
Waddington Galleries, London
Christie's, New York, 12 December 1996, lot 5
Mr. & Mrs. Anton C.R. Dreesman, Netherlands
Christie's, London, 9 April 2002, lot 69
Private collection
Sotheby's, New York, 2 November 2010, lot 52

Exhibitions
1900 Paris, Galerie de la Revue Blanche, *Georges Seurat 1860–1891: Œuvres peintes et dessinées*, no. 9
1908 Paris, Galerie Georges Seligmann
1908–09 Paris, Galerie Bernheim-Jeune, *Georges Seurat*, no. 32
1920 Paris, Galerie Bernheim-Jeune, *Georges Seurat*, no. 15
1952–53 Paris, Musée Carnavalet, *Chefs d'Œuvre des Collections Parisiennes: Ecole française du XIX siècle*, no. 94
1957 Paris, Musée Jaquemart-André, *Seurat*, no. 21
1958 Stockholm, Nationalmuseum, *Fem Sekler Fransk Konst*, no. 163
1963 Hamburg, Kunstverein, *Wegbereiter der modernen Malerei: Cézanne, Gauguin, Van Gogh, Seurat*, no. 97
1969 Phoenix, Museum of Art (on loan)
1974 Los Angeles, County Museum of Art (on loan)
2004 Chicago, The Art Institute of Chicago, *Seurat and the Making of the Grande Jatte*, no. 10
2015 Vaduz, Hilti Art Foundation / Kunstmuseum Liechtenstein, *Hilti Art Foundation – Painting and Sculpture. From Classical Modernism to the Present Day*, p. 50, no. 12

Literature
Coquiot 1924, p. 246
Laprade 1945, fig. no. 17
Rewald 1959, no. 22, fig. p. 21
Herbert 1959, p. 24
Hauke 1961, no. 102, fig. p. 63
Homer 1963, p. 284
Chastel and Minervino 1973, no. 45
Grenier 1990, no. 43
Distel 1991, no. 12, fig. p. 154
Wieczorek 2015, p. 50. no. 12

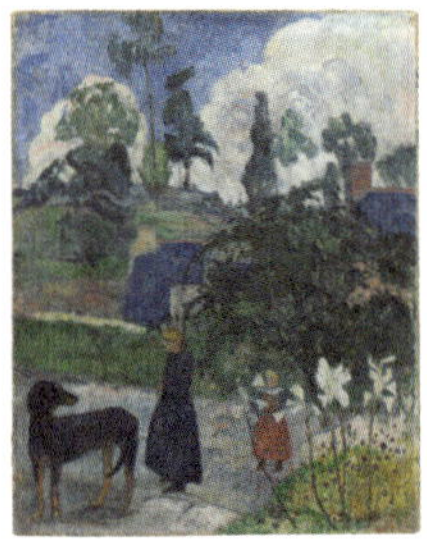

002

Paul Gauguin
Entre les lys
1889

Provenance
Hôtel Drouot, Paris, 23 February 1891, no. 5
M. Matthissen, Paris (acquired at Drouot 1891)
Fritz Bendix, Copenhagen
Paul Cassirer, Berlin
Galerie Bernheim-Jeune, Paris
Otto Feldmann
Mario Arbini, Frankfurt am Main
Galerie Thannhauser, Berlin
Rudolf Staechlin, Basel
Sotheby's, New York, 15 November 1989
Private collection, Japan
Private collection, Switzerland
Galerie Beyeler, Basel

Exhibitions
1893 Copenhagen, Bâtiment des Expositions libres, *Fortegnelse Over Kunstvoerkerne Paa den Frie Udstilling*, no. 151
1928 Basel, Kunsthalle, *Paul Gauguin 1848–1903*, no. 47 and 52 (2nd ed.)
1947–89 Basel, Kunstmuseum (on loan)
1949 Paris, Orangerie des Tuileries, Exposition du Centenaire, *Gauguin*, p. 30, no. 18
1949–50 Basel, Kunstmuseum, *Paul Gauguin zum 100. Geburtstag*, 1949–50, p. 31, no. 27
1956 Basel, Kunstmuseum, *Sammlung Rudolf Staechlin*, no. 33
1964 Paris, Musée National d'Art Moderne, *Fondation Rudolf Staechlin. De Corot à Picasso*, no. 27
1997 Basel, Galerie Beyeler, *Joie de vivre*, no. 26
1998–2004 Basel, Kunstmuseum (on loan)
2004–05 Madrid, Museo Thyssen-Bornemisza, *Gauguin and the Origins of Symbolism*, p. 228, no. 104 and p. 324
2005 Vaduz, Kunstmuseum Liechtenstein, *Werke aus der Hilti Art Foundation. Von Paul Gauguin bis Imi Knoebel*, p. 12, no. 1
2007–08 Riehen / Basel, Fondation Beyeler, *Die andere Sammlung. Hommage an Ernst und Hildy Beyeler*, p. 23
2011 Copenhagen, Ny Carlsberg Glyptotek, *Gauguin. Polynesia*, p. 50, no. 27 and p. 363
2015 Vaduz, Hilti Art Foundation / Kunstmuseum Liechtenstein, *Hilti Art Foundation – Painting and Sculpture. From Classical Modernism to the Present Day*, p. 54, no. 13
2016 Vaduz, Hilti Art Foundation / Kunstmuseum Liechtenstein, *Hilti Art Foundation – Kirchner, Léger, Scully & more. Works from the Collection*, p. 16, no. 1
2019 Vaduz, Hilti Art Foundation / Kunstmuseum Liechtenstein, *Composition '19 – Thomas Struth at the Hilti Art Foundation*, p. 123

Literature
Malingue 1948, no. 139
Lewandowski (Lee van Dovski) 1950, p. 345, no. 176
Wildenstein 1964, p. 140, no. 366
Pichon 1986, p. 131
Schneider 2005, p. 12, no. 1
Dickson 2010–11, p. 112
Schneider 2015, p. 54, no. 13
Schneider 2016, p. 16, no. 1
Wieczorek 2019, p. 123

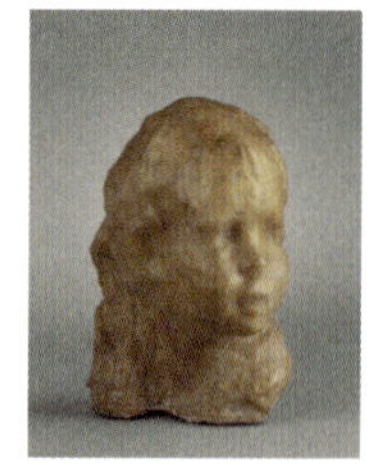

003

Medardo Rosso
Bambino ebreo
c. 1892–93

Provenance
Private collection, Italy
Private collection, Switzerland
Kunsthandel Wolfgang Werner, Bremen / Berlin

Exhibitions
2016 Vaduz, Hilti Art Foundation / Kunstmuseum Liechtenstein, *Hilti Art Foundation – Kirchner, Léger, Scully & more. Works from the Collection*, p. 28, no. 6
2018 Vaduz, Hilti Art Foundation / Kunstmuseum Liechtenstein, *Hilti Art Foundation – Rosso, Klee, Sonnier & more. Works from the Collection*, p. 12, no. 1

Literature
Santiago de Compostela 1996, fig. 40–48
Cooper / Hecker 2003, p. 44 and fig. 9–12 (different casts)
Caramel 2004, p. 140
Wieczorek 2016, p. 28, no. 6
Wieczorek 2018, p. 12, no. 1

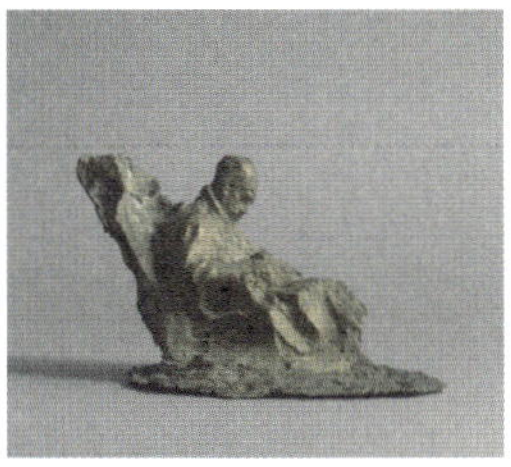

004

Medardo Rosso
Malato all'ospedale
1889 (cast c. 1906)

Provenance
Francesco Rosso (the artist's son)
Gift from Francesco Rosso to the lawyer Giovanni Bolognesi, Milan 1929
Private collection, Florence
Private collection, USA
Galleria Pieter Coray, Montagnola

Exhibitions
2016–17 St. Louis, USA, Pulitzer Arts Foundation, *Medardo Rosso – Experiments in Light and Form*, p. 53, no. 14 and p. 137
2018 Vaduz, Hilti Art Foundation / Kunstmuseum Liechtenstein, *Hilti Art Foundation – Rosso, Klee, Sonnier & more. Works from the Collection*, p. 16, no. 3

Literature
Borghi 1950, p. 65
De Sanna 1985, p. 128
Mola / Vitucci 2009, p. 353, no. III. 10e
Schenkenberg 2018, p. 53, no. 14
Wieczorek 2018, p. 16, no. 3

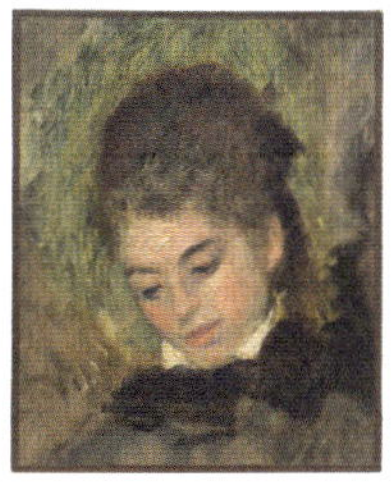

005

Pierre Auguste Renoir
Portrait de Nini Lopez
1876

Provenance
M. Albert Hensana
Galerie Bernheim-Jeune, Paris, 1935
Paul Rosenberg & Co., New York
Wildenstein & Co., New York
Alfred Schaefer, Zurich, 1963
Galerie Beyeler, Basel
Private collection, Switzerland
Dickinson, London

Literature
Daulte 1971, no. 164

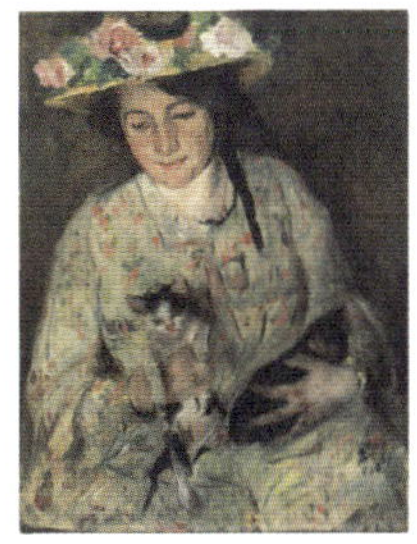

006

Lovis Corinth
Junge Frau mit Katzen
1904

Provenance
Samuel Siegbert Stern, Berlin
Johanna Margaretha Stern-Lippmann, Berlin, Amsterdam
Private collection, Wuppertal
Private collection, USA
Kunsthaus Bühler, Stuttgart
Verein der Freunde der Staatsgalerie Stuttgart
Restituted to Johanna Margaretha Stern-Lippmann, October 2011
Dickinson, London

Exhibitions
1918 Berlin, Secession, no. 42
1981 New York, The Metropolitan Museum of Art, *German Masters of the Nineteenth Century, Paintings and Drawings from the Federal Republic of Germany*, p. 72/73, no. 14
2006–07 Karlsruhe, Städtische Galerie, *Auf leisen Pfoten. Die Katze in der Kunst*, p. 16 und p. 87
2008–09 Regensburg, Kunstforum Ostdeutsche Galerie, *Lovis Corinth und die Geburt der Moderne*, p. 169

Literature
Pauli 1918, p. 338
Biermann 1922, p. 60
Scheffler 1923, p. 338
Heise / Berend-Corinth 1958, pp. 21–22, no. 5
Berend-Corinth 1958, no. 292
Berend-Corinth 1992, no. 292

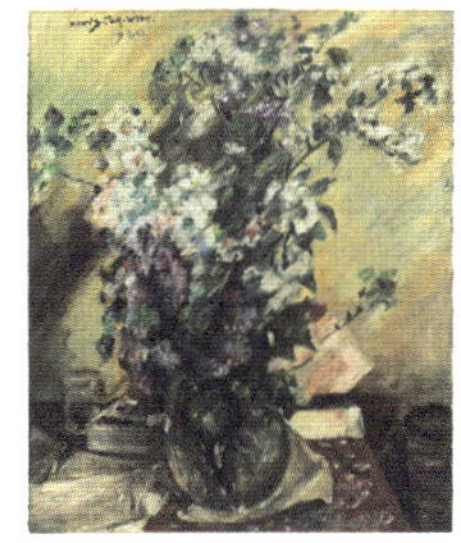

007

Lovis Corinth
Apfelblüten und Flieder
1920

Provenance
M. Feldberg, Stettin
Sammlung Nordmann, Berlin
Private collection, Ingolstadt
Private collection, Germany
Galerie Thomas, Munich

Exhibitions
1958 Berlin, Nationalgalerie, Schloss Charlottenburg, *Lovis Corinth zum 100. Geburtstag.*
1976 Cologne, Kunsthalle, *Lovis Corinth. Gemälde, Aquarelle, Zeichnungen und druckgraphische Zyklen*, no. 66

Literature
Berend-Corinth 1958, no. 796, fig. p. 730

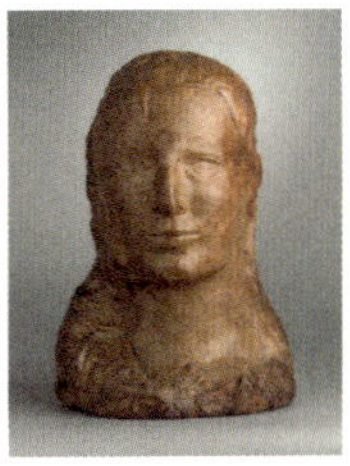

008

Pablo Picasso
Tête de femme (Fernande)
1906

Provenance
Ambroise Vollard, Paris
Jacques Ullman, Paris
Heinz Berggruen, Paris
Pierre Matisse Gallery, New York
Private collection, New York
Stephen Mazoh & Co., Inc., New York
Nathan and Marion Smooke, California, 1986–2001
Phillips de Pury & Luxembourg, New York, 5 November 2001, lot 10

Exhibitions
1983 New York, Stephen Mazoh & Co., Inc., *Twentieth Century Works of Art*, no. 15, fig. p. 32
1987 Los Angeles, Los Angeles County Museum of Art, *Degas to Picasso: Modern Masters from the Smooke Collection*, fig. p. 108
2005 Vaduz, Kunstmuseum Liechtenstein, *Werke aus der Hilti Art Foundation. Von Paul Gauguin bis Imi Knoebel*, p. 20, no. 4
2015 Vaduz, Hilti Art Foundation / Kunstmuseum Liechtenstein, *Hilti Art Foundation – Painting and Sculpture. From Classical Modernism to the Present Day*, p. 56, no. 14

Literature
Zervos 1942, vol. I, no. 323
Merli 1942, p. 292
Boeck and Sabartés 1955, p. 489, no. 68
Penrose 1967, pp. 17, 221, no. 6
Spies 1971, p. 301, no. 6
Johnson 1976, pp. 38–42, 165, no. 5
Palau i Fabre 1981, pp. 436–37, no. 1205
Spies and Piot 1983, pp. 28, 372, no. 61
Wilson 1987, p. 98
Baker 1987, p. 12
Spies 2000, pp. 31–32, 38, 394, no. 6
Schneider 2005, p. 20, no. 4
Schneider 2015, p. 56, no. 14

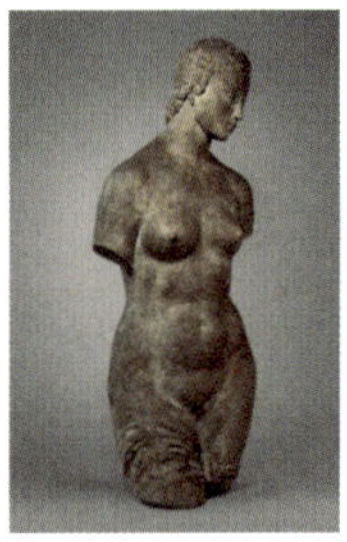

009

Wilhelm Lehmbruck
Torso der Grossen Stehenden
1910

Provenance
Leopold Badt
Kurt Badt and heirs
Christie's, London, 25 June 2001, lot 25
Private collection, Switzerland
Galerie Arnoldi-Livie, Munich

Exhibitions
2015 Vaduz, Hilti Art Foundation / Kunstmuseum Liechtenstein, *Hilti Art Foundation – Painting and Sculpture. From Classical Modernism to the Present Day*, p. 14, no. 1
2016 Vaduz, Hilti Art Foundation / Kunstmuseum Liechtenstein, *Hilti Art Foundation – Kirchner, Léger, Scully & more. Works from the Collection*, p. 18, no. 2
2018 Vaduz, Hilti Art Foundation / Kunstmuseum Liechtenstein, *Hilti Art Foundation – Rosso, Klee, Sonnier & more. Works from the Collection*, p. 18, no. 4
2019 Vaduz, Hilti Art Foundation / Kunstmuseum Liechtenstein, *Composition '19 – Thomas Struth at the Hilti Art Foundation*, p. 27

Literature
Badt 1920, pp. 169 (fig.), 172
Schubert 2001, p. 57
Schubert 2012, no. 7
Schneider 2015, p. 14, no. 1
Schneider 2016, p. 18, no. 2
Schneider 2018, p. 18, no. 4
Wieczorek 2019, p. 27

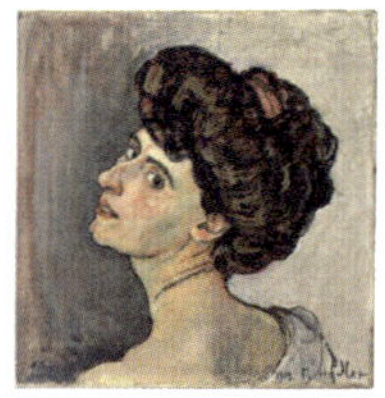

010

Ferdinand Hodler
Bildnis Valentine Godé-Darel (La Parisienne I)
1909

Provenance
Galerie Moos, Geneva
Private collection, Switzerland
Galerie Kornfeld, Bern, 15 June 2012, lot 59

Exhibitions
1910 Interlaken, *II. Internationale Kunst-Ausstellung in Interlaken (Kursaal)*, no. 34 (Frauenbildnis)
1918 Geneva, Galerie Moos, *Exposition suisse des beaux-arts*, no. 183
1918 Geneva, Galerie Moos, *Exposition Ferdinand Hodler*, no. 84 (La Parisienne)
1918 Geneva, Galerie Moos, *Salon d'été*, no. 46
1918 Geneva, Galerie Moos, *Expositions Peinture anglaise moderne. Hodler – Pierre Bertrand et A. Regnier*, no. 164
1919 Geneva, Galerie Moos, *Exposition Pietro Chiesa*, no. 143
1919 Basel, Kunsthalle, *Gedächtnisausstellung Ferdinand Hodler*, no. 56
1919 Geneva, Galerie Moos, *Salon d'été. Exposition particulière Alexandre Soldenhoff*, no. 61
1919 Bern, Kunsthalle, *Ferd. Hodler. E. de Fiori. W. Lehmbruck. Herm. Haller. H. Hubacher. E. Morgenthaler*, no. 26
1997 Trubschachen, 15. *Gemäldeausstellung Trubschachen. Schweizer Maler von A. Anker bis heute*, Kulturverein, no. 10
2015 Vaduz, Hilti Art Foundation / Kunstmuseum Liechtenstein, *Hilti Art Foundation – Painting and Sculpture. From Classical Modernism to the Present Day*, p. 16, no. 2
2016 Vaduz, Hilti Art Foundation / Kunstmuseum Liechtenstein, *Hilti Art Foundation – Kirchner, Léger, Scully & more. Works from the Collection*, p. 20, no. 3
2018 Vaduz, Hilti Art Foundation / Kunstmuseum Liechtenstein, *Hilti Art Foundation – Rosso, Klee, Sonnier & more. Works from the Collection*, p. 14, no. 2

Literature
Bloesch 1910, p. 31
Loosli 1919–20, no. 109
Loosli 1921–24, no. 1660
Loosli 1921–24, vol. 3, p. 119
Mühlestein / Schmidt 1942, p. 430
Fischer 1961, p. 9
Vignau-Wilberg 1973, p. 174
Kraft 1984, pp. 308/09
Affentranger-Kirchrath 1994, p. 301
Bätschmann / Brunner / Walter 2012, p. 217, no. 831
Wieczorek 2015, p. 16, no. 2
Wieczorek 2016, p. 20, no. 3
Wieczorek 2018, p. 14, no. 2

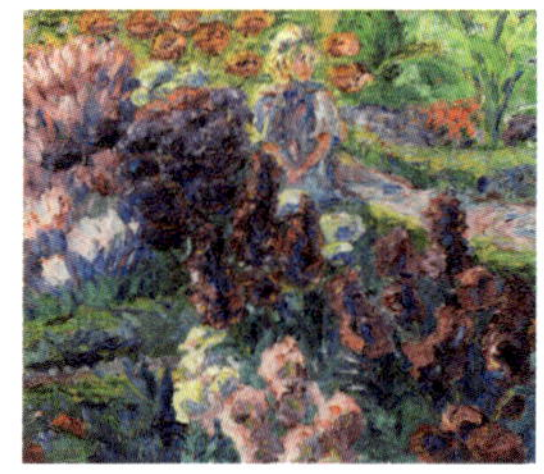

011

Emil Nolde
Blumengarten (Kleines Mädchen)
1908

Provenance
Emil Nolde Collection
Wilhelm and Edith Schulstad, Copenhagen
Flemming Vogg, Copenhagen
Private collection, Charlottenhof (Kiel)
Private collection, Germany
Private collection, Switzerland

Exhibitions
1958 Copenhagen, Schloss Charlottenborg, *Emil Nolde*, no. 119
2005 Vaduz, Kunstmuseum Liechtenstein, *Werke aus der Hilti Art Foundation. Von Paul Gauguin bis Imi Knoebel*, p. 24, no. 5
2010–11 Madrid, Museo Thyssen-Bornemisza, Fundación Caja Madrid, *Jardines impresionistas*, p. 278, no. 118

Literature
Urban 1987, p. 247, no. 276
Wieczorek 2005, p. 24, no. 5

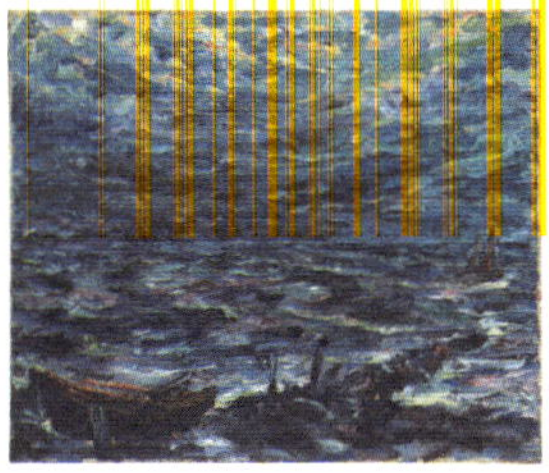

012

Emil Nolde
Dunkles Meer
1909

Provenance
Emil Nolde Collection
Dr. Paul Sudeck, Hamburg
Private collection, Germany
Private collection, Switzerland

Exhibitions
1912 Munich, Der Neue Kunstsalon, no. 43
1917 Hamburg, Hamburger Kunsthalle, *Hamburger Privatbesitz*, no. 93
1929 Kiel, Kunstverein Kiel, *Rohlfs, Nolde, Barlach*, no. 77
1987 Winterthur, Kunstmuseum, *Sommerausstellung der Sammlung*
1994 Lugano, Museo d'Arte Moderna, Villa Malpensa
1994–95 Vienna, Kunstforum der Bank Austria, *Emil Nolde*
2005 Vaduz, Kunstmuseum Liechtenstein, *Werke aus der Hilti Art Foundation. Von Paul Gauguin bis Imi Knoebel*, p. 26, no. 6

Literature
Urban 1987, p. 255, no. 286
Chiappini 1994, p. 46, no. 16
Wieczorek 2005, p. 26, no. 6

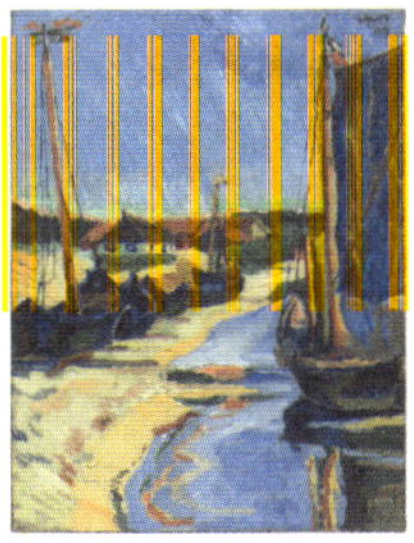

013

Max Pechstein
Geteerte Kähne
1909

Provenance
Private Collection, Heidelberg
Christie's London, March 1984, lot 26
Wolfgang Werner, Bremen
The Hoener Collection, USA
Phillips de Pury & Luxembourg, New York, 5 November 2001, lot 11

Exhibitions
1910 Darmstadt, Deutscher Künstlerbund, no. 183
1959 Berlin, Hochschule für Bildende Künste / Nationalgalerie, *Der junge Pechstein*, no. 39
1962 Heidelberg, Kunstverein Heidelberg, *Kunst des 20. Jahrhunderts aus Heidelberger Privatbesitz*, p. 38, no. 154
2005 Vaduz, Kunstmuseum Liechtenstein, *Werke aus der Hilti Art Foundation. Von Paul Gauguin bis Imi Knoebel*, p. 28, no. 7

Literature
Tobien 1987, p. 87
Wieczorek 2005, p. 28, no. 7

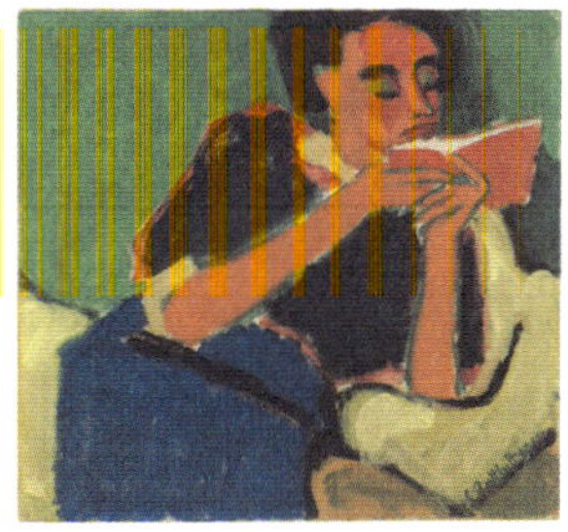

014

Karl Schmidt-Rottluff
Die Lesende
1911

Provenance
Alfred Hess, Erfurt
Städtisches Museum, Erfurt (now Anger-museum), gift of Alfred Hess, 1919
J. A. Benkert, Berlin
Galerie Ketterer, Munich 1976
Private collection, Munich
The Hoener Collection, USA
Phillips de Pury & Luxembourg, New York, 5 November 2001, lot 12

Exhibitions
1952 Florence, Museo della Commune di Firenze, *Mostra dell'Espressionismo*
1957 Oldenburg, Kunstverein, *Maler der Brücke in Dangast von 1907 bis 1912*, p. 79, no. 70
1964 London, Tate Gallery, *Painters of the Brücke*, p. 76, no. 253
1966 Paris, et al., Musée National d'Art Moderne, *Le Fauvisme Français et les Débuts de l'expressionnisme Allemand*, Paris, p. 350, no. 273
1989 Bremen, et al., Kunsthalle, *Karl Schmidt-Rottluff, Retrospektive*, p. 233, no. 83
2005 Vaduz, Kunstmuseum Liechtenstein, Werke aus der Hilti Art Foundation. Von Paul Gauguin bis Imi Knoebel, p. 30, no. 8

Literature
Niemeyer 1911
Apollonio 1952, p. 27, no. 75
Grohmann 1956, p. 284
Wietek 1955, p. 596, no. 211
Schneider 2005, p. 30, no. 8
Schneider 2015, p. 64, no. 15

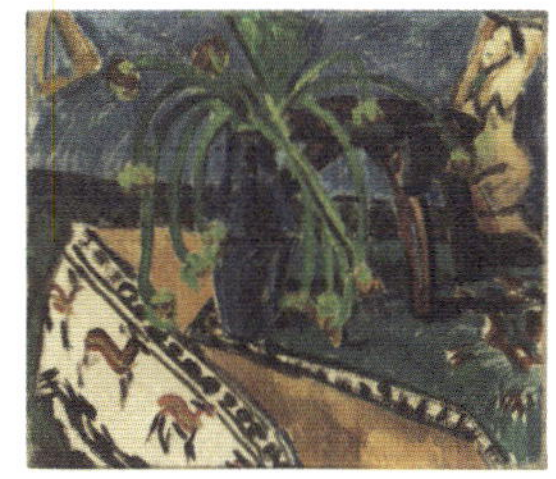

015

Erich Heckel
Stilleben mit blauer Vase
1912

Provenance
Kunstverein Barmen, 1923–1937
Deutsches Reich, Reichsministerium für Propaganda und Volksaufklärung, 1937–1941
Galerie Ferdinand Möller, Berlin, from 1941
Susanne Wenzl-Möller, Lucerne, until 1970
Villa Grisebach, Berlin, auction, 28 November 2003, lot 37
Private collection, Germany
Simon Theobald Ltd, London

Exhibitions
1923–1937 Kunstverein Barmen (Barmer Ruhmeshalle)
1953 Lucerne, Kunstmuseum, *Deutsche Kunst, Meisterwerke des 20. Jahrhunderts*, no. 18
1955 Berlin, Haus am Waldsee, *Deutsche Stilleben seit 1900*, no. 26
1961 Lucerne, Kunstmuseum, *Europäische Kunst des 19. und 20. Jahrhunderts aus Luzerner Privatbesitz*, no. 64
2010–11 Schleswig, Schloss Gottorf; Berlin, Brücke-Museum, *Erich Heckel, Aufbruch und Tradition, Eine Retrospektive*, no. 46

Literature
Platte 1964
Vogt 1965, no. 1912–46
Hüneke 2017, vol. 1, p. 173, no. 1912-17

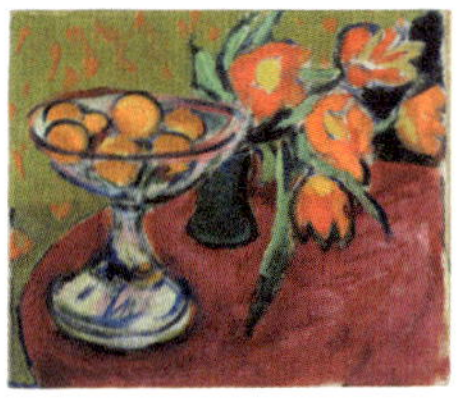

016

Ernst Ludwig Kirchner
Stilleben mit Orangen und Tulpen
1909

Provenance
Eberhard Grisebach Collection, Jena and Zurich
Private collection
Galerie Thomas, Munich

Exhibitions
1917 Jena, Kunstverein, *Ernst Ludwig Kirchner*, no. 9
1948 Bern, Kunsthalle, *Brücke*, no. 53
1952 Zurich, Kunsthaus Zürich, *Ernst Ludwig Kirchner*, no. 41
1960 Düsseldorf, Kunstverein für die Rheinlande und Westfalen, *Ernst Ludwig Kirchner*, no. 18 with fig.
1967 Basel, Kunsthalle, *E. L. Kirchner und Rot-Blau*, no. 20
1979–80 Berlin, Nationalgalerie, *Ernst Ludwig Kirchner*, no. 66
2001–02 Dresden, Staatliche Kunstsammlungen, Galerie Neue Meister, *Ernst Ludwig Kirchner*, p. 207, no. 254
2005 Madrid, Museo Thyssen-Bornemisza, *Brücke. El nacimiento del expresionismo alemán*, p. 226, no. 128
2006–07 Davos, Kirchner Museum Davos, *Ernst Ludwig Kirchner, Die Stilleben*, pp. 11, 15 (fig.), 88 (no. 15)
2009–10 Salzburg, Museum der Moderne, *Ernst Ludwig Kirchner*, pp. 45 (fig.), 296 (no. 6)
2016 Vaduz, Hilti Art Foundation / Kunstmuseum Liechtenstein, *Hilti Art Foundation – Kirchner, Léger, Scully & more. Works from the Collection*, p. 42, no. 10

Literature
Grisebach 1962, p. 64
Gordon 1968, no. 112
Wahl 1980, pp. 473–501
Henze 1980, pp. 23 (fig.), 24
Grisebach 1995, p. 28
Schick 2006, pp. 11, 15 (fig.)
Grisebach 2009–10, pp. 45 (fig.), 296 (no. 6)
Grisebach 2010, p. 275
Schneider 2016, p. 42, no. 10

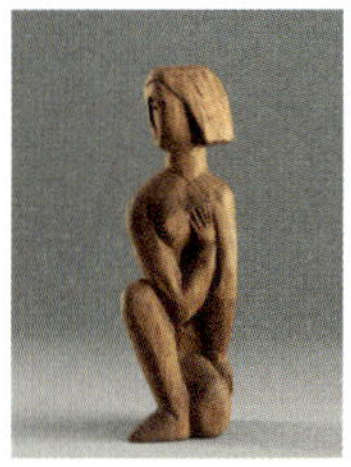

017

Ernst Ludwig Kirchner
Kniende, nach links gewandter Kopf, rechte Hand auf der linken Brust
1912

Provenance
Elisabeth Harkort, Hagen, c. 1915–2006/07
Christie's, London, 20 June 2012, lot 44
Private collection
Peter Raczeck Fine Art, New York

Exhibitions
2002–03 Davos, Kirchner Museum, *Ernst Ludwig Kirchner – Das plastische Werk*, no. 123
2003 Stuttgart, Staatsgalerie, *Ernst Ludwig Kirchner. Der Maler als Bildhauer*, no. 14
2015 Vaduz, Hilti Art Foundation / Kunstmuseum Liechtenstein, *Hilti Art Foundation – Painting and Sculpture. From Classical Modernism to the Present Day*, p. 68, no. 17
2016 Vaduz, Hilti Art Foundation / Kunstmuseum Liechtenstein, *Hilti Art Foundation – Kirchner, Léger, Scully & more. Works from the Collection*, p. 48, no. 12

Literature
Kirchner Archiv, V, no. 10
Nachbaur 1962, no. 90
Hesse-Frielinghaus 1974, nos. 1–4, p. 19 (fig.)
Gabler 1980, no. 37
Henze 2002, no. 1912–13, p. 330, fig. pp. 139, 140, 330
Schneider 2015, p. 68, no. 17
Schneider 2016, p. 48, no. 12

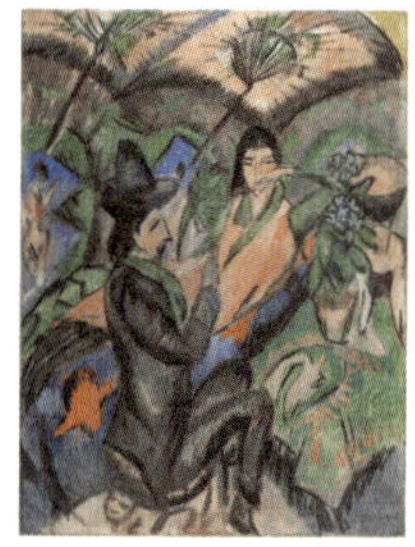

018

Ernst Ludwig Kirchner
Paar unter Japanschirm
1913

Provenance
Galerie Ludwig Schames, Frankfurt am Main
Ludwig and Rosi Fischer, Frankfurt am Main, c. 1916–18 until after 1945
Ernst Fischer, Richmond, Virginia
The New Gallery, New York
Larry Aldrich, New York
Parke-Bernet Galleries, New York, 1963
Marlborough Fine Art, London
The Yaseen Family Collection
Christie's, New York, 14 November 1990, lot 24
Private collection, Germany
Dickinson, London

Exhibitions
1958 Raleigh, North Carolina, The Museum of Art, *E. L. Kirchner, German Expressionist*, no. 18, fig. p. 78
1959 Richmond, The Virginia Museum of Fine Arts, *Paintings and Sculpture collected by Mr. and Mrs. Larry Aldrich*, no. 19, pl. 20
1960 Berkeley, University of California, *Art from Ingres to Pollock, Painting and Sculpture since Neoclassicism*, no. 27, with fig.
1963 New York, Marlborough-Gerson Gallery, *A Tribute to Curt Valentin*
1964 London, Tate Gallery, *Painters of the Brücke*, no. 84
1973 New York, Serge Sabarsky Gallery, *Expressionists: Major Paintings, Watercolors, Drawings and Sculptures by 17 German Expressionists*, fig. no. 25
1983–84 New York, Neuberger Museum, *Selections from the Yaseen Family Collection*
2002–03 Rome, Complesso del Vittoriano, *Gli Espressionisti*, fig. p. 71
2009–10 Salzburg, Museum der Moderne, *Ernst Ludwig Kirchner*, cat. no. 15, fig. p. 103
2010 Frankfurt am Main, Städel Museum, *Ernst Ludwig Kirchner. Retrospektive*, no. 47, fig. p. 126
2015 Vaduz, Hilti Art Foundation / Kunstmuseum Liechtenstein, *Hilti Art Foundation – Painting and Sculpture. From Classical Modernism to the Present Day*, p. 66, no. 16
2016 Vaduz, Hilti Art Foundation / Kunstmuseum Liechtenstein, *Hilti Art Foundation – Kirchner, Léger, Scully & more. Works from the Collection*, p. 46, no. 11
2017 Zurich, Kunsthaus Zürich, *Grossstadtrausch / Naturidyll. Kirchner – Die Berliner Jahre*, p. 144, no. 35

Literature
Kirchner Archiv, II, no. 31
Gordon 1968, no. 318
Branat, et al. 1987, p. 8
Grisebach 2009–10, pp. 103, 297, no. 15
Brandmüller 2010, p. 100
Schneider 2015, p. 66, no. 16
Schneider 2016, p. 46, no. 11

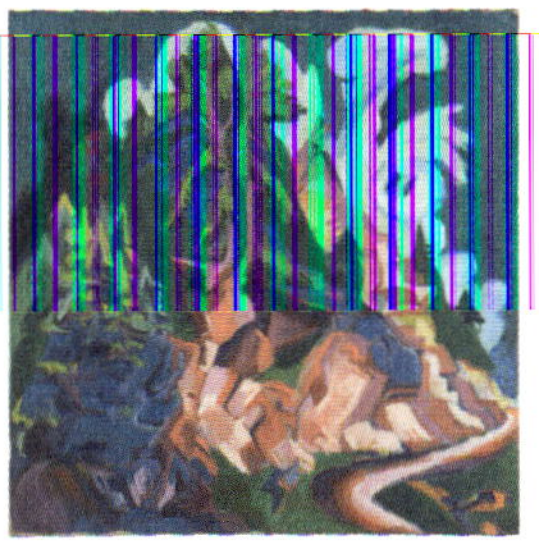

019

Ernst Ludwig Kirchner
Weg zur Staffel
1919

Provenance
The artist's estate
Roman Norbert Ketterer, Stuttgart / Campione d'Italia / Lugano
Private collection, Switzerland
Galerie Henze & Ketterer & Triebold, Riehen / Basel

Exhibitions
1922 Frankfurt, Galerie Ludwig Schames, *Schweizer Arbeit von E. L. Kirchner – 1916–1921*, p. 14 (there titled: *Der Berg*, 1918)
1950–51 Hamburg, Kunstverein HHBW, *Ernst Ludwig Kirchner. Werke aus dem Nachlass, zum ersten Male in Deutschland, aus Anlass seines 70. Geburtstages*, p. 19
1952 Zurich, Kunsthaus Zürich, *Ernst Ludwig Kirchner*, p. 63
1953 Chur, Kunsthaus, *Ernst Ludwig Kirchner. Gemälde und Graphik aus der Davoser Zeit*, p. 7
1956 Stuttgart, Württembergischer Kunstverein, *Ernst Ludwig Kirchner, zur Erinnerung an den 75. Geburtstag des Künstlers*, p. 32
1960–61 Bremen, Kunsthalle; Hanover, Kunstverein; The Hague, Gemeentemuseum; Cologne, Wallraf-Richartz-Museum; Zurich, Kunsthaus Zürich, *Meisterwerke des deutschen Expressionismus*, p. 40 (colour plate 32)
1965 Campione d'Italia, Galerie R. N. Ketterer, *Moderne Kunst II*, p. 75, fig. p. 109
2003–04 Basel, Kunstmuseum, *Ernst Ludwig Kirchner – Bergleben. Die frühen Davoser Jahre 1917–1926*, p. 21, fig. p. 78
2009 Trubschachen, 18. Kunstausstellung Trubschachen, *Schweizer Künstlerinnen und Künstler*, p. 12
2016 Vaduz, Hilti Art Foundation / Kunstmuseum Liechtenstein, *Hilti Art Foundation – Kirchner, Léger, Scully & more. Works from the Collection*, p. 52, no. 13

Literature
Ernst Ludwig Kirchner, Photoalbum III, fig. p. 147
Grohmann 1961, fig. p. 101
Gordon 1968, no. 570, fig. p. 357
Ketterer 1999, fig. p. 247
Lüttichau 2007, pp. 74–91
Delfs 2010, 1193, 1242, 1440
Busch et al. 1960, no. 40, fig. 32
Schneider 2016, p. 52, no. 13

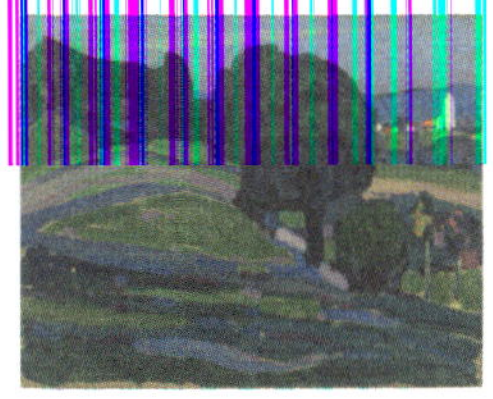

020

Wassily Kandinsky
Paysage à Murnau
(Landschaft mit dunklem Baum)
1908

Provenance
Gabriele Münter, Murnau
Marlborough Fine Art Ltd., London
Stephan Hahn, New York
Findlay Galleries, Chicago
Cynthia Warrick Kemper, New York
Jan Krugier, Geneva
Private collection, Switzerland
Galerie Jan Krugier, Geneva

Exhibitions
1957 Munich, Städtische Galerie im Lenbachhaus, *Kandinsky und Gabriele Münter*, no. 65
1961 London, Marlborough Fine Art Ltd., *Kandinsky, The Road to Abstraction*, no. 24
1965 Kansas City, William Rockhill Nelson Gallery of Art, Atkins Museum of Fine Art, *Kansas City Collects*, no. 36
1995 Lugano, Museo Cantonale d'Arte, *Kandinsky dans les collections suisses*, p. 158, no. 7
2003–04 Ludwigshafen am Rhein, Wilhelm-Hack-Museum, *Der Blaue Reiter, Die Befreiung der Farbe*, p. 121, no. 92
2005 Vaduz, Kunstmuseum Liechtenstein, *Werke aus der Hilti Art Foundation. Von Paul Gauguin bis Imi Knoebel*, p. 32, no. 9
2018 Vaduz, Hilti Art Foundation / Kunstmuseum Liechtenstein, *Hilti Art Foundation – Rosso, Klee, Sonnier & more. Works from the Collection*, p. 52, no. 19

Literature
Roethel / Benjamin, 1982, p. 196, no. 194
Wieczorek 2005, p. 32, no. 9
Wieczorek 2018, p. 52, no. 19

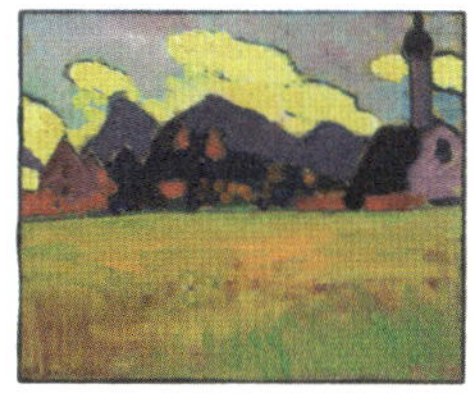

021

Alexej Jawlensky
Landschaft bei Murnau
c. 1910

Provenance
Private collection, Germany
Landau Fine Art, Montreal

Exhibitions
1956 Düsseldorf, Kunsthalle Düsseldorf, *Düsseldorfer Kaufleute sammeln moderne Kunst*, no. 66
1957 Hamburg, Hamburger Kunsthalle, *Jawlensky*, no. 15
2005 Vaduz, Kunstmuseum Liechtenstein, *Werke aus der Hilti Art Foundation. Von Paul Gauguin bis Imi Knoebel*, p. 34, no. 10
2010–11 Wiesbaden, Museum Wiesbaden, *Das Geistige in der Kunst. Vom Blauen Reiter zum Abstrakten Expressionismus*, p. 83
2012–13 Essen, Museum Folkwang, *Im Farbenrausch. Munch, Matisse und die Expressionisten*, p. 229, no. 53
2014 Murnau, Schlossmuseum Murnau, *Blaues Haus und Gelber Klang. Wassily Kandinsky und Alexej Jawlensky in Murnau*, p. 6, p. 70, no. 9
2018 Vaduz, Hilti Art Foundation / Kunstmuseum Liechtenstein, *Hilti Art Foundation – Rosso, Klee, Sonnier & more. Works from the Collection*, p. 54, no. 20

Literature
Weiler, p. 264, no. 540
The Alexej von Jawlensky Archive, 1991, p. 291, no. 358
Wieczorek 2005, p. 34, no. 10
Wieczorek 2018, p. 54, no. 20

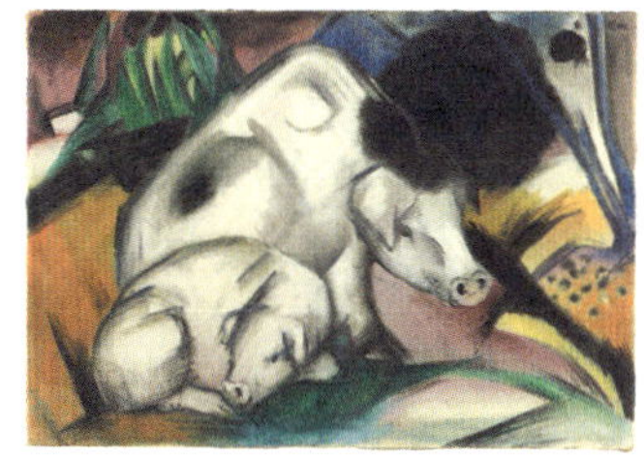

022

Franz Marc
Schweine (Mutterschwein)
1912

Provenance
Galerie Der Sturm, Berlin
Maria Marc, Ried
Fritz Schön, Berlin, 1920
Kronprinzenpalais Berlin (on loan from 1928–1933)
Robert C. Schön, 1937
Irene Freund (nee Schön), Toronto, c. 1938
M. Stern, Dominion Gallery Montreal, 1942
Fred S. Mendel, Saskatoon, 1942
Eva Miller (nee Mendel), c. 1970
Karl & Faber, Munich, 1977
Christie's, New York, November 1983, lot 74
Marlborough Fine Art Ltd., London, 1983–87
Private collection, Germany
Caspar H. Schübbe, Switzerland

Exhibitions
1913 Munich, Galerie Thannhauser, *Franz Marc*
1913 Jena, Kunstverein, *Tierbild-Ausstellung, Franz Marc et al.*
1913 Berlin et al., Galerie Der Sturm, 14th exhibition, *Franz Marc*
1928 Berlin, National-Galerie, *Neuere Deutsche Kunst aus Berliner Privatbesitz*, no. 113
1956 Ottawa, National Gallery / Montreal, Museum of Fine Arts 1956, *The Fred Mendel Collection*
1962 Ottawa, National Gallery, *Corot to Picasso*
1971–72 New Orleans, Museum of Fine Art, *German & Austrian Expressionism*, no. 59
1979–80 Berkeley, University Art Museum; Fort Worth, The Fort Worth Art Museum; Minneapolis, Walker Art Center, *Franz Marc: 1880–1916*, published in conjunction with the exhibition *Franz Marc: Pioneer of Spiritual Abstraction*, no. 19, fig. p. 78
1985 London, Royal Academy of Arts and Stuttgart 1986, Staatsgalerie, *German Art in the 20th Century. Painting and Sculpture 1905–1985*, no. 43 (no. 41 in Ger. ed.)
2005–06 Munich, Städtische Galerie im Lenbachhaus und Kunstbau, *Franz Marc – Die Retrospektive*, p. 148, no. 57
2015 Vaduz, Hilti Art Foundation / Kunstmuseum Liechtenstein, *Hilti Art Foundation – Painting and Sculpture. From Classical Modernism to the Present Day*, p. 72, no. 18

Literature
Walden 1919 (fig.)
Weiss 1933, fig. 43
Schardt 1936, 1-1012-10
Lankheit 1970, no. 179
Lankheit 1976, fig. 17
Rosenthal 1989, fig. 29
Hoberg / Jansen 2003, p. 216, no. 191
Wieczorek 2015, p. 72, no. 18

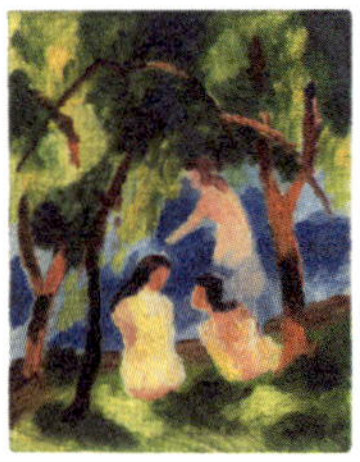

023

August Macke
Badende Mädchen
1913

Provenance
Joseph Haubrich, Cologne, until 1947
Private collection, Germany
Wolfgang Werner, Bremen, 1983
Diethelm Hoener, Germany
Phillips, de Pury & Luxembourg, New York, 5 November 2001, lot 24
Private collection
Sotheby's, New York, 2 November 2010, lot 19

Exhibitions
1914 Berlin, Erste Ausstellung der freien Secession, no. 145
1928 Berlin, Galerie Ferdinand Moeller, *Neuere deutsche Kunst aus Berliner Privatbesitz*, no. 15
1947 Cologne, Museen der Stadt Köln in der Alten Universität, *August Macke, Gedächtnisausstellung*, no. 48
1954 Braunschweig, Kunstverein, *August Macke*, no. 63
1957 Münster, Westfälischer Kunstverein, *August Macke, Gedenkausstellung zum 70. Geburtstag*, no. 78
1964 Amsterdam, Stedelijk Museum, *Expressionisme van Gogh tot Picasso*, no. 81
2015 Vaduz, Hilti Art Foundation / Kunstmuseum Liechtenstein, *Hilti Art Foundation – Painting and Sculpture. From Classical Modernism to the Present Day*, p. 76, no. 19

Literature
Cohen 1922, p. 710
Vriesen 1953, no. 436
Vriesen 1957, no. 436, p. 332
Gordon 1974, no. 145, p. 818
Heiderich 2008, no. 515, p. 484 with fig.
Wieczorek 2015, p. 76, no. 19

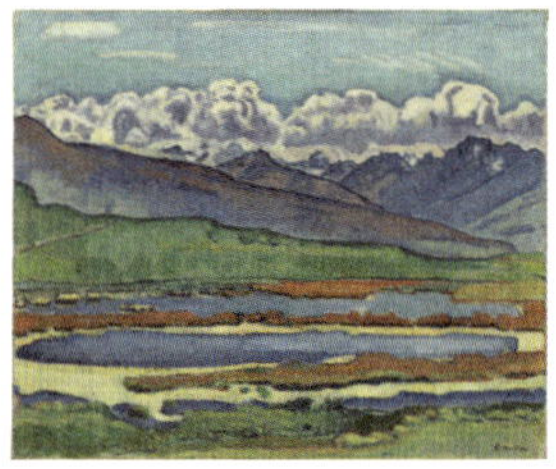

024

Ferdinand Hodler
Les Etangs longs bei Montana
1915

Provenance
Kunstsalon Wolfsberg, Zurich, 1917
Private collection, Switzerland, since 1917
Galerie Kornfeld, Bern, 15 June 2012, lot 59

Exhibitions
1917 Zurich, Kunsthaus, *Ferdinand Hodler*, no. 395
2013 Riehen / Basel, Fondation Beyeler, *Ferdinand Hodler*, pp. 62–63

Literature
Bender 1921, p. 25 b (colour plate)
Loosli 1921–24, vol. 3, p. 208
Loosli 1921–24 (GK), no. 1491
Rascher 1928, p. 17
Müller 1941, p. 214
Müller 1941 (LK), no. 542
Mühlestein / Schmidt 1942, p. 481
Doriot Galofaro 2005, pp. 58–59 (colour plate)
Bätschmann / Brunner / Walter 2008, vol. 1, p. 422, no. 534

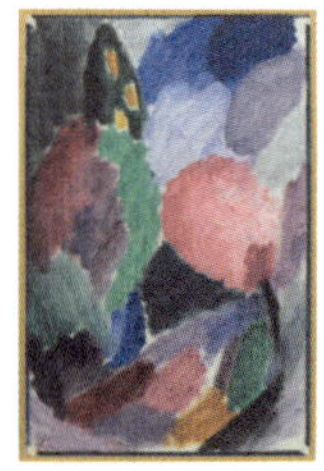

025

Alexej Jawlensky
Grosse Variation – Es stürmt
1916

Provenance
Private collection
Galerie Alex Vömel, Düsseldorf 1956–1982
Private collection, Munich
Private collection
Galerie Thomas, Munich

Exhibitions
1956 Düsseldorf, Gallery Alex Vömel, *Alexej von Jawlensky*
1957–58 Düsseldorf, Kunstverein für die Rheinlande und Westfalen; Hamburg, Kunstverein; Bremen, Kunsthalle, *Alexej von Jawlensky*, no. 67
1958 Stuttgart, Württembergischer Kunstverein; Mannheim, Städtische Kunsthalle, *Alexej von Jawlensky*, no. 72
1958 Berlin, Haus am Waldsee, *Alexej von Jawlensky*, no. 41
1967 Frankfurt, Kunstverein; Hamburg, Kunstverein, *Alexej von Jawlensky*, no. 94
1971 Bonn, Museum Städtischer Kunstsammlungen, *Alexej von Jawlensky*, no. 38
1983 Munich, Städtische Galerie im Lenbachhaus; Baden-Baden, Staatliche Kunsthalle, *Alexej von Jawlensky*, no. 130
2018 Vaduz, Hilti Art Foundation / Kunstmuseum Liechtenstein, *Hilti Art Foundation – Rosso, Klee, Sonnier & more. Works from the Collection*, p. 58, no. 22

Literature
Weiler 1959, no. 623
Weiler 1970, no. 1203
Jawlensky / Pieroni-Jawlensky / Jawlensky 1992, no. 844, p. 167
Wieczorek 2018, p. 58, no. 22

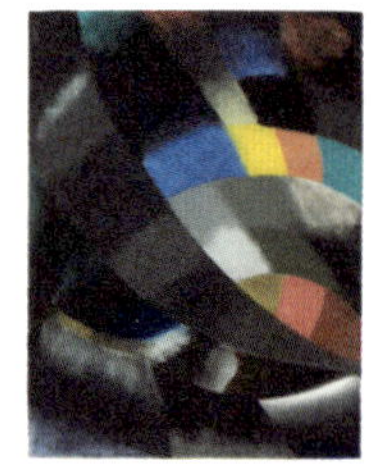

026

Otto Freundlich
Schiff im Sturm
1924

Provenance
Private collection
Galerie Berinson, Berlin

Exhibitions
1978 Bonn, Rheinisches Landesmuseum, *Otto Freundlich (1878–1943). Monographie mit Dokumentation und Werkverzeichnis*, no. 232, fig. 228
2017 Cologne, Museum Ludwig, *Otto Freundlich. Kosmischer Kommunismus*, pp. 170, 343

Literature
Heusinger von Waldegg 1978, no. 232, fig. 228
Franken 2017, p. 224

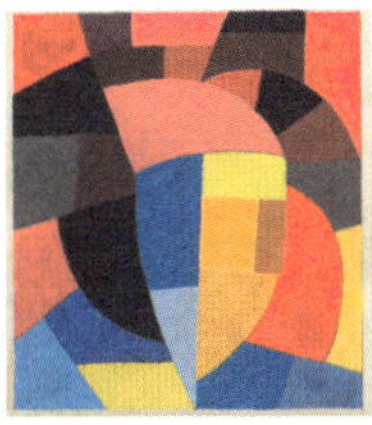

027

Otto Freundlich
Untitled
1937

Provenance
Sammlung Étienne Béothy, Paris
Galerie Lahumière, Paris

Exhibitions
2005 Vaduz, Kunstmuseum Liechtenstein, *Werke aus der Hilti Art Foundation. Von Paul Gauguin bis Imi Knoebel*, p. 66, no. 25

Literature
Wieczorek 2005, p. 66, no. 25

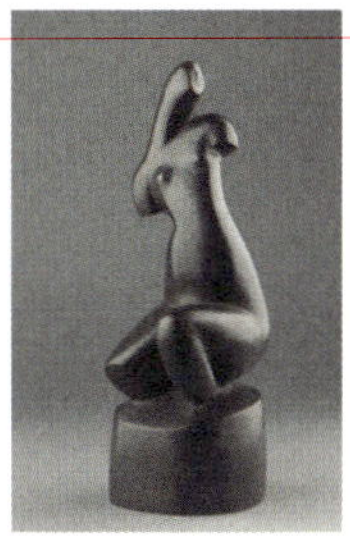

028

Alexander Archipenko
Black Seated Torso
1909

Provenance
Galerie Im Erker, St.Gallen (1962 directly from the artist)
Private collection, Switzerland
Galerie Widmer, St. Gallen

Exhibitions
1962–63 St. Gallen, Galerie Im Erker
2018 Vaduz, Hilti Art Foundation / Kunstmuseum Liechtenstein, *Hilti Art Foundation – Rosso, Klee, Sonnier & more. Works from the Collection*, p. 40, no. 13

Literature
Hofmann 1962, p. 2, no. 1
Karshan 1974, p. 38
Wieczorek 2018, p. 40, no. 13

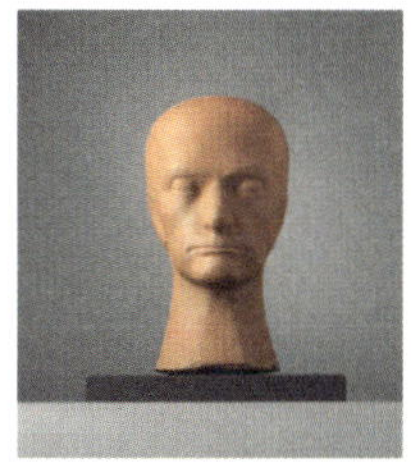

029

Raymond Duchamp-Villon
Baudelaire
1911

Provenance
Francis Picabia, acquired from the artist c. 1912
Gabriella Buffet-Picabia
Drouot-Richelieu, Paris, 22 November 1996, lot 151b
Private collection, France
Dickinson, London

Exhibitions
2015 Vaduz, Hilti Art Foundation / Kunstmuseum Liechtenstein, *Hilti Art Foundation – Painting and Sculpture. From Classical Modernism to the Present Day*, p. 18, no. 3

Literature
Cabanne 1997
Grandy-Pradel 1998, p. 145
Wieczorek 2015, p. 18, no. 3

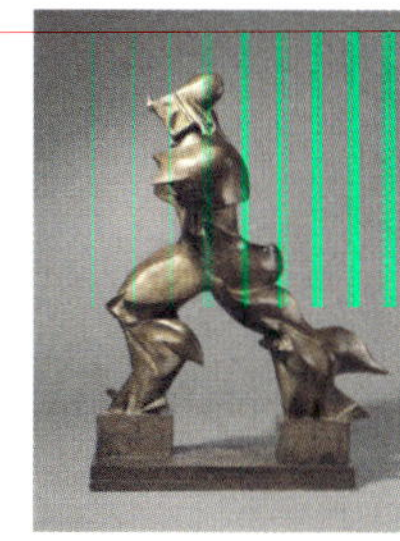

030

Umberto Boccioni
Forme uniche della continuità nello spazio
1913

Provenance
Private collection, Italy
Private collection, Switzerland
Caspar H. Schübbe, Switzerland

Exhibitions
2005 Vaduz, Kunstmuseum Liechtenstein, *Werke aus der Hilti Art Foundation. Von Paul Gauguin bis Imi Knoebel*, p. 40, no. 13
2014 Vaduz, Kunstmuseum Liechtenstein, *lens-based-sculpture. Die Veränderung der Skulptur durch die Fotografie*, p. 211
2015 Vaduz, Hilti Art Foundation / Kunstmuseum Liechtenstein, *Hilti Art Foundation – Painting and Sculpture. From Classical Modernism to the Present Day*, p. 20, no. 4

Literature
Alley 1981, pp. 60–61
Calvesi and Coen 1983, pp. 466–72
Coen 1988, pp. 216–18
Schneede 1994, pp. 142–51
Wieczorek 2005, p. 40, no. 13
Malsch 2014, p. 103
Wieczorek 2015, p. 20, no. 4

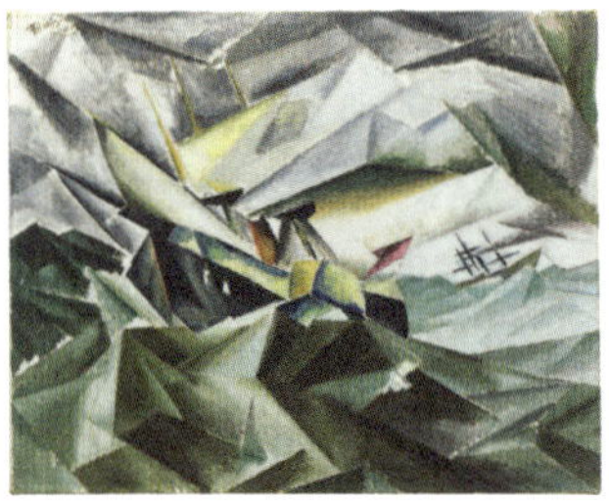

031

Lyonel Feininger
Der Raddampfer I
1913

Provenance
Lyonel Feininger, Berlin, Weimar, Dessau, until 1931
Galerie Dr. Goldschmidt / Dr. Wallerstein, Berlin
Galerie Ferdinand Möller, Berlin, Zermützel, Cologne, until 1956
Maria Möller-Garny, Cologne, Maienfeld, 1956–1971
Private collection, Switzerland
Wolfgang Wittrock Kunsthandel, Berlin

Exhibitions
1919–20 Hanover, Kestner-Gesellschaft e.V., XXIX. Sonderausstellung, *Paul Klee, Lyonel Feininger. Gemälde, Graphik*
1931 Essen, Museum Folkwang, *Jubiläumsausstellung Lyonel Feininger aus Anlass des 60. Geburtstages des Künstlers*
1931 Berlin, Nationalgalerie, *Lyonel Feininger*
1951–52 Cologne, Gallery Ferdinand Möller, Eröffnungs-Ausstellung. *Die Alten Meister der modernen Kunst in Deutschland*, no. 8
1960–61 Paris, Musée National d'Art Moderne, *Les sources du XXe siècle. Les Arts en Europe de 1884 à 1914*, no. 166
1966 Cologne, Dom Galerie (Angelika Fessler-Möller), Sammlung Ferdinand Möller, *Gedächtnisausstellung zu seinem 10. Todestag*
1966 Frankfurt a. M., Frankfurter Kunstverein, *Vom Impressionismus zum Bauhaus. Meisterwerke aus deutschem Privatbesitz*, no. 22
2001 Basel, Sonderausstellung auf der ART BASEL von Wolfgang Wittrock Kunsthandel, *Die Blaue Vier und Ferdinand Möller*
2005 Vaduz, Kunstmuseum Liechtenstein, *Werke aus der Hilti Art Foundation. Von Paul Gauguin bis Imi Knoebel*, p. 38, no. 12
2005 Hamburg, Hamburger Kunsthalle, *Seestücke. Von Caspar David Friedrich bis Emil Nolde*, p. 103, no. 58
2006 Wuppertal, Von der Heydt-Museum, *lyonel feininger*, p. 126
2018 Vaduz, Hilti Art Foundation / Kunstmuseum Liechtenstein, *Hilti Art Foundation – Rosso, Klee, Sonnier & more. Works from the Collection*, p. 56, no. 21

Literature
Hess 1959, p. 257, no. 105
Roters 1984
Luckhardt 1998, p. 84–85
Wieczorek 2005, p. 38, no. 12
Wieczorek 2018, p. 56, no. 21

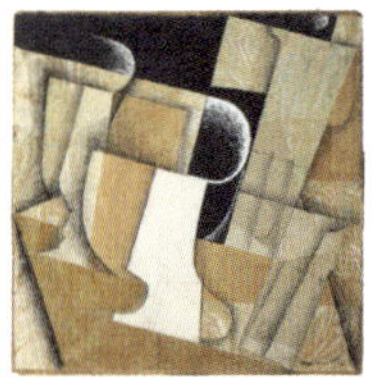

032

Juan Gris
Le verre
1914

Provenance
Daniel-Henry Kahnweiler, Bern
Galerie Simon, Paris
Howard Putzel, San Francisco
Adolfe Mack, San Francisco
Alexander Rabow Galleries, San Francisco
Perls Gallery, New York
Private collection, New York
Landau Fine Art, Montreal

Exhibitions
1940 San Francisco, San Francisco Museum of Art, *Contemporary Art*, no. 119
2015 Vaduz, Hilti Art Foundation / Kunstmuseum Liechtenstein, *Hilti Art Foundation – Painting and Sculpture. From Classical Modernism to the Present Day*, p. 78, no. 20
2018 Vaduz, Hilti Art Foundation / Kunstmuseum Liechtenstein, *Hilti Art Foundation – Rosso, Klee, Sonnier & more. Works from the Collection*, p. 36, no. 11
2019 Vaduz, Hilti Art Foundation / Kunstmuseum Liechtenstein, *Composition '19 – Thomas Struth at the Hilti Art Foundation*, p. 121

Literature
Cooper 1977, p. 170, no. 110
Wieczorek 2015, p. 78, no. 20
Wieczorek 2018, p. 36, no. 11
Wieczorek 2019, p. 121

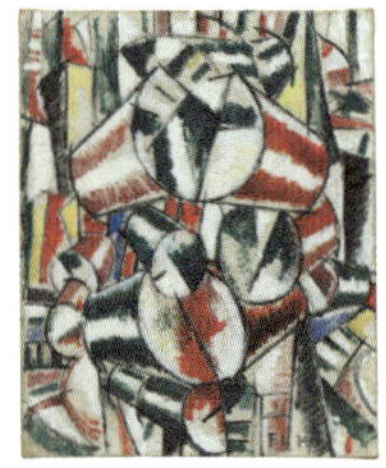

033

Fernand Léger
Contraste de formes
1914

Provenance
Maurice Laffaille, Paris
Ernst Beyeler Collection, Basel, since 1961
Galerie Beyeler, Basel

Exhibitions
1969 Basel, Galerie Beyeler, *Fernand Léger*, no. 5
1969 Madrid, *Colección Beyeler, Centro de Arte Reine Sofia*, p. 68
1969–70 Düsseldorf, Städtische Kunsthalle Düsseldorf, *Fernand Léger*, no. 15
1993 Berlin, Nationalgalerie, *Wege der Moderne – Die Sammlung Beyeler*, no. 61
1993 Basel, Kunstmuseum, et. al., *Fernand Léger 1911–1924. Der Rhythmus des modernen Lebens*, p. 96 and p. 244, no. 15
1996 Sapporo, Hokkaido Museum of Modern Art, et al., *The Exhibition from Swiss Private Collections*, no. 17, p. 50
1996–97 Sydney, The Art Gallery of South Wales, *Masterpieces of the Twentieth Century, The Beyeler Collection*, no. 35
2005 Vaduz, Kunstmuseum Liechtenstein, *Werke aus der Hilti Art Foundation. Von Paul Gauguin bis Imi Knoebel*, p. 44, no. 14
2007–08 Riehen / Basel, Fondation Beyeler, *Die andere Sammlung. Hommage an Ernst und Hildy Beyeler*, p. 128
2008 Riehen / Basel, Fondation Beyeler, *Fernand Léger. Paris – New York*, p. 31, no. 10 and p. 202
2015 Vaduz, Hilti Art Foundation / Kunstmuseum Liechtenstein, *Hilti Art Foundation – Painting and Sculpture. From Classical Modernism to the Present Day*, p. 80, no. 21
2018 Vaduz, Hilti Art Foundation / Kunstmuseum Liechtenstein, *Hilti Art Foundation – Rosso, Klee, Sonnier & more. Works from the Collection*, p. 38, no. 12
2019 Vaduz, Hilti Art Foundation / Kunstmuseum Liechtenstein, *Composition '19 – Thomas Struth at the Hilti Art Foundation*, p. 67

Literature
Jullian et al., 1969, no. 10
Néret 1990, no. 5
Bauquier 1990, no. 67, fig. p. 125
Los Pintores Cubistas, in: Saber Ver, 10 Contemporáneo del Arte, Mexico City 1993, p. 49
Fondation Beyeler, Sammlungskatalog, Basel 1997, no. 85, p. 31
Wieczorek 2005, p. 44, no. 14
Wieczorek 2015, p. 80, no. 21
Wieczorek 2018, p. 38, no. 12
Wieczorek 2019, p. 67

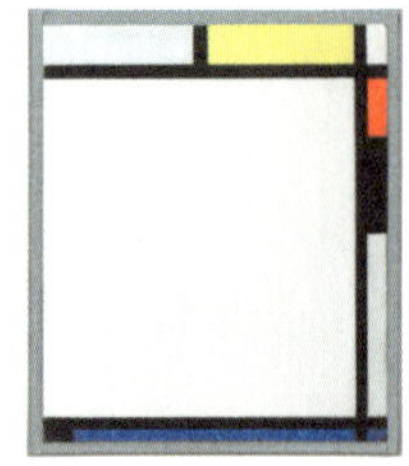

034

Piet Mondrian
Tableau No. VIII with Yellow, Red, Black and Blue
1925

Provenance
Sophie Küppers, Hanover / Dresden, 1925, from the artist
Kunstausstellung Kühl, Dresden, 1926–27, from Sophie Küppers
Kaiser Wilhelm Museum, Krefeld, c. 1929–50
Galerie Alex Vömel, Düsseldorf, after 1950 to 1955
Karl Anselmino, Wuppertal, c. 1955–77
Private collection, Germany, on loan 1977–88 to Staatsgalerie Moderner Kunst, Munich, inv. no. L 1641
Private collection
Dickinson, London

Exhibitions
1925 Dresden, Kunsthandlung Kühl und Kühn, *Piet Mondrian – Man Ray*
1926 Munich, Galerie Goltz, *Lissitzky: Moskau, Mondrian: Paris, Man Ray: New York*
1927 Mannheim, Städtische Kunsthalle, *Wege und Richtungen der Abstrakten Malerei in Europa*, no. 261
1929 Frankfurt am Main, Kunstgewerbemuseum, *Der Stuhl*
1958 Wuppertal, Kunsthalle, *Moderne Kunst in Wuppertaler Privatbesitz*, no. 99
1966 Recklinghausen, Städtische Kunsthalle, *Variationen (über ein Thema)*, no. 154
1967 Düsseldorf, Städtische Kunsthalle, *Kunst des 20. Jahrhunderts aus rheinisch-westfälischem Privatbesitz*, no. 247
1972 Wuppertal, Von der Heydt-Museum, *Um 1930: Bild, Bau, Gerät*, no. 128
2005 Vaduz, Kunstmuseum Liechtenstein, *Werke aus der Hilti Art Foundation. Von Paul Gauguin bis Imi Knoebel*, p. 62, no. 23
2015 Vaduz, Hilti Art Foundation / Kunstmuseum Liechtenstein, *Hilti Art Foundation – Painting and Sculpture. From Classical Modernism to the Present Day*, p. 82, no. 22
2018 Vaduz, Hilti Art Foundation / Kunstmuseum Liechtenstein, *Hilti Art Foundation – Rosso, Klee, Sonnier & more. Works from the Collection*, p. 90, no. 36
2019 Vaduz, Hilti Art Foundation / Kunstmuseum Liechtenstein, *Composition '19 – Thomas Struth at the Hilti Art Foundation*, p. 64

Literature
Piet Mondrian, letter to Til Brugman, 13 November 1924
Piet Mondrian, letter to S. B. Slijper from "Dinsdagavond", c. July 1925
Piet Mondrian, postcard to M. Seuphor, 9 August 1925
Sophie Küppers, Bilderliste, Hanover, 20 December 1926, no. 6, Komposition No. VIII, 25. 51/45. Mark 400
Stuhl-Ausstellung, in: Das Neue Frankfurt, p. 64 (with photograph of the exhibition), March 1929
Wember 1973, p. 21
Joosten and Welsh 1998, vol. II, p. 316, no. B 160
Wieczorek 2005, p. 62, no. 23
Wieczorek 2015, p. 82, no. 22
Wieczorek 2018, p. 90, no. 36
Wieczorek 2019, p. 64

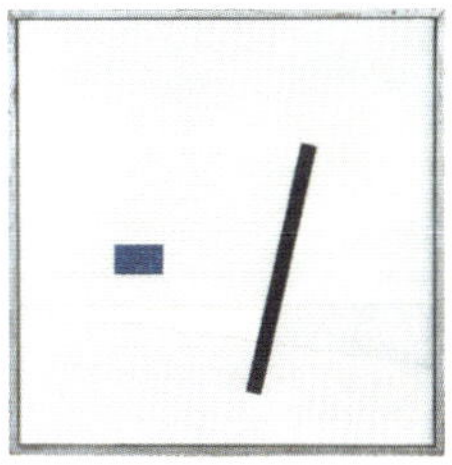

035

Friedrich Vordemberge-Gildewart
Komposition 78
1933

Provenance
Prof. Annie Müller-Widmann, Switzerland*
Nachlass Prof. Dr. Oskar Müller-Widmann, Basel
Sammlung Petzold-Müller, Basel
Von Bartha, Basel

Exhibitions
1934 Rome, Galleria Bragaglia fuori commercio, *Vordemberge-Gildewart*
1934 Milan, Galleria del Milione, *Vordemberge-Gildewart*
1975 Ulm / Münster, Ulmer Museum und Westfälisches Landesmuseum für Kunst und Kulturgeschichte, *Vordemberge-Gildewart*, Ulm / Münster, 1975
1997 Wiesbaden, Museum Wiesbaden, *Friedrich Vordemberge-Gildewart, Retrospektive*, p. 93

Literature
Schmidt no year, unpaginated (p. 19)
Helms / Valstar-Verhoff 1990, p. 279, K78
Rattemeyer / Helms / Valstar-Verhoff, 1996–97
Valstar-Verhoff 2018, K78

*Given to Frau Prof. Müller-Widmann on 17 June 37 for hospitality for dadá and me in spring 36 and spring-summer 37 (Vordemberge-Gildewart, in: studio-book)

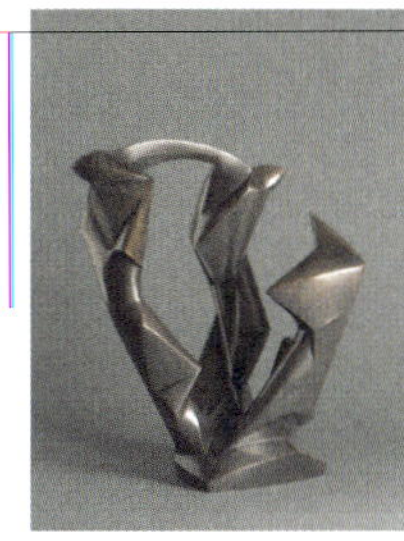

036

Rudolf Belling
Dreiklang
1919

Provenance
Galerie Wolfgang Werner, Bremen / Berlin

Exhibitions
2017 Berlin, Nationalgalerie, *Rudolf Belling. Skulpturen und Architekturen*, pp. 144–145

Literature
Nerdinger 1981, p. 229, no. 20
Hartog 2017, pp. 144–145

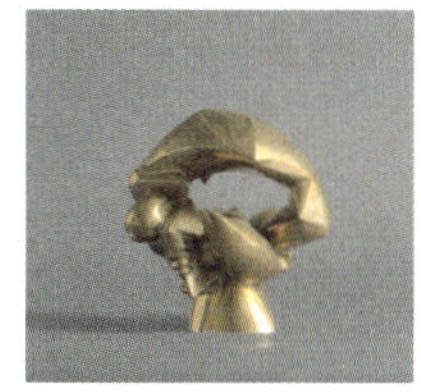

037

Rudolf Belling
Erotik
1920

Provenance
Josef Adolf Schmoll, gen. Eisenwerth (1971 from the artist)
Galerie Wolfgang Werner, Bremen / Berlin
Private collection, Monaco
Galerie Thomas, Munich

Literature
Westheim 1920, p. 375
Westheim / Einstein 1924, p. 13
Einstein 1926, p. 55
Schmoll gen. Eisenwerth 1971, pp. 30–31
Nerdinger 1981, p. 231, no. 25

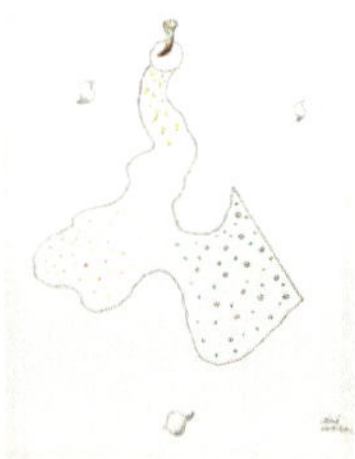

038

Joan Miró
Untitled
1924

Provenance
The New Gallery, New York
Richard L. Feigen & Co., Chicago
Leo Castelli Gallery, New York
Jane B. Holzer, New York
Private collection, USA
Landau Fine Art, Montreal

Exhibitions
2015 Vaduz, Hilti Art Foundation / Kunstmuseum Liechtenstein, *Hilti Art Foundation – Painting and Sculpture. From Classical Modernism to the Present Day*, p. 84, no. 23

Literature
Dupin / Lelong-Mainaud 2008, p. 102, no. 201
Schneider 2015, p. 84, no. 23

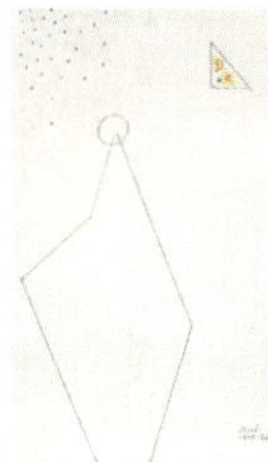

039

Joan Miró
Untitled
1924

Provenance
Serge Lifar (gift of the artist)
Galerie des 4 mouvements, Paris
Galerie Ubu, Knokke-Heist
Hopkins Custot Gallery, London

Literature
Dupin / Lelong-Mainaud 2008, no. 200, p. 103

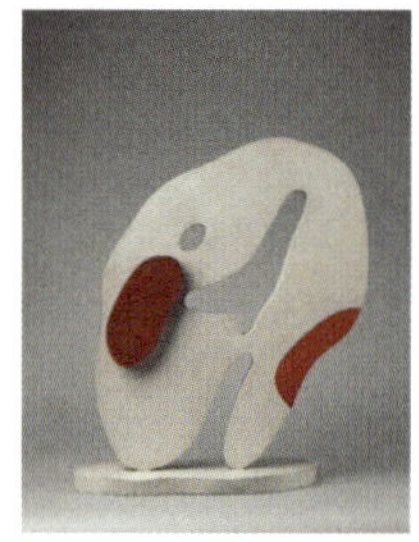

040

Hans Arp
Kopf-Stabile
1926

Provenance
Pierre Janlet, Brussels, 1930
Leo Simon, New York, 1969
Agenzia d'arte moderna, Rome
Johannes Wasmuth, 1982
Stiftung Hans Arp und Sophie Taeuber-Arp e.V., Remagen

Exhibitions
1994 Munich, Haus der Kunst, *Elan vital oder Das Auge des Eros. Kandinsky, Klee, Arp, Miró, Calder*, no. 46, fig. 122
1996 Rolandseck, Stiftung Hans Arp und Sophie Taeuber-Arp e.V., Bahnhof Rolandseck, *Hans Arp. Sophie Taeuber-Arp*, p. 98, no. 26, fig. p. 99 and cover
2004 Basel, Kunstmuseum, *Schwitters. Arp*, no. 29, fig. p. 108
2007 Rolandseck, Arp Museum Bahnhof Rolandseck, *Hans Arp. Die Natur der Dinge*, no. 49, fig. p. 129
2015 Vaduz, Hilti Art Foundation / Kunstmuseum Liechtenstein, *Hilti Art Foundation – Painting and Sculpture. From Classical Modernism to the Present Day*, p. 86, no. 24
2016 Vaduz, Hilti Art Foundation / Kunstmuseum Liechtenstein, *Hilti Art Foundation – Kirchner, Léger, Scully & more. Works from the Collection*, p. 74, no. 21
2018 Vaduz, Hilti Art Foundation / Kunstmuseum Liechtenstein, *Hilti Art Foundation – Rosso, Klee, Sonnier & more. Works from the Collection*, p. 64, no. 25

Literature
Marchiori 1964, p. 69, fig. p. 90
Trier 1968, no. V
Andreotti 1989, p. 9, fig. 21, S. 97
Hartog/Fischer 2012, p. 60, fig. V
Schneider 2015, p. 86, no. 24
Schneider 2016, p. 74, no. 21
Von Asten 2017, p. 16, fig. 1, p. 17
Schneider 2018, p. 64, no. 25

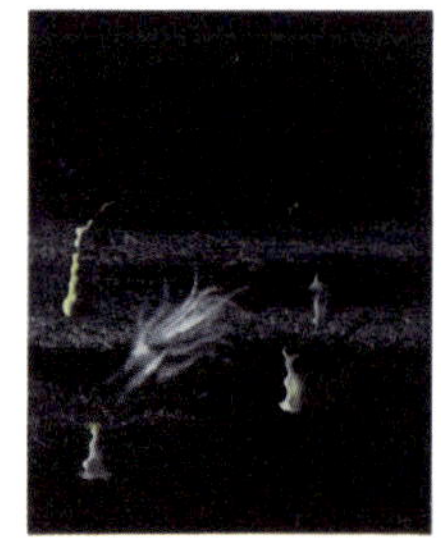

041

Yves Tanguy
Titre inconnu (noyer indifférent)
1929

Provenance
Kunsthaus Zürich (acquired from the artist)
Carl Gustav Jung, Zurich (1929–61)
Private collection, Switzerland
Christie's, London, 6 February 2001, lot 58
Jan Krugier Estate
Sotheby's, New York, 8 May 2014, lot 357

Exhibitions
1929 Zurich, Kunsthaus Zürich, *Abstrakte und Surrealistische Malerei und Plastik*, no. 136
1982–83 Baden-Baden, Staatliche Kunsthalle, *Yves Tanguy, Retrospektive 1925–1955*, no. 34
2000 Stuttgart, Staatsgalerie Stuttgart, *Yves Tanguy und der Surrealismus*, no. 31
2007 Munich, Kunsthalle der Hypo-Kulturstiftung, *Das ewige Auge: Von Rembrandt bis Picasso. Meisterwerke der Sammlung Jan Krugier und Marie-Anne Krugier-Poniatowski*
2015 Vaduz, Hilti Art Foundation / Kunstmuseum Liechtenstein, *Hilti Art Foundation – Painting and Sculpture. From Classical Modernism to the Present Day*, p. 94, no. 27

Literature
Matisse 1963, no. 90, fig. p. 68
Waldberg 1977, fig. p. 78
Hohl, 1982, pp. 64–65
Jung 1986, no. 4
Maur, 2000, pp. 58–59
Bihan, Mabin, Sawin 2001, pp. 58–59
Cariou 2007, p. 114
Berk 2009 (cover page)
Wieczorek 2015, p. 94, no. 27

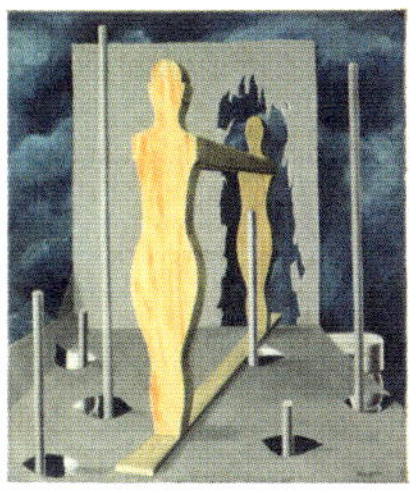

042

René Magritte
La chambre du devin
1926

Provenance
Galerie Le Centaure (P. G. van Hecke), Brussels
E.L.T. Mesens, Brussels, 1931
Grosvenor Gallery, London, 1961
Private collection, Monte Carlo
Studio Bellini, Milan
Private collection, 1996
Christie's, London, 18 June 2013, lot 37

Exhibitions
1927 Brussels, Galerie Le Centaure, *Exposition Magritte*, no. 35
1931 Liège, Palais des Beaux-Arts, Salon quatriennal de Belgique, no. 134
1956 Antwerp, Zaal Comité voor Artistieke Werking, *De Vier hoofdpunten van het surrealisme: René Magritte, Max Ernst, Joan Miró, Yves Tanguy*, no. 20
1961 London, Grosvenor Gallery, *Magritte*, no. 12
1979 Venice, Palazzo Grassi, *La pittura metafisica*, no. 118
2015 Vaduz, Hilti Art Foundation / Kunstmuseum Liechtenstein, *Hilti Art Foundation – Painting and Sculpture. From Classical Modernism to the Present Day*, p. 88, no. 25

Literature
Van Hecke 1927, p. 445
Sylvester and Whitfield 1992, no. 88, p. 174
Sylvester 2009, pp. 82, 111 and 424 (fig. p. 78)
Wieczorek 2015, p. 88, no. 25

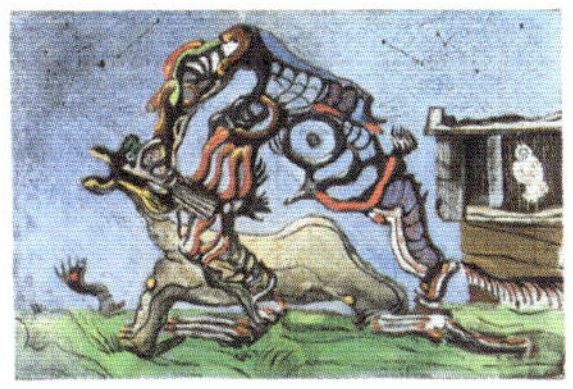

043

Max Ernst
Le paradis
1927

Provenance
Paul Gustave van Hecke, Brussels
Victor Servranckx, Brussels
Private collection, Switzerland
Caspar H. Schübbe, Switzerland

Exhibitions
1927 Brussels, Galerie Le Centaure
1949 Ostende and The Hague, *Hommage à Ensor*, no. 71
2005 Vaduz, Kunstmuseum Liechtenstein, *Werke aus der Hilti Art Foundation. Von Paul Gauguin bis Imi Knoebel*, p. 56, no. 20
2007–08 Vienna, Belvedere, *Wien – Paris. Van Gogh, Cézanne und Österreichs Moderne 1880–1960*, p. 355
2009–10 Münster, Westfälisches Landesmuseum, *„Max Ernst lässt grüssen". Peter Schamoni begegnet Max Ernst*, p. 51
2013 Riehen / Basel, Fondation Beyeler, *Max Ernst – Retrospektive*, p. 215, no. 131
2015 Vaduz, Hilti Art Foundation / Kunstmuseum Liechtenstein, *Hilti Art Foundation – Painting and Sculpture. From Classical Modernism to the Present Day*, p. 90, no. 26

Literature
Spies 1976, p. 147, no. 1076
Malsch 2005, p. 56, no. 20
Schneider 2015, p. 90, no. 26

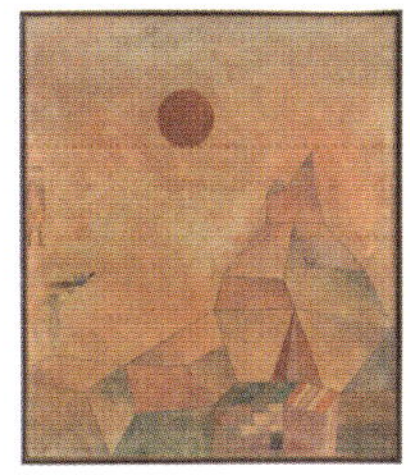

044

Paul Klee
Märchen
1929
132 (D2)

Provenance
Anhaltische Gemäldegalerie, Dessau, 1929–37
Curt Valentin (Buchholz Gallery / Valentin Gallery), Berlin / New York, until 1939
Galka E. Scheyer, Braunschweig / New York / San Francisco / Hollywood, from 1939
Douglas Cooper, London / Argilliers / Monte Carlo, until 1955
Berggruen & Cie, Paris, from 1955
William A. M. Burdon, New York
Galerie am Lindenplatz, Vaduz

Exhibitions
1933 Dessau, exhibition of works acquired by the city of Dessau between 1931–32 and on permanent loan to the Staatliche Gemäldegalerie.
1939 New York, Buchholz Gallery, Curt Valentin, *Dessau Contemporary European Painters & Sculptors.*
1945–46 London, The Tate Gallery in the National Gallery London, *Paul Klee 1879–1940*
2005 Vaduz, Kunstmuseum Liechtenstein, *Werke aus der Hilti Art Foundation. Von Paul Gauguin bis Imi Knoebel*, p. 54, no. 19
2016 Vaduz, Hilti Art Foundation / Kunstmuseum Liechtenstein, *Hilti Art Foundation – Kirchner, Léger, Scully & more. Works from the Collection*, p. 70, no. 19
2018 Vaduz, Hilti Art Foundation / Kunstmuseum Liechtenstein, *Hilti Art Foundation – Rosso, Klee, Sonnier & more. Works from the Collection*, p. 60, no. 23
2019 Vaduz, Hilti Art Foundation / Kunstmuseum Liechtenstein, *Composition '19 – Thomas Struth at the Hilti Art Foundation*, p. 120

Literature
Grohmann 1954
Brion 1955
Spiller 1956, p. 517
Janda 1986, p. 46–51 Hopfengart 2000, pp. 68–92
Paul-Klee-Stiftung 2001, vol. 5, fig. p. 309, p. 336, no. 4888
Malsch 2005, p. 54, no. 19
Schneider 2016, p. 70, no. 19
Schneider 2018, p. 60, no. 23
Wieczorek 2019, p. 120

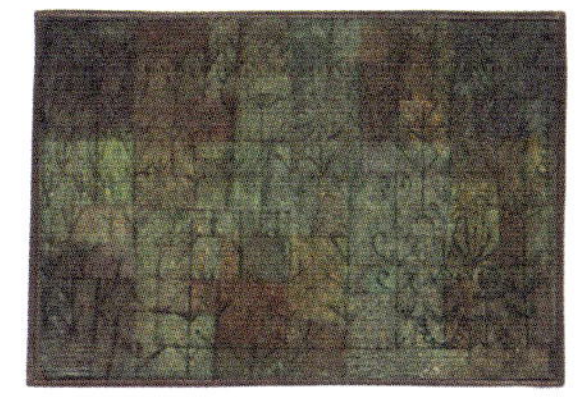

045

Paul Klee
Gemüsegarten
1925
14 (K4)

Provenance
Alfred Flechtheim, Düsseldorf / Berlin / Paris / London
Rudolf Probst, Galerie Neue Kunst Fides & Das Kunsthaus, Dresden / Mannheim
Hans and Erika Meyer-Benteli, Bern
Ted and Meret Schaap-Meyer, Vallamand-Dessous
Max Kohler, Zurich

Exhibitions
1926 Zurich, Kunsthaus Zürich, *Paul Klee, Paul Altherr, R. Th. Bosshard, Emil Bressler, Willy F. Burger, Max Burgmeier, Eugen Maurer, August Speck*, no. 40
1926 Wiesbaden, Neues Museum, August-Exhibition 1926, no. 36
1926 Dresden, Galerie Ernst Arnold, Sonderausstellung von 100 Gemälden und Aquarellen von Paul Klee aus den Jahren 1908–1926
1927 Mannheim, Städtische Kunsthalle Mannheim, *Wege und Richtungen der abstrakten Malerei in Europa*, no. 140
1927 Düsseldorf, Galerie Alfred Flechtheim, *Landschaften aus Cagnes und Stilleben von Auguste Renoir, Paul Klee. Ölgemälde und Aquarelle*, no. 17
1929 Berlin, Juryfreie Kunstschau Berlin. Landesausstellungsgebäude am Lehrter Bahnhof, no. 600
1935 Bern, Kunsthalle Bern, *Paul Klee*, no. 25
1935 Basel, Kunsthalle Basel, *Paul Klee*, no. 18
1936 Lucerne, Kunstmuseum, *Paul Klee, Fritz Huf*, no. 35
1941 Basel, Kunsthalle Basel, *Gedächtnisausstellung Paul Klee*, no. 297
1950 Basel, Kunstmuseum, *Paul Klee, 1879–1940*, Exhibition of works from Swiss private collections, commemorating the 10th anniversary of Klee's death, 29 June 1950, no. 8
1952 Winterthur, Kunstmuseum, *Paul Klee*, no. 44
1956 Bern, Kunstmuseum, *Paul Klee*, exhibition with the Paul Klee Foundation, no. 524
2003–04 Ludwigshafen am Rhein, Wilhelm-Hack-Museum, *Der Blaue Reiter, Die Befreiung der Farbe*, p. 141, no. 114
2012–13 Bern, Kunstmuseum, et. al., *Itten – Klee. Kosmos Farbe*, p. 250, no. 93 and p. 365
2016 Vaduz, Hilti Art Foundation / Kunstmuseum Liechtenstein, *Hilti Art Foundation – Kirchner, Léger, Scully & more. Works from the Collection*, p. 78, no. 23

Literature
Paul Klee Stiftung 2001, vol. 4, fig. p. 290, no. 3695, fig. p. 322
Schneider 2016, p. 78, no. 23

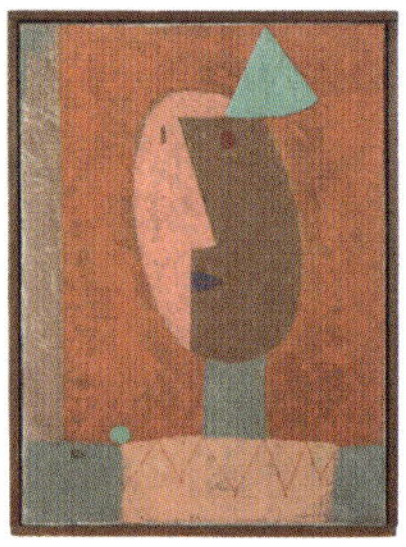

046

Paul Klee
Clown
1929
133 (D3)

Provenance
Ida Bienert, Dresden / Munich, until 1952
Curt Valentin, Buchholz Gallery / Valentin Gallery, Berlin / New York, 1952–54
Gertrude Lenart Bernoudy, St. Louis, 1954–94
The Gertrude Bernoudy Trust, 1994
Private collection, Switzerland
Galerie Beyeler, Basel

Exhibitions
1929 Berlin, Galerie Alfred Flechtheim, *Paul Klee*, no. 116
1950 Munich, Haus der Kunst, *Die Maler am Bauhaus*, no. 140
1953 New York, Curt Valentin Gallery, *Paul Klee*, no. 19
1967 New York, The Solomon R. Guggenheim Museum, *Paul Klee 1879–1940. A Retrospective Exhibition*, no. 104
1987–88 New York, Museum of Modern Art, et al., *Paul Klee*, no. 22
1995 Basel, Galerie Beyeler, *Joie de vivre*, no. 37
2000–01 Turin, Galleria Civica d'Arte Moderna e Contemporanea, *Paul Klee*
2005 Vaduz, Kunstmuseum Liechtenstein, *Werke aus der Hilti Art Foundation. Von Paul Gauguin bis Imi Knoebel*, p. 48, no. 16
2006–07 Dresden, Staatliche Kunstsammlungen, Galerie Neue Meister, *Von Monet bis Mondrian. Meisterwerke der Moderne aus Dresdner Privatsammlungen der ersten Hälfte des 20. Jahrhunderts*, p. 76 and p. 198, no. 75
2007 Bern, Zentrum Paul Klee, *Überall Theater*, p. 156, p. 171 and p. 269
2007–08 Riehen / Basel, Fondation Beyeler, *Die andere Sammlung. Hommage an Ernst und Hildy Beyeler*, p. 195
2009 Ulm, Ulmer Museum, *Paul Klee und die Romantik*, p. 79, no. 50, p. 143 and front cover
2010 Bern, Zentrum Paul Klee, *Klee trifft Picasso*, p. 160, p. 171 and p. 269
2012–13 Bern, Kunstmuseum, et al., *Itten – Klee. Kosmos Farbe*, p. 264, no. 106 and p. 366
2015 Vaduz, Hilti Art Foundation / Kunstmuseum Liechtenstein, *Hilti Art Foundation – Painting and Sculpture. From Classical Modernism to the Present Day*, p. 98, no. 29
2016 Vaduz, Hilti Art Foundation / Kunstmuseum Liechtenstein, *Hilti Art Foundation – Kirchner, Léger, Scully & more. Works from the Collection*, p. 72, no. 20
2018 Munich, Pinakothek der Moderne, *PAUL KLEE – Konstruktion des Geheimnisses*, p. 331, no. 93
2018 Vaduz, Hilti Art Foundation / Kunstmuseum Liechtenstein, *Hilti Art Foundation – Rosso, Klee, Sonnier & more. Works from the Collection*, p. 62, no. 24

Literature
Documents, 1st vol., no. 5, October 1929, p. 286f.
Grohmann 1929, fig.
Hirsch 1929, fig. p. 210
Crevel 1930, fig. p. 61
Einstein 1931, fig. p. 548
Volné směry, vol. 29, no. 7–8, November 1932, pp. 187, 195, fig.
Grohmann 1933, pp. 14, 21, fig.
Giedion-Welcker 1952, fig.
Grohmann 1954, p. 246, fig.
San Lazzaro 1957, fig. 78
Plant 1978, pp. 43, 76, 97, 118, fig.
Müller 1979, p. 112, note 1
Kagan 1983, p. 102, fig.
Löffler 1986, p. 45
Bischoff 1992, fig.
Roskill 1992, fig.
Paul-Klee-Stiftung 2001, p. 336, no. 4889
Malsch 2005, p. 48. no. 16
Biedermann 2006, p. 76
Schneider 2015, p. 98, no. 29
Schneider 2016, p. 72, no. 20
Schneider 2018, p. 62, no. 24

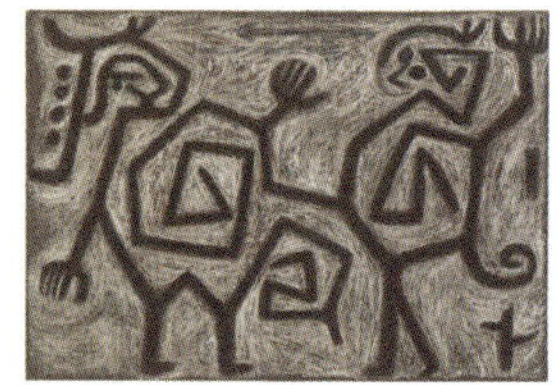

047

Paul Klee
Zank=Duett
1938

Provenance
Paul Klee, Bern 1938
Galerie Simon, Paris 1938
Nierendorf Gallery, New York 1938–39
Ludwig Mies van der Rohe, Chicago 1939–50
Bequest Mies van der Rohe family
Wolfgang Wittrock Kunsthandel, Berlin

Exhibitions
1967–88 Munich, Haus der Kunst (on loan)
1985 London, Royal Academy of Arts, *German Art in the 20th Century. Painting and Sculpture 1905–1985*, no. 195
1986 Stuttgart, Staatsgalerie, *Deutsche Kunst im 20. Jahrhundert. Malerei und Plastik 1905–1985*, no. 193
1988–2009 Düsseldorf, Kunstsammlung Nordrhein-Westfalen (on loan)
2008–09 Berlin, Neue Nationalgalerie, *Das Universum Klee*, fig. p. 339
2009–10 Berlin, Museum Berggruen (on loan)
2010–15 Düsseldorf, Kunstsammlung Nordrhein-Westfalen (on loan)
2016–17 Aachen, Ludwig Forum; Schweinfurt, Museum Georg Schäfer, *Mies van der Rohe. Die Collagen aus dem MoMA*
2018 Vaduz, Hilti Art Foundation / Kunstmuseum Liechtenstein, *Hilti Art Foundation – Rosso, Klee, Sonnier & more. Works from the Collection*, p. 66, no. 26

Literature
Renne / Serbanne 1945, 32, vol. 23, p. 675
Hayter 1946, vol. 39, pp. 126–30, fig. p. 130
Verdi 1985, pp. 452
Dessauer-Reiners 1996, pp. 179, fig. 34
Schmalenbach 1996, pp. 178
Paul-Klee-Stiftung 2001, vol. 7, p. 336, no. 7350
Endicott Barnett 2001, p. 99, p. 124, fig. p. 105
Hopfengart 2008, p. 76, fig. p. 339
Wieczorek 2018, p. 66, no. 26

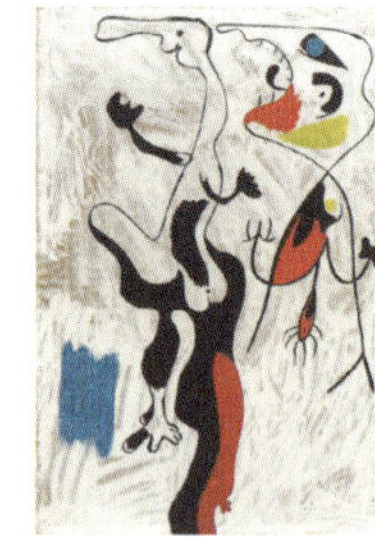

048

Joan Miró
Homme et femme
1935

Provenance
Pierre Matisse Gallery, New York
Jane Mitchell, New York
Knoedler & Company, New York
Galerie Beyeler, Basel
Galerie Melki, Paris
Galerie Daniel Malingue, Paris
Didier Imbert Fine Art, Paris
Private collection
Christie's, New York, 12 November 2015, lot 24C
Landau Fine Art, Montreal

Exhibitions
1986–87 Zurich, Kunsthaus; Düsseldorf, Kunsthalle, *Joan Miró*, no. 95
1988–89 Barcelona, Fundació Joan Miró, *Impactes: Joan Miró*, p. 68, no. 37

Literature
Greenberg 1948, p. 74, fig. XXXIII
Dupin 1961, p. 416, no. 411
Dupin 1962, p. 532, no. 411
Dupin / Lelong-Mainaud 2000, p. 132, no. 494

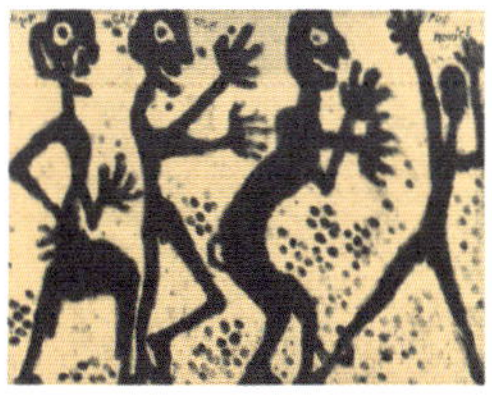

049

Louis Soutter
Vierges cruelles – Pur novice
1937–1942

Provenance
Private collection, Switzerland
Galerie Kornfeld, Bern, Auction 250, 18 June 2010, lot 140
Galerie Haas AG, Zurich

Literature
Thévoz 1976, no. 2710

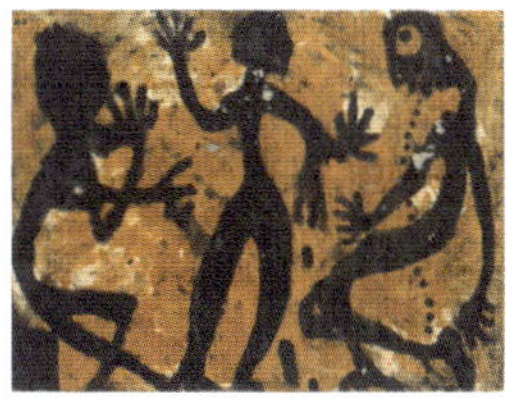

050

Louis Soutter
Lasse tête / Les caillots / Dernières perles
1937–1942

Provenance
Cadeau de Soutter à Monsieur et Madame Marcel Poncet, Switzerland, c. 1939
Poncet collection, Switzerland
Private collection, Switzerland
Steinfels Art Consulting AG, Zurich

Literature
Thévoz 1974, p. 121, no. 56
Thévoz 1976, no. 2706

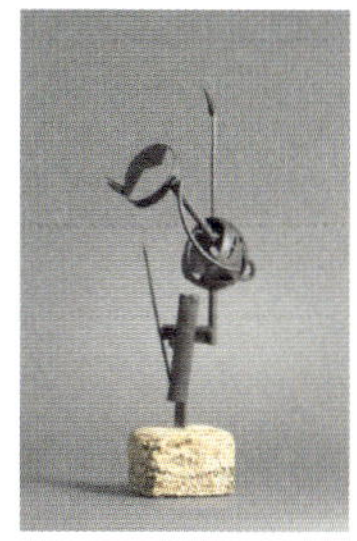

051

Julio González
Le rêve / Le baiser
c. 1934

Provenance
Roberta González, Paris
Nachlass Julio González, Paris
Galerie de France, Paris
Private collection, Paris
Galleria Pieter Coray, Montagnola

Literature
Merkert 1987, pp. 157, no. 154, 0

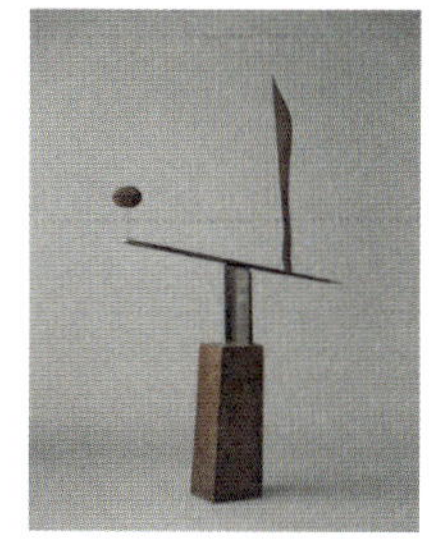

052

Alexander Calder
Untitled
1935
(A00236)

Provenance
Galerie Claude Bernard, Paris
Henry Hecht, New York
Ralph and Helyn Goldenberg, Chicago
Sotheby's, New York, 14 November 2007, lot 34
Mitchell-Innes & Nash, New York

Exhibitions
1936 New York, Pierre Matisse Gallery, *Mobiles and Objects by Alexander Calder*
1969 Saint-Paul de Vence, Fondation Maeght, et al., *Calder*
1974 Chicago, Museum of Contemporary Art, *Alexander Calder: A Retrospective Exhibition* (Works from 1925–1974)
1977 New York, Whitney Museum of American Art, *Calder's Universe*, fig. p. 226
1987–88 New York, Whitney Museum of American Art, *Alexander Calder: Sculpture of the Nineteen Thirties*
1998 Washington D.C., National Gallery of Art, et al., *Alexander Calder: 1898–1976*, no. 79
2005 Houston, The Menil Collection, *The Surreal Calder*, fig. 50, fig. p. 130
2015 Vaduz, Hilti Art Foundation / Kunstmuseum Liechtenstein, *Hilti Art Foundation – Painting and Sculpture. From Classical Modernism to the Present Day*, p. 96, no. 28
2019 Vaduz, Hilti Art Foundation / Kunstmuseum Liechtenstein, *Composition '19 – Thomas Struth at the Hilti Art Foundation*, p. 36

Literature
Arnason 1971, fig. 20
Fondation Maeght 1971, fig. p. 51
San Lazzaro 1972, fig. p. 226
Schneider 2015, p. 96, no. 28
Wieczorek 2019, p. 36

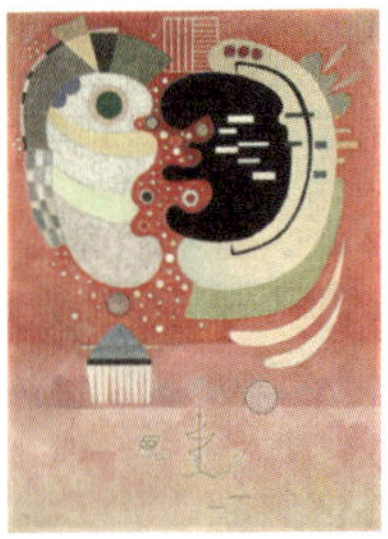

053

Wassily Kandinsky
Entre Deux
1934

Provenance
Nina Kandinsky, Neuilly-sur-Seine
Pierre Peissi (acquired c. 1950 from Nina Kandinsky)
Private collection
Galerie Beyeler, Basel

Exhibitions
1934 Paris, Galerie Cahiers d'Art, *Kandinsky: peintures de toutes les époques, aquarelles et dessins*
1936 London, Alex Reid and Lefèvre Ltd., *Abstract and Concrete: An International Exhibition of Paintings and Sculpture*
1937 Bern, Kunsthalle Bern, *Kandinsky and French Masters*, no. 55
1937 Paris, Musée du Jeu de Paume, *Origines et développement de l'art international indépendant*
1938 London, Guggenheim Jeune, *Contemporary Painting and Sculpture*, no. 10
1946 Zurich, Kunsthaus Zürich, *Georges Braque, Wassily Kandinsky, Pablo Picasso*, no. 72
1947–48 The Hague, Gemeente Museum; Amsterdam, Stedelijk Museum, *Kandinsky*, no. 63
1948 Buenos Aires, Instituto de Arte Moderno, *Arte abstracto en Francia*, no. 31
1949 São Paulo, Museu de Arte Moderno, *Figurativismo – Abstractionismo*, no. 41
1950 Lille, Palais des Beaux-Arts, *Un demi-siècle de peinture française, 1900–1950*
1963 Paris, Musée National d'Art Moderne de la Ville de Paris, *Wassily Kandinsky 1866–1944: exposition rétrospective*, supplément no. 124
1972 Paris, Musée National d'Art Moderne de la Ville de Paris, *Hommage de Paris à Wassily Kandinsky: La conquête de l'abstraction, l'époque parisienne*, no. 19
2005 Vaduz, Kunstmuseum Liechtenstein, *Werke aus der Hilti Art Foundation. Von Paul Gauguin bis Imi Knoebel*, p. 64, no. 24
2010–11 Wiesbaden, Museum Wiesbaden, *Das Geistige in der Kunst. Vom Blauen Reiter zum Abstrakten Expressionismus*, p. 296
2015 Bern, Zentrum Paul Klee, *Klee & Kandinsky. Nachbarn, Freunde, Konkurrenten*, p. 239, no. 177
2015–16 Munich, Städtische Galerie im Lenbachhaus, *Klee & Kandinsky*, p. 239, no. 177
2016 Vaduz, Hilti Art Foundation / Kunstmuseum Liechtenstein, *Hilti Art Foundation – Kirchner, Léger, Scully & more. Works from the Collection*, p. 76, no. 22

Literature
Wassily Kandinsky, Handliste IV, no. 601 (handwritten list of the artist's works in the archives of the Musée National d'Art Moderne, Centre Georges Pompidou, Paris, Nina Kandinsky Estate)
Zervos 1934, no. 5/8, pp. 149 ff.
Bill 1951
Grohmann 1958, p. 340, no. 601
Damase 1963, photographs of Pierre Peissi's living room with the painting on the wall
Jong 1963, p. 221
Vallier 1966, pp. 72 ff., no. 27
Roethel / Benjamin 1984, p. 936, no. 1038
Barnett 1985, pp. 61 ff., no. 10
Wieczorek 2005, p. 64, no. 24
Zieglgänsberger 2013, p. 37, fig. p. 38
Wieczorek 2016, p. 76, no. 22

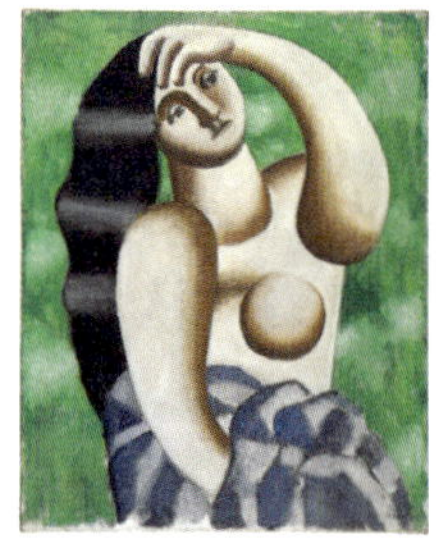

054

Fernand Léger
La danseuse
1929

Provenance
Paul Rosenberg, Paris
Mrs. Sinclair Collection
Daniel Varenne Collection, Geneva
Galerie Beyeler, Basel
Private collection, USA
Galerie Beyeler, Basel

Exhibitions
1989–90 Basel, Galerie Beyeler, *L'éternel féminin*, no. 33
1994–95 Basel, Galerie Beyeler, *Fernand Léger, Œuvres 1925–1955*, no. 19
2005 Vaduz, Kunstmuseum Liechtenstein, *Werke aus der Hilti Art Foundation. Von Paul Gauguin bis Imi Knoebel*, p. 58, no. 21
2007–08 Riehen / Basel, Fondation Beyeler, *Die andere Sammlung. Hommage an Ernst und Hildy Beyeler*, p. 135
2016 Vaduz, Hilti Art Foundation / Kunstmuseum Liechtenstein, *Hilti Art Foundation – Kirchner, Léger, Scully & more. Works from the Collection*, p. 30, no. 7
2018 Vaduz, Hilti Art Foundation / Kunstmuseum Liechtenstein, *Hilti Art Foundation – Rosso, Klee, Sonnier & more. Works from the Collection*, p. 42, no. 14

Literature
Elgar 1954
Bauquier 1996, no. 652 (fig. p. 86)
Wieczorek 2005, p. 58, no. 21
Wieczorek 2016, p. 30, no. 7
Wieczorek 2018, p. 42, no. 14

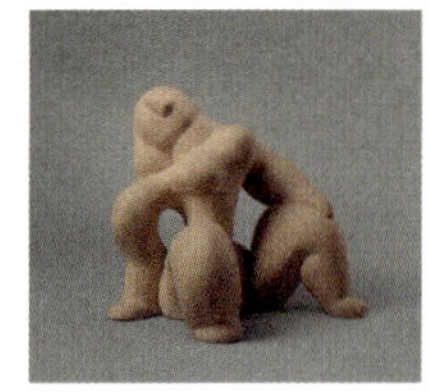

055

Henri Laurens
Flora
1939

Provenance
Private collection
Landau Fine Art, Montreal

Exhibitions
1998 Paris, Galerie Louise Leiris, *Henri Laurens – 60 Terres cuites*, no. 51, fig.
2016 Vaduz, Hilti Art Foundation / Kunstmuseum Liechtenstein, *Hilti Art Foundation – Kirchner, Léger, Scully & more. Works from the Collection*, p. 36, no. 9

Literature
Hofmann 1970, p. 202
Schneider 2016, p. 36, no. 9

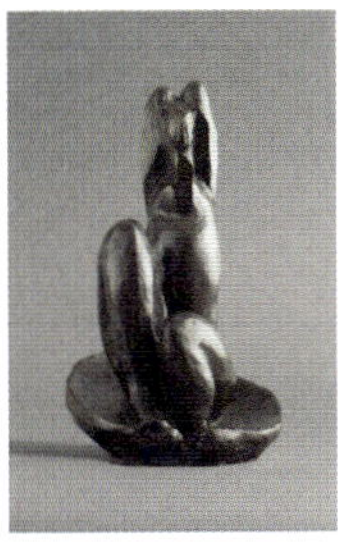

056

Henri Matisse
Vénus à la coquille I
1930 (cast 1954)

Provenance
Theodor Ahrenberg, Stockholm
Sotheby's London, 7 July 1960, lot 47
David Gibbs & Co. Ltd., London
Sir Charles Clore, London
Private collection, London and Monaco
Dickinson, London

Exhibitions
1957–58 Helsinki, Helsingin Taidehalli, *Henri Matisse. Apollon*, Nr. 167
1958 Liège, Musée des Beaux-Arts, *Apollon. Collection Theodor Ahrenberg*, Nr. 167
1958 Stockholm, National Museum, *Henri Matisse. Apollon*, Nr. 39
1959 Zurich, Kunsthaus Zürich, *Henri Matisse. Das plastische Werk*, Nr. 65
1960 Gothenburg, Konsthallen, *Henri Matisse ur Theodor Ahrenbergs Samling*, Nr. 209
2018 Vaduz, Hilti Art Foundation / Kunstmuseum Liechtenstein, *Hilti Art Foundation – Rosso, Klee, Sonnier & more. Works from the Collection*, p. 48, no. 17

Literature
Duthuit / De Guébriant 1997, no. 79
Wieczorek 2018, p. 48, no. 17

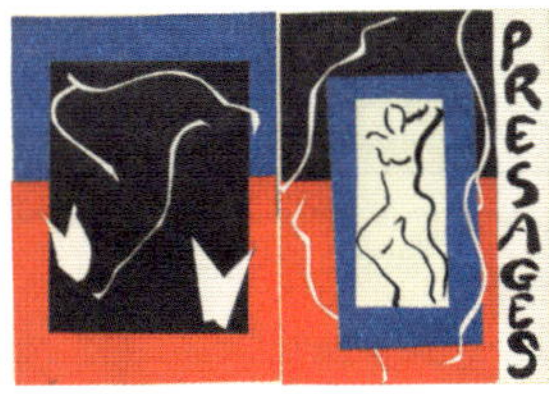

057

Henri Matisse
PRESAGES
1937

Provenance
Tériade collection, Paris
Private collection, Paris

Exhibitions
2013 Le Cateau-Cambrésis, Musée Matisse, *Matisse, La couleur découpée, Une donation révélatrice*, p. 34/35
2014–15 London, Tate Modern; New York, The Museum of Modern Art, *Henri Matisse, The Cut-Outs*, p. 101, no. 11

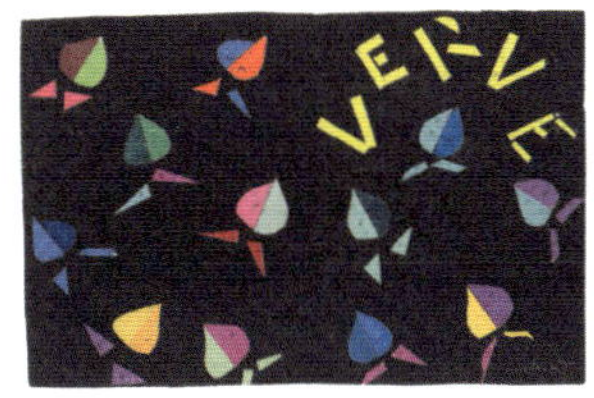

058

Henri Matisse
Symphonie chromatique
1939

Provenance
Tériade collection, Paris

Exhibitions
1977–78 Washington D.C., National Gallery of Art; Detroit, Detroit Institute of Arts; St. Louis, St. Louis Art Museum, *Henri Matisse: Paper Cut-Outs*, p. 97
2013 Le Cateau-Cambrésis, Musée Matisse, *Matisse, La couleur découpée. Une donation révélatrice*, p. 20–21
2014–15 London, Tate Modern; New York, The Museum of Modern Art, *Henri Matisse. The Cut-Outs*, p. 102, no. 13

Literature
Anthonioz 1987, p. 124
Berggruen / Hollein 2006, p. 26–27
De Chassey / Ovaere 2009, p. 21

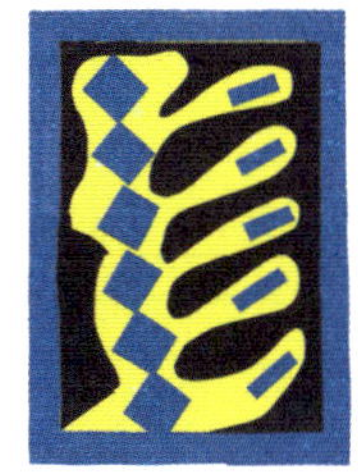

059

Henri Matisse
Composition, Jaune, Bleu et Noir
1947

Provenance
Berggruen et Cie., Paris
Theodor Ahrenberg, Stockholm
Thomas Gibson Fine Art Ltd, London
Private collection
Dickinson, London

Exhibitions
1949 Paris, Musée National d'Art Moderne, Henri Matisse: *Œuvres Récentes, 1947–48*
1953 Paris, Berggruen et Cie., *Henri Matisse, papiers découpés*
1954 Stockholm, Nationalmuseum, *Modern utländsk Konst ur Svenska privatsamlingar*
1958 Helsinki, Helsingin Taidehalli, *Henri Matisse, Apollon*
1958 Liège, Musée des Beaux-Arts, *Henri Matisse, Apollon, Collection Theodor Ahrenberg*
1959 Zurich, Kunsthaus Zürich, *Henri Matisse, Das Plastische Werk, Sämtliche Plastiken des Meisters sowie Zeichnungen, Graphik und Collagen als Leihgaben der Sammlung Ahrenberg, Stockholm*
1960 Gothenburg, Konsthallen, *Henri Matisse ur Theodor Ahrenbergs Samling*
1961 Copenhagen, Radhus, Frederiksberg, *Moderne Verdenskunst fra Ahrenbergs Samling*
1977–78 Washington D.C., National Gallery of Art; Detroit, The Detroit Institute of Arts; St. Louis, The St. Louis Art Museum, *Henri Matisse. Paper Cut-Outs*, p. 144
2004–05 Le Cateau-Cambrésis, Musée Matisse; London, Royal Academy of Art; New York, The Metropolitan Museum of Art, *Matisse et la couleur des tissus*
2014–15 London, Tate Modern; New York, The Museum of Modern Art, *Henri Matisse. The Cut-Outs*, p. 140, no. 58

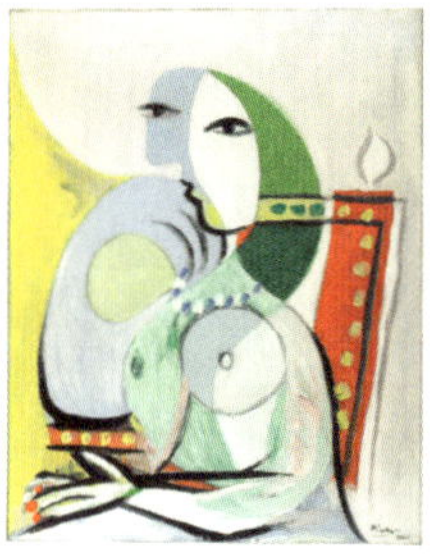

060

Pablo Picasso
Femme dans un fauteuil
1932

Provenance
Valentine Dudensing, New York
Ernst Zeisler, Chicago
Richard L. Feigen & Co., New York
Charles Yalem, St. Louis, 1963
Richard L. Feigen & Co., New York, 1966
Robert L. Livingston, New York, 1967
Mollie Parnis Livingston, USA
Collection of the Phoenix Assurance Company, Africa
Christie's, London, 3 February 2003, lot 72
Galerie Beyeler, Basel

Exhibitions
1967 Dallas, Museum of Fine Arts, *Picasso – Two Concurrent Retrospective Exhibitions*
2002 Tel Aviv, Museum of Art, *Picasso*, p. 25
2005 Vaduz, Kunstmuseum Liechtenstein, *Werke aus der Hilti Art Foundation. Von Paul Gauguin bis Imi Knoebel*, p. 60, no. 22
2006–07 Riehen / Basel, Fondation Beyeler, *Eros*
2007 Vienna, BA-CA Kunstforum, *Eros*, p. 113 and p. 195
2015 Vaduz, Hilti Art Foundation / Kunstmuseum Liechtenstein, *Hilti Art Foundation – Painting and Sculpture. From Classical Modernism to the Present Day*, p. 28, no. 5
2016 Vaduz, Hilti Art Foundation / Kunstmuseum Liechtenstein, *Hilti Art Foundation – Kirchner, Léger, Scully & more. Works from the Collection*, p. 34, no. 8
2018 Vaduz, Hilti Art Foundation / Kunstmuseum Liechtenstein, *Hilti Art Foundation – Rosso, Klee, Sonnier & more. Works from the Collection*, p. 44, no. 15

Literature
Zervos 1957, Bd. 8, no. 154
Picasso Project 1997, p. 128
Schneider 2005, p. 60, no. 22
Schneider 2015, p. 28, no. 5
Schneider 2016, p. 34, no. 8
Schneider 2018, p. 44, no. 15

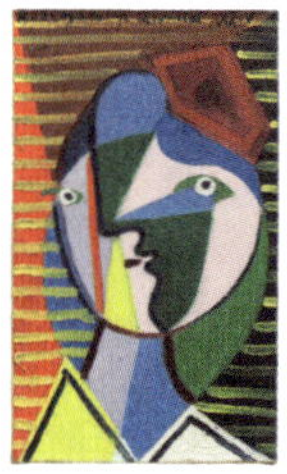

061

Pablo Picasso
Figure, Femme de trois-quarts gauche
1934

Provenance
Collection Marina Ruiz Picasso
Galerie Jan Krugier, Geneva
Galerie Beyeler, Basel
Private collection, Switzerland
Galerie Beyeler, Basel

Exhibitions
1981 Basel, Galerie Beyeler, *Picasso – A Centennial Selection*, no. 29
1986 Basel, Galerie Beyeler, *Picasso – le peintre et ses modèles*, no. 16
1992 Basel, Galerie Beyeler, *Hommage to Francis Bacon*, no. 40
1995 Basel, Galerie Beyeler, *Who is afraid of Red...?*, no. 59
1995–96 Basel, Galerie Beyeler, *Surrealismus, Traum des Jahrhunderts*, no. 84
2002–03 Chemnitz, Kunstsammlungen Chemnitz, *Picasso et les femmes*, p. 183
2004 Münster, Graphikmuseum Pablo Picasso, *Pablo Picasso und Marie-Thérèse Walter. Zwischen Klassizismus und Surrealismus*, p. 94
2005 Vaduz, Kunstmuseum Liechtenstein, *Werke aus der Hilti Art Foundation. Von Paul Gauguin bis Imi Knoebel*, p. 50, no. 17
2010 Bern, Zentrum Paul Klee, *Klee trifft Picasso*, p. 197 and p. 277
2016–17 Bern, Zentrum Paul Klee, *Paul Klee und die Surrealisten*, p. 254, no. 203
2018 Vaduz, Hilti Art Foundation / Kunstmuseum Liechtenstein, *Hilti Art Foundation – Rosso, Klee, Sonnier & more. Works from the Collection*, p. 46, no. 16

Literature
Zervos 1957, vol. VIII, no. 243
Schneider 2005, p. 50, no. 17
Schneider 2018, p. 46, no. 16

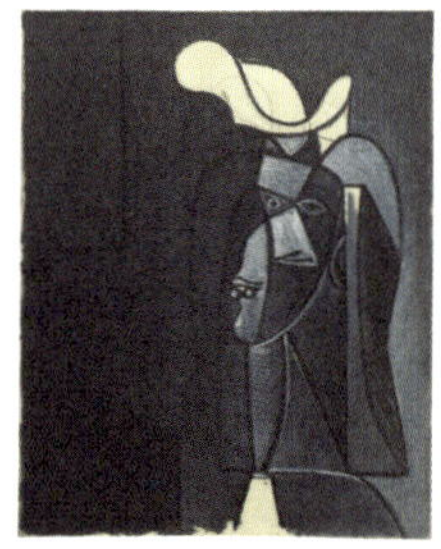

062

Pablo Picasso
Visage gris foncé au chapeau blanc
1947

Provenance
Claude Ruiz-Picasso
Gagosian Gallery, New York
Private collection
Gagosian Gallery, New York

Exhibitions
1995 New York, Matthew Marks Gallery, *Picasso: Works from the Rue des Grands-Augustins Studio, 1939–1947*, no. 10
2003–04 Málaga, Museo Picasso, *El Picasso de los Picasso*, p. 156, no. 58
2006–07 Venice, Palazzo Grassi, *La Joie de Vivre 1945–1948*, p. 118
2009 Antibes, Musée Picasso, *Picasso 1945–1949: l'ère du renouveau*, p. 17, fig. p. 163
2011 Paris, Galeries Nationales, Grand Palais, *Aimé Césaire, Lam, Picasso, "Nous nous somme Trouvés"*
2012–13 New York, Guggenheim Museum; Houston TX, Museum of Fine Arts, *Picasso: Black and White*, no. 86 and p. 224
2018 Vaduz, Hilti Art Foundation / Kunstmuseum Liechtenstein, *Hilti Art Foundation – Rosso, Klee, Sonnier & more. Works from the Collection*, p. 28, no. 9
2019 Vaduz, Hilti Art Foundation / Kunstmuseum Liechtenstein, *Composition '19 – Thomas Struth at the Hilti Art Foundation*, p. 107

Literature
Zervos 1965, vol. 15, no. 61
The Picasso Project 2000, no. 47-038, p. 182
Andral 2009, p. 17, fig. p. 163
Wieczorek 2018, p. 28, no. 9
Wieczorek 2019, p. 107

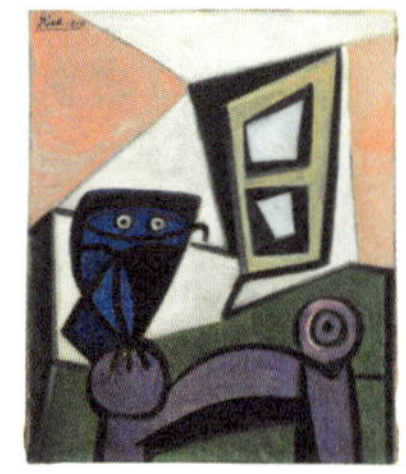

063

Pablo Picasso
Hibou sur une chaise
1947

Provenance
Galerie Cardo, Paris
Sotheby's, New York, 4. November 2004, lot 59

Exhibitions
1952 Paris, Galerie André Weil, *Exposition Picasso, au profit du Musée d'Antibes*
1953 Lyon, Musée des Beaux-Arts, Palais Saint-Pierre, *Picasso*
1980 New York, Museum of Modern Art, *Pablo Picasso*
2005 Vaduz, Kunstmuseum Liechtenstein, *Werke aus der Hilti Art Foundation. Von Paul Gauguin bis Imi Knoebel*, p. 50, no. 17 (not in catalogue)
2009 Antibes, Musée Picasso, *Picasso 1945–1949: l'ère du renouveau*, p. 14 and fig. p. 151
2010–11 Vienna, Albertina, *Picasso. Peace and Freedom*, no. 36
2018 Vaduz, Hilti Art Foundation / Kunstmuseum Liechtenstein, *Hilti Art Foundation – Rosso, Klee, Sonnier & more. Works from the Collection*, p. 50, no. 18

Literature
Andral 2009, p. 14 und fig. p. 151
Wieczorek 2018, p. 50, no. 18

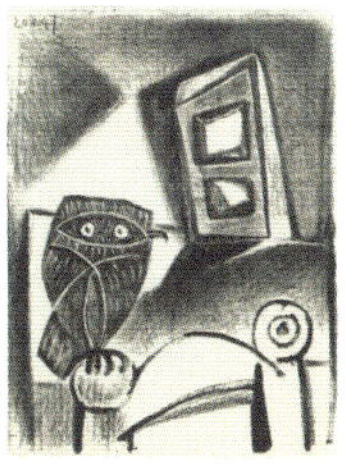

064

Pablo Picasso
Hibou à la chaise
1947

Lithograph on vellum
Dated on the stone upper left: 20.1.47
Signed and numbered on verso: Picasso 15/50
65.5 × 49.5 cm

Inv. no. G49T / Acquired 2011

This lithograph has the same date as the painting *Hibou sur une chaise* in the collection of the Hilti Art Foundation (Inv. no. P28T). The subject matter is basically the same in both works.

Provenance
Ketterer Kunst, Munich, 14 May 2011, lot 459

Literature
Bloch 1971, no. 409
Mourlot 1950, no. 54
Reusse 2000, no. 163

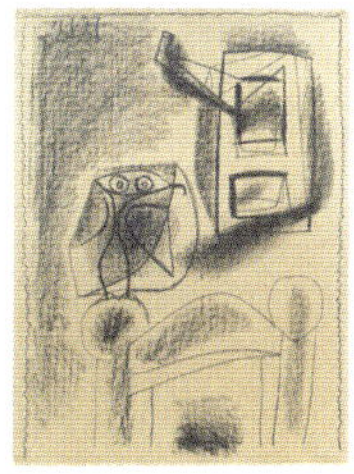

065

Pablo Picasso
Hibou au crayon
1947

Crayon lithograph on vellum
Dated on the stone upper left: 21.1.47
Signed and numbered on verso: Picasso 14/50
65.2 x 49.8 cm

Inv. no. G50T / Acquired 2011

Unlike the painting and lithograph of the previous day (20.1.47), Picasso has here done almost entirely without spatial depth, restricting the motif to the chair with the owl and the window (or the door). The function of the bent pipe attached to the window with a cord (?) cannot be clearly defined.

Provenance
Ketterer Kunst, Munich, 14 May 2011, lot 458

Literature
Bloch 1971, no. 412
Mourlot 1950, no. 57

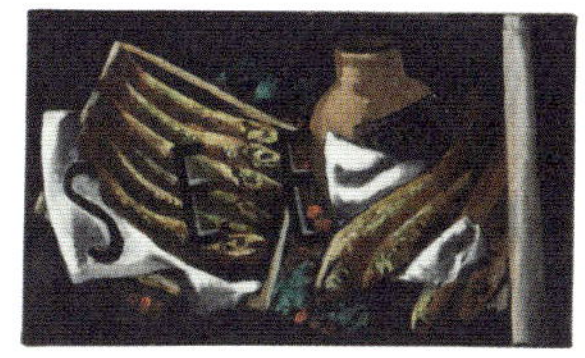

066

Max Beckmann
Bücklinge
1928

Provenance
The artist's studio
Julius Meier-Graefe, Berlin
Alfred Flechtheim, Berlin
I. B. Neumann, New York
G. David Thompson, Pittsburgh
Galerie Beyeler, Basel
Private collection
Galerie Thomas, Munich

Exhibitions
1928 Munich, Galerie Günther Franke, *Max Beckmann*, no. 19
1928 Stuttgart, Kunsthaus Schaller, *Max Beckmann*
1929 Berlin, Galerie Alfred Flechtheim, *Max Beckmann. Neue Gemälde und Zeichnungen*, no. 7
1929 Frankfurt, Kunstverein, *Max Beckmann*, no. 36
1930 Basel, Kunsthalle, *Max Beckmann*, no. 71
1930 Zurich, Kunsthaus Zürich, *Max Beckmann*, no. 57
1932 Berlin, Galerie Alfred Flechtheim, *Max Beckmann*, no. 17
1960–61 Zurich, Kunsthaus Zürich, *G. David Thompson Collection*, no. 7
1961 Düsseldorf, Kunstmuseum, *G. David Thompson Collection*, no. 7
1961 Pasadena, The Pasadena Art Museum, *German Expressionism*, no. 4
1964 Kassel, Museum Fridericianum, documenta III, no. 8, p. 6
1968–69 Paris, Musée National d'Art Moderne; Munich, Haus der Kunst; Brussels, Palais des Beaux-Arts, *Max Beckmann*, nos. 37, 34, 37
1999 Zurich, Kunsthaus Zürich; Saint Louis, The Saint Louis Art Museum, *Max Beckmann and Paris*
2013 Kochel, Franz Marc Museum, *Max Beckmann. Kleine Stillleben*, p. 50
2016 Vaduz, Hilti Art Foundation / Kunstmuseum Liechtenstein, *Hilti Art Foundation – Kirchner, Léger, Scully & more. Works from the Collection*, p. 56, no. 14

Literature
Glaser 1929, p. 223
Hausenstein 1930
Reifenberg / Hausenstein 1949, p. 71, no. 259
Göpel 1976, vol. 1, no. 284, p. 206, fig. vol. 2, plate 100
Schulz-Hoffmann 2013, p. 50
Wieczorek 2016, p. 56, no. 14

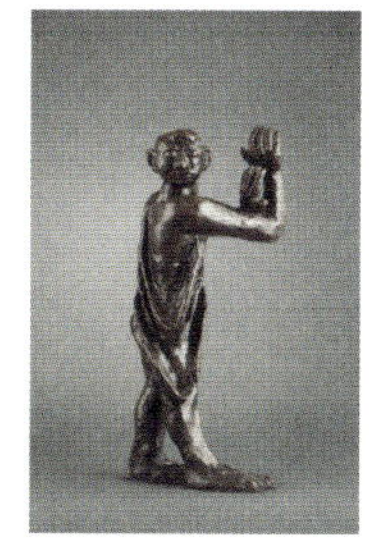

067

Max Beckmann
Mann im Dunkeln
1934

Provenance
Galerie Springer, Berlin
Private collection, Germany
Dickinson, London

Exhibitions
2015 Vaduz, Hilti Art Foundation / Kunstmuseum Liechtenstein, *Hilti Art Foundation – Painting and Sculpture. From Classical Modernism to the Present Day*, p. 34, no. 7
2016 Vaduz, Hilti Art Foundation / Kunstmuseum Liechtenstein, *Hilti Art Foundation – Kirchner, Léger, Scully & more. Works from the Collection*, p. 58, no. 15

Literature
Fischer 1972, pp. 116–17, fig. no. 34
Lackner 1979, p. 22, fig. 25
Amyx 1981, p. 98
Beckmann 1982, p. 60, fig. p. 57
Dube 1982, p. 70
Beckmann 1983, p. 21
Uthemann 1983–84, p. 40, fig. p. 41
Lackner 1984, pp. 64–65
Franzke 1984, pp. 93ff., fig. no. 1, p. 95
Stabenow 1984–85, pp. 139ff., fig. no. 2, p. 140
Erpel 1985, no. 144/A, fig. no. 152
Rosenthal 1985, no. 90
Wiese 1985, fig. 4
Franzke 1987, pp. 26–29, fig. no. 1
Noll 2002, pp. 26–51, fig. pp. 30–31
Rainbird 2003, pp. 157–64
Schneider 2015, p. 34, no. 7
Schneider 2016, p. 58, no. 15

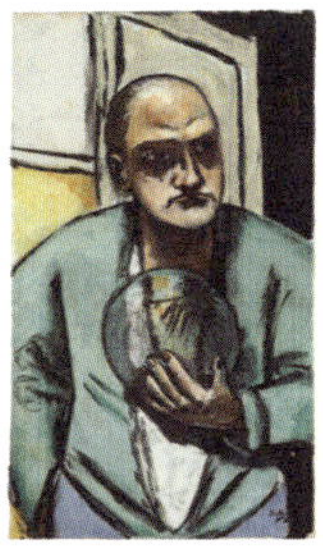

068

Max Beckmann
Selbstbildnis mit Glaskugel
1936

Provenance
Max Beckmann's studio
Rudolf Freiherr von Simolin, Berlin, later Seeseiten
Private collection (bequeathed within the family until 2005)
Sotheby's, New York, 3 May 2005, Impressionist & Modern Art, Part One, lot 27
Private collection
Galerie Thomas, Munich

Exhibitions
1951 Munich, Haus der Kunst; Berlin, Schloss Charlottenburg, *Max Beckmann zum Gedächtnis 1884–1950*, no. 103
1951–52 Amsterdam, Stedelijk Museum, *Max Beckmann*, no. 36
1953–54 Braunschweig, Kunstverein Städtisches Museum und Haus Salve Hospes; Bremen, Kunsthalle, *Max Beckmann*, no. 51
1955–56 Zurich, Kunsthaus Zürich, *Max Beckmann 1884–1950*, no. 74
1956 Basel, Kunsthalle, *Max Beckmann*, no. 64
1956 The Hague, Gemeentemuseum, *Max Beckmann*, no. 54
1963 Karlsruhe, Badischer Kunstverein, *Max Beckmann – Das Portrait, Gemälde, Aquarelle, Zeichnungen*, no. 40
1968–69 Paris, Musée National d'Art Moderne; Munich, Haus der Kunst; Brussels, Palais des Beaux-Arts, *Max Beckmann*, no. 58 (in Munich no. 56)
1993 Hamburg, Kunsthalle; Munich, Staatsgalerie Moderner Kunst, no. 18
2003 Riehen, Fondation Beyeler, *Expressive!*
2015 Vaduz, Hilti Art Foundation / Kunstmuseum Liechtenstein, *Hilti Art Foundation – Painting and Sculpture. From Classical Modernism to the Present Day*, p. 30, no. 6
2016 Vaduz, Hilti Art Foundation / Kunstmuseum Liechtenstein, *Hilti Art Foundation – Kirchner, Léger, Scully & more. Works from the Collection*, p. 60, no. 16
2018 Vaduz, Hilti Art Foundation / Kunstmuseum Liechtenstein, *Hilti Art Foundation – Rosso, Klee, Sonnier & more. Works from the Collection*, p. 20, no. 5

Literature
MB-Liste 1936: Selbstbildnis mit Glaskugel. Simolin
Lackner 1938
Bihalji-Merin 1955, fig. XXXII
Busch 1957, vol. 12, p. 10, no. 1 with fig.
Buchheim 1959, no. 61
Busch 1960, pp. 31–32, 66, fig. 12
Jedlicka 1962, pp. 124–25
Max Beckmann Gesellschaft 1962, p. 262, fig. 58
Overy 1965, p. 120
Lackner 1967, p. 38 and p. 62
Lackner 1969, p. 41 and 59
Zahn 1968–69, fig. p. 54
Schade 1969, vol. 94, pp. 236–37, fig. 4
Kessler 1970, p. 156
Fischer 1972, p. 52 and p. 119, fig. no. 18
Göpel 1976, vol. I, no. 434, p. 286; vol. II, fig. 148
Zenser 1984, p. 23, fig. no. 33
Erpel 1985, no. 145, fig. 151
Selz 1992, p. 65, fig. p. 64
Buck 1993, p. 35 and p.94, no. 18
Spieler 1994, fig. p. 12
Wieczorek 2015, p. 30, no. 6
Wieczorek 2016, p. 60, no. 16
Wieczorek 2018, p. 20, no. 5

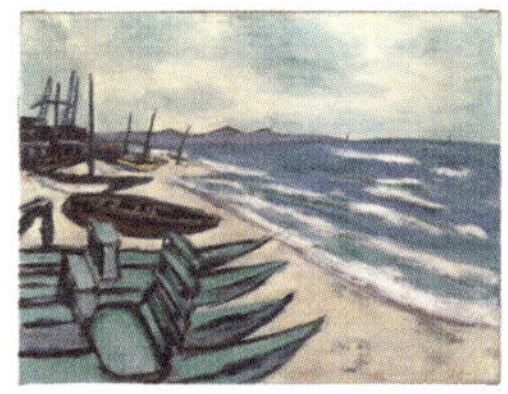

069

Max Beckmann
Strand mit Booten an der Riviera
1938

Provenance
The artist's studio
C. J. Leembruggen, The Hague
Galerie Walter Feilchenfeldt, Zurich
The Deutsche Bank Collection, Frankfurt a. M.
Dickinson, London

Exhibitions
1990 Leipzig, Museum der bildenden Künste; Frankfurt, Städelsches Kunstinstitut, *Max Beckmann, Gemälde 1905–1950*, no. 61
1998 Hamburg, Kunsthalle; Bielefeld, Kunsthalle; Vienna, Kunstforum, *Max Beckmann, Landschaft als Fremde*, no. 50
2001 Oldenburg, Landesmuseum für Kunst und Kulturgeschichte; Aschaffenburg, Kunsthalle Jesuitenkirche, *Landschaften eines Jahrhunderts aus der Sammlung Deutsche Bank*
2003 Hamburg, Bucerius Kunstforum, *Max Beckmann. Menschen am Meer*, p. 57, no. 18
2011–12 Basel, Kunstmuseum, *Max Beckmann. Die Landschaften*, p. 168, no. 50
2016 Vaduz, Hilti Art Foundation / Kunstmuseum Liechtenstein, *Hilti Art Foundation – Kirchner, Léger, Scully & more. Works from the Collection*, p. 64, no. 17

Literature
Göpel 1976, vol. 1, p. 320, no. 505, fig. vol. 2, plate 177
Peter 1998, p. 51
Stotz 2011–12, p. 159
Wieczorek 2016, p. 64, no. 17

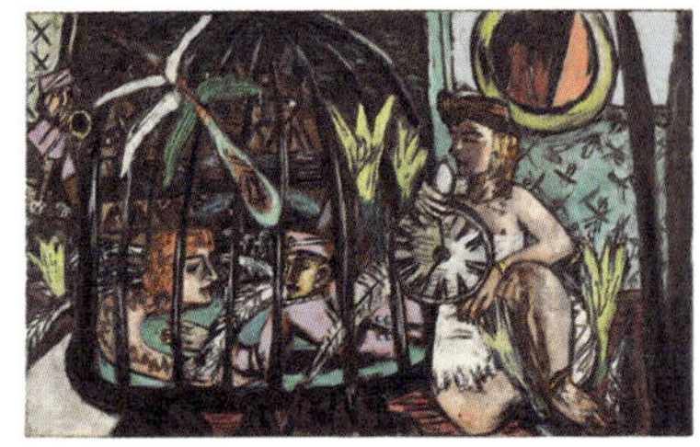

070

Max Beckmann
Traum des Soldaten
1942–43

Provenance
The artist's studio
Buchholz Gallery, Curt Valentin, New York
Elise V.H. Ferber, Washington D.C., 1946
Private collection
Galerie Thomas, Munich

Exhibitions
1948–49 St. Louis, Saint Louis City Art Museum, et al., *Max Beckmann 1948. Retrospective Exhibition*
1950 Northampton, Smith College, *Works of Art Belonging to Alumnae*, no. 37
1957 Boston, Museum of Fine Arts, *European Masters of our time*, no. 6, fig. 106
1959 Northampton, Smith College , *Works of Art Belonging to Alumnae*, no. 33
1961 Kansas City, William Rockhill Nelson Gallery of Art and Mary Atkins Museum of Fine Art, *The Logic of Modern Art*, no. 10 with fig.
1984 Munich, Haus der Kunst, et al., *Max Beckmann – Retrospektive*
2007 Munich, Pinakothek der Moderne, *Max Beckmann. Exil in Amsterdam*, no. 21
2012 Munich, Pinakothek der Moderne, *Frauen. Picasso, Beckmann, de Kooning*, no. 84
2013–14 Mannheim, Kunsthalle, *Dix / Beckmann: Mythos Welt*, no. 62, fig. p. 181
2015 Vaduz, Hilti Art Foundation / Kunstmuseum Liechtenstein, *Hilti Art Foundation – Painting and Sculpture. From Classical Modernism to the Present Day*, p. 100, no. 30
2016 Vaduz, Hilti Art Foundation / Kunstmuseum Liechtenstein, *Hilti Art Foundation – Kirchner, Léger, Scully & more. Works from the Collection*, p. 66, no. 18
2018 Vaduz, Hilti Art Foundation / Kunstmuseum Liechtenstein, *Hilti Art Foundation – Rosso, Klee, Sonnier & more. Works from the Collection*, p. 22, no. 6

Literature
MB-Liste Amsterdam 1942
Reifenberg 519
Swarzenski 1948, p. 8
Göpel 1976, vol. 1, p. 372, no. 616, vol. 2, fig. 222, no. 616
Schulz-Hoffmann 2007, p. 192, no. 21
Schulz-Hoffmann 2012, p. 288, no. 84
Von Bormann 2013, p. 159
Schneider 2015, p. 100, no. 30
Schneider 2016, p. 66, no. 18
Schneider 2018, p. 22, no. 6

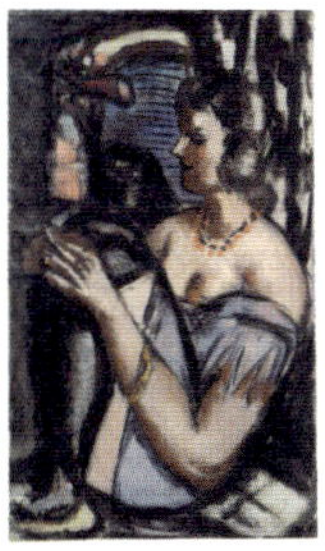

071

Max Beckmann
Frau mit Zigarette in Blauviolett
1944

Provenance
The artist's studio
Dr Helmuth Lütjens, Amsterdam
Marie Anne Strengholt, Amsterdam (1945)
E. J. van Wisselingh & Co., Amsterdam
Dr Werner Rusche, Cologne
Galerie Marbach, Bern
Roman Norbert Ketterer, Stuttgart
Lilo Behr (c.1956)
Private collection, Germany
Galerie Thomas, Munich

Exhibitions
1994 Stuttgart, Staatsgalerie Stuttgart, *Max Beckmann, Meisterwerke*, p. 152
2005 Vaduz, Kunstmuseum Liechtenstein, *Werke aus der Hilti Art Foundation. Von Paul Gauguin bis Imi Knoebel*, p. 70, no. 27
2016 Vaduz, Hilti Art Foundation / Kunstmuseum Liechtenstein, *Hilti Art Foundation – Kirchner, Léger, Scully & more. Works from the Collection*, p. 22, no. 4
2018 Vaduz, Hilti Art Foundation / Kunstmuseum Liechtenstein, *Hilti Art Foundation – Rosso, Klee, Sonnier & more. Works from the Collection*, p. 24, no. 7

Literature
Buchheim 1959, p. 167
Anonymous description, in: *Scala international*, German edition, Frankfurt am Main 1961, no. 11, pp. 21–28 and no. 12, colour fig. p. 22 and cover
Göpel 1976, vol. I, no. 675, fig. vol. II, plate 246
Wieczorek 2005, p. 70, no. 27
Wieczorek 2016, p. 22, no. 4
Wieczorek 2018, p. 24, no. 7

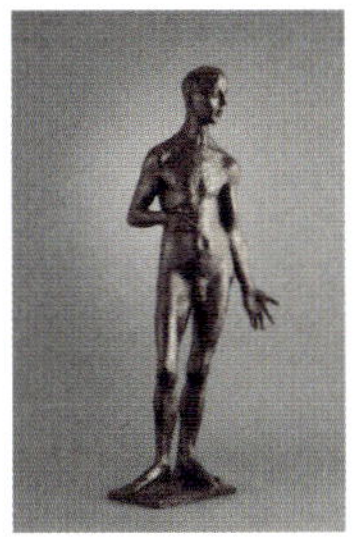

072

Germaine Richier
Juin 40
1940

Provenance
Jean Richier, 1950
Private collection
Dickinson, London

Exhibitions
1942 Winterthur, Kunstmuseum, *René Auberjonois, Gemälde und Zeichnungen – Germaine Richier, Plastiken* (a different cast on view)
1946 Geneva, Galerie Georges Moos, *Germaine Richier*, no. 2 (a different cast on view)
1963 Zurich, Kunsthaus Zürich, *Germaine Richier*, no. 63 (a different cast on view)
1996 Saint-Paul-de-Vence, Fondation Maeght, *Germaine Richier, Rétrospective*, no. 6 (a different cast on view)
1997 Berlin, Akademie der Künste, *Germaine Richier*, no. 6 (a different cast on view)
2013–14 Bern, Kunstmuseum; Mannheim, Kunsthalle, *Germaine Richier. Retrospektive*, no. 17, fig. pp. 80–81 (a different cast on view)
2015 Vaduz, Hilti Art Foundation / Kunstmuseum Liechtenstein, *Hilti Art Foundation – Painting and Sculpture. From Classical Modernism to the Present Day*, p. 36, no. 8

Literature
Francastel 1954, pp. 316–20, p. 399
Wieczorek 2015, p. 36, no. 8

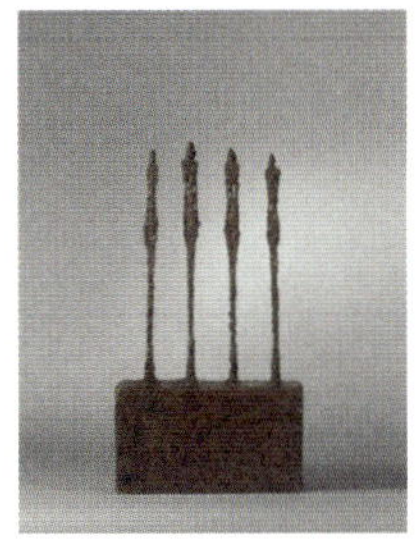

073

Alberto Giacometti
Quatre femmes sur socle
1950

Provenance
Collection Berggruen, Geneva
Galerie Beyeler, Basel

Exhibitions
1969–70 Paris, Orangerie des Tuileries (Gal. Berggruen), p. 57, no. 63
1990 Basel, Galerie Beyeler, *Alberto Giacometti*, pp. 44–45, no. 18
1991–92 Paris, Musée d'Art Moderne de la Ville de Paris, *Alberto Giacometti, Sculptures, Peintures, Dessins*, p. 240, no. 139
1996 Vienna, Kunsthalle; Edinburgh, Scottish National Gallery of Modern Art, *Alberto Giacometti 1901–1966*, p. 255, no. 155
1997 Basel, Galerie Beyeler, *Joie de vivre*
2005 Vaduz, Kunstmuseum Liechtenstein, *Werke aus der Hilti Art Foundation. Von Paul Gauguin bis Imi Knoebel*, p. 74, no. 29
2007–08 Riehen / Basel, Fondation Beyeler, *Die andere Sammlung. Hommage an Ernst und Hildy Beyeler*, p. 234
2016 Vaduz, Hilti Art Foundation / Kunstmuseum Liechtenstein, *Hilti Art Foundation – Kirchner, Léger, Scully & more. Works from the Collection*, p. 26, no. 5
2018 Vaduz, Hilti Art Foundation / Kunstmuseum Liechtenstein, *Hilti Art Foundation – Rosso, Klee, Sonnier & more. Works from the Collection*, p. 26, no. 8

Literature
Ponge 1951, p. 87 (different cast)
Dupin 1962, p. 253 (different cast)
Zurich 1971, no. 39 (different cast)
Hohl 1971, p. 139 (different cast)
Rotzler 1982, p. 425, no. 39 (different cast)
Bonnefoy 1991, p. 343, no. 316 (different cast)
Malsch 2005, p. 74, no. 29
Schneider 2016, p. 26, no. 5
Schneider 2016, p. 26, no. 8

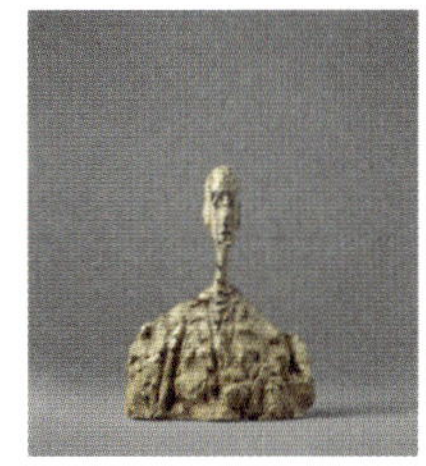

074

Alberto Giacometti
Petit buste d'homme
1950–51

Provenance
Herbert Matter
Harold Diamond, New York
Galerie Beyeler, Basel, 1971
Private collection, Germany, 1974
Sotheby's, New York, 3 May 2005, lot 60

Exhibitions
1977 Duisburg, Wilhelm Lehmbruck Museum, *Alberto Giacometti*, p. 223, no. 32
1987–88 Berlin, Nationalgalerie SMPK, et al., *Alberto Giacometti*, p. 248, no. 143
1991–92 Paris, Musée d'Art Moderne de la Ville de Paris, *Alberto Giacometti*, p. 217, no. 121
2015 Vaduz, Hilti Art Foundation / Kunstmuseum Liechtenstein, *Hilti Art Foundation – Painting and Sculpture. From Classical Modernism to the Present Day*, p. 110, no. 33

Literature
Hohl / Honisch / Beye 1987–88, p. 248, no. 143
Page 1991–92, p. 121, fig. p. 217
Schneider 2015, p. 110, no. 33

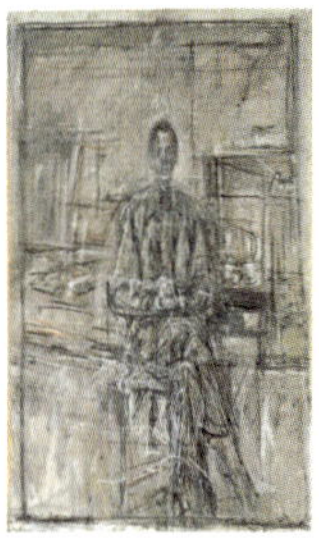

075

Alberto Giacometti
Diego dans un intérieur
1949–50

Provenance
Christoph Bernoulli, Basel
(acquired from the artist)
Sotheby's, London, 4 December 1984, lot 58
Thomas Ammann Fine Art, Zurich
Private collection, USA
Vivian Horan Fine Art, New York
Private collection, New York
Dickinson, London

Exhibitions
1960 Paris, Musée d'Art Moderne, et al., *Swiss Art from Hodler to Klee*, no. 17
2002–03 Zurich, Kunsthaus Zürich (loan)
2005 Vaduz, Kunstmuseum Liechtenstein, *Werke aus der Hilti Art Foundation. Von Paul Gauguin bis Imi Knoebel*, p. 72, no. 28
2011 Wolfsburg, Kunstmuseum, et al., *Alberto Giacometti. Der Ursprung des Raumes*, pp. 142, 252
2015 Vaduz, Hilti Art Foundation / Kunstmuseum Liechtenstein, *Hilti Art Foundation – Painting and Sculpture. From Classical Modernism to the Present Day*, p. 38, no. 9
2019 Vaduz, Hilti Art Foundation / Kunstmuseum Liechtenstein, *Composition '19 – Thomas Struth at the Hilti Art Foundation*, p. 125

Literature
Wieczorek 2005, p. 72, no. 28
Wieczorek 2015, p. 38, no. 9
Wieczorek 2019, p. 125

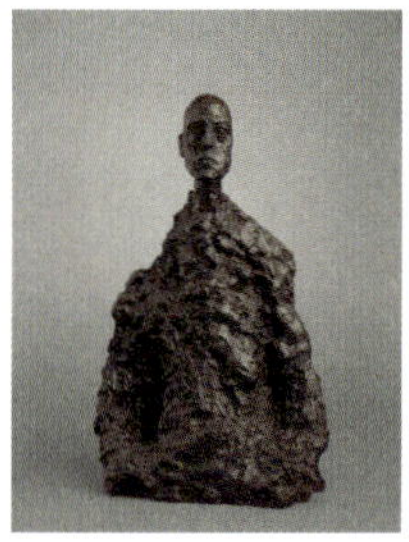

076

Alberto Giacometti
Buste d'homme (Eli Lotar II)
1964–65
(AGD 1620)

Provenance
Annette Giacometti
Thomas Gibson Fine Art, London, 1987
Private collection, New York
Galerie Michael Blaszczyk, Bad Homburg

Exhibitions
1977 Duisburg, Wilhelm-Lehmbruck-Museum, *Alberto Giacometti. Plastiken. Gemälde. Zeichnungen*, no. 54
1992 Basel, Galerie Beyeler, *Homage to Francis Bacon*, no. 25
2015 Vaduz, Hilti Art Foundation / Kunstmuseum Liechtenstein, *Hilti Art Foundation – Painting and Sculpture. From Classical Modernism to the Present Day*, p. 40, no. 10
2016 Vaduz, Hilti Art Foundation / Kunstmuseum Liechtenstein, *Hilti Art Foundation – Kirchner, Léger, Scully & more. Works from the Collection*, p. 90, no. 26
2018 Vaduz, Hilti Art Foundation / Kunstmuseum Liechtenstein, *Hilti Art Foundation – Rosso, Klee, Sonnier & more. Works from the Collection*, p. 30, no. 10
2019 Vaduz, Hilti Art Foundation / Kunstmuseum Liechtenstein, *Composition '19 – Thomas Struth at the Hilti Art Foundation*, p. 80

Literature
Salzmann 1977, no. 54, fig. p. 166
Schneider 2015, p. 40, no. 10
Schneider 2016, p. 90, no. 26
Schneider 2018, p. 30, no. 10
Wieczorek 2019, p. 80

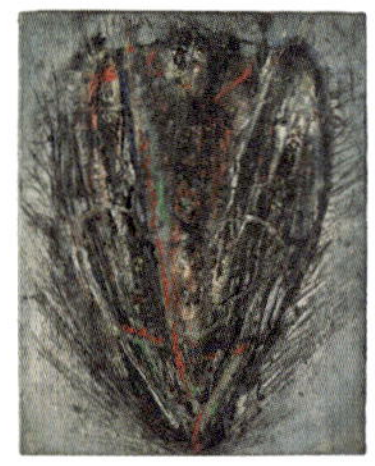

077

Wols
La flamme
1946–47

Provenance
Galerie René Drouin, Paris
Private collection (Bernard Collin), Paris, 1948
Sotheby's, Paris, 31 May 2011, lot 5

Exhibitions
1947 Paris, Galerie René Drouin, *Wols*
1949 Milan, Galleria del Milione, *Wols*
1957 Paris, Studio Paul Facchetti, *Jean Dubuffet, Henri Michaux, Wols*, fig.
1958 Venice, XXIX Esposizione Biennale Internazionale d'Arte, p. 152, no. 3
1973 Berlin, Nationalgalerie SMPK, *Wols 1913–1951. Gemälde, Aquarelle, Zeichnungen*, no. 20, fig. p. 52
1973–74 Paris, Musée d'art moderne de la ville de Paris, *Wols 1913–1951*, no. 16
1974 Ginals, Abbaye de Beaulieu en Rouergue, Centre d'art contemporaine, *Matière e Mémoire. L'informel, l'expressionisme abstrait, cobra…*
1989–90 Zurich, Kunsthaus Zürich; Düsseldorf, Kunstsammlung NRW, *Wols. Bilder, Aquarelle, Zeichnungen, Photographien, Druckgraphik*, no. 220, fig. p. 274
1990 Edinburgh, Scottish National Gallery of Modern Art, *Wols. Paintings, Watercolours, Photographs and Prints*, no. 3
1995–96 Paris, Musée d'art moderne de la ville de Paris, *Passions privées. Collections particulières d'art moderne et contemporain en France*, p. 297, no. 18, fig.
2013 Bremen, Kunsthalle, *Wols: Die Retrospektive*, p. 227, no. 189 and p. 270
2015 Vaduz, Hilti Art Foundation / Kunstmuseum Liechtenstein, *Hilti Art Foundation – Painting and Sculpture. From Classical Modernism to the Present Day*, p. 106, no. 32
2016 Vaduz, Hilti Art Foundation / Kunstmuseum Liechtenstein, *Hilti Art Foundation – Kirchner, Léger, Scully & more. Works from the Collection*, p. 94, no. 27
2019 Vaduz, Hilti Art Foundation / Kunstmuseum Liechtenstein, *Composition '19 – Thomas Struth at the Hilti Art Foundation*, p. 65

Literature
Anonymous 1955, fig. p. 19, upper right
Roh 1958, fig. p. 258
Hofmann 1959, p. 183
Platschek 1959, 3rd fig. after p. 40
Restany 1962, fig. p. 56
Celebonovic 1965, fig. p. 11
Chiba 1974, p. 107
LeCris-Bergmann, 1976, no. 163
Glozer 1978, p. 8, fig. 2
Damme 1985, no. 428, p. 270
Bonnefoi 1988, fig. cover
Lévêque 2001, fig. cover
Schneider 2015, p. 106, no. 32
Schneider 2016, p. 94, no. 27
Wieczorek 2019, p. 65

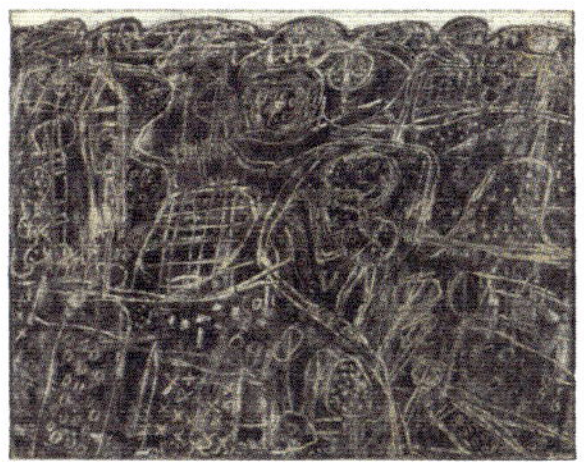

078

Jean Dubuffet
Paysage noir avec joueur de fifre
1949

Provenance
Pierre Matisse, New York
Kunsthandel Wolfgang Werner, Bremen / Berlin

Exhibitions
1994 Avignon, Palais des Papes, *Dubuffet. Haute Lieux, Paysages 1944–1984*, fig. p. 37
2001 Paris, Centre Georges Pompidou, *Dubuffet*, fig. p. 113
2010 Berlin, Wolfgang Werner, *Dubuffet*, no. 2
2015 Vaduz, Hilti Art Foundation / Kunstmuseum Liechtenstein, *Hilti Art Foundation – Painting and Sculpture. From Classical Modernism to the Present Day*, p. 104, no. 31
2016 Vaduz, Hilti Art Foundation / Kunstmuseum Liechtenstein, *Hilti Art Foundation – Kirchner, Léger, Scully & more. Works from the Collection*, p. 82, no. 24

Literature
Loreau 1965, WV no. 58, fig. p. 40
Schneider 2015, p. 104, no. 31
Schneider 2016, p. 82, no. 24

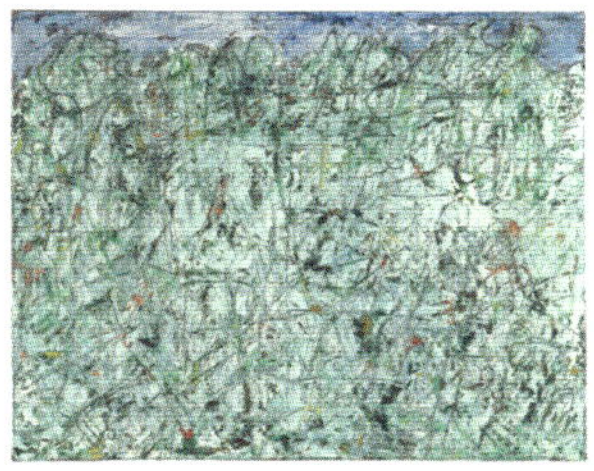

079

Jean Dubuffet
Riant été
1954

Provenance
Pierre Matisse Gallery, New York
William Motter Inge, Los Angeles
Robert Elkon Gallery, New York
Catherine Schlumberger Jones, Washington, D.C.
Sotheby's, New York, 13 November 1990, lot 50
Galerie Urban, Tokyo
Sotheby's, London, 2 July 1992, lot 32
Private collection USA
Galerie am Lindenplatz, Vaduz

Exhibitions
1955 London, Institute of Contemporary Art
1956 New York, Pierre Matisse Gallery, *Dubuffet Paintings and Assemblages d'empreintes*
1967 New York, Stephan Hahn Gallery, *Dubuffet 1941–1961*
2016 Vaduz, Hilti Art Foundation / Kunstmuseum Liechtenstein, *Hilti Art Foundation – Kirchner, Léger, Scully & more. Works from the Collection*, p. 86, no. 25

Literature
Loreau 1969, Vol. 10, p. 75, no. 99
Schneider 2016, p. 86, no. 25

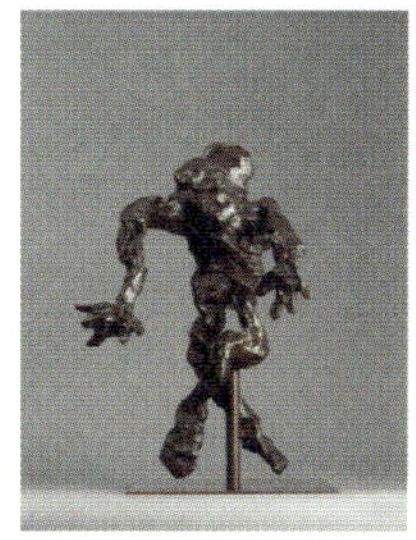

080

Willem de Kooning
Cross-Legged-Figure
1972

Provenance
Estate of Willem de Kooning
The Pace Gallery, New York
Private collection, New York
Mnuchin Gallery, New York

Exhibitions
1975 Chicago, The Art Institute of Chicago, *The 34th Annual Society for Contemporary Art Exhibition: The Small Scale in Contemporary Art*, no. 26
2011 New York, The Pace Gallery, *Willem de Kooning, The Figure: Movement and Gesture*, fig. no. 25, p. 44
2011–12 New York, The Museum of Modern Art, *De Kooning, A Retrospective*, fig. no. 162, p. 414
2015 Vaduz, Hilti Art Foundation / Kunstmuseum Liechtenstein, *Hilti Art Foundation – Painting and Sculpture. From Classical Modernism to the Present Day*, p. 46, no. 11

Literature
Gaugh 1983, no. 89, p. 100 (fig.)
Neff 1984, p. 59
Joosten 1984, no. 440
Sollers 1988, no. 76 (fig.)
Washington D.C., 1994
Yard 1997, no. 86, p. 101 (fig.)
Hess 2004, p. 65
Wieczorek 2015, p. 46, no. 11

Bibliography

Affentranger-Kirchrath, Angelika: Die Frage nach dem Menschen. Portraitmalerei um 1900 am Beispiel Ferdinand Hodlers und Edvard Munchs, in: Zeitschrift für Schweizerische Archäologie und Kunstgeschichte, no. 4, 1994

Alley, Ronald: Catalogue of The Tate Gallery's Collection of Modern Art, other than works by British Artists, London, 1981

Amyx, Clifford: Max Beckmann: Die Ikonographie der Triptychen, in: Max Beckmann. Die Triptychen im Städel, exh. cat., Frankfurt am Main, 1981

Andral, Jean-Louis: l'ère du renouveau, in: Picasso 1945–1949: l'ère du renouveau, exh. cat., Musée Picasso, Antibes, 2009

Andreotti, Margherita: The Early Sculpture of Jean Arp, London, 1989

Anonym: Wols, in: I 4 soli. Rassegna d'arte attuale, 2/5, 1955

Anthonioz, Michel: L'Album Verve, Paris, 1987 (Verve, The Ultimate Review of Art And Literature, 1937–1960, New York, 1988)

Apollonio, Umbro: Die Brücke e la Cultura dell'Espressionismo, Venice, 1952

Arnason, H. Harvard: Calder, New York, 1971

Asten, Astrid von: Die Reliefs im Œuvre von Hans Arp, in: Arp. Vorwände. Bestandskatalog der Reliefs im Arp Museum Bahnhof Rolandseck, Remagen, 2017

Badt, Kurt: Die Plastik Wilhelm Lehmbrucks, in: Zeitschrift für Bildende Kunst, 55. Jahrgang, Leipzig, 1920

Bätschmann, Oskar / Brunner, Monika / Walter, Bernadette: Ferdinand Hodler, Catalogue raisonné der Gemälde, vol. 1, Die Landschaften, Zurich, 2008

Bätschmann, Oskar / Brunner, Monika / Walter, Bernadette: Ferdinand Hodler, Catalogue raisonné der Gemälde, vol. 2, Die Bildnisse, Zurich, 2012

Baker, Kenneth: The Modern and the Ancient, San Francisco Chronicle, May 31, 1987

Barnett, Vivian Endicott: Kandinsky and Science: The Introduction of Biological Image in the Paris Period, in: Kandinsky in Paris, 1934–1944, exh. cat., The Solomon R. Guggenheim Museum, New York, 1985

Bauquier, Georges: Fernand Léger, Catalogue raisonné de l'œuvre peint, vol. 1, Paris, 1990

Bauquier, Georges: Fernand Léger, Catalogue raisonné de l'œuvre peint, vol. 4, Paris, 1996

Beckmann, Peter: Max Beckmann, Leben und Werk, Stuttgart / Zurich, 1982

Beckmann, Matilda Q.: Mein Leben mit Max Beckmann, Munich, 1983

Bender, Ewald: Das Leben Ferdinand Hodlers, Zurich 1921

Berend-Corinth, Charlotte: Die Gemälde von Lovis Corinth, Munich, 1958

Berend-Corinth, Charlotte: Die Gemälde von Lovis Corinth, 2nd ed., Munich, 1992

Berggruen, Olivier / Hollein, Max: Henri Matisse, Drawing with Scissors, Masterpieces from the Late Years, Munich / London, 2006, exh. cat., pp. 26–27

Berk, Tjeu van den: Eigenzinnig kunstzinnig, De visie van Carl Gustav Jung op kunst, Zoetermeer / Kapellen, 2009 (Jung on Art: The Autonomy of the Creative Drive, New York, 2012)

Biedermann, Heike: Ida Bienert – Avantgarde als Lebensgefühl, in: Von Monet bis Mondrian, Meisterwerke der Moderne aus Dresdner Privatsammlungen der ersten Hälfte des 20. Jahrhunderts, exh. cat., Staatliche Kunstsammlungen, Galerie Neue Meister, Dresden, 2006

Biermann, Georg: Lovis Corinth, Berlin, 1922

Bihalji-Merin, Oto: Savremena Nemačka Umetnost (German Art of the Present), Belgrade, 1955

Bihan, René le / Mabin, Renée / Sawin, Martica: Yves Tanguy, Plougstall-Daoulaz, 2001

Bill, Max: Wassily Kandinsky, Paris, 1951

Bischoff, Ulrich: Paul Klee, Munich, 1992

Bloch, Georges: Pablo Picasso, Catalogue de l'Œuvre gravé et lithographié 1904–1967, Bern, 1971

Bloesch, Hans: Zur internationalen Kunstausstellung in Interlaken, in: Die Alpen. Monatsschrift für schweizerische und allgemeine Kultur, 5, 1910, no. 1, pp. 25–32

Boeck, Wilhelm / Sabartés, Jaime: Picasso, New York, 1955

Bonnefoi, Geneviève: Les années fertiles 1940–1960, Paris, 1988

Bonnefoy, Yves: Alberto Giacometti, Paris, 1991

Borghi, Mino: Medardo Rosso, Milan, 1950

Bormann, Beatrice von: Triebträume – Von Bordell und Lustmord, in: Dix / Beckmann. Mythos Welt, Mannheim, 2013

Branat, F. / Hight E. / Kistler A. / Schultz S.: German Expressionist Art, The Ludwig and Rosy Fischer Collection,Virginia Museum of Fine Arts, 1987

Brandmüller, Nicole: Der Expressionist in Berlin, in: Ernst Ludwig Kirchner. Retrospektive, exh. cat., Städel Museum, Frankfurt am Main, 2010

Brion, Marcel: Paul Klee, Paris, 1955

Buchheim, Lothar-Günther: Max Beckmann, Feldafing, 1959

Buck, Matthias: Der erneuerte Mythos. Zu einigen Selbstbildnissen Max Beckmanns, in: Max Beckmann, Selbstbildnisse. exh. cat., Hamburger Kunsthalle / Staatsgalerie Moderner Kunst, Munich, 1993

Busch, Günter: Max Beckmann, in: Mededelingen Gemeentemuseum, The Hague, vol. 12, 1957

Busch, Günter: Max Beckmann, Eine Einführung, Munich, 1960

Busch, Günter et al.: Meisterwerke des deutschen Expressionismus, Stuttgart-Bad Cannstatt, 1960

Calvesi, Maurizio / Coen, Ester: Boccioni, Milan, 1983

Caramel, Luciano: Medardo Rosso: Der Ursprung der modernen Skulptur, exh. cat., MART Rovereto, GAM Turin, Milan, 2004

Cariou, André: Yves Tanguy. L'Univers surréaliste, exh. cat., Musée des Beaux-Arts Quimper & Museu Nacional d'Art de Catalunya, Barcelona, 2007

Celebonovic, Aleska: Novi oblici u posleratnom slikarstvu, in: Umetnost, April–June 1965

Chastel, A. / Minervino, F.: Tout l'œuvre peint de Seurat, Paris, 1973

Chiappini, Rudy: Emil Nolde, Milan, 1994

Chiba, Shigeo: L'œuvre de Wols (Diss.), Paris, 1974

Clemenz, Manfred: Der Mythos Paul Klee. Eine biographische und kulturgeschichtliche Untersuchung, Cologne, Weimar, Vienna, 2016

Coen, Ester: Umberto Boccioni, New York, 1988

Cohen, Walter: August Macke, in: Der Cicerone, Leipzig, 1922

Cooper, Douglas: Juan Gris, Catalogue raisonné de l'œuvre peint, vol. 1, Paris, 1977

Cooper, Harry / Hecker, Sharon: Medardo Rosso. Second Impressions, exh. cat., Fogg Art Museum of the Harvard University Art Museums (HUAM), Cambridge, Massachusetts, 2003

Coquiot, Gustave: Seurat, Paris, 1924

Crevel, René: Paul Klee, Peintres nouveaux, Paris, 1930

Damase, Jaques: Vassily Kandinsky, père de l'art abstrait, in: Maison et Jardin, May 1963

Damme, Claire van: Kunst als catharsis en psychogenese. Het extreem subjectivistisch kunstscheppen van de Duitse surrealistische en informele kunstnaar Wols 1913–1951, Ghent, 1985

Daulte, François: Auguste Renoir, Catalogue Raisonné de l'oeuvre peint, vol. I, Figures 1860–1890, Lausanne, 1971

De Chassey, Éric / Ovaere, Émilie: Ils ont regardé Matisse: Une réception abstraite États-Unis / Europe 1948–1968, exh. cat., Montreuil, 2009

De Sanna, Jole: Medardo Rosso o la Creazione dello Spazio Moderno, Milan, 1985

Delfs, Hans: Ernst Ludwig Kirchner – Der gesamte Briefwechsel, Zurich, 2010

Dessauer-Reiners, Christine: Das Rhythmische bei Paul Klee. Eine Studie zum genetischen Bildverfahren (Manuskripte zur Kunstwissenschaft in der Wernerschen Verlagsgesellschaft, vol. 51), Worms, 1996

Dickson, Amy: Landscape and Rural Narrative, in: Gauguin. Maker of Myth, exh. cat., Tate Modern, London, 2010–11

Distel, Anne: Seurat, Chêne, Paris, 1991

Doriot Galofaro, Sylvie: Les paysages de Ferdinand Hodler, in: Un siècle de tourisme à Crans-Montana. Lectures du territoire, Ayer: Edition Porte-Plumes, 2005

Dube, Wolf-Dieter: Auferstehung im Werke Max Beckmanns, in: Kunst und Kirche 2, 1982

Dupin, Jacques: Miró, Paris, 1961

Dupin, Jacques: Joan Miró, Life and Work, Paris, 1962

Dupin, Jacques: Alberto Giacometti, Paris, 1962

Dupin, Jacques / Lelong-Mainaud, Ariane: Joan Miró: Catalogue raisonné. Paintings, vol. 2 (1931–1941), Paris, 2000

Dupin, Jacques / Lelong-Mainaud, Ariane: Joan Miró: Catalogue Raisonné of Drawings, vol. 1 (1909–1937), Paris, 2008

Duthuit, Claude / De Guébriant, Wanda: Henri Matisse. Catalogue raisonné de l'œuvre sculpté, Paris 1997

Einstein, Carl: Die Kunst des 20. Jahrhunderts, Propyläen-Kunstgeschichte, vol. XVI, Berlin, 1926

Einstein, Carl: Die Kunst des 20. Jahrhunderts, 3rd ed., Berlin, 1931

Elgar, Frank: Picasso et Léger: deux hommes, deux mondes, Paris, 1954

Endicott Barnett, Vivian: The Architect as Collector, in: Mies in America, exh. cat., Whitney Museum of American Art, New York, 2001 / Canadian Center for Architecture, Montreal, 2002 / Museum of Contemporary Art, Chicago, 2002

Erpel, Fritz: Max Beckmann, Leben im Werk. Die Selbstbildnisse, Berlin, 1985

Fischer, Friedhelm Wilhelm: Max Beckmann, Symbol und Weltbild, Munich, 1972

Fischer, Marcel: Sammlung Arthur Stoll. Skulpturen und Gemälde des 19. und 20. Jahrhunderts, ed.: SIK, Zurich / Stuttgart, 1961

Fondation Maeght, Alexander Calder, Stabiles, Saint Paul, France, 1971

Francastel, Pierre: La nouvelle sculpture, Richier Germaine, Les sculpteurs célèbres, Paris, 1954

Franken, Verena: Zur Maltechnik von Otto Freundlich am Beispiel des Spätwerks, in: Otto Freundlich. Kosmischer Kommunismus, exh. cat., Museum Ludwig, Cologne/Kunstmuseum Basel, Munich, 2017

Franzke, Andreas: Max Beckmanns Skulpturen, in: Max Beckmann, exh. cat., Josef-Haubrich-Kunsthalle, Cologne, 1984

Franzke, Andreas: Max Beckmann, Skulpturen, Munich, 1987

Gabler, Karlheinz: E. L. Kirchner: Dokumente, Fotos, Schriften, Briefe, Aschaffenburg, 1980

Gaugh, Harry F.: Willem de Kooning, New York, 1983

Giedion-Welcker, Carola: Paul Klee, London, 1952

Glaser, Curt: in: Kunst und Künstler 27, Berlin, 1929

Glozer, Laszlo: Wols. Photograph, Munich, 1978

Göpel, Erhard and Barbara: Max Beckmann, Katalog der Gemälde, vol. I and II, Bern, 1976

Gordon, Donald E.: Ernst Ludwig Kirchner, Munich, 1968

Gordon, Donald E.: Modern Art Exhibitions 1900–1916, Munich, 1974

Grandy-Pradel, Marie-Noëlle de: Duchamp-Villon, exh. cat., Centre Georges Pompidou, Paris, 1998

Greenberg, Clement: Joan Miró, New York, 1948

Grenier, Catherine: Seurat, Catalogo Completo, Milan, 1990

Grisebach, Lothar: Maler des Expressionismus im Briefwechsel mit Eberhard Grisebach, Hamburg, 1962

Grisebach, Lucius: Ernst Ludwig Kirchner 1880–1938, Cologne, 1995

Grisebach, Lucius: Ernst Ludwig Kirchner, exh. cat., Museum der Moderne, Salzburg, 2009–10

Grisebach, Lucius: Bilder an der Wand. Die Kunstsammlung von Eberhard und Lotte Grisebach in Jena 1909 bis 1931, in: Weimar-Jena: Die grosse Stadt 3/4, Edition und Dokumentation, Jena, 2010

Grohmann, Will: Paul Klee, with contributions by René Crevel, Paul Eluard, Roger Vitrac, Tristan Tzara, Louis Aragon, Philippe Soupault and Jean Lurçat, Paris, 1929

Grohmann, Will (ed.): Privatsammlungen neuer Kunst. Die Sammlung Ida Bienert Dresden, vol. 1, Potsdam, 1933

Grohmann, Will: Paul Klee, Geneva / Stuttgart, 1954

Grohmann, Will: Schmidt-Rottluff, Stuttgart, 1956

Grohmann, Will: Wassily Kandinsky, Life and Work, New York, 1958

Grohmann, Will: Ernst Ludwig Kirchner, New York, 1961

Hartog, Arie / Fischer, Kai: Hans Arp, Skulpturen – Eine Bestandsaufnahme, Ostfildern, 2012

Hartog, Arie: Belling be(tr)achten. Rudolf Belling, die deutschen Bildhauer und der Raum, in: Rudolf Belling. Skulpturen und Architekturen, exh. cat., Nationalgalerie Berlin, 2017

Hauke, Cesar M.: Seurat e son Œuvre, vol. 1, Paris, 1961

Hausenstein, Wilhelm: Meister und Werke, Munich, 1930

Hayter, Stanley William: Paul Klee. Apostle of Empathy, in: Magazine of Art, New York, 1946

Hecke, P.G. van: René Magritte, peintre de la pensée abstraite, in: Sélection, Antwerp, 1927

Heiderich, Ursula: August Macke, Gemälde, Werkverzeichnis, Ostfildern, 2008

Heise, Carl Georg / Berend-Corinth, Charlotte: Bildnisse der Frau des Künstlers, Stuttgart, 1958

Helms, Dietrich / Valstar-Verhoff, Arta: Vordemberge-Gildewart, The Complete Works, Munich, 1990

Henze, Anton: Ernst Ludwig Kirchner, Leben und Werk, Stuttgart / Zurich, 1980

Henze, Wolfgang: Die Plastik Ernst Ludwig Kirchners. Monografie mit Werkverzeichnis, Wichtrach-Bern, 2002

Herbert, Robert L.: Seurat and Puvis de Chavannes, in: Yale University Art Literature Gallery Bulletin, October 1959

Hess, Hans: Lyonel Feininger, Stuttgart, 1959

Hess, Barbara: Willem de Kooning, Inhalt als flüchtiger Eindruck, Cologne, 2004

Hesse-Frielinghaus, Herta: Ernst Ludwig Kirchner und das Museum Folkwang Hagen. Briefe von ihm, an und über ihn, in: Westfalen 52, 1974, nos. 1–4

Heusinger von Waldegg, Joachim (ed.): Otto Freundlich (1878–1943), Monographie mit Dokumentation und Werkverzeichnis, Bonn, 1978

Hirsch, Karl Jakob: Maler Paul Klee, in: Musaion, vol. 9, Prague, December 1929

Hoberg, Annegret / Jansen, Isabelle: Franz Marc. Werkverzeichnis, vol. 1, Gemälde, Munich, 2004

Hofmann, Werner: Der Maler Wols, in: Werk. Schweizer Monatsschrift für Architektur, Kunst und künstlerisches Gewerbe 46, 1959

Hofmann, Werner: Alexander Archipenko, Galerie "Im Erker", St. Gallen, 1962

Hofmann, Werner: Henri Laurens. Sculptures, Teufen, 1970

Hohl, Reinhold: Alberto Giacometti, New York, 1971

Hohl, Reinhold: Tanguy und die surrealistische Figuration, in: Yves Tanguy, exh. cat., Staatliche Kunsthalle Baden-Baden, 1982–83

Hohl, Reinhold / Honisch, Dieter / Beye, Peter: Alberto Giacometti, in: Alberto Giacometti, exh. cat., Nationalgalerie Berlin, Staatsgalerie Stuttgart, 1987–1988

Homer, W. I.: Seurat's Paintings and Drawings, in: Burlington Magazine, London, June 1963

Hopfengart, Christine: Klee an den deutschen "Museen der Gegenwart", 1916–1933, in: Oskar Bätschmann and Josef Helfenstein (eds.), Paul Klee. Kunst und Karriere, Schriften und Forschungen zu Paul Klee, vol. 1, Bern, 2000

Hopfengart, Christine: Der Magier als Quotenkünstler. Paul Klee und sein Aufstieg zum Klassiker der Moderne, in: Das Universum Klee, exh. cat., Neue Nationalgalerie Berlin, 2008

Hopfengart, Christine: Verschobene Gesichter, in: Klee trifft Picasso, exh. cat., Zentrum Paul Klee, Bern, 2010

Hüneke, Andreas: Erich Heckel, Werkverzeichnis der Gemälde, Wandbilder und Skulpturen, 2 vols., Munich, 2017

Janda, Annegret: Paul Klee und die Nationalgalerie 1919–1937, in: Paul Klee. Vorträge der wissenschaftlichen Konferenz in Dresden am 19. und 20. Dezember 1984, Dresden / Berlin, 1986

Jawlensky, Maria / Pieroni-Jawlensky, Lucia / Jawlensky, Angelica: Alexej von Jawlensky, Catalogue Raisonné of the Oil Paintings, vol. 2, 1914–1933, London, 1992

Jedlicka, Gotthard: Max Beckmann in seinen Selbstbildnissen, in: Blick auf Beckmann, Dokumente und Vorträge, Munich, 1962

Johnson, Ron: The Early Sculpture of Picasso, 1901–1914, New York, 1976

Jong, Casper de: Paintings of the Western World, New York, 1963

Joosten, Joop M.: Twenty Years of Collecting, Stedelijk Museum Amsterdam, 1984

Joosten, Joop M. / Welsh, Robert P.: Piet Mondrian, Catalogue Raisonné of the Work of 1911–1944, Antwerp, 1998

Jullian, René et al.: Fernand Léger, Edition Beyeler, Basel, 1969

Jung, Carl Gustav: Ein moderner Mythus. Von Dingen die am Himmel gesehen werden (Zurich and Stuttgart 1958), in: Zivilisation im Übergang, Freiberg, 1986

Kagan, Andrew: Paul Klee. Art & Music, Ithaca / London, 1983

Karshan, Donald H.: Archipenko, The Sculpture and Graphic Art, Catalogue Raisonné, Tübingen, 1974

Kessler, Charles S.: Max Beckmann's Triptychs, Cambridge, 1970

Ketterer, Roman Norbert: Legenden am Auktionspult. Die Wiederentdeckung des deutschen Expressionismus, Munich, 1999

Kraft, Hartmut: Objektverlust und Kreativität – eine Darstellung anhand Ferdinand Hodlers Werkzyklus über Valentine Godé-Darel, in: Psychoanalyse, Kunst und Kreativität heute. Die Entwicklung der Kunstpsychologie seit Freud, Cologne, 1984

Lackner, Stephan: Das Welttheater des Malers Max Beckmann, 1938, in: Benno Reifenberg und Wilhelm Hausenstein, Max Beckmann, Munich, 1949

Lackner, Stephan: Ich erinnere mich gut an Max Beckmann, Mainz, 1967

Lackner, Stephan: Max Beckmann, Memories of a Friendship, Coral Gables, FL, 1969

Lackner, Stephan: Max Beckmann, Cologne, 1979

Lackner, Stephan: Max Beckmann, in: Skulptur des Expressionismus, exh. cat., Josef-Haubrich-Kunsthalle, Cologne, 1984

Lankheit, Klaus: Franz Marc. Katalog der Werke, Cologne, 1970

Lankheit, Klaus: Franz Marc. Sein Leben und seine Kunst, Cologne, 1976

Laprade, Jacques de: Georges Seurat, Monaco, 1945

LeGris-Bergmann, Françoise: Composantes plastiques et pôles référentiels dans l'œuvre de Wols (Diss.), Paris, 1976

Lévêque, Jean-Jacques: Wols, Neuchâtel, 2001

Lewandowski, Herbert (Lee van Dovski): Gauguin oder die Flucht vor der Zivilisation, Olten, Bern, 1950

Löffler, Fritz: Theodor Däubler sowie Ida Bienert und Klee, in: Akten, Dresden, 1986

Loosli, Carl Albert: Ferdinand Hodler, Zurich, 1919–20

Loosli, Carl Albert: Ferdinand Hodler, Leben, Werk und Nachlass, 4 vols., Bern, 1921–24

Loosli, Carl Albert: (GK) Generalkatalog, in: C.A. Loosli, Ferdinand Hodler. Leben, Werk und Nachlass, Bern, 1921–24

Loreau, Max: Catalogue des travaux de Jean Dubuffet, vol. V, Paysages grotesques, Lausanne, 1965

Loreau, Max: Catalogue des travaux de Jean Dubuffet, vol. X, Vaches. Petites statues de la vie précaire, Lausanne, 1969

Luckhardt, Ulrich: Lyonel Feininger, Munich, New York, 1998

Lüttichau, Mario-Andreas von: Zwischen Freude und Niedergeschlagenheit, in: Ernst Ludwig Kirchner. Die Deutschlandreise 1925–26, Kunstsammlungen Chemnitz, Chemnitz, 2007

Malingue, Maurice: Gauguin, Le peintre et son œuvre, Paris, 1948

Malsch, Friedemann: in: Werke aus der Hilti Art Foundation. Von Paul Gauguin bis Imi Knoebel, exh. cat., Kunstmuseum Liechtenstein, Vaduz, 2005

Malsch, Friedemann: Avantgarde als Antizipation. Futuristische Experimente zwischen Fotografie, Skulptur, Raum und Medien, in: lens-based-sculpture. Die Veränderung der Skulptur durch die Fotografie, exh. cat., Kunstmuseum Liechtenstein, Vaduz, 2014

Marchiori, Giuseppe: Arp. Cinquante ans d'activité, exh. cat., Bruno Alfieri, Milan, 1964

Matisse, Pierre: Yves Tanguy, Un Recueil de ses œuvres, Paris, 1963

Maur, Karin von: Yves Tanguy oder "Die Gewissheit des Niegesehenen", in: Yves Tanguy und der Surrealismus, exh. cat., Staatsgalerie Stuttgart, Stuttgart, 2000

Max Beckmann Gesellschaft: Blick auf Beckmann, Munich, 1962

Merkert, Jörn: Julio González, Catalogue raisonné des sculptures, Milan, 1987

Merli, Juan: Picasso, el artista y la obra de nuestro tiempo, Buenos Aires, 1942

Mola, Paola / Vittucci, Fabio: Medardo Rosso, Catalogo Ragionato della Scultura, Milan, 2009

Mourlot, Fernand: Picasso Lithographe II. 1947–1949, Monte Carlo, 1950

Mühlestein, Hans / Schmidt, Georg: Ferdinand Hodler 1853–1918. Sein Leben und sein Werk, Zurich, 1942

Müller, Carola: Das Zeichen in Bild und Theorie bei Paul Klee (Diss.), Technische Universität, Munich, 1979

Müller, Werner Y.: Die Kunst Ferdinand Hodlers. Gesamtdarstellung. vol. 2, Reife und Spätwerk 1885–1918, Zurich, 1941

Müller, Werner Y.: (LK) Landschaftskatalog, in: Werner Y. Müller, Die Kunst Ferdinand Hodlers. Gesamtdarstellung. vol. 2. Reife und Spätwerk 1885–1918, Zurich, 1941

Nachbaur, Wenzel: Verzeichnis der Plastiken Ernst Ludwig Kirchners, 1962

Neff, Terry Ann R.: Selections from the Permanent Collection, vol. I, exh. cat., The Museum of Contemporary Art, Chicago, 1984

Nerdinger, Winfried: Rudolf Belling und die Kunstströmungen in Berlin 1918–1923 mit einem Katalog der plastischen Werke, Berlin, 1981

Néret, Gilles: Fernand Léger, Paris, 1990

Niemeyer, Wilhelm: Malerische Impressionen und koloristischer Rhythmus. Denkschrift des Sonderbundes, Düsseldorf, 1911

Noll, T.: Max Beckmann – Mann im Dunkeln, in: Christian Lenz, Max Beckmann, Aufsätze, Max Beckmann Archiv, Munich, 2002

Overy, Paul: Three German Self-Portraits, in: Apollo, vol. 81, London 1965

Page, Suzanne: Alberto Giacometti. Sculptures. Peintures. Dessins, in: exh. cat., Musée d'Art Moderne de la Ville de Paris, Paris, 1991–92

Palau i Fabre, Josep: Picasso – The Early Years 1881–1907, New York, 1981

Paul-Klee-Stiftung, Kunstmuseum Bern (ed.): Paul Klee, Catalogue Raisonné, vol. 5, 1927–1930, Bern, 2001

Pauli, Gustav: Lovis Corinth, in: Kunst und Künstler 16, Berlin, 1918

Penrose, Roland: The Sculpture of Picasso, exh. cat., The Museum of Modern Art, New York, 1967

Peter, Nina: Déjà vu. Die Bildquellen der Landschaften von Max Beckmann, in: Max Beckmann. Landschaft als Fremde, exh. cat., Hamburg / Bielefeld / Vienna, 1998–99

Picasso Project (ed.): Picasso's Paintings, Watercolours, Drawings and Sculpture – Surrealism 1930–1936, San Francisco, 1997

Pichon, Yann le: Sur les traces de Gauguin, Paris, 1986

Plant, Margaret: Paul Klee: Figures and Faces, London, 1978

Platschek, Hans: Neue Figuration. Aus der Werkstatt der heutigen Malerei, Munich, 1959

Platte, Hans: Erich Heckel, Baden-Baden, 1964

Ponge, Francis: Réflexions sur les statuettes, figures et peintures d'Alberto Giacometti, in: Cahiers d'Art, Paris, XXVI, 1951

Prather, Maria: Willem de Kooning, exh. cat., National Gallery of Art, Washington D.C., 1994

Rainbird, Sean: A Gathering Storm: Beckmann and Cultural Politics 1925–38, in: Max Beckmann, exh. cat., The Tate Gallery, London, 2003

Rascher, Max: Ferdinand Hodler und andere Schweizer Künstler. Reproduktionen und Radierungen des Verlages Rascher & Cie. A.-G., Zurich, Leipzig, Stuttgart, 1928

Rattemeyer, Volker / Helms, Dietrich / Valstar-Verhoff, Arta: Friedrich Vordemberge-Gildewart. Retrospektive, IVAM Centre Julio Gonzalez Valencia/Museum Wiesbaden, 1996–97

Reifenberg, Benno / Hausenstein, Wilhelm: Max Beckmann, Munich, 1948

Renne, René / Serbanne, Claude: Paul Klee ou la passivité, in: Cahiers du Sud, vol. 32, 1945

Restany, Pierre: Une peinture existentielle. Wols, in: XXe siècle, 24/19, 1962

Reusse, Felix: Pablo Picasso. The Lithographs, Ostfildern, 2000

Rewald, H. Dorra and John: Seurat, Paris, 1959

Roethel, Hans K. / Benjamin, Jean K.: Kandinsky, Catalogue Raisonné of the Oil Paintings, vol. 1 (1900–1915), London, 1982

Roethel, Hans K. / Benjamin, Jean K.: Kandinsky, Catalogue Raisonné of the Oil Paintings, vol. 2 (1916–1944), London, 1984

Roh, Franz: Geschichte der deutschen Kunst von 1900 bis zur Gegenwart. Deutsche Kunstgeschichte, vol. VI, Munich, 1958

Rosenthal, Mark: German Art in the 20th Century, exh. cat., Royal Academy, London, 1985

Rosenthal, Mark: Franz Marc, Munich, 1989

Roskill, Mark: Klee, Kandinsky, and the Thought of Their Time. A Critical Perspective, Urbana / Chicago, 1992

Roters, Eberhard: Galerie Ferdinand Möller. Die Geschichte einer Galerie für Moderne Kunst in Deutschland 1917–1956, Berlin, 1984

Rotzler, Willy: Die Geschichte der Alberto Giacometti Stiftung, Bern, 1982

Salzmann, Siegfried: Alberto Giacometti. Plastiken. Gemälde. Zeichnungen, exh. cat., Wilhelm-Lehmbruck-Museum, Duisburg, 1977

San Lazzaro, Gualtieri di: Klee. La vie et l'œuvre, Paris, 1957

San Lazzaro, Gualtieri di: XXe Siècle: Hommage à Calder, Paris, 1972

Moure, Gloria: Medardo Rosso, exh. cat., Centro Galego de Arte Contemporánea, Santiago de Compostela, 1996

Schade, Herbert: Max Beckmann, Gestaltung ist Erlösung, in: Stimmen der Zeit, Freiberg, 1969

Schardt, Alois J.: Franz Marc. Mit hundertfünfzehn Abbildungen, Berlin, 1936

Scheffler, Karl: Lovis Corinth, in: Kunst und Künstler 21, Berlin, 1923

Schenkenberg, Tamara H.: "You Cannot Divide or Stop the Air". Dimensions of Space in Medardo Rosso's Sculpture, in: Medardo Rosso, Experiments in Light and Form, exh. cat., Pulitzer Arts Foundation, St. Louis, MO, 2018

Schick, Karin: Ruhelose Ordnung. Ernst Ludwig Kirchner und das Stilleben, in: Ernst Ludwig Kirchner, Die Stilleben, exh. cat., Kirchner Museum, Davos, 2006

Schmalenbach, Werner: Die Lust auf das Bild. Ein Leben mit der Kunst, Berlin, 1996

Schmidt, Georg: In memoriam Oskar Müller-Widmann, 1887–1956, Basel, 1956

Schmoll gen. Eisenwerth, Josef Adolf: Rudolf Belling, St. Gallen, 1971

Schneede, Uwe M: Umberto Boccioni, Stuttgart, 1994

Schneider, Angela: in: Werke aus der Hilti Art Foundation. Von Paul Gauguin bis Imi Knoebel, exh. cat., Kunstmuseum Liechtenstein, Vaduz, 2005

Schneider, Angela: in: Hilti Art Foundation, Painting and Sculpture – From Classical Modernism to the Present Day, exh. cat., Hilti Art Foundation/Kunstmuseum Liechtenstein, Vaduz, 2015

Schneider, Angela: in: Hilti Art Foundation, Kirchner, Léger, Scully & more, Works from the Collection, exh. cat., Hilti Art Foundation / Kunstmuseum Liechtenstein, Vaduz, 2016

Schneider, Angela: in: Hilti Art Foundation, Rosso, Klee, Sonnier & more, 36 Works from the Collection, exh. cat., Hilti Art Foundation / Kunstmuseum Liechtenstein, Vaduz, 2018

Schubert, Dietrich: In ihrer wunderbaren Gusshaut, in: Frankfurter Allgemeine Zeitung, no. 137, 16 June 2001

Schubert, Dietrich: Anmerkungen zur ersten Ausstellung der "Freien Secession"" in Berlin, April 1914, in: Jahrbuch der Berliner Museen, vol. 52, 2012

Schulz-Hoffmann, Carla: in: Max Beckmann. Exil in Amsterdam, exh. cat., Pinakothek der Moderne, Munich, 2007

Schulz-Hoffmann, Carla: Frauen. Picasso, Beckmann, de Kooning, exh. cat., Pinakothek der Moderne, Munich, 2012

Schulz-Hoffmann, Carla: in: Max Beckmann. Kleine Stillleben, exh. cat., Franz Marc Museum,Kochel am See, 2013

Selz, Peter: Max Beckmann, The Self-Portraits, New York, 1992

Sollers, Philippe: De Kooning, Vite, Paris, 1988

Spieler, Reinhard: Max Beckmann – Der Weg zum Mythos, Cologne, 1994

Spies, Werner: Pablo Picasso. Das plastische Werk, Stuttgart, 1971

Spies, Werner: Max Ernst, Oeuvre-Katalog, Werke 1925–1929, Cologne, 1976

Spies, Werner / Piot, Christine: Picasso. Das plastische Werk, Bonn, 1983

Spies, Werner: Picasso, The Sculptures: Catalogue Raisonné of the Sculptures, Ostfildern / Stuttgart, 2000

Spiller, Jürg (ed.): Paul Klee. Das bildnerische Denken. Form- und Gestaltungslehre, vol.1, Basel / Stuttgart, 1956

Stabenow, Cornelia: Metaphern der Ohnmacht. Zu den Plastiken Max Beckmanns, in: Max Beckmann Retrospektive, exh. cat., Munich et al., 1984–85

Stotz, Maren: Amsterdam 1937–1947, in: Max Beckmann. Die Landschaften, exh. cat., Kunstmuseum Basel, 2011–12

Swarzenski, Hanns: Max Beckmann 1948. Retrospective Exhibition, exh. cat., Saint Louis City Art Museum, St. Louis, MO, 1948–49

Sylvester, David / Whitfield, Sarah: René Magritte, Catalogue Raisonné, vol. 1, oil paintings, 1916–1930, Antwerp, 1992

Sylvester, David: Magritte, Brussels, 2009

The Alexej Jawlensky Archive (Maria Jawlensky, Lucia Pieroni-Jawlensky, Angelica Jawlensky Bianconi): Alexej von Jawlensky, Catalogue Raisonné of the Oil Paintings, vol. 1 (1890–1914), London, 1991

The Picasso Project: Picasso's Paintings, Watercolors, Drawings and Sculpture: A Comprehensive Illustrated Catalogue 1885–1973, Alan Wofsy Fine Art, San Francisco, 2000

Thévoz, Michel: Louis Soutter ou l'écriture du désir, Editions L' Âge d'Homme, Lausanne, Institute suisse pour l'étude de l'art, Zurich, 1974

Thévoz, Michel: Catalogue raisonné de l'oeuvre de Louis Soutter, Editions L'Âge d'Homme, Lausanne, Institute suisse pour l'étude de l'art, Zurich, 1976

Tobien, Felicitas: Die Künstlergruppe Brücke, Berghaus, 1987

Trier, Eduard: Hans Arp. Skulpturen 1957–1966, Stuttgart, 1968

Urban, Martin (ed.): Emil Nolde, Werkverzeichnis der Gemälde, vol. 1, 1895–1914, Munich, 1987

Uthemann, Ernest W.: Mann im Dunkeln, in: Max Beckmann, Werke aus der Sammlung des Kunstmuseums Hannover mit Sammlung Sprengel, Hanover, 1983–84

Vallier, Dora: Son Fil d'Ariane, la couleur, in: XXe siècle, Centenaire de Kandinsky, Paris, 1966

Valstar-Verhoff, Arta: Friedrich Vordemberge-Gildewart – The New Publication. Including the New Œuvre-Catalogue of the Paintings and Works on Paper by Friedrich Vordemberge-Gildewart, Rapperswil, Switzerland, 2018.

Verdi, Richard: Der späte Klee, in: Deutsche Kunst im 20. Jahrhundert. Malerei und Plastik 1905–1985, exh. cat., Staatsgalerie Stuttgart, Munich, 1986

Vignau-Wilberg, Peter: Gemälde und Skulpturen. Museum der Stadt Solothurn, Zurich, 1973

Vogt, Paul: Erich Heckel, Catalogue raisonné, Recklinghausen, 1965

Vriesen, Gustav: August Macke, Stuttgart, 1953

Vriesen, Gustav: August Macke, Stuttgart, 1957

Wahl, Volker: Ernst Ludwig Kirchner und Jena. Ein Beitrag zur Bibliographie des Künstlers anlässlich seines 100. Geburtstages, in: Staatliche Museen, Forschungen und Berichte, vol. 20/21, 1980

Waldberg, Patrick: Yves Tanguy, Brussels, 1977

Walden, Herwarth: Die neue Malerei, Berlin, 1919

Weiler, Clemens: Alexej Jawlensky, Cologne, 1959

Weiler, Clemens: Alexej Jawlensky, Köpfe Gesichte Meditationen, Hanau, 1970

Weiss, Elisabeth: Franz Marc. Elin Versuch zur Deutung expressionistischer Stilphänomene und ihrer Voraussetzungen (Diss.), Frankfurt am Main, 1933

Wember, Paul: Kunst in Krefeld. Öffentliche und private Kunstsammlungen, Cologne, 1973

Westheim, Paul: Das Kunstblatt, Berlin, 1920

Westheim, Paul/Einstein, Carl: Rudolf Belling – Skulpturen, in: Das Kunstblatt, Potsdam, 1924

Wieczorek, Uwe: in: Werke aus der Hilti Art Foundation. Von Paul Gauguin bis Imi Knoebel, exh. cat., Kunstmuseum Liechtenstein, Vaduz, 2005

Wieczorek, Uwe: Hilti Art Foundation, Painting and Sculpture – From Classical Modernism to the Present Day, exh. cat., Hilti Art Foundation/Kunstmuseum Liechtenstein, Vaduz, 2015

Wieczorek, Uwe: Hilti Art Foundation, Kirchner, Léger, Scully & more, Works from the Collection, exh. cat., Hilti Art Foundation / Kunstmuseum Liechtenstein, Vaduz, 2016

Wieczorek, Uwe: Hilti Art Foundation, Rosso, Klee, Sonnier & more, 36 Works from the Collection, exh. cat., Hilti Art Foundation / Kunstmuseum Liechtenstein, Vaduz, 2018

Wieczorek, Uwe: Composition '19, Thomas Struth in der Hilti Art Foundation, exh. cat., Hilti Art Foundation / Kunstmuseum Liechtenstein, Vaduz 2019

Wiese, Stephan von: Max Beckmann, in: Moeller, Magdalena M. (ed.), Sprengel Museum Hannover. Malerei und Plastik des 20. Jahrhunderts, Hanover, 1985

Wietek, Gerhard: Schmidt-Rottluffs Oldenburger Jahre 1907–1912, Mainz, 1955

Wildenstein, Georges: Gauguin, Paris, 1964

Wilson, William: A Heartfelt Compendium of Modernism, Los Angeles Times, April 26, 1987

Yard, Sally: Willem de Kooning, New York, 1997

Zenser, Hildegard: Max Beckmann, Selbstbildnisse, Munich, 1984

Zervos, Christian: Pablo Picasso, Catalogue raisonné, Paris, 1932–1978

Zervos, Christian: Notes sur Kandinsky, A propos de sa récente exposition à la Galerie des Cahiers d'Art, Paris, 1934

Zieglgänsberger, Roman: "nichts – und alles". Der De Stijl-Künstler Friedrich Vordemberge-Gildewart, exh. cat., Museum Wiesbaden, 2013

Kunsthaus Zürich (ed.): Die Sammlung der Alberto Giacometti Stiftung, Zurich, 1971

Epigraph: J. W. von Goethe,
Maxims and Reflections,
translated by Elisabeth Stopp,
London 1998

Imprint

Feldkircherstrasse 100
9494 Schaan
Liechtenstein

Museum address:
Städtle 32
9490 Vaduz
Liechtenstein

www.hiltiartfoundation.li

///

Hirmer Publishers
Bayerstraße 57–59
80335 Munich
Germany

www.hirmerpublishers.com

PUBLISHER
Michael Hilti
President
Hilti Art Foundation
Schaan / LI

EDITOR
Uwe Wieczorek
Curator
Hilti Art Foundation
Schaan / LI

PROJECT ADMINISTRATION
Isabel Fehr
Michèle Frey-Hilti
Hilti Art Foundation
Schaan / LI

PROJECT MANAGEMENT
Rainer Arnold
Hirmer Publishers
Munich / DE

TEXTS
Angela Schneider
Berlin / DE
Uwe Wieczorek
Schaan / LI

TRANSLATION
Catherine Schelbert
Weggis, Hertenstein / CH

COPY EDITING, PROOFREADING
Louise Stein
London / UK

REPRODUCTIONS
Günter König
Ruggell / LI
Heinz Preute
Vaduz / LI

INSTALLATION PHOTOGRAPHS
Günter König
Ruggell / LI
Thomas Struth
Berlin / DE
(Pages 112/113, 140/141, 196/197)

ARCHITECTURAL PHOTOGRAPHS
Valentin Jeck
Stäfa / CH

VISUALS
prepressstudio
Günter König
Ruggell / LI

GRAPHIC DESIGN, TYPESETTING
Kurt Dornig
Dornbirn / AT

TYPEFACES
Novel Pro / Christoph Dunst
Allegra / Jost Hochuli

PAPERS
Pergraphica Classic Rough
Arctic Silk+

PRINTING, BINDING
Kösel GmbH & Co. KG
Altusried / DE

ISBN 978-3-7774-3342-4

Printed in Germany

COVER ILLUSTRATIONS

Hans Arp
KOPF-STABILE
(cat. 40)

Max Beckmann
Selbstbildnis mit Glaskugel
(cat. 68)

Umberto Boccioni
Forme uniche della continuità nello spazio
(cat. 30)

Alberto Giacometti
Buste d'homme (Eli Lotar II)
(cat. 76)

Alberto Giacometti
Diego dans un intérieur
(cat. 75)

Juan Gris
Le verre
(cat. 32)

Ferdinand Hodler
Les Etangs longs bei Montana
(cat. 24)

Ernst Ludwig Kirchner
Stilleben mit Orangen und Tulpen
(cat. 16)

Paul Klee
Clown
(cat. 46)

Fernand Léger
Contraste de formes
(cat. 33)

Fernand Léger
La danseuse
(cat. 54)

Henri Matisse
Composition, Jaune, Bleu et Noir
(cat. 59)

Piet Mondrian
Tableau No. VIII
with Yellow, Red, Black and Blue
(cat. 34)

Pablo Picasso
Femme dans un fauteuil
(cat. 60)

Georges Seurat
La tas de pierres
(cat. 1)